ROMANIA

Marxist Regimes Series

Series editor: Bogdan Szajkowski,
Department of Sociology, University College,
Cardiff

Ethiopia Peter Schwab
Romania Michael Shafir

Further Titles

Afghanistan
Albania
Angola
Benin and The Congo
Bulgaria
Cape Verde, Guinea-Bissau and São Tomé and Príncipe
China
Cuba
Czechoslovakia
German Democratic Republic
Ghana
Grenada
The Co-operative Republic of Guyana
Hungary
Kampuchea
Democratic People's Republic of Korea
Laos
Madagascar
Mongolia
Mozambique
Nicaragua
Poland
Somalia
Soviet Union
Surinam
Vietnam
People's Democratic Republic of Yemen
Yugoslavia
Zimbabwe
Marxist State Governments in India
Marxist Local Governments in Western Europe and Japan
The Diversification of Communism
Comparative Analysis
Cumulative Index

ROMANIA

Politics, Economics and Society
Political Stagnation and Simulated Change

Michael Shafir

Frances Pinter (Publishers), London

Lynne Rienner Publishers, Inc., Boulder

© Michael Shafir 1985

First published in Great Britain in 1985 by
Frances Pinter (Publishers) Limited
25 Floral Street, London WC2E 9DS

First published in the United States of America in 1985 by
Lynne Rienner Publishers, Inc.
948 North Street
Boulder, Colorado 80302

British Library Cataloguing in Publication Data

Shafir, Michael
    Romania: politics, economics and society.—
    (Marxist regimes)
    1. Romania
    I. Title
    949.8'03   DR205
    ISBN 0-86187-438-2
    ISBN 0-86187-439-1 Pbk

Library of Congress Cataloging in Publication Data

Shafir, Michael.
    Romania, politics, economics, and society.

    Bibliography: p
    Includes index.
    1. Romania—Politics and government—20th century.
    2. Communism—Romania.   3. Romania—Economic conditions.
    4. Romania—Social conditions.   I. Title.
    DR264.S53   1985   306'.09498   84–62183

ISBN 0-931477-02-6
ISBN 0-931477-03-4 (pbk.)

Typeset by Joshua Associates, Oxford
Printed by SRP Ltd., Exeter

Editor's Preface

The study of Marxist regimes has for many years been equated with the study of communist political systems. There were several historical and methodological reasons for this.

For many years it was not difficult to distinguish the eight regimes in Eastern Europe and four in Asia which resoundingly claimed adherence to the tenets of Marxism and more particularly to their Soviet interpretation—Marxism–Leninism. These regimes, variously called 'People's Republic', 'People's Democratic Republic', or 'Democratic Republic', claimed to have derived their inspiration from the Soviet Union to which, indeed, in the overwhelming number of cases they owed their establishment.

To many scholars and analysts these regimes represented a multiplication of and geographical extension of the 'Soviet model' and consequently of the Soviet sphere of influence. Although there were clearly substantial similarities between the Soviet Union and the people's democracies, especially in the initial phases of their development, these were often overstressed at the expense of noticing the differences between these political systems.

It took a few years for scholars to realize that generalizing the particular, i.e. applying the Soviet experience to other states ruled by elites which claimed to be guided by 'scientific socialism', was not good enough. The relative simplicity of the assumption of a cohesive communist bloc was questioned after the expulsion of Yugoslavia from the Communist Information Bureau in 1948 and in particular after the workers' riots in Poznań in 1956 and the Hungarian revolution of the same year. By the mid-1960s, the totalitarian model of communist politics, which until then had been very much in force, began to crumble. As some of these regimes articulated demands for a distinctive path of socialist development, many specialists studying these systems began to notice that the cohesiveness of the communist bloc was less apparent than had been claimed before.

Also by the mid-1960s, in the newly independent African states 'democratic' multi-party states were turning into one-party states or military dictatorships, thus questioning the inherent superiority of liberal democracy, capitalism and the values that went with it. Scholars now began to ponder on the simple contrast between multi-party democracy and a one-party totalitarian rule that had satisfied an earlier generation.

More importantly, however, by the beginning of that decade Cuba had a revolution without Soviet help, a revolution which subsequently became to many political elites in the Third World not only an inspiration but a clear military, political and ideological example to follow. Apart from its romantic appeal, to many nationalist movements the Cuban revolution also demonstrated a novel way of conducting and winning a nationalist, anti-imperialist war and accepting Marxism as the state ideology without a vanguard communist party. The Cuban precedent was subsequently followed in one respect or another by scores of regimes in the Third World who used the adoption of 'scientific socialism' tied to the tradition of Marxist thought as a form of mobilization, legitimation or association with the prestigious symbols and powerful high-status regimes such as the Soviet Union, China, Cuba and Vietnam.

Despite all these changes the study of Marxist regimes remains in its infancy and continues to be hampered by constant and not always pertinent comparison with the Soviet Union, thus somewhat blurring the important underlying common theme—the 'scientific theory' of the laws of development of human society and human history. This doctrine is claimed by the leadership of these regimes to consist of the discovery of objective causal relationships; it is used to analyse the contradictions which arise between goals and actuality in the pursuit of a common destiny. Thus the political elites of these countries have been and continue to be influenced in both their ideology and their political practice by Marxism more than any other current of social thought and political practice.

The growth in the number and global significance, as well as the ideological political and economic impact, of Marxist regimes has presented scholars and students with an increasing challenge. In meeting this challenge, social scientists on both sides of the political divide have put forward a dazzling profusion of terms, models, programmes and varieties of interpretation. It is against the background of this profusion that the present comprehensive series on Marxist regimes is offered.

This collection of monographs is envisaged as a series of multi-disciplinary textbooks on the governments, politics, economics and society of these countries. Each of the monographs was prepared by a specialist on the country concerned. Thus, over fifty scholars from all over the world have contributed monographs which were based on first-hand knowledge. The geographical diversity of the authors, combined with the fact that as a group they represent many disciplines of social science, gives their individual analyses and the series as a whole an additional dimension.

Each of the scholars who contributed to this series was asked to analyse such topics as the political culture, the governmental structure, the ruling party, other mass organizations, party-state relations, the policy process, the economy, domestic and foreign relations together with any features peculiar to the country under discussion.

This series does not aim at assigning authenticity or authority to any single one of the political systems included in it. It shows that depending on a variety of historical, cultural, ethnic and political factors, the pursuit of goals derived from the tenets of Marxism has produced different political forms at different times and in different places. It also illustrates the rich diversity among these societies, where attempts to achieve a synthesis between goals derived from Marxism on the one hand, and national realities on the other, have often meant distinctive approaches and solutions to the problems of social, political and economic development.

University College
Cardiff

Bogdan Szajkowski

To the memory of my father

Contents

List of Tables

Acknowledgements

Children and books share common traits. Both are born in pain and both are expected to bring joy. Some children, and some books, come to life easier than others. Some children, though born bastards, defy the establishment and become famous. So do some books. What the fate of this book will be is not for me to prophesy. I know, however, that it was born in pain. The greater the reason, therefore, for expressing my gratitude to those who attempted to ease the pangs of birth.

My thanks go first to the editor of the series, Bogdan Szajkowski, who provided encouragement and showed appreciation of my insignificant abilities at moments when this was needed. I hope I have not betrayed his trust. I would also like to thank my research assistant, Hagit Brown, without whose efficiency and promptness I would never have coped with the administrative side of this endeavour. My gratitude goes also to Ginette Avram, Librarian of the Soviet and East European Research Centre of the Hebrew University, Jerusalem, who was of great assistance in my search for Romanian and other publications, and to the staff of the Russian and East European Research Centre of the University of Tel Aviv. Without the watchful eye of my good friend Iulia Azriel, Librarian at the National Library in Jerusalem, I might never have benefited from some rare Romanian works quoted in this book. Morissa Amittai and Sylvia Weinberg of the Tel Aviv University typing pool did a splendid job in deciphering my impossible hieroglyphics and in coping with an impossible deadline. I am also grateful for a small grant received from the Social Sciences Faculty of the University of Tel Aviv which was spent on photostats and similar requirements.

Last, but not least, my family has patiently learned to endure the slings and arrows of an outrageous fortune and to bear with me during this project. For better or worse, I can promise no rest.

Jerusalem
1 September 1984

Basic Data

Official name	The Socialist Republic of Romania
Population	22,352,635 (1981 estimate)
Population density	94.1 per sq. km.
Population growth (% p.a.)	.0.3 (1983)
Urban population (%)	51.1 (1981)
Total labour force	10,375,500 (1981)
Life expectancy	69.82 (1976-8)
Infant death rate (per 1,000)	28.6 (1981)
Ethnic groups	88.1% Romanians; 7.9% Hungarians; 1.6% Germans; 0.2% Ukrainians; 0.1% Serbians; 0.1% Jews and others (1977 census)
Capital	Bucharest, 2.1 million (1981)
Land area	237,500 sq. km., of which 41% is arable land, 27% forest, 19% pasture and cornfields, 3% vineyards and orchards and 3% rivers and lakes.
Official language	Romanian
Administrative division	40 counties and the Bucharest municipality, 237 cities (of which 56 municipalities) and 2,705 communes
Membership of international organizations	UN since 1955; CMEA since 1949; WTO since 1955; FAO, GATT, IMF, IAEA, IBRD, ICAO, ICJ, ILO, IMCO, ITU, UNESCO, UPU, WHO, WIPO, WMO, BIS, CCC, IBEC, IIB, ITC, PCA
Foreign relations	Diplomatic and consular relations with 137 states (1981)
Political structure	
Constitution	As of August 1965
Highest legislative body	Grand National Assembly of 369 members
Highest executive body	Council of Ministers
Prime minister	Constantin Dăscălescu (Prime Minister of the SRR since 1982)

President   Nicolae Ceaușescu
Food self-sufficiency   Bread rationing introduced in October 1981
                                             and food prices raised by 35% in 1982. Virtual
                                             rationing introduced in 1982 in the form of
                                             limitations in calorie intake.
Growth indicators (% p.a.)

	1971-80	1981	1982
national income*	9.2	2.2	2.6
industry†	11.2	2.6	NA
heavy	11.9	2.5	NA
consumer	9.4	2.8	NA
agriculture†	5.1	−0.9	7.5

* Net material product, excluding services in housing, education, cultural, health and administrative sectors.
† Gross output

Exports: US$12,610 m (1981)
Imports: US$12,456 m (1981)
Exports as % of GNP   13%

Main exports %   Machine equipment and transportation 29.0;
                                             fuel, raw materials and metals 27.8; industrial
                                             consumer goods 15.7; chemical products, fer-
                                             tilizers, rubber 9.4; food commodities 8.1
                                             (1981)

Main imports %   Fuel, raw materials and metals 48.6; machine
                                             equipment and transportation 23.6; non-
                                             edible raw materials 6.9; raw materials for
                                             food production 6.6; chemical products, ferti-
                                             lizers and rubber 6.2 (1981)

Destination of exports (%)   Socialist countries 53.0
                                             Non-socialist countries 47.0 (1983)

Main trading partners: USSR; West Germany; USA; Iraq; Iran; East
                                             Germany; France; People's Republic of China
                                             (1981).

Foreign debt: US$9,300-9,500 bn. (estimated, 1983).
Ruling party   Romanian Communist Party
Secretary General of   Nicolae Ceaușescu (since 1965)
   the party
Party membership   3,370,343 (1983). In 1982 14.4 per cent of
                                             total estimated population and 31 per cent of
                                             total active population.

Armed forces:	Total regular forces: 189,500 (109,000 conscripts); Reserves: 45,000; Border guards: 17,000; Security Forces: 20,000; Patriotic Guard: 900,000; Youth Homeland Defence: 650,000.
Education and health:	
School system:	Pre-school, 3 years; primary (grades I–IV) + high school (grades V–VIII) + lyceum first step (grades IX–X), 10 years, free and compulsory; lyceum second step, 2 years; vocational schools and schools for foremen, 2 years; pedagogical institutes, 2 years; higher education, 4–6 years; universities and institutes of higher education: Bucharest, Iaşi, Cluj-Napoca, Timişoara, Craiova, Braşov, Galaţi, Ploieşti, Tîrgu Mureş, Petroşani, Sibiu, Piteşti, Baia Mare, Reşiţa, Hunedoara, Constanţa, Suceava, Oradea, Bacău.
Adult literacy (%)	98% (1976)
Population per hospital bed	107.1 (1981)
Population per physician	538 (1981)
Economy:	
GNP	US$92–98.9m (1982 estimated)
GNP per capita	US$4,096–4,403 (1982 estimated)
GDP by %	industry 63.8; construction 9.0; agriculture 13.6; transportation and telecommunications 5.2 (1981).
State budget (expenditure):	271,823.2 million lei (1981)
Defence expenditure % of state budget	3.8
Monetary unit:	Leu (17 lei = $1)
Main crops:	maize, wheat and rye, sugar beet, potatoes, vegetables, barley and two-oat barley
Land tenure:	About 200 sq.m. per peasant household for private cultivation
Main religions:	Romanian Orthodox, Roman Catholic, Lutheran, Calvinist, Unitarian, Uniate (outlawed), Jewish, Moslem
Rail network:	11,093 km. (1981)
Road network:	73,364 km. (1981)

Population Forecasting

The following data are projections produced by Poptran, University College Cardiff Population Centre, from United Nations Assessment Data published in 1980, and are reproduced here to provide some basis of comparison with other countries covered by the Marxist Regime Series.

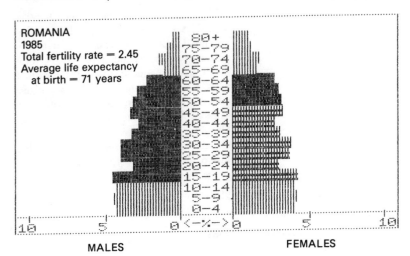

ROMANIA
1985
Total fertility rate = 2.45
Average life expectancy
   at birth = 71 years

MALES   FEMALES

Projected Data for Romania 1985

Total population ('000)	23,152
Males ('000)	11,449
Females ('000)	11,703
Total fertility rate	2.45
Life expectancy (male)	69.0 years
Life expectancy (female)	73.7 years
Crude birth rate	17.4
Crude death rate	9.6
Annual growth rate	0.78%
Under 15s	25.03%
Over 65s	9.55%
Women aged 15–49	23.86%
Doubling time	90 years
Population density	97 per sq. km.
Urban population	51.6%

Romania—Regions and Major Towns

Part I
History and Political Traditions

1   The Environmental Dimension

That nationalism and Marxism are the two main conflicting ideologies of our time appears to be a truism in no need of postulation. Yet if the spectre of communism still haunts the ghost of nationalism, it is not less true that the contradiction has become 'non-antagonistic' at the 'intra-systemic' (state) level through a veritable dialectical performance. Marxism, which is international in its aspirations and appeal has managed to absorb the seemingly incompatible ('bourgeois') phenomenon of nationalism into its reconstrued doctrinary tenets. The equation is not less valid when read the other way around: by absorbing Marxism into its own definitional categories, nationalism survives and flourishes in a political 'praxis' when, according to Marxist 'theory', it should have vanished. The blend, however, creates great antagonism in the 'extra-systemic' order— including the international communist movement.

Placed in that cradle of nationalism that Eastern Europe has always been, Romania is no exception to the rule. On the contrary, it is perhaps the epitome of it. History, naturally, is everywhere contingent on geography. In its attempt to combine Marxism and nationalism, however, the regime of President Nicolae Ceauşescu has turned not only history, but also historical materialism, into a function of geographic location. It is therefore important to consider first of all Romania's 'environmental' dimensions, i.e., the physical as well as the ideological background in which the system was generated and developed.

The evidence concerning the birth and formation of the Romanian nation is still controversial and somewhat obscure.[1] The Daco-Roman race, to which the origins of most of the present inhabitants of the country can be traced, vanished for a thousand years from recorded history, then reappeared in the thirteenth and fourteenth centuries in the form of the *viovodates* of Wallachia and Moldavia. Transylvania, historically the third province of Romania, was by that time part of the Kingdom of Hungary. Turkish suzerainty over the *voivodates* was established in the fifteenth century. Modern Romanian nationalism was born in the eighteenth century, and stemmed from two parallel sources: the influence of Western liberal ideas, which penetrated the Romanian principalities of Moldavia and Wallachia under the influence of the Greek phanariote princes, and the parallel rediscovery of the Latin origins of the nation by the Transylvanian Bishop Inocenţiu Micu-Klein and his disciples (Georgescu, 1971; Fischer-Galati, 1971, pp. 374–7). In the immediate geo-political context of a transitional Romanian society subject to, on one hand, its first exposure to modernization, and on the other, to the struggle for power and influence between the then superpowers of the region, Russia, Turkey and Austria, liberalism, in the eyes of the young *boyars* of that time, meant largely the right to self-determination (Shafir, 1983b, p. 399). The birth of the modern Romanian state may be traced back to the mid-nineteenth century—more precisely, to the 1859 unification of Moldavia and Wallachia under Prince Alexandru Ioan Cuza. Skilfully manœuvering in favourable international circumstances, and driven by surprisingly intense (considering their relatively recent vintage) nationalist motives, the local political circles of the time managed to start the process of state building in the Romanian lands. The United Principalities won formal independence from Turkey as a result of the Russo-Turkish war of 1877-78. At the end of the war, however, the country found itself territorially smaller than it had been at the outset. For, despite the considerable contribution of the Romanian army to the war effort, the Russians recompensed their allies by annexing (or rather re-annexing) Bessarabia. These ancient Romanian lands had first been annexed by Russia in 1812, when Turkey ceded them to Tsar Alexander I (Dima, 1982, pp. 7-18).

The foreign policy of the 'Old Kingdom' in the immediate post-independence period was aimed above all at the establishment of 'România Mare' (Greater Romania), comprising all the territories inhabited by the Romanian population and, if possible, their hinterlands as well. The dream became a reality as a result of the First World War and the October Revolution in Russia. As one of the victorious powers, Romania was awarded Transylvania and the formerly Austrian northern Bukovina. In Bessarabia the 'Sfatul Țării' (Bessarabian Assembly), a more or less representative body, first proclaimed autonomy, then reunification with Romania. Already in 1913, as a result of the Second Balkan War, Romania had acquired the territory of southern Dobruja (the 'Cadrilater') from Bulgaria. Territorially, the country more than doubled in size, while the population also doubled. About a quarter of the total population, however, was made up of national minorities (Lendvai, 1970, p. 271; Turnock, 1974, p. 11). It was against this background of historical enmity that the ruling Romanian elites in the inter-war period attempted to mould a formula for 'political integration'. Faced with serious social and economic cleavages, and both unwilling and incapable of coping with such problems, these elites often chose to deflect attention from much-needed reforms to external affairs, blaming Romania's 'historical enemies', i.e. Russia and Hungary, and the national minorities, for the country's difficulties.

The issue of national identity and patriotism consequently became the main integrative device, from which important consequences arose. For national identities are not established in terms of positive reference alone—'what we are'—but also in terms of negative reference—'what we are not'. The latter is just as important, perhaps even indivisible, from the former. As Karl Deutsch observes in an article devoted to nation building, the 'choice of national alignments and national identity is related to the decision to choose a common enemy. This is indeed a decision, even if it has been made unconsciously' (Deutsch, 1966, pp. 10-11).

This suspicious attitude towards the country's neighbours, moreover, seemed to be vindicated by subsequent international developments. Greater Romania was sacrificed on the altar of the Soviet-German pact of August 1939. In June 1940 Moscow presented the Romanian government with a twenty-four hour ultimatum, demanding the return of Bessarabia and the incorporation of northern Bukovina into the Soviet Union. In early August of the same year southern Dobruja was ceded to Bulgaria as a result of German pressure and at the end of that month northern Transylvania was reincorporated into Hungary, following the Vienna award. When Germany launched its attack against the Soviet Union Romania joined the war on the side of the Axis.

The country's present borders were established in the wake of the Second World War, in circumstances analysed elsewhere in this book. Contemporary Romania is the second-largest state in south-eastern Europe. To the east and the north it is bordered by the Soviet Union—more precisely by Bessarabia and northern Bukovina. Present-day Romanian historiography, however, overtly treats these territories as part of historical Romania. Even the validity of Bessarabia as a geographical term of reference has come to be negated, and the province is referred to as 'Eastern Moldavia', to reflect the historical links of the region with the body of the Romanian state (Felea & Tănăsescu, 1980, p. 41). In a book originally published in 1976, two Romanian historians indicate that the territory 'had been named Bessarabia because it had once been part of Wallachia under the reign of the Basarab family', and trace Russian endeavours to annex not only this region, but the principalities of Wallachia and Moldavia as a whole. The authors bluntly describe the machinations of the tsarist governments leading to the territory's incorporation into Russia in 1812, the aggrandizement of the plunder in 1829, their short-lived return to Moldavia in 1856 and the re-annexation of 1878. The 1918 reunification with Greater Romania is deemed to have been an act 'which crowned the struggle waged for more than a century by the Bessarabian Romanians to preserve their national identity'. Northern Bukovina, and its reunification with Romania in the wake of the collapse of the Austro-Hungarian Empire, is similarly treated (Muşat & Ardeleanu, 1982, pp. 11-17).

Such a presentation is by no means consonant with pronouncements of the regime at the outset of communist rule, but it reflects the subsequent focusing of the regime's search for legitimacy on national history as an integral part of a process which will be discussed further in this book. At this point it is sufficient to indicate that the evolution of post-war Romanian historiography demanded—and still demands—careful and propitious 'timing' on the part of the highest decision-making party and state bodies. That this process is a long and tortuous one is revealed, among other ways, by the first edition of the book just quoted, which appeared in 1971 without the inclusion of the 'sensitive' chapter later added to the revised version (Muşat & Ardeleanu, 1971). However, Romanian historiography had already travelled a long way from the days of party historian M. Roller, according to whom the reunification of Bessarabia with Romania in 1918 had been nothing but 'occupation', carried out by a 'reactionary' Romanian government which had exploited the temporary weakness of the 'young Soviet Republic' (Roller, 1956, pp. 545–6).

To the west, Romania is bordered by both Yugoslavia (to the south) and Hungary (to the north). The Yugoslav border has never been a subject of prolonged dispute, except for some disagreement over the partitioning of the formerly Hungarian Banat region in the wake of the First World War, which was eventually settled. Relations with Hungary, however, have plagued the country almost without interruption. Transylvania is an extremely complicated regional sore spot, for both nations regard this as the traditional repository of their national awareness. As one observer of East European affairs put it, 'for both Romanians and Hungarians, Transylvania is a political category which is regarded as having made the crucial contribution to the two communities', having 'ensured their autonomous survival'. Consequently, myth and reality became impossible to separate and Transylvania itself has been turned by both states into 'a category of meta-communication', negatively affecting their relations (Schöpflin, 1983b).

So far as Romania is concerned, the rediscovery of the Latin origins of the nation by the Transylvanian Latinist School was a milestone in the process of nation building. In the Romanian case–as indeed in other instances of nascent nation-states in this area–nation building, i.e. the development of awareness of a common bond uniting the members of a specific entity, preceded the process of state building, by which I mean the institutional framework within which that entity functions. Although the Latinist School was not originally politically motivated,[2] it was from Transylvania that the idea of a separate and common identity, uniting all Romanians inhabiting the three historical provinces, spread to Wallachia and Moldavia (Iorga, 1915, pp. 100–2; Fischer-Galati, 1971, pp. 374–5). Hence, the additional symbolic significance of this area to contemporary Romania, to which it should be added that the Dacian entity which is considered to be in part the ancestor of the nation, was also centred in the Transylvanian mountains. In view of this, and in the face of disputed historical evidence, myth and symbol were bound to acquire supreme importance.

According to the official doctrine now employed (or rather re-employed) in Romanian historiography, nation building was a 'long historical process', and developed 'as a consequence of the struggle for the defence of the nation being waged over centuries ... by the Romanians on both slopes of the Carpathian mountains'. These people, it is held, were 'the descendants of the Romanized Dacian population that has been uninterruptedly living in the Carpathian Danubian territory, a population with its centre in Transylvania and laying the basis of the formation of the Romanian people' (Institute of Political Sciences and of the Study of the National Question, 1976, p. 5). In recent years, hardly a week passes without the appearance in Romanian scientific (and less than scientific) publications, of a plethora of articles dedicated to the 'continuity' issue.

As in the case of Bessarabia, such pronouncements mark a return to the traditional lines of Romanian political historiography, which, in the Stalinist period, was subjected to total 'revision'. In this case it was not the 'Romanity' of

Transylvania that was in question, but that of the Romanians themselves. In the 1950s the Roman forefathers were turned into 'conquerors' and 'exploiters' of the native Dacians, in striking contrast to the alleged benevolent influence later exercised by the neighbouring Slavs.[3] Until 1965 even the official name of the country was Romînia—an attempt to diminish the association with historical Rome and with the West in general.[4]

The southern Dobruja problem has not affected relations between Bulgaria and Romania since the Second World War. Nevertheless, official Romanian pronouncements, including speeches by President Ceauşescu, emphatically state that the post-1918 territorial agreements, i.e. the country's southern boundaries as well as its other borders, have been legitimately established. Moreover, on two occasions at least the issue has been presented by Romanian historians in a decidedly controversial manner. In a collection of articles published in 1977 Ion Calafeteanu compared inter-war Bulgarian policies directed at the reacquisition of territory lost in 1913 to 'Horthyst revisionism'. 'The Bulgarian Premier G. Kiosseivanov', he wrote, 'conditioned any rapprochement and co-operation of his country with her neighbours on the acquisition of territories from them, and above all southern Dobruja'. Romania, however, could not possibly accept such claims, for, 'following the 1918 dismemberment of the Austro-Hungarian and Czarist Empires, she had achieved the completion of the national unitary state' (Calafeteanu, 1977, pp. 356-7). Similarly, a history of the region published in 1979 (quoted in Ghermani, 1981, pp. 188-9) establishes that the incorporation of the 'Cadrilater' had been historically warranted. Whether or not such utterances constitute a Romanian reaction to (possibly Soviet-prompted) hints by Bulgarian historians that the dormant issue of *northern* Dobruja could be re-awakened in a not too distant future (King, 1976) is, of course, difficult to establish. Since both countries are involved in pseudo-historical debates concerning areas to which much greater importance is attached (Bessarabia, Bukovina, Transylvania and Macedonia), it is unlikely that the near future will bring an escalation of this issue.

With the partial, though not insignificant, exception of the intellectuals (Shafir, 1983b, pp. 400-1), the integrationist policies pursued by Romanian elites in the inter-war period could hardly be qualified as successful. There is, indeed, a virtual consensus among scholars that state and society in pre-communist Romania were divided by serious cleavages. A small political elite, composed of landed gentry and some industrialists, ignored the great mass of impoverished peasantry, whose needs were habitually met too late and too reluctantly (Roberts, 1969; Turczinski, 1971, pp. 102-3 and *passim*; Jowitt, 1974a, p. 1179; Janos, 1978).

At the beginning of this century the most striking feature of the Romanian social and political system was the schisms between the *pays légal* and the *pays réel*. Western political reforms, gradually introduced since the middle of the nineteenth century, found no parallel in socio-economic reforms. As Constantin Dobrogeanu-Gherea, the 'founding father' of Romanian socialism, put it in 1894, Romania had 'a liberal constitution, but in actual situation which, in some of its aspects, is worse than that of autocratic countries'. According to the letter of the law, Gherea wrote, sovereignty belonged to the people, 'but in reality, the country is mastered by an oligarchy of a few thousand'. Officially, 'over thirty years have passed since we abolished feudal serfdom legality, replacing it with a bourgeois, liberal one'. However, 'in reality, and above all in administration, feudal relationships are acknowledged' (Dobrogeanu-Gherea, 1976-8, Vol. 3, p. 183). Although land reform was introduced in the wake of the First World War, by 1930 75 per cent of all land-holdings were under five hectares (approximately twelve acres), whereas, according to that year's census, nearly 77 per cent of the population still lived in rural areas (Roberts, 1969, p. 370; Republica Socialistă Romănia. Direcţia Centrală de Statistică, 1975, p. 9; Zach, 1979, p. 193; King, 1980, p. 23).

Although occasional outbursts of revolt, such as the 1907 peasant *jacquerie*, have been recorded in modern Romanian history, socio-economic inequities of the kind previously mentioned should not be automatically associated with political unrest. For, if political integration was unlikely to be achieved in a basically underdeveloped society on the strength of nationalist values alone, identification with the 'centre' none the less came about as a result of the transfer of loyalties from the wider bonds characteristic of peasant societies. These bonds, as K. Jowitt shows, are 'corporate' and 'patriarchical'. Consequently, 'references of national identification were religious and personal, and, for the majority of the population, they were likely to be understood in terms of mass ("small boy") deference to privileged "big men"' (Jowitt, 1978a, p. 20).

Claims of the contemporary Romanian leadership notwithstanding, in the inter-war period the working class were numerically weak and certainly possessed no proletarian class consciousness. As late as 1930 only 7.7 per cent of the population belonged to the industrial sector (Connor, 1979, p. 31). By 1938 the modern industrial proletariat (according to post-war communist data which should, however, be suspected of some degree of inflation) had reached the unimpressive figure of some 400,000, out of a population of nearly 20 million (Scurtu, 1982, pp. 20-1; Roberts, 1969, p. 355). Urbanization, and the growth of a 'third estate'—both conducive to development of positive attitudes towards group and individual autonomy[5] (Boehm, 1930, p. 334), and consequently to political activism—had been slow to arrive in Romania. Although some cities underwent considerable growth in the second part of the nineteenth century, a very large proportion of their population was made up of foreign elements (Chirot, 1976, pp. 107-8, 145-6; Zach, 1979, p. 188), which should partially account for the local attitude of xenophobic anti-modernization displayed by intellectual elites. As Andrew Janos indicates, whereas in Western Europe 'social mobilization implied the rising of public awareness of masses who had already been detached from norms of the traditional *Gemeinschaft* by experience of the market economy', the bulk of the Romanian population had not been 'accultured into the impersonal norms of the modern *Gesellschaft*' and continued to seek 'the moral and emotional support of kinship, household and community' (Janos, 1978, pp. 100-1). Romania, in other words, was basically a 'status' rather than a 'class' society, i.e. one whose 'basic social units, organizational models and cultural matrices were the peasant household and village community'. Such entities are 'based on personal-affective ties subordinating economic considerations and manipulating them in light of their own status-based meanings' (Jowitt, 1978a, p. 21).

Patronage and nepotism, both known to have been characteristic of political life, may be explained by such traditional peasant social attitudes, though only partially so. The historical legacy of an oriental mentality—not unknown to corrupt by offering material privileges in exchange for acquiescence and deference—as well as influences stemming from a dominant religion in which the accent is on externalization rather than on internalization of values (Shafir, 1983b, pp. 406-9), must have played an equal part in moulding inter-war political culture and behaviour.

Dissenting from views which emphasize the state-society gulf in the inter-war period, Paul Shapiro writes that the 'traditional' or 'historical' parties had been rather successful in their attempts to bridge such a gap (Shapiro, 1981). Conventional wisdom, he claims, 'often proves no wisdom at all', whence he proceeds to demonstrate that earlier authors who dealt with this question would have been less 'harsh', had they taken the trouble to study 'trends rather than isolated events'. Such trends, he claims, indicate that the parties were transforming themselves from regional organizations into organizations with a national constituency, and that the Romanian political system was making its first steps towards transformation 'from one of passive acceptance of the status quo by the voter to one of more conscious mass participation in the determination of the country's future course'. These conclusions are based on election returns from Greater Romania's parliamentary elections, which Shapiro himself qualifies as 'not entirely reliable'. Even allowing for the legitimate attempt to overcome such unreliability by various techniques, Shapiro fails to distinguish between the integration of the (previously regionally orientated) *political parties* into Romanian society and the integration of the bulk of *society* into Romanian politics, which, unlike the former, obviously did not go very deep. It is consequently difficult to subscribe to his conclusion that the disappearance of the political system, seen to have 'succumbed in 1938' to the rise of extremism 'inside Romania and abroad' and to attacks 'on the territorial integrity of the state', was 'an indication of fragility, however, not of bankruptcy'. The proof of the *mămăligă*, after all, should have been in its eating.

Without diminishing the importance of the 'external factor', the destruction of the political system at the end of the third and the beginning of the fourth decade of the century is to be understood above all in intra-systemic terms. The ideational activities of the revolutionary Romanian right combined the nationalist ethos of the intelligentsia with protest against the wretched state of the peasantry as well as against the corrupt practices of traditional elite 'politicking'—labelled in Romania '*politicianism*' (Weber, 1966; Turczynski, 1971). This ideology had its roots in the 'traditionalist' school of thought, originally moulded by the conservative right. Born as a reaction to emulative attitudes displayed in the mid-nineteenth century by the 'evolutionists', who propagated Western ideas and political institutions, the traditionalist school rejected the adoption of 'forms' devoid of local 'essence', i.e. the Romanian national identity. By the end of the century the traditionalists had gained the upper hand in letters, in philosophy and in historiography. Cultural figures such as the national poet Mihai Eminescu, the 'Moldavian bard' Vasile Alecsandri, the overtly anti-semitic historian, literary critic and politician Nicolae Iorga, founder of the nationalist conservative school of 'sowism', the writer and philosopher Constantin Stere, who adopted a Russian-inspired populist approach to local conditions in his *Volkish* school of *poporanism*, contributed each in their own way to the accumulation of system-delegitimization trends (Oldson, 1973; Turczynski, 1971; Kitch, 1975; Shafir 1983a, 1983b). It is here that the roots of political stances later taken up by such figures as the poet-politician Octavian Goga, the right-wing existentialist philosopher Nae Ionescu, or the overtly fascist poet Nichifor Crainic, are to be found.

Romanian fascism, in other words, was far from being a foreign-imported bourgeois 'diversion', as the Comintern-inspired version has it in Bucharest even today. On the contrary, like fascism elsewhere, it was anti-bourgeois, and it sought to return to an idealized past, sanctified by the bond of 'blood and soil', as embodied by the peasantry and founded in religion. In other words, it combined intellectual nationalism with social protest. Such origins help to explain the Iron Guardist (the Romanian Fascist Movement) adoration of the national poet Eminescu (Weber, 1966, p. 507). Indeed, it was the fascist leader Corneliu Zelea Codreanu himself who established that 'before being a political, theoretical, financial, economic movement, the Legionary Movement is a spiritual school' (Weber, 1964, p. 169). It is the autochthonous nature of such roots that also explains why revolutionary-inclined Romanian youths could more easily identify with the Iron Guardist ethos than with communist doctrines. To understand this, however, it is necessary to review the birth and development of the socialist, and later the communist, movement in that part of the world.

2 Marxism in Romania: the early stages

The rise and development of socialist thought in Romania was hindered by three main factors: the socio-economic structure of society, which was predominantly agricultural; the non-Romanian ethnic origin of many of the original and later exponents of socialist and communist ideas; and, last, but by no means least, the disregard displayed by the Romanian Communist Party (RCP) towards tradi-tional national aspirations, as a result of its absolute subservience to Moscow (Ionescu, 1964, pp. 1-28, 41-6; Fischer-Galati, 1967, pp. 1-16; King, 1980, pp. 9-38; Shafir, 1981b, pp. 593-7).

In an outline for a history of Romanian socialism published in 1925, L. Ghelerter, one of the more prominent members of the movement in the inter-war period, connects the beginnings of socialist activities in the country with the arrival in Romania of a group of Russian revolutionary socialists, such as N. Zubcu Codreanu, Eugen Lupu, Z. Arbore and, above all, Constantin Dobrogeanu-Gherea (Ghelerter, 1980, pp. 242-9). With apparently substantial omissions, this outline is included in a posthumous volume of Ghelerter's writings, re-issued in 1980. An editorial note, however, indicates that the beginnings of such activities should be attributed to a considerably earlier period. This note attests to the regime's current endeavours to demonstrate that the doctrine is deeply embedded in national history, and that, consequently, the RCP is entitled to a rightful claim to seniority in the international movement. Similar considerations lay behind President Ceauşescu's declaration of 1973, according to which the founding of the first country-wide organized labour movement, the Romanian Social-Democratic Workers' Party (RSDWP) in the spring of 1893, should be considered as marking 'the true beginnings of the Romanian Communist Party' (Ceauşescu, 1970-83, vol. 8, p. 273).

Despite contemporary attempts to demonstrate the existence of 'socialist' activity as early as the third decade of the last century (Ceauşescu, 1970-83, Vol. 8, p. 259; Ornea, 1975), the only 'genuine' Romanian 'contribution' to Marxism before the 1880s can be attributed to the self-proclaimed 'prince' I. Racoviţă, who shot Ferdinand Lassalle in a duel over a woman (Dobrogeanu-Gherea, 1976-8, Vol. 1, pp. 185-6).

Before the First World War the Romanian socialist movement was dominated by two figures who were as similar in some respects in background as they were different in the positions they were to adopt in the face of like circumstances: Constantin Dobrogeanu-Gherea and Christian Rakovsky. Born Solomon Katz in the Ukrainian village of Slavinka, in the Ekaterinoslav district, Gherea first set foot in Romania in 1875.[1] By that time, though barely twenty years of age, he was already a refugee, fleeing the long arm of the tsarist *Okhrana*, for already in his Kharkov high school days he had become involved in the activities of the *narodnik* movement. The young man, who was in due course to become one of Romania's foremost literary critics, knew no word of the language and apparently had no intention of settling there. He travelled on to Switzerland, but soon returned, entrusted with smuggling revolutionary literature into neighbouring Russia. The 1877-8 Russo-Turkish war brought him ill-fortune, for the *Okhrana*'s 'long arm', now present in the Romanian principalities alongside tsarist troops, finally caught up with him. Robert Jinks (as he was called in the American passport he had managed to obtain) was abducted *imenem gosudaria* (in the name of the Tsar) and held in the notorious fortress of Petropavlovsk, only to be later banished to Menzen, on the shores of the White Sea. A year later he managed to escape, and by September 1879 he was back in Romania where his wife was expecting their second child, Alexandru (Sasha). A potential tragedy was thus ending as another was about to be born, for Alexandru Dobrogeanu-Gherea, a future founding member of the RCP, was to meet his death in a Stalinist deathcamp in December 1937 (Dobrogeanu-Gherea, 1956, Vol. 2, pp. 388-400; Dobrogeanu-Gherea, 1972, pp. 3-4, 109; Cruceanu & Tănăsescu, 1971, pp. 64-125; Ornea, 1982, p. 480).

In view of his personal experience it is hardly surprising that Gherea became the life-long enemy of 'Europe's gendarme' (Russia). Admittedly, the 'Eastern question' was by then viewed in a similar light by many members of the European socialist movement, including a significant number of refugees who had found temporary shelter in Romania. One of the earliest local socialist publications (1879) was named *Bessarabia*. Far from alluding to the split national identity of its contributors (as one might mistakenly conclude from a reading of the past from contemporary perspectives), the publication's name indicated that the editorial board shared the national resentment generated by the province's forced in-corporation into Russia, in the wake of a war in which the two countries had been one-time allies. Among *Bessarabia*'s sponsors were Dr N. Russel, one of the most colourful figures of East European socialism,[2] Zubcu-Codreanu, and Gherea himself. For Gherea, however, the experience of 1878 had added a personal element to his political involvement. When, in 1916, Romania once more found herself allied with Russia, he thought it prudent to leave the country temporarily, for, as he put it in a letter in 1909, he had learnt by then that while an involuntary visit to Russia might be simple, the return journey would prove more difficult (Dobrogeanu-Gherea, 1972, p. 4).

The outbreak of the 1917 revolution in Russia and the victory of the Bolsheviks produced no radical change in his attitude, for, having evolved from a Bakuninist position to Marxism, Gherea was essentially a Plekhanovist and regarded developments in what was to become the Soviet Union with suspicion. Socialism, he wrote in November 1919, is not supposed to 'organize starvation and a shining poverty'. Shortly before his death in 1920 he warned that, should the endeavour be attempted before a proper evolution of society had been brought about, society might 'develop regressively, towards medieval society, towards primitive communism' (Dobrogeanu-Gherea, 1976-8, Vol. 5, pp. 236, 269).

Yet Gherea's position on the national question can by no means be considered to be identical with that of Romania's ruling elites of the time, for, as a socialist, he made it clear that he rejected the concept of 'nation' in terms of one, united 'family'. The 'family-nation', a concept he attributed, in 1886, to the Romanian Liberal revolutionaries of 1848, was in his eyes but 'a sentimental ideological-utopian fallacy', which 'never existed, does not exist and never will exist' (Dobrogeanu-Gherea, 1976-8, Vol. 2, p. 134).

Gherea's differences of opinion applied to practical politics too, and particularly to divergences concerning the feasibility of a 'Greater Romania' and its envisaged ethnic and geographical borders. He opposed Romania's entry into the Second Balkan War in 1913, seeing it as an imperialist reflection of the ruling oligarchy's internal policies, and supported instead the Rakovsky plan for a Balkan federation, as a possible solution to the region's border conflicts. In the wake of the war, he condemned the incorporation of the 'Cadrilater' into Romania, warning that the conflict with Bulgaria would only play into the hands of the tsarists, and— at various stages and for a variety of reasons, all somehow connected with his anti-Russian views—advocated either neutrality (as a matter of socialist pacifist principle) or an alliance with Austro-Hungary against the 'Eastern menace'. Although a supporter of Romanian claims in Transylvania, once the hostilities of the First World War had broken out, he rebuked the voices that called for an immediate march on Transylvania, warning that, at worst, the Habsburg empire's designs on the Romanian state could lead to temporary loss of *state* independence, whereas an alliance with Russia would endanger Romanian *nationhood*. In what reads as a surprising insight into present-day political concepts, Gherea seems to have differentiated between 'nation building' and 'state building', warning, at the same time, that both could be 'unbuilt'. For, although both empires were multinational, he wrote, Transylvanian Romanians had been capable of safeguarding national rights and a separate identity, whereas an eventual incorporation into the tsarist empire—likely to follow an alliance with Russia, as demonstrated by the 1878 Bessarabian, and by other, precedents—would be followed by enforced Russification (Dobrogeanu-Gherea, 1976-8, Vol. 5, pp. 237-76).

Such views led to an altercation in Parliament, where a deputy accused Gherea of lack of loyalty towards his host-nation, demanding revocation of the citizenship he had acquired in 1890 (Ornea, 1982, p. 449). Although without further repercussions, the incident was symptomatic. Already in 1888 he had been forced to request an audience with his literary adversary Titu Maiorescu, at that time a minister in the Conservative government, fearing expulsion on grounds of socialist agitation (Ornea, 1982, pp. 339-40). The legal mechanism for such steps was not lacking, for a 'Law on the status of foreigners', adopted in 1881 in the wake of a socialist demonstration commemorating the Paris Commune, had already been applied to Pavel Axelrod and to Dr Russel, and would be invoked against Rakovsky and others in 1907 (Cîncea, 1974, pp. 115, 137; Ornea, 1982, pp. 207, 359; Felea & Tănăsescu, 1980, p. 34; Rakovsky, 1974, pp. 393-5; Conte, 1975, Vol. 1, pp. 93-7).

By the turn of the century socialism was regarded by the majority of

Romanian intellectuals as an 'imported exotic plant' (Dobrogeanu-Gherea, 1956, Vol. 1, pp. 216-17, 1976-8, Vol. 1, pp. 369-74, 386-94, 404-7, Vol. 2, pp. 60-1), with Gherea himself considered by many to be its chief prophet. The accusation was not without foundation, for as Gherea confessed in a letter to Karl Kautsky in 1894, when he had 'first arrived in Romania as a Russian refugee, not even the word "socialism" was known' there (Dobrogeanu-Gherea, 1972, p. 35). The situation had made Axelrod extremely pessimistic. After some time spent in the country in Gherea's company he predicted that 'not even the greatest optimist would dare entertain hopes that modern socialist ideas could take root' there (quoted in Haupt, 1967, p. 31).

The handful of intellectuals who adhered to socialist ideas in the 1880s were known as the 'Generous', to indicate the abdication of relatively privileged social positions and dedication to building a more egalitarian society (Georgescu, 1970a, p. 21). Running under the banner of the 'Socialist formation' (Partida socialistă), the group succeeded in getting two of its members elected to parliament in 1888, a performance nowadays evinced to demonstrate the strength of the movement by the end of the ninth decade (Muşat & Ardeleanu, 1982, p. 231). Less partial contemporary Romanian sources, however, admit that in one of these two cases the deputy in question, V. G. Morţun, scion of a well-to-do Moldavian family, made use of 'traditional' methods and family resources, to buy off the electorate (Ornea, 1982, p. 253). Morţun was re-elected to the Assembly of Deputies in 1891, 1892 and again in 1895 (Muşat & Ardeleanu, 1982, p. 231).

In the absence of any real proletarian electorate, and both unable and unwilling to bear the stigma of 'rootlessness', many of the intellectuals who in 1893 had constituted the backbone of the RSDWP joined the Liberal Party in 1899, in an act later to be known as the 'treason of the Generous'. 'What is the result of our socialist movement? The creation of a socialist headquarters of some seventy to eighty people', socialist leader G. Diamandi stated at the last (sixth) congress of the party, while Morţun complained that the socialists had been unable to get their policies known because their pamphlets were not understood. Significantly, this splinter group originally decided to change the party's name to *National*-Democratic, having previously opposed the demands of the Ghelerter-led 'Lumina' circle to intensify activities aimed at extending suffrage rights to Jews (Institutul de studii istorice, 1969, pp. 684, 689, 701-7; Shafir, 1984b). The rebirth of the socialist party in Romania had to await the arrival of a new prime mover, in the person of Rakovsky.

Meanwhile, some of the 'Generous' turned against their former colleagues, whom they constantly accused of attempting to sow artifical ideological seeds in Romanian soil. Among these was Stere, an ethnic Romanian from Bessarabia, who, although never a formal member of the RSDWP, had been close to the party's leadership. Like Gherea, he arrived from Russia imbued with *narodnik* ideas, but unlike him, his thinking evolved in a nationalist direction. Attempting to justify this ideological switch, Stere explained that young intellectuals who had arrived in Romania with noble socialist ideas, valid in other situations, had founded the RSDWP, only to realize after some time that they had been campaigning for a virtually non-existent social class. Such intellectuals were 'spiritually foreign' to the people among whom they had settled, and followed the 'tyranny of abstract formulas', while the peasant 'in vain keeps waiting for the liquidation of ancient debts' (quoted in Ornea, 1972, p. 200). Stere equated the 'tyranny of abstract formulas' with another cardinal sin, the disregard of 'national essence'—a leitmotif later to be embraced by the Romanian extreme right wing. The solution, according to his *poporanist* (populist) doctrines, lay in avoiding the evils of capitalist industrialization, and in creating a society with institutions that corresponded to its national peasant character and that served rural interests (Roberts, 1969, pp. 143-7, 161-2 and *passim*; Ionescu, 1970, pp. 97-106; Kitch, 1975).

In his major work, *Neo-Serfdom (Neoiobăgia)*, Gherea refuted the *poporanist* argument, alongside the 'traditionalist' (*Junimist*) theories of 'forms without essence'. To do this, however, he proceeded in a Marxist manner, i.e. adopting the *Junimist* epistemology and producing its critique 'from inside out'. Gherea's theory about the evolution of capitalism in underdeveloped nations, which constitutes the backbone of his argument in *Neo-Serfdom* (1910), had been outlined as early as 1886, in his first substantial theoretical pamphlet, 'What Do Romania's Socialists Want'. The Liberal revolutionaries of 1848, he claimed, had indeed imported from the West ideas which were 'foreign' to local conditions, but, far from having thereby committed a 'crime', they had acted as the (mostly unconscious) tools of social evolution. History's *List der Vernunft*, to use Hegel's term, of necessity required that advanced capitalism should spread its influence in search of markets, whereby smaller, less-developed nations would benefit by being pushed into the modern world (Dobrogeanu-Gherea, 1976-8, Vol. 2, pp. 7-126). Without claiming that the underdeveloped nations of Europe had vegetated in a state of 'oriental despotism', as Marx did in his critique of colonialism in Asia, his argument none the less stemmed from similar premises concerning modernization (Avineri, 1969, pp. 1-31). And from these premises Gherea was to prophesy in *Neo-Serfdom* that socialism would be brought to the underdeveloped countries of Eastern Europe on Western wings.

The introduction of contemporary capitalist models in the Romanian principalities, indicated Gherea, had not been accompanied by corresponding social transformations. Whereas in Western Europe the introduction of a capitalist superstructure had in fact been an outcome of the process of economic growth, in states such as Romania, Bulgaria and Serbia, the process had begun at the level of the superstructure, as a result of the influence of the more developed nations. But it had also stopped there. This situation, he believed, was dissimilar to that of Russia, where the feudal superstructure, i.e. authoritarian rule, had not yet disappeared. Its special characteristic consisted in the gap between the *pays légal* and the *pays réel*.

Having outlined these historical developments, 'What Do Romania's Socialists Want' proceeded to lay down future tasks for socialists at the local level, in a section unmistakably inspired by Chernyshevski's famous *What Is To Be Done*, and bearing the same name. But if the title was identical to Lenin's book of similar inspiration (published, nevertheless, sixteen years later), the solution envisaged was totally different. Rather than planning Leninist tactics, the Romanian socialists copied the Erfurt Programme of German social democracy (Ghelerter, 1980, p. 246), which Gherea had transposed to local conditions. Socialist activity, according to Gherea, should be directed at 'pouring content' into empty 'forms'; the 'content' should be bourgeois, however, though this would eventually further socialist aims too. Romania's socialists, as he put it in an article in 1894, must be 'legalists', for strict adherence to the letter of bourgeois law meant universal suffrage, the extension of other civil rights, and land reform bringing capitalist forms of production to the countryside as soon as possible, all of which would hasten the approach of a socialist order. In other words, before the socialist order could be envisaged, the bourgeois order of things had to be universalized.

It is not difficult to see why, on coming to power,[3] the then Soviet-orientated Romanian communist leadership castigated the 'Menshevik' orientation of Gherea and of the early Romanian socialists (Gheorghiu-Dej, 1952, pp. 518-19). It was, however, Christian Rakovsky, Romanian socialism's second 'founding father', who, in thought and deed, had already turned from Gherea's legacy after the 1917 revolution in Russia, and possibly even earlier. Like Gherea, Rakovsky was not Romanian by birth.[4] Born in 1873 in the Bulgarian town of Kotel, he was the son of a tradesman who was the head of one of the most prosperous families in town. On his mother's side he belonged to a long line of nationalist revolutionaries. Like Gherea, he became a rebel at a very young age, and was twice expelled from high school for revolutionary activity. Like Gherea, he was a man of broad interests and culture, and like his predecessor in the Romanian socialist movement, he was well known to, and respected by, the revolutionary figures of the time, such as Engels, Axelrod, Plekhanov, Rosa Luxemburg, Vera Zasulich, Wilhelm Libnecht, Jules Guesde, Karl Kautsky, Lenin, and, above all, Trotsky, for whose friendship he was to pay with his life in 1941.

Rakovsky's political career may be said to have been moulded from beginning to end by the shadow of Russia, in a love-hate, or rather—chronologically more accurate—hate-love relationship. According to his autobiography, he had conceived, from early childhood, a strong and passionate sympathy for Russia, not only because his family's revolutionary activities had mainly been connected with Moscow, but also because he had personally witnessed the war of 1877-8, in which the Russian army had fought for the liberation of Bulgaria from the Turks. He had become aware of the current of revolution in the tsarist empire, for some of the officers stationed in the Rakovsky residence had contacts with underground organizations. 'We are liberating you', he later recalled them telling their Bulgarian friends, 'but who will liberate us?' (Rakovsky, 1974, p. 384).

As in Gherea's case, Rakovsky's 'Romanian connection' was a direct outcome of the 1877-8 war, for his parents' estate was in Romanian Dobruja, and the future revolutionary found himself evacuated to that region, eventually to become a

Romanian citizen. By the time he was in high school he had become a convert to Marxism and when, in 1890, he set off for Geneva to enter the medical faculty of the university, his mind was more preoccupied with the ills of society than with those of the human body. Consequently, he attended more revolutionary meetings than medical lectures, and by the time he received his degree in 1897, he had moved from Geneva to Berlin, to Zurich, and finally to Montpellier. When not due to expulsion for revolutionary activities, the moves were determined by his desire to further contacts with the social democratic circles of the time, and above all with the Russian Marxist revolutionaries. Under the influence of Plekhanov he was strengthened in both his Marxist convictions and in his hatred for Russian tsarism. Rakovsky consequently followed Plekhanov's dictum that 'Czarist Russia must be isolated in her foreign relations', and, on graduation, he published a book in Bulgaria entitled *Russia na istok* (Russia in the East), which, in his own words, 'for years to come provided ammunition not only for the Bulgarian Socialist Party against Russian Tsarism, but also for all so-called rusophobe tendencies in the Balkans' (Rakovsky, 1974, p. 387). This earned him the hatred of slavophile Bulgarian nationalist circles, with whom he was to clash again and again (Conte, 1975, Vol. 1, pp. 93-5). Ironically enough, this enemy of Bulgarian nationalism would soon become the object of attacks launched against him in Romania, where he was accused of being a Bulgarian by birth and by loyalty (Conte, 1975, Vol. 1, p. 67).

It was only from 1905 onwards that Rakovsky became a 'Romanian' socialist, but his crucial contribution to the revival of the party is beyond doubt. His name, according to Gheorghe Cristescu, the first Secretary General of the RCP, 'is connected with the most important activities' of the movement during this period (Cristescu, 1972, p. 147).[5] He saw his main task as orientating socialist activities 'to the formation of trade unions, so as to provide a proletarian base, different from that of the dissolved Romanian SD Party, which had mainly consisted of intellectuals and members of the *petit bourgeoisie*' (Rakovsky, 1974, p. 392). With this in mind, he founded, together with Gherea and others, the publication *România muncitoare*. The new party, now called 'the Romanian Social-Democratic Party (RSDP)', came into being in 1910. Rakovsky's relations with Gherea, for whom he had great respect, were friendly (Conte, 1975, Vol. 1, p. 65). This is attested by their correspondence, among other things, and the fact that in 1913 they both played host to Trotsky, influencing his dispatches to *Kievskaya misl* on the Balkan War (Dobrogeanu-Gherea, 1972, pp. 52-6; Shafir, 1984b). Gherea was by then devoting most of his time to writing and was partially incapacitated by illness and old age. Consequently it is to Rakovsky that the relative radicalization of the Romanian movement can be attributed, as well as its gradual 'deviation' from 'legalist' Marxism.

Under his leadership, in 1905, the socialists were active in securing political asylum for the sailors of the battleship *Potemkin* and, probably at his insistence, the movement began to concentrate on the rural areas as well. Whether availing itself of the opportunity, or whether in fact it suspected serious incitement by socialist circles, the Liberal government accused 'foreign-inspired' elements of having engineered the 1907 peasant uprising. Even if such activities were part of the tactics of foreign-inspired deflection, it is nevertheless true that, during the uprising, Rakovsky had appealed to soldiers to act 'against the real enemy, and, if necessary and possible, cross over to the insurgents' (quoted in Conte, 1975, Vol. 1, p. 75). As a result, he was declared an 'undesirable alien' and refused permission to return to Romania from Germany, where he had been attending a conference of the Socialist Internationale.

Contesting the legality of his expulsion (unlike other expelled activists, Rakovsky was a Romanian citizen), the socialist leader made several attempts to cross the border, but was banished each time. The story of these attempts reads as a prelude to the Trotsky saga, for Romania's neighbours refused to allow Rakovsky to cross their borders, and he was bounced from one border to another. He was finally allowed to return in 1912, following a change of government. Since the Conservative government which had allowed him to come back would eventually become the partisan of Romania's adherence to the Central Powers, it was later alleged that Rakovsky owed his return to a 'German connection'. The Germans were thought to have an interest in strengthening anti-Russian elements in Romania. To what extent this is true it is not possible to establish. On the other hand, it has been proved beyond doubt that (like many other members of the Russian revolutionary movement) Rakovsky availed himself of German funds for anti-war propaganda on the eve of Romania's entry into the First World War and during the war itself. Such activities no more make him a 'German agent' in fact than Lenin could have been accused of being. However, they were to constitute the backbone of Vyshinski's accusations against him at his trial in 1938 (Conte, 1975, Vol. 1, pp. 99-101, 129-37, 166-7).

Immediately on his return Rakovsky became engaged in denunciations of the Balkan Wars. Taking a position similar to that of 1907, he published an appeal to new recruits in *România muncitoare*, calling on them to turn their weapons on those who had sent them to the front line. The guns were 'paid for with our sweat, they have often been pointed at our hearts'. The proletarian soldier should not become the defender of 'a deceitful country'. Rather, he should be 'a defender of the class to which he belongs', one 'who will some day wage a bitter war on the most merciless enemy the working classes can have—the governing possessing class'. It was, he concluded, for 'that war, and for that war alone' that workers 'must make every preparation, and learn every stratagem' (quoted in Clark, 1927, p. 186).

The appeal was bound to fall on deaf ears, however, the more so since the mass of the soldiers whom he attempted to persuade were peasants, a category most unlikely to be attracted to Rakovsky's recommendations for 'the socialization of all means of production, including land'—and by force, if necessary (Rakovsky in Institutul de studii istorice, 1968, pp. 57-67). Where the propaganda was understood, it generated hostility. The more emancipated members of the peasantry supported Stere's *poporanist* policies, against which Rakovsky and his friends had been fiercely campaigning (Institutul de studii istorice, 1968, p. 10). Consequently, when the socialist leader ran for Parliament in two successive elections in 1914, he won scarcely more than two hundred votes. He was to do worse in 1916, when he received only 109 votes (Clark, 1927, p. 187).

On the eve of the outbreak of the First World War and throughout the period of Romania's neutrality which ended in 1916, Rakovsky became one of the most vociferous opponents of an alliance with the Entente powers. His position was based on two differing, though complementary views. First, the war *per se* was seen by him as a blatant form of imperialist diversionist tactics, and in September 1914 *România muncitoare* changed its name to *Jos răsboiul* (*Down with the War*) (Institutul de studii istorice, 1968, p. 583). Rakovsky became involved in propaganda for the Balkan Federation, a scheme he had supported ever since 1908, drawing on ideas which had been generating in the area during the eighteenth century, and which enjoyed considerable support in local socialist circles (Conte, 1975, Vol. 1, pp. 95-6). The 'nation-state', he declared, was 'an institution without future'. Such utterances annoyed the nationalist ruling circles of the day and, according to present-day Romanian historiography, the federation he envisaged was a 'non-realistic, utopian solution', which 'disregarded concrete historical conditions' (Institutul de studii istorice, 1968, p. 600). In the eyes of Rakovsky and his friends, however, the national problem could be solved only by socialist revolution, resulting from the disappearance of national boundaries for, as he put it as early as 1905, if patriotism meant 'race prejudice, international and civil war, political tyranny and plutocratic domination', then he was not a patriot. Foreshadowing the approach he would take towards Romania's national problems after 1917, Rakovsky stated that he recognized 'no country but the common country of the international proletariat' (quoted in Clark, 1927, p. 183). The foreign policies of bourgeois circles, directed at the establishment of 'Greater Romania', were castigated as 'bankrupt'—an analysis which contemporary RCP historians qualify as 'mistaken' (Institutul de studii istorice, 1968, pp. 654-5). In the summer of 1915 Rakovsky organized a conference of Balkan social-democratic parties in Bucharest which demanded the immediate cessation of hostilities. Within a few months he became one of the main initiators of the Zimmerwald Conference (Cristescu, 1972, p. 153; Conte, 1975, Vol. 1, pp. 147-51).

The second reason for Rakovsky's opposition to Romania's entry into the war is to be found in his persistent determination to prevent the alliance with tsarist Russia. With this in mind, he did not hesitate to cast the socialist movement as the true and only defender of Romanian historical rights in Bessarabia. On his return to the country in 1912 one of his first political acts was to participate in a ceremony of mourning, marking the anniversary of Bessarabia's annexation, where he protested against the continuance of tsarist rule over the territory (Clark, 1927, p. 185). In February 1913 he wrote that

had there been a Socialist Party in Romania in 1879, it would not have remained impassive before the annexation of Bessarabia, as the governmental parties did, and if it could not have prevented this crime by its protests and efforts, it would have sowed hopes for the future in the spirits of the Bessarabian Romanians.

Finally, in January 1915, arguing against the position of French socialists, he wrote in a Russian journal published in Paris:

> Our French comrades assure us that the Allies, including Russia, are fighting for the principle of nationality. We who live in Eastern Europe, in immediate propinquity to the Muscovite Empire, ask liberty to doubt that . . . We admit the imperialistic policy of Austria in the Balkans, but who can deny that a similar danger exists from Russia toward Romania and Bulgaria who lie in her pathway toward the Straits? [quoted in Clark, 1927, pp. 185-7].

Yet only two years later Rakovsky became the chief communist advocate of Russian hegemony in Eastern Europe, including Bessarabia. In fact it is no exaggeration to assume that the vassal status of the RCP, as well as its 'foreign' image, were established even before the official foundation of the party in 1921; and although Rakovsky never became a member of that particular section of the Third Internationale, no other leader was more responsible for this state of affairs.

After Romania joined the Entente in August 1916 the RSDP virtually disintegrated, following some harsh measures taken by the government as a reaction to socialist anti-war propaganda, as well as to disturbances which took place during the spring. Rakovsky was put under arrest and when the government had to withdraw to Iaşi, the capital of Moldavia, he was also taken there. The outbreak of the February revolution in Russia brought about a revival of the party's activities, the more so since the population had come under the influence of Russian troops stationed in Moldavia. At the beginning of April the social-democratic groups which had managed to escape imprisonment even sent a message to the Odessa soviet, expressing the hope that a new age was about to break for all of Europe's oppressed nations, including the Romanians (Hitchins, 1968, pp. 268-71). The government seemed to panic, and a new wave of arrests followed. Among those detained was Max Vexler, a founding member of the 'Lumina' circle, who was shot in the back while allegedly attempting to escape. A week after this incident, on 1 May 1917, the Romanian socialists, aided by the soviets of Russian soldiers, organized a demonstration in Iaşi, which ended in a march on the local prison and the liberation of Rakovsky and several other socialists (Felea & Tănăsescu, 1980, p. 43). Fearing re-arrest, the freed prisoners fled to Odessa. The 'Romanian chapter' in Rakovsky's eventful career was coming to an end.

In Odessa the leaders of the Romanian movement, led by Rakovsky and Mihai Bujor, set up the Romanian Committee of Social Democratic Action, which very soon began to emulate the Russian model, demanding the overthrow of 'tsarism' in Romania and the extension of the revolution 'beyond the Prut' (*Documente din istoria Pardidului Communist din România*, 1953, Vol. 1, pp. 13, 15-16; Hitchins, 1968,

p. 273). This committee was in close touch with the Russians, but from the beginning it was distrusted by the mass of RSDP members in Romania, who suspected it of having come under Russian domination. It is here that one may discern the roots of the schism which was to occur in the movement in 1921, with the formation of the RCP. In July 1917 the RSDP publicly disavowed the committee, declaring that its actions contravened the party's past and present policies (Ionescu, 1964, p. 6).

Although Rakovsky originally felt closer to the Mensheviks, he evolved rather quickly into a Bolshevik position, apparently under the influence of Trotsky (Conte, 1975, Vol. 1, pp. 173, 190-2). From Stockholm, where he was attending a conference of the Zimmerwald left in November 1917, he sent a telegram to the victorious Bolshevik faction, expressing regret that 'at this grandiose and decisive moment for the entire proletariat, the Romanian proletariat is in no position to extend its full aid to the Russian revolution', but none the less promising that 'the Romanian comrades will do their duty'. Their hopes, he indicated, 'turn above all to the socialist government of Russia' (*Izvestia*, 29 November 1917, as quoted in Conte, 1975, Vol. 1, pp. 182-3). By the end of December the Odessa Committee began organizing a Romanian Military Revolutionary Committee, the purpose of which was to recruit soldiers who would fight alongside their Russian comrades for the defence of the revolution. The troops came from among ethnic Romanians who had fought in the Austro-Hungarian armies and had become prisoners of war, as well as from Romanian soldiers stationed in southern Russia (Cherestesiu & Copoiu, 1967; Cruceanu & Ciobanu, 1970, pp. 40-1; Hitchins, 1971, pp. 127-8). According to a declaration issued by the Military Revolutionary Committee on 8 February 1918, it was considered a 'revolutionary duty' to declare that the Romanian revolutionaries would not hesitate to use their weapons against their own government (*Izvestia*, 8 February 1918, quoted in Conte, 1975, Vol. 1, p. 199). These troops did indeed participate in the military confrontation at Bender and in the subsequent Russian offensive in Bessarabia, but were eventually beaten back and forced to withdraw to Odessa.

When Rakovsky arrived in Moscow in April 1918 he was immediately put in charge of the Romanian desk at the People's Commissariat for Foreign Affairs, and in January 1919 he became head of the Soviet government in the Ukraine. It was in this capacity that—against Lenin's express orders[6]—he planned an invasion of Romania in order to join up with Béla Kún's forces in Hungary. On 1 May 1919 he sent an ultimatum to the Romanian government, demanding the immediate evacuation of Bessarabia (Degras, 1953, Vol. 1, pp. 155-7), to which, foreshadowing the events of 1940, Bukovina was added in a second ultimatum, on the following day (Conte, 1975, Vol. 1, pp. 244-5). It was also Rakovsky who, on two occasions at least, in 1921 and 1924, exercised his 'Romanian expertise' to prevent *de jure* Soviet recognition of Bucharest's sovereignty over Bessarabia (King, 1980, p. 28; Ionescu, 1964, pp. 22-3). When, in 1920, in circumstances yet to be discussed, a delegation of the RSDP went to Moscow to negotiate affiliation with the Third Internationale, he was among those who exercised considerable pressure on his former colleagues to agree to total submission to Comintern domination (Cristescu, 1972, p. 154).

Such positions, as a virulently anti-communist Western observer remarked many years ago (Clark, 1927, p. 188), make the reading of Rakovsky's post-1917 views on the 'Romanian question'—particularly those on Bessarabia (Rakovsky, 1925)—an amusing pasttime, when placed in juxtaposition with the opinions he aired before. The contrast, though blatant, is none the less not disconsonant, for, as F. Conte points out, while all of tsarist Russia's conquests were in Rakovsky's eyes despicable, wars waged by the first socialist state were wars of liberation, by definition (Conte, 1975, Vol. 1, p. 106). It is precisely here that Gherea and Rakovsky parted ways: not in fact because Gherea remained a loyal citizen of his adopted country (though, of course, that was also true) but because the older leader entertained very serious doubts about the feasibility of inculcating socialist norms of behaviour in the population of an underdeveloped country—and possibly in its leadership as well. Had he lived long enough, Gherea would in all probability have refused to endorse Soviet territorial irredentism, if only because in his eyes the 'first workers' motherland' was simply not a socialist country, and her message, consequently, could not be one of liberation. Such significant differences were none the less of little importance for the emerging image of Romanian socialism. In their endeavours to project Marxism as an ethnically and socially subversive doctrine, inter-war Romanian politicians found a reliable ally in the Comintern.

3 The Socialist Movement in the Inter-war Period

In May 1966, in a speech delivered on the occasion of the forty-fifth anniversary of the founding of the RCP, Secretary General Ceauşescu departed from the hitherto customary idealized presentation of the party's activities in the period of illegality. To particular criticism, reiterated since on several occasions (Ceauşescu, 1970-83, Vol. 4, p. 368; Vol. 8, p. 275; Vol. 10, p. 242; Vol. 22, pp. 523-4), were now subjected Soviet-inspired policies regarding Greater Romania's territorial integrity, the cadre and leadership policies deriving therefrom, attitudes towards middle and lower classes of the peasantry,[1] as well as the question of collaboration with democratic, non-communist forces. The 'tactical orientations and indications' issued by the Comintern, according to the Romanian party leader, contradicted the Romanian 'economic, social, political and national conditions'. The Third Internationale, moreover, had added insult to injury by 'appointing leadership cadres, including the Secretary General, who were not familiar with the life and with the preoccupations of the Romanian people' (Ceauşescu, 1968-9, Vol. 1, pp. 357-61).

This speech amounted, in part, to an oblique admission of party failure in attracting any significant support from among Romania's ethnic majority. As it turns out, these Comintern directives had overshadowed RCP prospects from the very beginning. In autumn 1920, Ceauşescu told his hearers, 'the Romanian socialists sent to Moscow a delegation for the purpose of discussing affiliation to the Communist Internationale'. Lenin, Rakovsky, Bukharin, and the other Soviet officials whom the delegation met, insisted on strict adherence to the '21 Conditions', including the prerogative for the Comintern to interfere in the party's cadre and personnel policies. The six-member delegation, composed of Gheorghe Cristescu, Constantin Popovici, Eugen Rozvan, Alexandru Dobrogeanu-Gherea, D. Fabian and I. Fluieraş (Muşat & Ardeleanu, 1982, p. 250), was apparently not united in its attitude *vis-à-vis* Soviet demands. According to Ceauşescu, Cristescu, Popovici and Rozvan, while adhering to 'the Leninist principles concerning the new type of party', raised some objections to assessments by the Comintern concerning the situation in Romania, which stemmed from 'lack of knowledge concerning realities in our country'. The three dissenting members of the Romanian delegation also objected to 'Comintern interference with the composition of the leading organs of the Romanian Communist Party, expressing the view that this was an inalienable attribute of the party itself'.

It is nowadays admitted in Romania that the brutality of Soviet demands, as well as their ultimata concerning the expulsion of 'undesirable' elements from the movement (Felea & Tănăsescu, 1980, p. 64), ultimately led to schism.

Contemporary Romanian official historiography finds itself in an uneasy dilemma concerning these developments, for, on the one hand, it clearly cannot condemn the formation of the RCP without impinging on the ideological legitimacy of the present ruling elite, while, on the other hand, it clearly—though not always openly—sides with the more independent and more nationally responsive views of the anti-Comintern elements.[2]

The schism which was to occur in May 1921 began to develop, as observed, during the days of the Odessa-based and Rakovsky-led Military Revolutionary Committee. It would, however, be inaccurate to attribute pro-Comintern or 'extreme leftist' attitudes to ethnically non-Romanian elements alone. A very important part in the radicalization of the movement, for instance, was played by Alecu Constantinescu, who headed the more militant faction of the party in Rakovsky's absence. By summer 1918 this faction was calling itself the 'Maximalist Federation of Romania', with 'maximalism' as a kind of parallel version of 'bolshevism' (Hitchins, 1968, pp. 282-5). The 'minimalist' faction, on the other hand, recommended that the party abide by its 1919 programme, which, although it was undeniably radicalized, still basically envisaged legalist evolutionism. The party's name was changed from Social-Democratic to Socialist (RSP) and its main goal was deemed to be the 'gaining, by whatever means, of political power held by the bourgeoisie and the establishment of the dictatorship of the proletariat with a view to attaining the communist ideal' (Muşat & Ardeleanu, 1982, p. 238; Hitchins, 1968, p. 285). Somewhere half-way between these two opposing groups were the 'centrists' or the 'unitary socialists', who came to support affiliation to the Comintern, provided this did not overlook the 'specific' (i.e. national) interests of the Romanian movement and did not infringe its independence (Felea & Tănăsescu, 1980, p. 65).

The first confrontation between these opposing factions took place in January/February 1921, on the return of the RSP delegation from Moscow, at a conference of the party's General Council and the trade-union movement. According to post-war Romanian historiography, the communist motion was endorsed by eighteen votes, the 'unitary socialists' received ten votes and the 'minimalists' eight (Muşat & Ardeleanu, 1982, p. 250). As a result, the 'rightist' faction decided to leave the party. The early 1921 conference decided to convene a party congress in early May, the main question on the agenda being affiliation to the Third Internationale.

As Robert King indicates in his *History of the Romanian Communist Party*, there are considerable differences in the evaluation of the significance of this forum's decisions (King, 1980, p. 17). C. Titel Petrescu, one of the socialist leaders of the inter-war period, writes in his sketchy history of the movement in Romania, published in 1944, that the decision was adopted in the absence of many socialist leaders, who had been imprisoned by the authorities. Police provocateurs, according to this version, eventually sided with the 'maximalists' in order to provide justification for reprisals (Petrescu, 1944, p. 359). According to Ceauşescu's speech of May 1966, the decision to transform the RSP into the RCP and to accept affiliation was adopted by 'an overwhelming majority'. The size of the majority, however, is by no means clear. In the early sixties, official party historiography put it at 380 out of 540 delegates, a figure which was subsequently cited in several Western versions of the event (Liveanu, 1962; Ghermani, 1977, p. 12; Ghermani, 1981, p. 25; Shafir, 1981b, p. 594). More recent data, on the other hand, has it that 428 votes were cast for unconditional affiliation and 111 votes for affiliation with some reservations (Muşat & Ardeleanu, 1982, p. 251; Scurtu, 1982, p. 75).

The congress of 8-13 May 1921 is counted as the First Congress of the RCP. However, the gathering never concluded its agenda, for on 12 May the authorities closed the conference and put under arrest most of the delegates who had voted in favour of affiliation. The Second Congress took place on 3-4 October 1922 in the industrial town of Ploieşti, and may be regarded as a continuation of the work of the First Congress, which, owing to its termination, had failed to adopt a programme and most of the resolutions envisaged. It was in October 1922 that the party adopted its statutes imposed by the Comintern and elected Gheorghe Cristescu as its first Secretary General (Muşat & Ardeleanu, 1982, p. 251; Scurtu, 1982, p. 77).

The impact of the affiliation was immediate: at the insistence of the Comintern, the 'unitary socialists' were expelled from the RCP in early 1922 (Felea & Tănăsescu, p. 67). In October 1923 the schism was carried into the trade-union movement, with the communists seceding from the common umbrella organization and joining the International 'Red' Syndicates. They would eventually return to the united movement in 1935-6, once more following Soviet directions, arising from 'United Front' politics (Scurtu, 1982, pp. 79, 173). Nowhere, however, were the Soviet 'orientations and indications' more blatant than in the policies that the party had to adopt *vis-à-vis* Romania's national questions. In December 1923 the Balkan Communist Federation, following Rakovsky's directives, adopted a resolution which established the task of the Romanian 'section' as supporting the rights of national minorities to self-determination, 'up to and including complete secession from the existing state' (Gruber, 1974, p. 186; Scurtu, 1982, pp. 79-80). Preparations for the establishment of a 'Moldavian' Soviet Autonomous Republic (October 1924) were by then under way and, to make matters worse, the new republic was toasted by its first President—a Russian by birth—as 'the cradle of Soviet Romania' (Dima, 1982, p. 23). The Fifth Comintern World Congress in June/July 1924 reiterated the 1923 instructions, following the failure of negotiations between Romania and the Soviet Union (Gruber, 1974, pp. 131-3).

Within the ranks of the RCP, the directives once more generated a three-fold division. Cristescu, Romanian by birth, pointed out that the adoption of such a line by the party could lead to proscription, as indeed proved to be the case. At the other end of the spectrum, Elek Köblös (Bădulescu) and Sándor Körösi-Krizsán (Georgescu), both Hungarians from Transylvania, were in favour of acceptance, as indeed were other members from that region. A centrist group, led by Alexandru Dobrogeanu-Gherea, and more intellectual in outlook, hesitated between the two alternatives and finally proposed that the issue be discussed by the Comintern Executive Committee. A delegation was dispatched to Moscow in September 1923, and despite Cristescu's reluctance to accept what would obviously greatly affect the party's national image, the visit ended in virtual capitulation to Bukharin's pressures (Körösi-Krizsán, 1966; King, 1980, pp. 30-1). Shortly thereafter Cristescu was replaced by a Directorate, with Köblös acting as Secretary General on an *ad interim* basis (Cruceanu, 1967, pp. 154-5).

At the Third RCP Congress, which took place in Vienna in August 1924, Köblös was formally elected to the leadership of the party. The Congress duly included 'self determination' and the 'right to secession' in its resolution, as indeed it would do at the Fourth (1928) and the Fifth (1931) Congresses, held in Kharkov and Moscow, respectively (Scurtu, 1982, pp. 80, 82-3, 134-6; King, 1980, p. 31; Shafir, 1981b, p. 594). The resolution, as Cristescu had predicted, led the party into illegality, for the December 1924 'Mârzescu law' which outlawed the RCP had little difficulty in presenting the organization as fundamentally an agent of foreign interests. According to this resolution, the 'workers and peasants of Bessarabia' entertained the constant hope 'that their national revolution will unite them with the Union of Soviet Socialist Republics' (*Documente din istoria Partidului Comunist din România*, 1953, Vol. 2, p. 257).

The Fourth Congress once more replaced the leader of the party with a 'foreign' element, now 'electing' as Secretary General Vitali Holostenko (Barbu), formerly a member of the Ukrainian Communist Party (Scurtu, 1982, p. 82). What was not changed, however, was the line on Bessarabia and on the right to secession, to which, moreover, Bukovina was now added for the first time (*Documente din istoria Partidului Comunist din România*, 1953, Vol. 2, p. 567). According to Romanian historiography, the gathering 'not only failed to provide the necessary answers to questions which preoccupied the RCP . . . but, through measures adopted, generated further difficulties in the activity of communists in our country' (Scurtu, 1982, pp. 82-3).

Between the Fourth and the Fifth Congresses the party morale was at its lowest, for membership was very low, prospects poor, owing to lack of popularity, and the leadership was engaged in a bitter factional struggle. The two main opponents were Holostenko and Marcel Pauker. Both factions claimed fidelity to the Comintern—both apparently in good faith. Personal dislikes and antipathies, however, brought about the virtual paralysis of any meaningful activity, and by the end of 1931 the Internationale had to intervene once more—and more forcefully than ever (Ionescu, 1964, pp. 27-8; Scurtu, 1982, p. 134).

Apart from imposing stricter discipline and a worker recruitment policy, the Fifth Congress nominated as Secretary General Alexandru Danieluk Ştefanski (Gorun), a member of the Polish Communist Party. He fulfilled this function until 1934, being then followed on an *ad interim* basis by Eugen Iacobovici. In June 1936 it was the turn of a Bulgarian, Boris Ştefanov, to be designated leader of the RCP (Scurtu, 1982, pp. 135-6, 173). Ştefanov was one of the numerous Bulgarians to hold leading positions in the Romanian party in these 'formative' years, alongside D. Donchev (shot dead by the police in 1931), G. Kroşnev, D. Ganev, and D. Kolev (Dumitru Coliu) (Oren, 1971, pp. 138-43). Ştefanov held on to the position for a record of almost four years, being replaced by the Hungarian Ştefan Foriş in 1940—once again on the orders of the Comintern.

Among its other resolutions, the Fifth Congress branded the Social-Democrats 'social fascists'. In connection with such epithets, it is interesting to note that within the framework of efforts aimed at discrediting the bourgeois 'historical' parties, post-war Romanian historiography often evinced the electoral 'non-aggression' pact concluded in 1937 by Iuliu Maniu, the National Peasant Party (NPP) leader, with the Romanian fascist *Führer*, Corneliu Codreanu (Fătu, 1972). It is obliquely admitted nowadays, however, that on Soviet instructions the communists also supported Maniu's candidates at these elections, which amounted to indirect collaboration with the Iron Guardists (Nedelcu, 1973, pp. 149-50). Such support, it should be added, was but one of many Comintern-imposed contortions of RCP tactical collaboration. A few years earlier, at the Fifth Congress, any and all non-communist parties or organizations had been branded 'fascist' or 'proto-fascist' (Ioniţă, 1971, p. 514). Abiding by the new instructions of 1937, the RCP continued to endorse NPP candidates, unlike the Social-Democrats, who withdrew their support for Maniu's party in the wake of his 'understanding' with Codreanu. This position, it is now admitted, 'had serious consequences on the feasibility of setting up a Popular Anti-Fascist Front' (Nedelcu, 1973, pp. 122-3).

The contortions imposed by the Soviets' changing interests were indeed extreme and created embarrassing situations. If such oscillations were not very significant, it was only because by that time the RCP could count on very few cadres or sympathizers. After the Fifth Congress, the Soviet grip on the RCP was virtually absolute, but there was hardly any party to speak of. As our scrutiny has shown, many of its leaders belonged to the Hungarian minority. Apart from those already mentioned, one should identify here names such as K. Berger, I. Ranghet, and V. Luca. Classified statistics of the RCP for the year 1933 indicate that some 26.58 per cent of party members were of Hungarian origin. The relative popularity of the RCP among Hungarians could partly be attributed to the fact that Transylvanian towns were more industrialized than other parts of the country. The proportion of party members living in this region was in fact the highest of all Romania's provinces—some 36 per cent (Graham, 1982, p. 31). Nevertheless, as Robert King demonstrates, such support was mainly the result of antipathy to Greater Romania policies (King, 1980, pp. 33-4). The Jewish minority, in 1933, was the third largest ethnic group in the party, after the Hungarians and the Romanians (22.65 per cent). It comprised 18.12 per cent of the membership of the organization. The significance of these figures[3] can only be grasped in relation to the proportion of these groups in the population at large, as illustrated in Table 1.

What may have counted more than the proportion of the membership was the striking prominence of members of minorities in the leadership. Among Jews,

Table 1   RCP Membership by Ethnic Group in the 1930s*

	Party[†] %	Total population %
Hungarians	26.58	7.9
Romanians	22.65	71.9
Jews	18.12	4.0
Russians and Ukrainians	10.27	3.2
Bulgarians	8.45	2.0
Others	10.21	11.0

* Figures are worked out from *Institutul central de statistică*, 1938, p. xxiv, and Graham, 1982, p. 30.

† Figures add up to less than 100% because of calculation to the first two decimal points only.

names such as Alexandru Dobrogeanu-Gherea, Marcel and Ana Pauker, E. Iacobovici, L. Bechenau, M. Kahana, B. Brainer, R. Kofler, P. Borilă, I. Chişinevschi, L. Răutu and S. Toma, were unlikely to generate identification with the RCP in an atmosphere where the myth of 'Judeo-Bolshevism' was widely fostered. Neither the fact that the mass of the Jewish minority by no means identified itself with the RCP,[4] nor the purge of a number of communist activists (A. Dobrogeanu-Gherea, M. Pauker, E. Filipovici, E. Köblös, etc.)[5] in the Soviet Union significantly altered the party's 'foreign image'. To make matters worse, some of these leaders were what in the eyes of the Romanian majority was probably the worst combination— Bessarabian (Chişinevschi, Răutu) or Hungarian (Berger) Jews. Finally, names such as P. Tkachenko and, later, E. Bodnăraş, should be added to those belonging to the leadership's Slavic 'tributaries'. It is not difficult to understand why, in the heavily chauvinist inter-war years, members of national minorities should be attracted by an apparently internationalist doctrine. For the same reasons, however, the 'costs of identifying' with the nationalist-revolutionary right wing were considerably less for members of the mobilized reform-minded majority, than for those adhering to an organization widely perceived as serving the 'historical enemy' (Jowitt, 1971, p. 87). It is relevant to point out here that, in 1933, only 28.70 per cent of RCP members lived in the 'Old Kingdom', whereas 70.72 per cent were residents of the '*occupied* territories' (annexed after 1918), i.e. the bulk of the membership came from regions with a high proportion of national minorities (figures calculated from Graham, 1982, p. 31; emphasis mine).

The lack of popularity of the RCP affected efforts at recruitment. By 1922 the party had some 2,000 members (King, 1980, p. 18). In the elections which took place in that year (the only such confrontation before the RCP was banned), it managed to get 0.8 per cent of the ballot in the 'Old Kingdom', the only province where it put forward candidates. By 1924 the RCP had barely added 500 members to the 1922 figure. At the time of the Fifth Congress, when its stance on Bessarabia had become widely known, membership had fallen to 1,200 (King, 1980, p. 18) and, according to the classified statistics quoted earlier, in 1933 the figure stood at a mere 1,665 (Graham, 1982, p. 30). Nevertheless, in the elections which took place in June 1931, the Workers' and Peasants' Bloc (WPB), a communist front organization, managed to gain 73,716 votes, obtaining five mandates in parliament, although these were subsequently invalidated (Ziemer, 1969, p. 1065; Scurtu, 1982, pp. 137-8). Among the Bloc's deputies was Lucreţiu Pătrăşcanu, who later became a victim of Stalinist party-purges. To what extent such success indicated successful 'image-mending' is, however, difficult to establish. The SDP leadership claimed that most votes cast for the Bloc's candidates came from districts where the proportion of national minorities was high, and that in their electoral propaganda the communists had appealed to irredentist aspirations in the border regions. The former claim, in any case, seems to be corroborated by statistical evidence (King, 1980, p. 34).

Western estimates concerning the size of the party at the time of its emergence from illegality in 1944 put its membership at from 884 to between 1,000 and 2,000, with an unknown number of unregistered sympathizers (Burks, 1966, p. 95; Fischer-Galati, 1970, p. 75; Jowitt, 1971, p. 79; Ghermani, 1977, p. 13; Vago, 1977, p. 113). According to an article published in the Soviet publication *Bolshevik* in 1950, on 23 August 1944 the Romanian party had fewer than 1,000 members. In proportion to the population it was, according to the same source, the smallest communist party in Eastern Europe, while in absolute numbers its membership equalled that of the Albanian party (Grigorian, 1950, p. 14).

The socialists did better than the RCP—but not excessively so. Present-day Romanian figures put membership in the RSP on the eve of the split at some 150,000 (Scurtu, 1982, p. 72). Soviet figures, on the other hand, indicate a considerably more modest 45,000 (quoted in Jackson, 1966, p. 83). Be that as it may, at the 1919 elections, the first in which the party's candidates appeared on the ballot paper, following an absence of two decades, the RSP succeeded in having seven (according to other sources, nine) candidates elected to parliament (Muşat & Ardeleanu, 1982, p. 259; Scurtu, 1982, p. 72). In the following year it did even better, with twenty members elected—a performance all the more impressive since the number of seats had been reduced from 568 to 369 (Muşat & Ardeleanu, 1982, p. 259). However, two years later the party's strength in the legislature was drastically reduced, to two (Ziemer, 1969, p. 1061).[6]

Although this followed the split in the movement, the socialists' failure in 1922 should by no means be attributed to a move to the communists. Not only did the socialists succeed in outstripping their communist competitors in the trade union movement (King, 1980, p. 21), but in elections which took place in the period 1926-37, the Romanian Social-Democratic Party (as the movement once more called itself from 1927 on) did better than the communist-run WPB, the Ploughmen's Front and the League of Work.

The Romanian socialist movement, however, was plagued by constant rifts

Table 2   Socialist Parties Versus Communist Front Organizations, 1926–37*

	1926		1927		1928		1931		1932		1933		1937	
Social-Democrats	1.6	—	1.8	—	†	9	3.3	6	3.4	7	1.3	—	0.9	—
Independent Socialists	—	—	—	—	—	—	—	—	0.2	—	—	—	—	—
Unitary Socialists	—	—	—	—	—	—	—	—	—	—	0.1	—	—	—
Workers' and Peasants' Bloc	1.5	—	1.3	—	1.3	—	2.5	5	0.3	—	—	—	—	—
Ploughmen's Front	—	—	—	—	—	—	—	—	—	—	0.3	—	—	—
League of Work	—	—	—	—	—	—	—	—	—	—	0.1	—	—	—

* Figures in the first column indicate percentage of total number of votes cast received by the party; figures in the second column indicate seats in Parliament.
† In electoral cartel with the National Peasant Party and the German Party, the common list obtaining 77.8 per cent.
Sources: Figures calculated from Ziemer, 1969, pp. 1064–5; Georgescu, 170b, p. 416; Shapiro, 1981, pp. 46--7; Scurtu, 1982, p. 139.

schisms and re-alliances. As mentioned earlier, the 'rightist' faction of the RSP decided to leave the organization rather than abide by the decision to join the Comintern. Calling themselves the Social-Democratic Party of Romania, the rightists were active from 1921 to 1927 within the Federation of Romanian Socialist Parties, the other members of which were the Bukovinian Social Democratic Party, the Socialist Party of the Banat and the Socialist Party of Transylvania. All these organizations were relatively nationalist in outlook, for historical reasons. In 1922, following their ouster from the RCP on the orders of the Comintern, the former 'unitaries' organized themselves into the Socialist Party of Romania, but before the year was out they had rejoined forces with the rightists, as the RSP (Felea & Tănăsescu, 1980, pp. 66–7; Scurtu, 1982, p. 83). In May 1827 the Federation was transformed into the Social-Democratic Party (SDP), the Executive Committee of which was formed by C. Titel Petrescu, Ghelerter, L. Rădăceanu, I. Moscovici, I. Fluieraş, I. Jumanca and others.

Following a poor showing at the polls in 1927 (see Table 2), the SDP decided to form an electoral alliance with the NPP in early 1928 (Muşat & Ardeleanu, 1981, p. 208; Felea & Tănăsescu, 1980, pp. 85–6; Scurtu, 1982, p. 84). The decision brought about an immediate schism, when a leftist-inclined group led by Ghelerter and Ştefan Voitec contested the envisaged collaboration with a 'bourgeois party' and split the movement. This faction called itself the Romanian Workers' Socialist Party (July 1928). In 1932 they were followed by the former Secretary General of the RCP, Gheorghe Cristescu, the party's name being once more changed to Independent Socialist. Two years later a new splinter-group of the SDP, led by Constantin Popovici, joined forces with the Independent Socialists,[7] and the party's name was changed once again, this time to the Unitary Socialist Party (Petric & Ţrui, 1967, p. 13; Felea & Tănăsescu, 1980, p. 93). Ghelerter was elected party President, while Voitec and Popovici acted as Secretaries (Scurtu, 1982, pp. 139–40). Popovici, however, was expelled in 1936 for collaboration with the RCP, whereupon he re-established the Socialist Party (Scurtu, 1982, p. 176).

Meanwhile, the burden of the struggle against the rising tide of the forces of the extreme right was carried by the SDP, not by the Communists. As will be recalled, in 1937 the former ceased collaboration with the NPP following the Maniu–Codreanu 'non-aggression pact', which the RCP failed to do. Moreover, following Comintern instructions, the Communists opened a virulent campaign against other socialist organizations (Jurca, 1978, pp. 35-59). In 1937 also the Unitary Socialists returned to the ranks of the SDP, with the object of checking the strength of the right, but a year later, the nationalistic Bukovinian and Transylvanian leadership of the Social Democrats, including the party's President and Vice-President, G. Grigorovici and I. Fluieraş, were to join the official ranks of Carol II's royal dictatorship—the Front of National Rebirth[8] (Felea & Tănăsescu, 1980, p. 103; Jurca, 1978, p. 113; Scurtu, 1982, pp. 239-40).

Since Popovici's Socialist Party had virtually ceased its activities, the socialist (non-communist) movement was now reunited for the first time since 1928—though not for long. The leadership (including, during the underground years, C. Titel Petrescu as President, as well as figures such as Voitec, Ghelerter, Rădăceanu and Moscovici) was split once more in 1943, when L. Rădăceanu left the SDP, joining forces with the splinter-group of the NPP headed by M. Ralea, to form the Workers' and Peasants' Union, which was subsequently renamed the Socialist Peasant Party. The loss was partially balanced by the SDP's fusion with another dissident group of the NPP, the Iunian faction, which joined the party in June 1944, following the death of its leader several years earlier. During the same month, however, the Rădăceanu group also returned to the SDP, most probably as a preparatory step to 'take-over from within' tactics envisaged by the RCP, whose directives he was now following (Fătu, 1979, p. 92; Scurtu, 1982, pp. 277-8, 297). With the RCP following in the footsteps of the advancing Red Army, the fate of the independent socialist movement in Romania was as good as sealed.

4 The Everchanging Past:
Formation of the New Regime

An inherent danger, almost universally present in historiography, is history-telescoping. Such pitfalls account for Western versions which attribute to the Romanian leadership 'independence orientated' designs *vis-à-vis* the Soviet Union prior to the 1960s. The mistake of writing yesterday's story in the light of contemporary events, as it turns out, is not confined to communist historians alone.

In monopolistic regimes, on the other hand, historiography plays a major role in the process of overt and covert socialization directed from above. Under such regimes there are no *mis*-interpretations of history—only *re*-interpretations. In this environment, the reading *of* history becomes a corollary to reading *into* history values claimed by the regime to be 'functional' for the creation of its hegemony and for the consolidation of power of its leaders. As both Robert R. King and this author pointed out in the same year (King, 1980, pp. 1-3; Shafir, 1980, p. 273), the categories developed by Nancy Wittier Heer (1971, pp. 16-28) for the analysis of historiography in the Soviet Union are fully applicable to the Romanian case as well. Among these, the 'informal' functions of history-writing, and, above all, its use as an agent of legitimation for the present system and leadership and for rationalization of present policies, make the task of the political scientist both easier and more difficult. It is easier because these functions reflect the fluctuations in the policies of the regime and of its self-projected image. It is, however, more difficult, in as much as such fluctuations, more often than not, replace one half-truth with another. This state of affairs appears to be particularly relevant as we proceed to a survey of accounts of the formation of the new regime in Romania.

With the Red Army advancing on Romanian territory in 1944, a number of politicians attempted to approach the Western powers, urging Marshal Ion Antonescu, Romania's arch-conservative leader, to surrender, in the hope of avoiding Soviet occupation. Armistice feelers were put out with Antonescu's tacit approval, in what in retrospect appear as naïve endeavours at best (Nano, 1952; Cretzianu, 1957; Ionescu, 1964, pp. 74-8; Fischer-Galati, 1967, pp. 19-20; Vago, 1977, pp. 111-12; Simion, 1979, pp. 320-421[1]). As early as October 1943, the Allies had decided that any and all negotiations concerning the surrender of a Reich ally would be conducted jointly (Churchill, 1962, Vol. 5, pp. 254-5). The decision gave the Soviets considerable advantage, in view of the movement of their troops towards Eastern Europe. So far as Romania was concerned, the British-Soviet 'percentage agreement' of October 1944 (Churchill, 1962, Vol. 6, pp. 196-7) only acknowledged the existing situation, for by then Soviet troops had occupied the country. Seen from this angle, Yalta had only symbolic significance.

In April 1944 Soviet troops penetrated Romanian territory. The Russian offensive triggered dramatic internal developments. Lucreţiu Pătrăşcanu negotiated the establishment of a United Workers' Front (UWF) with the Social Democrats in April. The UWF was a significant extension of the Patriotic Anti-Hitlerite Front which had been established in 1943,[2] for SDP participation in this umbrella organization provided the communists with what they had always lacked—national legitimacy. On 26 May the RCP reached an understanding with the splinter-Liberal group led by Gheorghe Tătărăscu, an extremely controversial opportunist figure, who had been active in the establishment of Carol II's dictatorship (Nedelcu, 1973, pp. 37–41 and *passim*; Popişteanu & Pânzaru, 1974, p. 17). On 20 June the UWF allied itself with the two historical parties, the NPP and the National Liberal Party (NLP), becoming the National Democratic Bloc (NDB).

In the afternoon of 23 August Marshal Antonescu was arrested at the Royal Palace. The purpose of the coup was to topple his regime before Russian troops had entered Bucharest, and to turn arms against the Germans, thus avoiding occupation as a defeated Nazi ally. In so far as the King and the NPP-NLP leaderships were concerned, a parallel, and by no means secondary, purpose of the coup was to avoid an immediate communist take-over, in a scheme which eventually proved feasible as a short-term tactic only.

The course of events which led to the coup constitutes the subject of considerable dispute. It does not simply involve Western versus communist interpretations. Studies produced in the West vary mainly according to the preponderance attributed to the democratic components of the NDB or to the King and his immediate entourage[3] in planning the coup. There is, however, a broad consensus that the RCP, at best, played only a minor role. The variations in communist historiography are substantially more pronounced, reflecting typical fluctuations. These appear to have been induced by two main factors—personal and personnel policies, on the one hand, and the search for intra-systemic legitimacy triggered by the conflict with the Soviet Union from the 1960s onwards, on the other.

Up to the mid-sixties the events of August 1944 were presented as a solo performance by the RCP, led mainly by Gheorghe Gheorghiu-Dej (*Scînteia*, 31 July 1964; King, 1980, pp. 40–1). Dej had been one of the leaders of the 1933 strikes at the Bucharest Griviţa works. In circumstances which still remain obscure, he became leader of the party in the spring of 1944, when Foriş came under suspicion of acting in the service of the secret police (Shafir, 1981b, p. 585). In fact, the former party head's liaison with the Antonescu regime had been established with Soviet approval, in order to establish conditions for Romania's surrender (Fischer-Galati, 1967, p. 21).

Although Dej's escape from prison was not engineered until 9 August, post-war Romanian historiography has asserted that the RCP carried out the 'armed insurrection', on his personal initiative, without mentioning either Pătrăşcanu's role as chief liaison officer with the 'historical' parties and with the Royal Palace, or the key role played by King Michael I and by army officers loyal to him. The 'bourgeois parties', Dej asserted in May 1961, had 'self-dissolved already during Carol II's dictatorship'. For the first time since the establishment of the new regime the King's involvement in events was mentioned, in this speech, but this was deemed to have been caused by his attempt to 'eschew the heavy responsibility' which lay on his shoulders for 'having dragged Romania into the war against the USSR'. Consequently, Dej claimed, the royal entourage 'was forced to accept the action-plan established by the Communist Party, the only genuine political force active in the toppling of Antonescu's government' (Gheorghiu-Dej, 1961, pp. 438-40).

Shortly after Dej's death in 1965, however, Ceauşescu embarked on a process of 'de-Dejification', aimed at consolidating power at the expense of any potential rivals who could claim closer association with the former leader (see Chapter 6). The history of the August days consequently underwent significant revisions. The story of the establishment of a Marxist regime, as it turns out, is also a function of who happens to be in charge of the existing establishment. Pătrăşcanu's gradual rehabilitation, made official in April 1968, paved the way for the restoration of historical accuracy, at least as far as the personal contribution of the RCP leaders to the preparation of the 'insurrection' is concerned. The key role, it was now revealed, had been played by Pătrăşcanu and by Emil Bodnăraş, the Moscow emissary dispatched to Romania for the purpose of either persuading Antonescu to surrender or engineering a revolt against him (Fischer-Galati, 1967, p. 20; King, 1980, p. 163n.) Bodnăraş's role had previously been acknowledged, but primarily as a trusted Dej lieutenant.

An article published in 1969 in *Studii*, a journal of historical research, accused the published accounts of the period of having relied on 'quotations' instead of primary sources, i.e. of having taken the Dej version at face value (Rusenescu, 1969, p. 718). Only eight months after the former leader's death, the journal of the RCP's Institute of Historical and Social-Political Studies (IHSPS) had published the memoirs of a royal adjutant who had participated in the August 1944 events (Ionescu, 1965). This article was the first in a plethora of such reminiscences to appear in succeeding years, which amended the record significantly. The arrests of Ion Antonescu and his deputy, Mihai Antonescu, were now said to have been carried out in conformity with plans elaborated jointly *with* RCP representatives, i.e. not *by* these representatives. Only after the arrest of the Marshal by the King's forces, as acknowledged by Ceauşescu in 1966, was he handed to the 'patriotic' (RCP) forces, and transferred to lodgings belonging to the conspirators. (Ceauşescu, 1968-9, Vol. 1, p. 379; Rusenescu, 1969, p. 722). *The Programme of the Romanian Communist Party*, adopted in December 1974, attributes the 'insurrection' to the RCP '*in collaboration with* other democratic, patriotic forces' (*Programul Partidului*, 1975, p. 49; emphasis mine). A 500-page volume published in 1979 by IHSPS historian A. Simion at present constitutes the most detailed account of these events.

Such fluctuations notwithstanding, contemporary Romanian historiography continues to ascribe to the Communist Party the initiation of, and the main role in, the events of August (Zaharia, 1969). The tiny membership of the party at the time makes such claims highly implausible, and at present, attempts to tackle this aspect vary from the ridiculous to the pitiful. Arguing against Western historians in 1969, *Studii* claimed that 'a party's force does not rest solely in numbers, but [also] in its cohesion and its organizationary and action-capacities, and, above all, in its programme, in its ideas' (Chiper, 1969, p. 746). Ceauşescu's authoritative pronouncement on this issue, in March 1970, sounded just as persuasive:

> Some ask how could the Romanian Communist Party, which emerged from illegality with a relatively small number of members, lead struggles of such amplitude. Those who do so prove they are not familiar with the history of the Romanian Communist Party, that they do not know the Romanian Communist Party. The Romanian Communist Party was capable of fulfilling its historic role first, because its entire activity has been guided by the ever-victorious Marxist-Leninist conception. Secondly, it knew how to apply creatively the general validities of the proletariat's revolutionary theory . . . to our country's concrete situation. Thirdly, the party could fulfill its role because its entire being identified with the interests of the working masses, with aspirations for justice and national and social liberty [Ceauşescu, 1970-83, Vol. 4, pp. 639-40].

More candid, but still far from accurate, was party historian Gh. I. Ioniţă in 1983. He admitted that the official version of the August events sounded implausible to Western ears. However, according to Ioniţă, the Romanian historians 'never wrote and never claimed [sic] that in those crucial moments, the Romanian Communist Party had been the *exclusive* factor in determining the revolution's triumph'. Rather, 'due to the malleability of its tactical and strategic line, this party was capable of bringing about a coalition of large forces, which followed it [sic] in a difficult struggle, embued with responsibility and sacrifice' (Ioniţă, 1983, p. 82; emphasis in original).

Of no less significance in the presentation of the events leading to the establishment of the new regime is the handling of the role played by the Soviet army. Among Western historians there is a complete consensus that without the threat of the Red Army, no Marxist regime could have come into being in Romania. One of these historians goes so far as to qualify the take-over solely as 'a function of Soviet power', indicating that without a Russian military presence, neither the *de facto* seizure of power in March 1945, nor the *de jure* installation of the new regime in 1947, would have been feasible (Fischer-Galati, 1975). The Soviet role was originally acknowledged in the Constitution adopted in 1952, according to which the Romanian People's Republic had come into being 'as a result of the historic victory of the Soviet Union over German fascism and of Romania's liberation by the glorious Soviet army' (Triska, 1968, p. 362). As late as May 1961, Dej was still referring to the 'glorious freedom-bringing Soviet army' (Gheorghiu-Dej, 1962, p. 440). *Throughout the 1950s, the role which the RCP claimed for itself in the 'liberation' was symbiotic, not a substitution, for that ascribed to the Soviet Union.*

Yet, according to at least one interpretation, communist participation in the plot against Antonescu had spoilt the Soviet scenario for take-over. This interpretation is probably the best illustration of the pitfalls inherent in the telescoping of history. The scheme, it is claimed, envisaged immediate installation of a puppet regime, headed by the 'Moscow faction' of the party, led by Ana Pauker and Vasile Luca, and the liquidation of the 'home communists', led by Dej (Fischer-Galati, 1975, p. 310). This version is seemingly corroborated by accusations made at a party plenum in November/December 1961, nearly a decade after the purging of the 'Muscovites'. According to Dej, on their return from the Soviet Union in September 1944, Pauker and Luca criticized the party's participation in the organization of the coup and its collaboration with the democratic parties for this purpose. Romania's withdrawal from the war, the 'Muscovites' indicated, had unnecessarily prolonged the process of seizing power (Dej in *Scînteia*, 7 December 1961).

That such accusations were directed by the 'home communists' at their competitors for power, there is little reason to doubt. There is also no reason to question the Dejist version, according to which, while in exile, Pauker and her group had formed an 'external Bureau' of the party, regarding themselves as its actual leaders, and counting on taking over with the aid of the 'Tudor Vladimirescu' division of Romanian POWs, which they had set up in 1943 (Coliu in *Scînteia*, 19 December 1961). There are plenty of reasons, however, for questioning the attribution of such a design to *the Soviets*.

The evidence rests primarily in Bodnăraş's participation in both the preparations for Dej's escape from prison and in the events leading to the actions of 23 August. There is no uncertainty about Bodnăraş's 'Moscow-connection' (Ionescu, 1964, p. 350), a view shared by, among others, Professor Fischer-Galati (1967, pp. 18-20). Had Bodnăraş entertained any doubts concerning Soviet intentions, it is highly unlikely he would have participated in talks with other members of the NDB, not to mention commanding the communist guards who took charge of Antonescu after his arrest, as he apparently did. Even less likely, in retrospect, appears a version which shows the chief Soviet liaison man supporting the take-over of the party leadership by the faction sentenced by Moscow to 'liquidation'. For, according to Fischer-Galati's own account, Bodnăraş was active in the purging of Foriş and his replacement by Dej on 4 April 1944 (Fischer-Galati, 1967, p. 21).

Soviet cynicism probably accounts for the decision to get rid of the leader involved in armistice negotiations with Antonescu, once that option proved unfeasible or unsatisfactory. The Dejist version of this episode, presented by none other than Ceauşescu in 1961, alleged that, on their return, Pauker and Luca questioned the legality of Foriş's dismissal (*Scînteia*, 7 December 1961). This should be taken with more than a pinch of salt. At the April 1968 CC plenum, at which Foriş was posthumously rehabilitated, Ceauşescu presented a different, and probably more realistic account. According to this version, Foriş's liquidation (without trial) in 1946 had been ordered by both Dej and the 'Muscovites'

(*Plenara*, April 1968, p. 74). Foriş, it was now claimed, had not been 'guilty of treason', but merely of 'serious deficiencies and grave mistakes' (Rusenescu, 1969, p. 720), i.e. of implementing Soviet orders to establish contacts with Antonescu. Albeit for different reasons, both factions in the RCP were interested in obliterating this episode. Regardless of the competition between them, it appears that at the time both factions identified with Soviet-inspired policies, and both competed for Soviet support.

Moscow was undoubtedly aware of the rivalry, but not even at the outset of communist emergence from illegality did it side with the Pauker group. The Romanian situation did not encompass a dual 'patron-client' relationship, but rather a triangular one of 'patron-*clients*', even if the 'Muscovite' group was persuaded otherwise. Furthermore, as Vago points out (1977, p. 113), neither of the two competing factions was strictly cohesive, and the division into 'home communists' and 'Muscovites' is more a reflection of the needs of scholarly (or rather scholastic) categorization than of the real, fluid situation. The struggle for power which occurred in the late forties and in the early fifties involved groupings and regroupings along personal rather than strictly ideological, not to mention national, dividing lines. Miron Constantinescu, a 'home communist' imprisoned together with Dej, for example, took the Pauker-Luca side, while such 'pure breed Muscovites' as Chişinevschi and L. Răutu put their eggs in Dej's basket—at least for the time being. As Kenneth Jowitt demonstrates, the only genuine nationalist at this time was Pătrăşcanu. His hasty execution by Dej in 1954, at a time when the Soviet Union was encouraging the emergence of East European leaderships with local appeal, as well as Dej's anti-Titoist stances (Jowitt, 1971, pp. 125-7), hardly qualify the RCP First Secretary for the 'national communist' mantle, so generously thrown over his shoulders when attributing to him efforts 'to bring about the socialist transformation of Romania without exclusive dependence on Russia' (Fischer-Galati, 1967, p. 31).

Credentials given to the Soviet role in the 'liberation' of Romania, up to, and including, the early sixties, appear to add to the weight of this interpretation. The first signs of the forthcoming change became discernible in 1962. Following the widening gulf with Moscow, generated by the disagreement over the issue of 'specialization' within Comecon, the party leadership under Dej hesitantly began a process of exchanging 'derivative' for autochthonous legitimacy. This process would ultimately lead, under Ceauşescu, to nationalist excesses unparalleled elsewhere in Eastern Europe, and to the practical integration of all things Romanian, *including* traditional anti-Russian sentiments, into the new version of party history.

In late 1962 the journal of the IHSPS published a review of a book printed in the Soviet Union, the subject of which was Germany's wartime foreign policy. The author, V. B. Ushakov, was reproached by the Romanian reviewer with attributing the credit for Antonescu's arrest to non-communist forces, i.e. with doing precisely what Romanian historians would themselves do shortly after. Ushakov's main 'crime', however, appeared to consist in passing over in silence the 'insurrection', thereby ascribing the 'liberation' to Soviet forces alone, and in ignoring the contribution of Romanian armies to the defeat of the Nazis. According to the Romanian reviewer, the Soviet offensive had merely created 'favourable conditions' for the 'insurrection'. By implication, it followed that most of the credit for the August reversal should go to the Romanians themselves (Niri, 1962, p. 184). The 'symbiosis' of the 1950s was to be replaced by Romanian unicausality. By 1966 Ceauşescu no longer mentioned the Soviets' 'liberating' role, indicating merely that the victories of the Red Army in 1943-4 had 'weakened fascism' and 'animated' the Romanian people in its own struggle for 'liberation from the fascist yoke'. On the other hand, the Romanian leader stressed that his country's armies had fought 'shoulder to shoulder' with the Russians for the liberation of Romania, Hungary and Czechoslovakia, and that this contribution had consisted not only in a considerable loss of life, but also in great economic sacrifices (Ceauşescu, 1968-9, Vol. 1, pp. 378-9). As part of their quest to establish for themselves an 'equal among equals' status, the Romanians nowadays cite their part in the Allied effort against the Nazis (Popescu-Puţuri, Zaharia *et al.*, 1965; Anescu, Bantea and Cupşa, 1966; Zaharia, 1969, p. 44; Ioniţă, 1969, pp. 722-3; Simon, 1979, p. 491; Ţuţu, 1983). Furthermore, a book published in 1978 goes as far as to reproach the Soviets with having broken their promise to grant Romania co-belligerent status, and with ignoring her contribution to the war effort at the Paris peace conference in 1946 (Lache & Ţuţui, 1978).

The reference to the 'Soviet liberators' was dropped from the national anthem in the 1960s, and in 1977 the regime ordered the anthem's replacement by an old patriotic tune, revised to combine nationalist values with socialist glorification.[4] Eventually, the rift with the Soviets and the search for intra-systemic legitimacy would lead Romanian historiography into a total revision of the period of the war as well. In 1966 Ştefan Voicu, then Editor-in-chief of the RCP's theoretical journal, mentioned for the first time the 1940 Soviet ultimatum to Romania as such (Voicu, 1966, p. 78). In the same year Ion Popescu-Puţuri, director of the IHSPS, argued at a convention in Budapest that post-1918 Romania could by no means be considered an 'imperialist' country, since it had itself had been subject to imperialist designs[5] (Popescu-Puţuri, 1966, p. 35). This was a considerable departure from earlier evaluations (Roller, 1951, pp. 201, 208) and challenged the Soviet view that Bessarabia's unification with Romania had been generated by 'imperialist' machinations of the ruling Romanian oligarchy (Voturin, Petrov & Slepenchuk, 1965, p. 77). Inter-war 'bourgeois' foreign policies aimed at the preservation of the country's territorial integrity were in fact gradually vindicated, with the Soviet Union now reproached with having virtually thrown Romania into the hands of Nazi Germany, because of revisionist policies and her ill-will displayed *vis-à-vis* the 'Transylvanian question' (Popescu-Puţuri, 1966, pp. 42-50; Campus, 1966, 1968a, 1968b; Zaharia & Petri, 1966; Zaharia & Botoran, 1981; Moisiuc, 1969, 1971; Moisiuc *et al.*, 1977). The epitome of this process was the virtual rehabilitation of Antonescu's Bessarabian policies by Simion in 1979.

The period 1944-8 is described in contemporary Romanian accounts as a 'phase of transition' to 'socialist edification' (Ceterchi, 1981, p. 18n). Also labelled 'the phase of the popular-democratic revolution' (Surpat, 1981, pp. 25-6), the period is said to have 'objectively surpassed the tasks of the completion of the bourgeois-democratic revolution', because it prepared the way for the succeeding epoch. Whereas the bourgeois parties considered the act of 23 August as one *concluding* the period of re-establishment of bourgeois democracy, this act is claimed by the RCP as a prelude to new *beginnings* (Ceauşescu, 1970-83, Vol. 4, p. 625; Surpat *et al.*, 1980, pp. 30-1). At the same time, it is obliquely admitted that these intentions were not revealed at the time. In a book published in 1980 it is admitted that, despite its long-term policies, the party's proclamations after 23 August included 'only the most general, common and strictly utilitarian paragraphs, evincing the necessity to solve major tasks of a national, anti-fascist and general democratic character' (Surpat *et al.*, 1980, p. 31). In other words, as elsewhere in Eastern Europe, 'camouflage' tactics (Hammond, 1975, pp. 20-7) were part and parcel of the Romanian way of taking over.

Whether this process is analysed within the typology designed by Hugh Seton-Watson (1956, pp. 167-71), as King convincingly does (1980, pp. 47-51), or whether a different scheme is devised (Szajkowski, 1982), it makes little difference to the essentials of evolution towards a Leninist system. The Romanian variant has been scrutinized in detail (Markham, 1949; Prost, 1954, pp. 168-211; Cretzianu, 1956; Fischer-Galati, 1957 and 1970, pp. 70-108; Ionescu, 1964, pp. 94-125; Roberts, 1969, pp. 242-331; Vago, 1977; Franck, 1977) and is in no need of any but the briefest recapitulation, i.e. gaining control of key ministries (Justice, Propaganda, Interior) and subversion of government apparatus; penetration and internal splitting of rival parties and of mass organizations; the use of terror against political rivals, under the benevolent eye of the Soviet-dominated Allied Control Commission; disenfranchisement of genuine or allegedly fascist political rivals, coupled with communist recruitment of former Iron Guardists; control of the press, etc.

The three successive governments (Sănătescu, August-November 1944, November-December 1944, and Rădescu, December 1944-March 1945) which had included the bourgeois parties were continually subjected to the famous Rákosi 'salami-tactics'. The last slice to be swallowed, in September 1947, was Tătărăscu. He had continued to serve as Minister of Foreign Affairs in the National Democratic Front (NDF)[6] government headed by Dr Petru Groza since March 1945. Groza, a fellow-traveller who had once belonged to the leadership of the National Party alongside Octavian Goga, had led the Ploughmen's Front (Scurtu, 1980, pp. 51, 137) since 1933. His government had been imposed on the King by Soviet Deputy Foreign Minister A. Vyshinski, who threatened that Romania might otherwise cease to exist as an independent nation (Franck, 1977, p. 120), an episode now obliquely acknowledged by Ceauşescu himself (Ceauşescu, 1970-83, Vol. 4, p. 635). The immediate pay-off for this concession was Soviet recognition of Romanian sovereignty over all Transylvania, the future of which had been kept deliberately uncertain (Lahav, 1977).

At the 'elections' held in November 1946 the NDF allotted to itself 347 seats, with thirty-three seats going to the NPP and three to the NLP. Two seats were also given to the Democrat Peasant Party (Dr Lupu) (Ziemer, 1969, p. 1067). On 30 December 1947 Mihai I was forced to abdicate. A new constitution, adopted on 13 April 1948 and valid until September 1952, reflected the new social-economic structure of the state, providing for a new administrative organization, and outlining new measures intended to set Romania on the path of economic development. Articles 5 to 15 of this document attested to the new regime's determination to obliterate capitalism and to reorganize the economy on the basis of central planning (Surpat *et al.*, 1980, p. 46). The nationalization of industry in June 1948 was the most significant step taken in this direction (Surpat, 1980). This measure also marked the beginning of a new phase in the party's rule. A review of this, and of the stages that followed, warrants discussion in a separate chapter.

5 Rulers and Ruled from 'People's Republic' to the 'Multilaterally Developed Socialist Society': A Revised Framework of Political Analysis

Beyond the 'phase of transition', said to have marked the change from capitalist relations of production to the institution of socialist forms of labour and labour relations (Ceterchi, 1981, p. 18), Romanian RCP theoreticians divide the evolution of the regime into three main phases. The years 1948 to 1965 are seen to have encompassed the 'building of the base of socialist society' (Surpat, 1981, p. 27), which ended in 'the triumph of socialist relationships' in the economic system (Ceterchi, 1981, p. 18). The second phase covers the period 1965 to 1969, and is labelled 'consolidation of the socialist society'. Finally, the present stage is said to be that of the 'multilaterally developed socialist society', and is envisaged as lasting through several Five-Year Plans (Ceterchi, 1981, p. 18; Surpat, 1981, p. 30).

This allocation of periods has been subject to repeated alteration, particularly as far as the inherent features of each phase are concerned. In 1969, for example, former party ideologue Paul Niculescu-Mizil wrote that the 'edification of socialism', in the sense of *perfection* and completion, had started from the outset of socialist construction and should be viewed as an endless process, for one should always strive for the better (Niculescu-Mizil, 1969, p. 4). None the less, latter-day interpretations stress the perfecting of socialism (or 'socialist democratization') as a developmental feature characteristic of the Ceauşescu period alone[1] (Surpat *et al.*, 1980, p. 78). Until the early years of the present decade, such 'democratization' was presented as the consolidation of the dictatorship of the proletariat. In June 1982, however, Ceauşescu decreed that dictatorship of the proletariat was a thing of the past, since the concept no longer reflected the present stage of socialist construction. It was consequently replaced by a new name—the 'state of workers' democracy' (Ceauşescu, 1982, p. 18).

Such alterations of theory do not necessarily reflect any substantial change in party-society relationships. Rather, as discussed at the beginning of this chapter, they are part and parcel of pre-emptive regime postures, designed to ensure the continued dominance of the RCP. At the same time, such 'simulated change' (as discussed later) was induced in Romania by elite-perceived dangers of 'diffusion of political innovation' from related systems, such as Czechoslovakia or Hungary (Shafir, 1984b). Bearing in mind the suspicious coincidence of offical periodization with the rise to power of Ceauşescu and the subsequent institutionalization of his leadership, one is forced to conclude that little can be learned from Romanian sources about the evolution of society. Theory appears to be as genuinely related to *praxis* as orthodox Marxism ever was to the reality of the

Romanian situation. In other words, 'socialist theory' in Bucharest is charged with fulfilling functions very similar to those of telescoped history writing—above all with cloaking justification for present leaderships and for their policies in a Marxist jargon. Consequently, the evolution of the regime will be scrutinized here within a different analytical framework, to be more precise, within a modified version of the 'developmental scheme' originally devised by Kenneth Jowitt.

In several studies dedicated to the development of Leninist systems, Jowitt employs the concept of 'breaking through', to analyse RCP motivations and strategies in the period following take-over. The aim of the process of 'breaking through' is complete transformation of societal structures and values. The concept refers to 'the decisive alteration or destruction of structures and behaviours which are perceived by a revolutionary political elite as comprising or contributing to the actual or potential existence of alternative centres of political power' (Jowitt, 1971, p. 7). More specifically, according to Jowitt the process is perceived by the party as conditioned by the achievement of an absolute monopoly of political power; by industrialization; and by collectivization of agriculture. Success in socialist construction is thus said to be perceived solely as a function of political, economic and social achievement, while the society's cultural transformation is said to be seen by the regime as 'basically a derivative accomplishment' (Jowitt, 1974a, p. 1175).

However, this is only true inasmuch as it refers to 'mass political culture'. As I have pointed out elsewhere (Shafir, 1983b, p. 395), from the earliest stage of the process of 'breaking through', alteration of the pre-revolutionary societal system of values is perceived by the new elites as a primary task. Consequently, long-range strategies of political socialization of the masses become an immediate function of the process of 'socializing the socializers', i.e. of the de-socialization and then re-socialization of 'high culture' agents. As the authors of a Romanian book on cultural affairs put it some time ago, under the new regime it became imperative for all 'cultural-artistic creation' to reflect 'the principle of party-mindedness'. This meant that writers and artists should be 'guided in their creative activity by the party's ideology and ethics, moulding an art . . . capable of exercising a strong moral-educational influence' (*Cultura socialistă*, 1974, p. 29). The institutional supervisory set up of cultural life thus came to reflect the same 'transformative' endeavours as all other areas of society (Gabanyi, 1975, pp. 23-33; Shafir, 1981a, pp. 71-90). A fourth element, pertaining to a 'cultural break-through', should consequently be added to Jowitt's list of 'transformative' tasks of the regime. For, being 'thoroughly transformational', Marxist-Leninist regimes, whatever their local variation, 'seek to demolish systematically old political institutions, social structures *and value orientations*, and to replace them with a new socio-political edifice, erected according to the Leninist ideological blueprint' (Perlmutter and Leo Grande, 1982, p. 778; emphasis mine). As can easily be seen, 'breaking through' amounts to total emulation of the Soviet model. The core of this model is, of course, the concept of the party's leading role, resulting 'in a political system in which the party is sovereign, acting as the chief arbiter of values, authority, relations, institutional arrangements, political practice and policy' (Perlmutter and Leo Grande, 1982, p. 779).

The transformation stage (Jowitt, 1974a, p. 1174) involves a confrontation between the regime and 'unreconstructed society'. It is followed by the 'consolidation' stage, which is defined as 'the attempt to create the nucleus of a new political community in a setting that ideally prevents existing social forces from exercising any uncontrolled and undesired influence over the development of the new community'. The former confrontation between rulers and ruled is now replaced by 'a structure of domination', in which 'the politically defeated but "hostile" society must be prevented from "contaminating" the nuclei of the new socialist society' (Jowitt, 1974a, p. 1174). As originally devised, this definition implicitly viewed the party as a monolithic organization in course of establishing its monopoly over other groups; however, it neglected the question of factional struggles within the party itself. Apparently aware of this weakness, in a subsequent elaboration, Jowitt added the very relevant qualification that such pre-emptive activities referred to 'the party elite (or a section thereof)' (Jowitt, 1975, p. 70).

Transformation and Consolidation under Dej

The offensive launched against actual or potential rivals outside the party began even before 1948; annihilation of the leaders of the opposition, however, started in earnest with the arrest of the NPP leaders I. Maniu and I. Mihalache in July 1947. They were brought to trial at the end of October and sentenced to life imprisonment (Ionescu, 1964, pp. 131-6; Vago, 1977, p. 123). Maniu died in prison, as did his former Liberal rival, D. Brătianu (Ierunca, 1973, p. 198; Franck, 1977, p. 241). Many other former politicians met a similar fate. In August 1947 the two 'historical' parties were banned.[2] The obliteration of the opposition, however, was only completed in 1948.

The most significant step in this direction was the merging of the Communist and Social-Democratic parties in February 1948. This is not to imply that the SDP enjoyed greater popularity than Maniu's movement. But, whereas in the case of the 'historical' parties, the communists faced a 'class enemy', the annihilation of the SDP was indicative of their monopolist ethos. Democratic centralism was incorporated into the resolution concerning unification, and the party's statutes provided for a six-month 'candidacy stage' for new members, purported to 'give party organs the possibility of verifying the quality and behaviour of the candidates'. The organization, as explained in a book published in Bucharest in 1967, could not 'tolerate . . . a mere formal unity, behind which there existed all sorts of factions and groupings' (Petric & Ţuţui, 1967, pp. 164, 167). The immediate aim of the communists was the cleansing of possible supporters of C. Titel Petrescu, the former leader of the SDP.

Some two years earlier, in March 1946, they had manœuvred a substantial part of the SDP leadership into supporting intensified collaboration within the UWF, and into excluding Petrescu and his friends from the party. The manœuver had been achieved by the use of 'penetration tactics', with L. Rădăceanu, Ş. Voitec, Th. Iordăchescu and S. Voinea (a former French citizen whose original name was Gaston Boeve) casting their lot with the RCP. The new party was initially to be called the Single Workers' Party (Partidul Unic Muncitoresc) but, in circumstances which remain obscure, it became the Romanian Workers' Party (RWP). February 1948 was counted as its first Congress until 1965, when Ceauşescu restored the party's former name (Communist) and the counting of congresses back to 1921. The elected leadership was in the hands of communists at all levels (Petric & Ţuţui, 1967, p. 151). According to latter-day party historiography, this 'Romanian experience' in 'party unification' would serve as an example to other communist movements in Eastern Europe (Petric & Ţuţui, 1967, p. 170).

As for Titel Petrescu and his followers, their fate was no different from that of other leaders of the 'potential or alternative centres of power' (Vago, 1977, pp. 123-4), although apparently Petrescu managed to survive prison.[3] Following his expulsion, he had formed a separate organization, the Independent Social Democratic Party, but at the elections of November 1946, his supporters were badly harassed and none of the candidates were elected.

The March 1948 elections were the last to have a multi-party façade. The communist-run Popular Democracy Front 'won' 405 out of 414 seats (Surpat *et al.*, 1980, p. 45), with seven seats allocated to Tătărăscu's group (now led by P. Bejan) and two seats given to the Dr Lupu formation. Before the year ended these last vestiges of pluralism had ceased to exist. Unlike some of its counterparts in Eastern Europe, the new Romanian elite saw no need to allow for non-communist organizations to exist beyond the 'phase of transition'—not even in fictitious guise. The 1952 Constitution incorporated entire paragraphs from the Soviet Constitution. It also designated the RWP as the 'leading political force' in state and social organizations (Surpat *et al.*, 1980, p. 122).

Between 1944 and 1947, but particularly since the designation of Teohary Georgescu as Under-Secretary at the Ministry of the Interior in December 1944, the police apparatus was infiltrated by what is nowadays described as 'working-class elements' (Surpat *et al.*, 1980, p. 120). On 30 August 1948 the regime set up the General Directorate of People's Security—the secret police—or, for short, the *securitate* (*Monitorul oficial*, 30 August 1948). This was followed, in January 1949, by the disbanding of the police and the gendarmerie, and their replacement by the *miliţia* (*Monitorul oficial*, 23 January 1949). As Ceauşescu would eventually acknowledge in 1968 (in circumstances to be discussed later), the *securitate* conducted itself 'abusively' and was often guilty of 'law infringement'. Such behaviour was explained by 'the atmosphere of distrust and suspicion' generated by factional struggles in the party, as well as by uncritical emulation of the mistaken (Soviet) thesis concerning the intensification of class struggle in the course of socialist reconstruction (Ceauşescu, 1968-9, Vol. 3, pp. 186, 197; Surpat *et al.*, 1980, p. 121).

This atmosphere was intensified by the adoption in 1949 of a new system of justice which abolished the separation of powers. As in the Soviet Union, the new system provided for the brief and hasty training of 'People's Assessors' (Surpat *et al.*, 1980, p. 119). The former penal code was replaced by laws providing for punishment of acts 'considered dangerous to society', even when the infringements were not 'specifically provided for in the law as crimes' (Free Europe Committee, *Penal Law and Justice in the Communist Regime of Rumania*, as quoted in Ionescu, 1964, p. 172). Many of those sentenced under the new laws perished in the huge labour camps of the Danube-Black Sea Canal, a project initiated in 1949 and abandoned in 1953, only to be revived (albeit in different circumstances) in the 1970s. After a short lull brought by the 'New Course', a new wave of terror was instituted with Decree No. 318 of July 1958 (Ionescu, 1964, pp. 290-1; Ierunca, 1973, pp. 196-7).

Such a high incidence of 'irrational violence', as Jowitt rightly points out (1971, p. 102), is not to be explained simply 'in terms of Soviet demands for detailed emulation', but also in terms of the Romanian leadership's uncertainty, owing to its lack of independent experience, as to how else to achieve an ideologically and politically correct breakthrough. Dependency, as Jowitt indicates elsewhere, 'may be a consequence of the premature but imperative adoption of a political format for which the appropriate social base is lacking'. In such circumstances 'adoption of the organizational and ideological idiom of the dominant powers becomes situationally necessary'. What is more, a 'small country's adoption of a particular ideological and institutional façade may be as much an effort to make a special claim on a great power in order to survive as a political unit as a choice to redefine its internal political organisation' (Jowitt, 1978a, p. 23).

The same applies to an inexperienced revolutionary elite. So uncertain was Dej of any local bonds that even in those few instances where he could reasonably attempt to trace the roots of his rule to local continuity (such as the legacy of C. Dobrogeanu-Gherea's theoretical contributions to Marxism), he preferred to emulate the Soviet model, repudiating any links with national (Marxist or other) appendages. Ironically enough, as a Romanian philologist told this author, it was the 'Muscovite' Pauker who courted and even protected the intellectuals, whereas the 'local communists' proved to be among the harshest Zhdanovists. It was they who had to demonstrate to Moscow where the genuinely trustworthy element in the Romanian party lay.

For both ideological and circumstantial reasons, therefore, during the stages of transformation and consolidation, the task of political integration was considered by the regime as secondary to that of 'system-building' (Jowitt, 1974a, pp. 1175). Legitimacy had to be built on 'primitive accumulation' (Meyer, 1972, p. 56), i.e. before the new elite could conceive of altering the pattern of dominance in society, it had to pursue the only blueprint known to have achieved success in destroying the institutional and cultural patterns of an *ancien* régime—the Leninist one. 'System-building', in other words, involved un-building as much as it involved re-building.

Industrialization and collectivization were very much a part of this 'package deal'. The 'command economy' system was immediately adopted on the national-ization of major industries in 1948, with a State Commission of Planning (even-tually transformed into the State Planning Committee) in charge of the whole economy since July of that year (*Monitorul oficial*, 2 July 1948). Two one-year plans were followed by two five-year plans and a six-year plan, covering the period 1951-65, and reflecting the leadership's determination to put Romania on the path of forced development. The major target was industrialization, with little care given to human costs. Investments were consequently orientated towards 'Group A' (heavy industry), with the ratio of investments to consumption as one of the highest in the world.[4] According to official data (Surpat *et al.*, 1980, p. 71), during the first Five-Year Plan (1951-55), over 57 per cent of the investments in the national economy were channelled to industry, of which nearly 87 per cent went to 'Group A'. In 1951 investments in this category were 7.3 times higher than those in the light and food industries, in 1952 8 times as high, and in 1953 9.8 times. Moreover (Surpat *et al.*, 1980, p. 72), a campaign for the 'fulfilment of the plan' in four (instead of five) years, put the country on the path of 'mobilization', defined by Montias as 'pressures on individuals and their families, usually channelled through local party cadres, to make them contribute as much as they can to the pursuit of the regime's economic goals' (Montias, 1970, p. 117).

The social and human costs of such developmental strategies can be grasped in full only when taking into account that in the earlier period of 'transformation', Romania had not only failed to receive any economic aid from the Soviet Union (unlike Bulgaria, for example), but had also to pay large sums to Moscow, as part of war reparations calculated at the unrealistic prices of 1938. In addition, the country faced unfavourable trade terms with Comecon (Ionescu, 1964, pp. 91-2, Jackson, 1977, p. 889). Her resources were drained by the Soviet-Romanian joint-stock companies, the 'Sovroms'; unlike other branches of industry, these had *not* been nationalized, and by 1948 their number stood at 193. The Sovroms were eventually disbanded between 1954 and 1956 (Surpat *et al.*, 1980, pp. 54, 57, 74).

In view of such impediments, Romanian economic growth between 1951 and 1956 is impressive, though perhaps the official figure of an average annual growth of 13.3 per cent (Surpat *et al.*, 1980, p. 79) is somewhat exaggerated.[5] It has occasionally been pointed out that 'a comparable growth of national income could have been achieved without forcing the population to forego so much consumption' (Raţiu, 1975, pp. 125-6). Indeed, in the 1950s and 1960s, the non-socialist economies of Southern Europe (Greece, Italy and Spain) grew at about the same per capita rate as the Romanian economy (Chirot, 1978, p. 473). But this is just as relevant as indicating that Israel's, or Iran's balance of payments under Khomeini, might have been greatly improved by exports deriving from intensified pig husbandry. The personal identification of Romania's rulers with the Leninist model of 'breaking through' simply obliterated any such option.

This applies, to an equal extent, to the agricultural policies pursued by the regime. As Chirot indicates, it is doubtful 'that collectivization was the best possible solution' for the country's agrarian problems; rather, 'a firm commitment to private agriculture might have had equally good or better results' (Chirot, 1978, p. 478). Indeed, in 1981 private agriculture (9.7 per cent of the total agricultural land area), together with the production of the private gardens of the peasants of the collectives (6.2 per cent of the land available for agriculture), provided nearly 14 per cent of the cereal output, over 22 per cent of the maize, more than 60 per cent of the potatoes, over 40 per cent of the vegetables, virtually the entire fruit production (93.9 per cent), almost 44 per cent of the meat, close to 60 per cent of the milk and the eggs, and over 46 per cent of the wool (Republica Socialistă România, Direcţia Centrală de Statistică, 1982, pp. 120, 148-9, 161, 178-9). The commitment of 'transformative' Romania to the Leninist model, however, again made such an option yet another non-choice.

The decision to start collectivization was adopted at the Central Committee plenum of 3-5 March 1949, and in July this forum and the government approved the setting up of the first five 'collective farms' (*Gospodării agricole collective*, later to be named *Cooperative agricole de producţie*) (Surpat *et al.*, 1980, pp. 60-1). Although this resolution provided for 'gradual' collectivization, based on the principle of 'free consent', the countryside was soon subjected to an unprecedented reign of terror. The March 1949 resolution had also provided for the application of 'class criteria' in the countryside, distinguishing between the *chiabur* (the Romanian version of the *kulak*) and other categories. The *chiabur* was to be affected more intensively by the quota system, but all peasants (including collectivized peasants) were to share in this version of 'primitive accumulation'. Furthermore, in their zeal to revolutionize the village and fulfil quotas designated by the central authorities, party activists had little time for scrupulous observance of class differentiation. The Stalinist ordeal was repeating itself in the Romanian countryside. Often, it is nowadays acknowledged, 'whether due to pressure of difficulties or to the desire to accelerate the process of collectivization, mistakes were made, some of them grave, forcing the rhythm of collectivization, constraining the poor peasantry [*ţăranii muncitori*] to join the collectives'. Moreover, 'public trials were organized, with numerous peasants sentenced without legal ground' (Surpat *et al.*, 1980, pp. 91-2).

By Dej's own admission, these trials affected some 80,000 peasants, accused of belonging to, or siding with, the 'class enemy' (Gheorghiu-Dej, 1962, pp. 206-7). Such 'excesses' were eventually attributed to Ana Pauker and her supporters. Nevertheless, it should be pointed out that at the time of her purge, in 1952, Pauker was accused of 'right-wing deviation', including disassociation from the process of rapid collectivization. One should not conclude from such statements that in the winter of its days, the Pauker group was more 'liberal' than Dej's faction. Had the group supported quite opposite policies, the resulting accusation, in all probability, would have been 'left-wing deviation'; as Fischer-Galati points out, 'No matter what the official reasons for Pauker's, Luca's and Georgescu's removal from power in 1952, the real ones are solely connected with the struggle for control of the party' (Fischer-Galati, 1967, p. 39). The accusation itself, on the other hand, demonstrates that Dej was just as committed to collectivization as his political rivals. Indeed, as soon as the purge had come to an end, the process of 'socializing the countryside' was intensified, with 'trustworthy' elements from urban centres replacing cadres suspected of local loyalties (Surpat *et al.*, 1980, p. 90).

Forced delivery quotas were virtually abolished by 1956, most probably under Soviet (post-Twentieth CPSU Congress) influence—yet one more proof of the umbilical cord which attached Dej to Moscow. The collectivization drive had been somewhat slowed down ('gradualized'), by introducing intermediate forms of association under the impact of Malenkov's 'New Course', but in 1955 it was re-instituted and intensified (Surpat *et al.*, 1980, p. 95), albeit in a less brutal manner. Whatever the reason for such fluctuations, it is obvious that at no point did the leadership envisage abandoning 'village transformation' as a strategic policy. The Ceauşescu team, it should be added, remains as committed to the strategy as its predecessor. As pointed out by Marvin Jackson, Romanian agriculture is untouched by economic reform, and even that symbol of agricultural Stalinism, the Machine and Tractor Stations, dismantled in other countries of the bloc, continue to act as party 'watchdogs' in the countryside.

Collectivization was decreed complete in April 1962. By that time only a few mountain areas had alone been left outside its range. The agricultural sector encompassed 96 per cent of arable land and 93.4 per cent of the agricultural land area, while 77.4 per cent of the arable land belonged to collective and state farms. The members of the former cultivated some 7.8 per cent of arable land in private plots, but these were not—and are still not—their own property (Republica Socialistă România, Direcţia Centrală de Statistică, 1970, pp. 250-3).

The drive for industrialization, achieved, as it was, to a great extent at the expense of agricultural investments, brought widespread social change. By 1965 the proportion of the labour force employed in agriculture and forestry had decreased from 74.3 per cent in 1950 to 56.7 per cent (see Table 3). The 1966 census, moreover, indicated that the rural labour force tended to be composed to an increasing extent of women and the elderly, since many men and younger members of collective farm families, attracted by higher incomes and relatively better conditions in the industrial sector, became commuters or migrated to urban centres (Jackson, 1977, p. 933). Despite acute housing shortages, the population of urban and suburban areas grew from 23.4 per cent in 1948 to 33.7 per cent in 1965 (see Table 4).

From the leadership's point of view, this indicated success. By the end of the 1950s the country had virtually reached 'take-off' point. The Six-Year Plan adopted at the Third RWP (Eighth RCP) Congress in June 1960 continued to provide for a high rate of industrial growth. Its most outstanding symbol was the new Galaţi steel plant, an ambitious project envisaging the production of some four million tons in 1970.

Table 3   Percentage of Labour Force by Sector

	1950	1965	1975	1980	1981
Industry	12.0	19.2	30.6	35.5	36.1
Construction	2.2	6.3	8.1	8.3	7.7
Agriculture	74.1	56.5	37.8	29.4	28.9
Forestry	0.2	0.2	0.3	0.4	0.4
Communication	0.3	0.6	0.7	0.8	0.8
Transportation	1.9	3.1	4.3	6.1	6.4
Commerce	2.5	4.0	5.5	6.0	6.0
Lower-level services	0.7	2.1	3.4	3.8	3.8
Higher-level services	5.3	7.0	8.1	8.4	8.6
Other	0.8	1.0	1.2	1.3	1.3

Source: Republica Socialistă România. Direcţia Centrală de Statistică, 1982, p. 60.

Table 4   Urban-Rural Distribution of Romania's Population, 1930-1981*

	Total	Percentage of total	
		Urban	Rural
29 December 1930[†]	14,280,729	21.4	78.6
25 January 1948[†]	15,872,624	23.4	76.6
21 February 1956[†]	17,489,450	31.3	68.7
1 July 1960	18,403,414	32.1	67.9
1 July 1965	19,027,367	33.7	66.3
15 March 1966[†]	19,103,163	38.3	61.7
1 July 1970	20,252,541	40.8	59.2
1 July 1975	21,245,103	43.2	56.8
5 January 1977[†]	21,559,910	47.5	52.5
1 July 1980	22,201,387	49.6	50.4
1 July 1981	22,352,635	50.1	49.9
1 January 1984	22,593,720	[‡]	[‡]

Source: Republica Socialistă România. Direcţia Centrală de Statistică, 1982, p. 12.
Scînteia, 3 March 1984.
   * Urban and suburban categories compiled.
   [†] Official census.
   [‡] No data available.

From Dej to Ceauşescu: Political Change and Political Stagnation

The most significant development in the last years of Dej's rule was the outbreak and development of the conflict with the Soviet Union. The dispute originated with what Khrushchev saw as the appropriate division of labour within the Comecon. This would have turned Romania into a major supplier of agricultural products to the industrially advanced members of the community (Brown, 1963 and 1965; Montias, 1964 and 1967, pp. 187-230; Thompson, 1964; Braham, 1964; Kaser, 1967; Jowitt, 1971, pp. 174-228). Dej was faced with the dilemma of choosing between the Soviet Union and the Soviet model. Paradoxically enough, it was to a large extent his strong identification with the Leninist–Stalinist values of industrialization that turned him into a 'national communist'. The process was gradual and by no means unilinear (Jowitt, 1971, pp. 198-232), for the Dejist elite naturally hesitated before proceeding to distinguish between the blueprint and its political impersonation.

By the end of the 1950s there were already signs of an unmistakable reorientation in Romanian foreign trade, with the total Soviet share reduced from 51.5 per cent in 1958 to 43.7 per cent in 1959 and 40.1 per cent in 1960 (Shafir, 1981b, pp. 603-5). This trend remained constant in the years that followed, although not immune to fluctuations mentioned elsewhere in this study. The reorientation was largely the result of Soviet unwillingness to support the further expansion of Romanian industrialization. As a result of these developments Bucharest turned to the West for credits and, eventually, for political support. As the conflict with the Russians became public knowledge, the leadership turned to society, in search of domestic support.

As long as the party had identified itself with the Soviet external referent, it had no choice but to pursue a course of 'primitive accumulation of legitimacy'. Now the political formula had to be altered. Gradually, it evolved into an obvious effort of the political elite to rid itself of its earlier, extra-systemic image, and to base its claim to power on historic intra-systemic continuity instead. From now on the party was determined to become not only the embodiment of industrial development, but also of national aspirations for independence.

A carefully concerted campaign of 'de-Sovietization' and 're-Romanianization' was the first step. It began with the restoration of the original Romanian names to streets and places that had been Russified, developing into the mass rehabilitation of historical and cultural figures associated with the struggle for political and economic independence. A particularly interesting illustration of the Romanian evolution is provided by the use—and abuse—of the national poet, Mihai Eminescu (1850-89). In 1948 he had been among the authors whose works were withdrawn from circulation because of their powerful (in particular, anti-Russian) tones. Eventually, during the periods of transformation and consolidation, he was 'cleansed' of undesirable values and, through a process of 'selected continuity' that obliterated unwarranted parts of his creation, the poet was transformed into a pseudo-forerunner of Romanian socialism. Such a metamorphosis, to be sure, originated less from a search for inner legitimacy, than from an attempt to establish links with the extra-systemic legitimacy inherent in the socialist idea. Once the conflict with the Soviet Union had reached a point of no return, the early 'protectionist' Romanian Liberal politicians and economists, whose slogan had been 'through ourselves' (*prin noi înşine*), were rehabilitated, since they provided a note of continuity to the party's current policies *vis-à-vis* Comecon (Montias,

Table 5   Romanian Foreign Trade by Major Areas, 1960-1980*

	1960	1965	(million devisa lei) 1970	1975	1980
CMEA Countries†					
Exports	2831.9	4,193.4	5,563.0	10,247.2	19,752.7
Imports	2,639.0	3,703.3	5,660.4	9,826.3	18,308.5
% of total Romanian trade	66.8	60.4	49.0	37.8	33.7
Other Socialist countries‡					
Exports	307.4	341.9	889.6	1,966.1	3,719.4
Imports	202.7	254.4	682.6	1,732.2	4,006.9
% of total Romanian trade	6.2	4.5	6.8	6.9	6.8
Advanced Capitalist countries§					
Exports	908.8	1,632.5	3,520.5	9,063.3	18,791.5
Imports	905.4	2,147.9	4,637.5	11,187.5	18,234.8
% of total Romanian trade	22.1	28.9	35.6	38.1	32.8
Developing countries¶					
Exports	244.8	428.1	1,104.6	4,984.8	10,724.7
Imports	136.7	356.1	772.5	3,412.9	17,815.7
% of total Romanian trade	4.6	6.0	8.2	15.8	25.2

Source: figures calculated from *Republica Socialistă România. Direcţia Centrală de Statistică*, 1981, pp. 526-39.

* Figures for 1981, as published in the *Romanian Statistical Yearbook*, 1982, are deliberately confusing and were consequently not included in the table.

† Includes Bulgaria, Czechoslovakia, the GDR, Hungary, Poland and the USSR for the entire period covered. Albania is included in the 1960 column only. Mongolia is included, beginning in 1965, Cuba in 1975, and Vietnam in 1980.

‡ Includes the People's Republic of China, North Korea and Yugoslavia for the entire period covered. Albania ceased to be active in CEMA in 1961 and is consequently also included in this category, beginning in 1965. Mongolia is included in the 1960 column only, since it became a CEMA member in 1962. Cuba joined CEMA in 1972, and is consequently included in the first three columns only. North Vietnam joined Comecon in 1978 and is consequently not included in the last column, but was counted in all the others.

§ Comprises all non-socialist European countries, as well as the USA, Canada, Japan and Australia.

¶ Comprises all countries not listed above, including Israel and New Zealand.

1967, pp. 91–2; Schöpflin, 1974, p. 85). Eminescu was turned into a similar link in the continuity chain. Although he had once been a fierce adversary of the Liberals, he now joined their 'illustrious' club, becoming overnight the defender of Romania's industrial self-sufficiency (Ivaşcu, 1964; Bulborea, 1969). The operation was part of what was termed 're-evaluation of the national heritage'. Within a relatively short span of time, it restored to the national pantheon figures such as the historian N. Iorga, the literary critic and politician T. Maiorescu, the ferociously nationalist poet and former Prime Minister, O. Goga, and many others who had previously been thrown into the dustbin of history.

Whenever possible, these forerunners of Romania's 'independent course' were attributed with 'progressive' social ideas, to make them fit into the hastily reconstructed chain of continuity, in which the distinction between the struggle for national independence and the fight for 'social justice' became more and more obscure (Maciu *et al.*, 1964; Bochiş, Dumitrescu & Oprea, 1965; Gogoneaţă and Ornea, 1965). The endeavour to construct such continuity reached a new stage with the publication of Marx's *Notes on the Romanians*, edited by the Romanian historian A. Oteţea and his Polish colleague S. Schwann (Marx, 1964). Communist ideology now proved perfectly compatible with anti-Russian nationalism, since the founder of scientific socialism himself (as it appeared from Marx's notes discovered by Schwann in Amsterdam) had denounced Russian encroachments on Romanian independence in general, and the annexation of Bessarabia in particular.

The *timing* of the publication is in itself illustrative of historiographical fulfilment of the function of rationalization of contemporary policies. There can be no doubt that by 1963 the Marx manuscripts were known to Romanian historians. An article published in the party's journal of historical and political studies in March/April 1963 mentioned several of Marx's pro-Romanian and anti-Russian views, as these had been reflected in articles devoted to the 'Eastern Question'. It was well known, the author claimed, 'that Marx left behind, in manuscript form', other works, and these were deemed likely 'to include other references to the history of the Romanian people' (Copoiu, 1963, p.93). According to the reference on the last page of *Notes on the Romanians*, the book had been ready for printing in January 1964. However, it had only been sent to the printer in October, an unusually long gap (Ghermani, 1967a, p. 153). With the benefit of hindsight, one can see that the delay was in fact a piece of very careful timing, for the publication of the *Notes* followed the famous 'Statement' of the RWP of April 1964, in which the neo-nationalist, independent course pursued by Bucharest found its expression (*Scînteia*, 23 April 1964).

The publication of Marx's *Notes* brought about a revision of the third volume of the *History of Romania*, published by the Romanian Academy. In the first volume of this work (1960), and even more so in the second volume (1962), one could discern a certain deviation from earlier interpretations of Romanian history. These, however, were limited to the issue of the 'origins and formation' of the Romanian nation, being apparently more anti-Hungarian than anti-Russian in essence. The third volume, on the other hand, was ostensibly more anti-Russian in tone, as was the fourth volume, which covered the period up to the War of Independence of 1877 (Academia, 1960-4). An unusual occurrence accompanied the publication of Volume III, for shortly after distribution to libraries, it was withdrawn and replaced with a new version, which included references to Marx's *Notes* and some considerably expanded anti-Russian arguments (Ghermani, 1967b; Shafir, 1981a, p. 136).

The sequel to these volumes should have been two further volumes, covering the period from 1878 to the present. The fifth volume, though printed, was never published (Georgescu, 1981, p. 38). From an article published in 1971, one could learn that the authorities decided to return it to the editors, for further modifications ('Pentru dezvoltarea . . .', 1971). A similar fate awaited the sixth volume, the main body of which had been finalized by 1969 ('Dezbaterile privind macheta . . .', 1969). What modifications were envisaged one can only guess at, in the light of the constant crescendo in Soviet-Romanian historic and pseudo-historic disputes. By the end of the 1970s, in any case, the former *History of Romania* project had been completely replaced by a new collective work. This new 'telescoped' version of the past is covered in ten volumes and—if ever released to the public—it will probably reveal interesting 'additions'. For the time being, as the author has learnt from a Romanian historian close to inner party circles, it is considered 'unwise' to provoke further Soviet wrath.

The line adopted by the RWP in the early 1960s proved extremely popular, the more so since, together with appealing to national sentiments, the party sought to increase its popularity by granting an amnesty to former 'class enemies' and/or 'chauvinist elements'. Furthermore, as discussed elsewhere, it opened its own ranks to sections of the population formerly perceived as ideologically harmful. Such increased popularity was in itself somewhat of a paradox, for the new support-recruitment policies were rooted in the RCP's own failure to re-socialize the population into its 'transformative', anti-nationalist and class-orientated value-system.

The core of the recently rediscovered formula for political integration appears in retrospect to have been as ancient as the history of the modern Romanian political system. Exploitation by the regime of unaltered nationalist traits of intellectual political sub-culture proved as effective as it has always been. Discontent and political dissent, instead of being chanelled into the system, as inputs were successfully deflected by the leadership towards external (Soviet and Hungarian) targets as outputs, in a manner reminiscent of tactics employed by pre-war governments.

Kenneth Jowitt is undoubtedly accurate when he attributes to Dej (as well as to other consolidation regimes) 'manipulation of nationalist symbols', as an integral part of the leadership's 'perceived needs to address imbalances between the regime and society in a context of continuing political distrust and avoidance of commitments to that society' (Jowitt, 1975, pp. 79-80). Such manipulation, he indicates, is an inherent feature of regimes which must resort to mobilization tactics in relations between party and society. Yet the distinction Jowitt makes between the Dejist consolidation period and the 'inclusive' regime of President Ceauşescu is likely to raise a number of questions.

To begin with, compared with the 'Ceauşescu era', Dejist manipulation of national symbols, and the extensive exploitation of national myth (Kövary, 1979) appear as childplay. Never, under the previous party leader, had the historical panegyrics even approached the ridiculous dimensions they were to attain as part of Ceauşescu's effort to exploit national historical symbols to his own advantage. What under Dej began as a relatively restrained 're-Romanianization' campaign, developed under Ceauşescu not only into the continued mass rehabilitation of historical and cultural figures associated with the struggle for independence, but also into a very obvious effort to cast the new leader as the virtual reincarnation of all ancestral courage and wisdom—from the Dacian King Burebista onwards. For the sake of accuracy it should be indicated that, according to Jowitt, inclusion regimes may, at times, slide back into the use of 'mobilization' techniques, which are an inherent feature of periods of transformation and consolidation. Such regression is explained as being complementary, though not conflicting, with 'inclusion' tactics (Jowitt, 1975, pp. 93-4). It appears at times of particular stress and, if my reading of Jowitt is correct, mobilization techniques are not the *favourite* strategy of inclusive regimes.

Yet it can easily be demonstrated that manipulation of nationalist symbols has been an inherent feature of the Ceauşescu period from the very beginning. No sooner had Ceauşescu taken over the helm, following Dej's death in March 1965, than he embarked on extensive tours of the country. A year or so following his succession, one of the leitmotivs of these visits became the continual reference to historical figures or events connected with the province visited, emphasizing local contributions to the struggle for national independence. The language was bombastic, the resort to symbol striking (Ceauşescu, 1968-9, Vol. 1, pp. 426-31, 434-5, 461-2, 472-4, 605; Vol. 2, pp. 16-17, 55, 305-7, 339). Audiences could not fail to comprehend that, when making a toast to 'Bukovina' in the town of Suceava, Ceauşescu was making a veiled reference to the *historical* Bukovina, which had included territories now incorporated into the Soviet Union (Ceauşescu,-9, Vol. 1, p. 437). Nor was it a matter of simple coincidence that he chose to pay a visit to the Putna Monastery on the eve of the celebration of the half millenium since this historical monument had been consecrated by Stephen the Great, the Moldavian ruler of Bessarabia. Several intellectuals exploited this opportunity to give vent— for the first time, but by no means the last—to hitherto suppressed national frustrations over the fate of this province (Giurescu, 1966; Berza, 1966; Streinu, 1966). The epitomy of this manipulation, in 1966 and 1967, were the 'personal encounters' staged with ancestral predecessors, such as the Roman centurion of Sibiu, Stephen the Great and Michael the Brave (played by actors), in a quest to project the image of direct descent from the high-school manual of national history (*Tribuna*, No. 10, 1966; *Scînteia*, 19 June 1967, 18 July 1967). This is not to imply that Ceauşescu's repeated references to the nation and to history are merely cynical prevarications. There can be no doubt that the Romanian leader's nationalism is genuine. The intensive use of myth and of national symbols from the earliest years of Ceauşescu's rule, however, makes Jowitt's distinction between consolidation and inclusive regimes problematic, were one to accept the employment of such a device as a yardstick for the periodization.

The distinction, moreover, is problematic for several additional reasons. As has already been pointed out, there is no justification for accepting at face value the official Romanian periodization. Above all, the attribution of the timing and the subsequent granting of all credit for generating a 'new era' in the country's evolution to the present party leader, is a gross exaggeration. The developmental scheme devised by Jowitt (although undoubtedly the best ever produced) is unwarrantedly acquiescent to such personification, for 'inclusion' is timed in the early Ceauşescu period. In reality, the Dej and Ceauşescu 'eras' are linked in more than one respect. To put it briefly, not only did the Romanian system evolve from strategies adopted in the early sixties, but, as acknowledged by Jowitt, the regime by the early seventies had begun to show pronounced tendencies towards returning to Dejist mobilization techniques in relation to society. Furthermore, the return was not confined to the political realm alone. As Marvin Jackson observed, economic strategies were similarly affected. Following a short lull, between 1965 and 1970, 'the Romanian system has been re-mobilised, a process that has affected policy, performance and organisation' (Jackson, 1977, p. 890).

An even more substantial question concerns Jowitt's use of the term 'manipulation' in the 'inclusive' sense. Inclusive regimes are described as 'attempts by the party elite to expand the internal boundaries of the regime's political, productive and decision-making systems, to integrate itself with the official (non-*apparatchik*) sections of society, rather than insulate itself from them' (Jowitt, 1975, p. 69). We learn that 'when inclusion becomes the core task, manipulation, rather than domination, becomes the defining relationship between regime and society' (Jowitt, 1975, p. 76). But does such re-definition imply a real shift away from patterns of dominance? According to Jowitt's own analysis, inclusion tactics come to prevent 'the possibility that the increasing range of articulate social audiences' (i.e. groups which are 'politically knowledgeable and oriented') might 'express itself as an articulated plurality of political-ideological definitions' (Jowitt, 1975, p. 71). In other words, inclusion tactics are pre-emptive by definition. They are aimed at safeguarding the party's leading role in society. This is achieved through the use of 'organizational', instead of 'symbolic' manipulation. Is the difference significant to any real degree?

A striking feature of the post-consolidation period is that the regime embarks on a process of 'political innovation'. At central, at intermediary and at peripheral levels, new institutions are created, or existing institutions are altered in order to enhance the sense of participation. Soviet-type 'real socialism', or the Romanian (nominally different) 'multilaterally developed socialist society' are cases in point. As emphasized by Chalmers Johnson (1970, p. 14) and by S. P. Huntington (1970, p. 32), these endeavours are attempts to deal with the dilemmas of institutionalization and participation, in societies whose political elites are faced with the danger of becoming 'victims of their own success'. In other words, having consolidated power, and at least partially transformed, i.e. industrialized, society, communist political elites are now faced with the task of finding a suitable formula which, without compelling them to 'go beyond Leninism' (Gitelman, 1972), will offer some opportunities for political expression to the new socio-economic groups. But it is not so much 'participation' as '*party*-cipation' that is involved here.

Genuine participation, as Sharlet indicates, refers to the 'input', rather than to the 'output' dimension of the system (Sharlet, 1969). The former necessitates the acceptance by the elite of 'value-pluralism' as a precondition for the existence of political pluralism (Harasymiw, 1971, p. 46). The latter is merely confined to elite-activation of society, i.e. to mobilization. The first 'implies that those who engage in political activities do so with a view towards choice between alternatives and elites' (Gilberg, 1981b, p. 149). The second, on the contrary, sees political participation as based 'on strong consensual interests' and as 'meant to facilitate the attainment of [party-designated] collective goals'. Consequently, 'institutions of mass participation are designed to facilitate the better integration of the fundamental values, and not to provide the mechanism for the advocacy of conflicting interests'. Whereas the theory of 'developed socialism' may recognize the existence of different interests in society, these are considered 'non-antagonistic' in character. Participatory procedures are not aimed at advancing 'the interests of separate groups', but rather at promoting 'the closer identification of individuals with the common values and objectives of society'. Such a pattern of 'participation' is, by definition, 'collectivist, integrative and unitary', with the communist party remaining 'the "best" interpreter of the common purpose', the activator of all social forces (Bielasiak, 1982, pp. 148-9). As Donald S. Schulz puts it, one is dealing here with polities where 'the rhetoric and façade of socialist participatory democracy' is aimed at helping 'legitimize and make palatable the reality of centralized party-state power', but where, in practice, the function of participation is 'largely restricted to policy intelligence and implementation' (Schulz, 1981, p. 55). What one is dealing with are 'mechanisms of mass participation which would increase a citizen's *sense* of involvement in socio-economic affairs, without significantly altering regime policy preference'. In other words, one deals with 'pseudo-participation' (Bielasiak, 1981, p. 89; emphasis in original: cf. also Shafir, 1981b, p. 603). Since 'mobilization' is only formally affected in such systems, it would appear that 'organizational manipulation' is not of such 'character defining' proportions as Jowitt sees it.

In my own modest contribution to an ideal-type developmental scheme (Shafir, 1981b, p. 602 ff.), I attempted to provide an incremental improvement on an earlier version (1974, p. 1174) of Jowitt's model, where 'inclusion' had been termed 'modernization'. Pointing out the manipulative character of 'participation', and the party's unaltered monopolist ethos, I suggested, at the time, the term 'modernization and containment'. At first sight this might appear to be a contradiction in terms. However, as Donald R. Kelley indicates, the contradiction is actually in-built in elite perceptions of society. Under 'real socialism' society is, on the one hand, 'envisaged as more complex, as responsive to more sophisticated economic and political administrative levers', but, on the other hand, it is also regarded as 'increasingly in need of the guiding and co-ordinating role of the Communist Party to assure stability and continued evolutionary development' (Kelley, 1982, p. 3). Since Jowitt accurately refers to inclusion regimes as 'attempts to control society from "within"' (Jowitt, 1975, p. 86) and, further, since such attempts are even officially embodied in the strategy of the RCP's Programme (as explained later), I am still persuaded that 'modernization and containment' is a better term than 'inclusion'. Jowitt, lest this caveat be misunderstood, remains, in my judgement, by far the best 'conceptualist' of communist-ruled societies in general, and of Romanian society in particular. But as construed by him, 'inclusion' puts too much emphasis on the means, and too little on the goals of the envisaged post-consolidational policies. What we are actually witnessing is nothing less—and also nothing more—than a set of alternative tactics for societal penetration, the purpose of which remains domination.

'Modernization', in the sense I should like to employ it as a corollary of 'containment', does not reflect the processes outlined by K. W. Deutsch in his well-known article on social mobilization and political development (Deutsch, 1961). To begin with, the concept of political development is value-loaded (Kesselman, 1973). It unwarrantedly assumes that socio-economic change generates pluralism. It also obliterates the distinction between development and change, allowing no room for retrogression (Huntington, 1965)[6], or, for that matter, for stagnation. Finally, the categories employed by Deutsch, if at all applicable, fit more into the earlier periods of transformation and consolidation, than into subsequent stages.

The 'containment' corollary serves to emphasize that Leninist regimes in the modernization period are, above all, regimes of *simulated change*, in the sense that 'value-pluralism' never becomes an integral part of elite core-values. It goes without saying that such a perspective is different from Andrzej Korbonski's, according to whom political change is 'a process or a movement, as a result of which various components of the political system become different, altered, modified, transformed, or converted' (Korbonski, 1977, p. 3). For, once more, what one should be examining are the goals, not the means, of structural transformations (as will be discussed later).

Under regimes of simulated change the party becomes the main focus of formal (though not substantive) democratization, and 'collective leadership' is emphasized as one of the Leninist (as opposed to Stalinist) norms of party life. Party statutes are often amended, so as to provide for further grass-root involvement in decision-making and in leadership control. Where such change occurs in a situation of fluidity, in which no leader or group in the party has established absolute control, manipulative 'democratization' is likely to be launched on many spheres of state and society in order to secure support for the power-contenders. Such measures may acquire a dynamic of their own, which makes the task of a 'return to normalcy' only the more urgent once the leadership crisis has been ended. Yet 'democratic' terminology is not abandoned after 'normalization', not only because it has a symbolic value of its own, but because it is useful for 'containment' purposes. 'Real-socialism' is thus based on an in-built systemic gap between the *parti légal* and the *parti réel*, as well as on a corresponding gap between the *pays légal* and the *pays réel*. The latter discrepancy is of particular significance for group or individual autonomy. While these are acknowledged in theory and promoted within the *caveat* of socialist communitarian goals, they remain confined to the realm of meta-communication. This argument should not be interpreted as claiming that no significant political change has ever occurred in communist regimes. The de-Stalinization process in the Soviet Union and Eastern Europe, or what I am tempted to call the 'Khrushchevian earthquake', undoubtedly signified a departure from such system-embracing 'rules of the game' as mass terror or the leader's ability to decide 'anything he wanted . . . unconstrained by the powers of any individual, group, institution or law' (Rigby, 1977, p. 60). My argument does, however, imply that no change of similar scope, *induced or condoned by these regimes* had been witnessed since that belated echo of the 'earthquake' which was the Czechoslovak Prague Spring.

The explanation for the absence of such change probably rests in the limitations of the Khrushchevian formula, which provided for a change in the number of 'rule makers' but not in the 'name of the game'. The transition from 'monocratic' to 'oligarchic' leadership—or rather the co-existence of 'leader' and 'leadership' roles within both the national leadership and the political establishment (Hodnett, 1975)—never envisaged, in other words, the institution of a 'public political arena'. That arena, as Rigby points out, remained as empty as ever, with debate limited to the *means* of achieving *regime-designated* tasks. The former one-man umpire, to paraphrase Rigby's analysis, was replaced by a 'collective umpire'—the party (Rigby, 1980, p. 26). There was a qualitative change from the Stalin period to that of Khrushchev (via Malenkov), but otherwise change was limited to quantitative (environmentally conditioned) variations, within the boundaries of which it was necessarily simulative. The net result, as indicated, is that 'participation' in the newly created or modified structures of government is constantly highlighted, yet the structures remain under strict party supervision.

There is, indeed, plenty of room for 'local' variations, and the circumstances under which policies and decisions are made may vary from place to place, and from one period to another. As long as the party has not lost its grip on society, however, such variations are unlikely to be significant. The precise format of the political integration formula may, of course, be influenced by numerous factors, ranging from the particularities of the dominant political culture, to historical experience and to alterations in the political environment as a result of either circumstantial, or more permanent, change. In the Romanian case, as indicated, the formula drew to a great extent on a combination of revived and officially sponsored nationalism, and on national pride in the country's industrial achievements. Such specific features, however, by no means affect the general validity of the suggested framework for the analysis.

To demonstrate how simulated change works in the Romanian case, it is necessary to trace the broad steps of Ceauşescu's rise to, and consolidation of, power (see Chapter 6). The simulation, however, affects many more aspects than mere leadership structures. Its impact, as indicated, is directed to no lesser extent to relations between party and society. This can be illustrated by a review of the concept of the 'multilaterally developed socialist society', both in its theoretical evolution and in its practical implementation. The endless 'encroachment' on society by the RCP has been the main feature of Romanian social and political life ever since the late 1960s.[7] Apart from considerations of foreign policy and foreign trade (see Chapters 8 and 10), which cause the Romanians to declare that socialist construction is undertaken nowadays at a developing, rather than a developed, stage (Nelson, 1982a, pp. 63-5), the blueprint is by no means different from that of other models of 'real socialism'. The nationalist particularities of the Romanian form of political integration, however, prevent her from adopting a similar nomenclature.[8] The 'multilaterally developed socialist society' was first mentioned by Ceauşescu at the Ninth Congress of the party in 1965, but began to be elaborated upon only after the Tenth Congress, in 1969 (*Congresul al IX-lea*, 1966, p. 33). Its main thrust could be defined as the 'withering away of society', which, for all practical purposes, is to be 'taken over from within' by the 'conscious factor' (Niculescu-Mizil, 1969, p. 29), i.e. by the party.

As Ceauşescu (1970-83, Vol. 4, p. 256; 1982, p. 26) and Niculescu-Mizil (1969, p. 5) indicated, the term '*multilateral* development' was chosen to indicate that the future of socialism in Romania was not only a function of structural development, but also one of superstructural achievement. Infrastructural (industrial) progress alone would not create socialist consciousness. And since this consciousness bore heavily on the entire mechanism of social development, material investments must be accompanied by the necessary 'spiritual investments'. The member of the 'multilaterally developed socialist society', the 'multilaterally developed new man', must master all its values. The realm of consciousness was thus declared to be no less decisive than that of material achievement. Consequently, the party could not conceivably abandon its leading role in either of them.

The programme adopted by the RCP in December 1974 envisages an ever-widening role of the party, a position that has been constantly reiterated ever since (Ceauşescu, 1970-83, Vol. 22, p. 33; 1982, pp. 21-2; Ceterchi, 1981, p. 22). According to this programme, the party will exist and lead as long as the process of socialist edification and construction continues. It will eventually wither away, but it will do so 'through its integration in society's life, through the ever more organic participation of party members in the entire social life' (*Programul Partidului*, 1975, p. 111). In other words, the process of withering away is conditioned by the take-over from within of all social structures. In this sense, the party becomes 'integrative and integrating' (Popescu-Puţuri, 1981, p. 22), or, as the programme puts it, it exercises leadership 'not from outside, but from inside social, state and economic organs' (*Programul Partidului*, p. 116). The aim is to achieve such leadership by raising the 'consciousness' of the citizens to a level where every 'expert' will be 'red', through a parallel process of developing expertise among party activists as well as through merging party and state functions (King, 1980, pp. 99-119).

The Romanian party, Ceauşescu claimed in March 1981, was well on its way to accomplishing some of these aims, for the party now numbered over 3 million members, which meant it should no longer be considered a 'vanguard' organization (*Scînteia*, 25 March 1981). Furthermore, in June 1982, he declared that people should cease to speak of the 'dictatorship of the proletariat' and search for a more appropriate notion—possibly 'workers' democracy' (Ceauşescu, 1982, p. 18). And 'workers' democracy' it officially became, at the National Party Conference in December 1982 (*Scînteia*, 21 December 1982).

One is entitled to suspect the Romanian leader here of attempting to cope with the influence of Polish political developments, for the evolution of the 'multilaterally developed socialist society' as an operative concept was influenced from the beginning by attempts to fend off 'undesirable' political innovations arising in other Eastern European countries (Shafir, 1981a, pp. 279-356, and 1984a), where ruling elites had been less successful in their strategies for 'system maintenance'. Thus, the establishment of the Socialist Unity Front in 1968 resembled the parallel body set up in Czechoslovakia, though in name only. Similarly, 'Workers' Councils' were set up in the early 1970s, when 'self-management' and 'self-financing' were also introduced for the first time, without, as will be described later, provision for such bodies to fulfil their declared purpose.

To a certain extent, such simulated changes were rooted not only in the party's manipulative aims, but also in Romanian political tradition. The gap between *pays légal* and *pays réel*, after all, had formed the basis of Gherea's criticism of the early twentieth century Romanian polity (see Chapters 1 and 2). The setting up of a fictional system of 'direct participation' was in line with these dissimulative traditions, described by one of Romania's greatest poets and satirists, Tudor Arghezi, as 'What we talk ain't what we smoke' (*una vorbim şi alta fumăm*). These bodies, however, were only one side of the Romanian coin of simulated innovation. The other was the joint party-state structures. Among such organizations are the Supreme Council for Economic Development, the Central Council of Workers' Control of Economic and Social Activity, the National Council for Science and Technology, the Defence Council, the Committee for Problems of People's Councils, etc. (Cismărescu, 1976; Ceterchi, 1979, pp. 118-19 and 1981, p. 22; Surpat, 1981, pp. 37-8; King, 1978a and 1980, pp. 106-9).

The first joint party-state organ to be set up was the Council for Socialist Culture and Education, which replaced the State Committee for Culture and Arts in September 1971. The essential difference between these two bodies is perhaps best illustrated by pointing out that whereas the State Committee for Culture and Arts was originally subordinate to the Council of Ministers, the new structure is accountable to both the Central Committee and the government (*Colecţie de legi, decrete, hotărîri şi dispoziţii*, May–June 1962; *Buletinul oficial*, pt. I, no. 108, 1971). Moreover, the regional branches of the new Council were declared to be under the 'direct' supervision of local party committees. In November 1972 a CC plenum added a further provision, by which the local secretary in charge of propaganda affairs was designated Vice-President of the People's Council and charged with co-ordinating the activities of the local committee and the party propaganda department (*Buletinul oficial*, pt. I, no. 133, 1972).

At the 1972 RCP National Conference Ceauşescu proclaimed the 'blending' of party and state functions to be a 'law governed' societal development. There could be no doubt, according to the Romanian leader, that one would eventually 'witness an ever increasing intertwining of party, state and other social organs, in a law-like process of socialist and communist development' (Ceauşescu, 1970-83, Vol. 7, p. 506). According to this view, the

> new circumstances created by socialism have brought about a change in the relationship between state and society. While in bourgeois society, the state used to display—and still does today—a tendency towards alienation from society, under socialism the reverse is true: the state is brought ever closer to society, and the two will finally merge in communism [Boboş and Deleanu, 1979, p. 173].

The blending, however, is achieved *through the party*, and subsequent developments have amply demonstrated that its purpose is to achieve party dominance over the state, over 'public organizations' (*organizaţii obşteşti*) and over mass organizations, while displaying a 'participatory' façade. 'Take-over from within' thus seems to be the Romanian answer to the 'take-over from without', to which Romanian society has been exposed as a result of events in Czechoslovakia and Poland.

In May 1971, in an important speech delivered on the occasion of the party's anniversary, Ceauşescu acknowledged the possible existence of 'contradictions' in socialism. Such contradictions, he added, might degenerate into 'antagonistic' conflicts, when not made explicit and settled in time (Ceauşescu, 1970-83, vol. 5, p. 904). More than a decade later, and once more under the impact of Polish developments, he reiterated this statement, explaining that 'in the period of socialist construction, some contradictions are maintained, or new contradictions may yet appear'. If these 'are not understood, and if no action is undertaken for their liquidation, they might acquire serious forms, they may trigger powerful social disturbances'. The laws of dialectics, Ceauşescu added, were applicable to socialist, probably even to communist, society, for contradictions will exist 'as long as there are classes and social categories, even if they are not antagonistic' (Ceauşescu, 1970-83, Vol. 22, p. 32). It was, as he put it in June 1982, 'incumbent on us to understand, to note in time, the appearance of contradictions, and to take measures to do away with them', thus 'consciously contributing to society's renovation' (Ceauşescu, 1982, p. 26). Only the 'conscious element', i.e. a truly enlightened and, at the same time, vigilant party, which has an 'overall' view of society, is capable of fulfilling this task (Popescu-Puţuri, 1981, pp. 8-9; Stroe, 1983, pp. 18-20). 'Therein', the Secretary General stated in his speech delivered on the occasion of the party's sixtieth anniversary, 'rests the party's leading political role'. At the same time, however, he made it quite clear that his statement should not be regarded as an indication of the party's intention to withdraw from daily interference in social life. In the new 'democratic structures' set up in the last years, communist party members were to carry 'an ever-increasing responsibility' (Ceauşescu, 1970-83, Vol. 22, p. 35).

For this purpose the party consults with other organizations, with which it 'homogenization' of different interests in society (Pânzaru, 1968; Ceauşescu, 1970-83, Vol. 7, p. 505, Vol. 22, p. 29) and thereby impede their 'antagonization'. Such 'homogenization' came to be suggested by the change of name of the party's main theoretical journal, *Lupta de clasă* (Class Struggle), which, in September 1972, became *Era socialistă* (The Socialist Era).

This demonstrative step, anticipating the 1981 announcement about the ending of the 'dictatorship of the proletariat', seemed to find further support in Ceauşescu's surprising promulgation of the concept of 'transmission belts' (organizations which transmit party will) as no longer fitting the role that trade unions should play at the present stage of development. The party leader made this announcement at a Central Committee (CC) plenary session in February 1971, repeated it at the congress of the General Union of Romanian Trade Unions in March 1971 (Ceauşescu, 1970-83, Vol. 5, pp. 485, 766), but never reiterated it since. Speaking at another plenary session, more than a decade later, the Secretary-General indicated that the Central Committee should 'fulfil the role of a genuine headquarters of the organization and leadership' of all activities, and that the structures of 'democratic participation' (the trade unions included) were to ensure '*mobilization* of the toilers for the purpose of fulfilling the plan'. This was termed '*organized participation*', which is as close as one can possibly get to what East European sarcasm is reputed to call 'organized spontaneity' (Ceauşescu, 1970-83, Vol. 23, pp. 88, 91; emphasis mine). It was not without significance that, although the Polish crisis of the 1980s put the Romanian leadership in a difficult position (due to its constant advocacy of the principle of non-interference in other countries' affairs), by mid-October 1980 Ceauşescu was criticizing 'the slogan of so-called independent trade unions'. These organizations, he stated flatly, could not be independent, for no one could act apart from the party's 'revolutionary conception'. Such slogans could only 'serve the interests of the bourgeoisie and of imperialism'. It was necessary to 'provide a resolute riposte to any form of anti-socialist activity' (Ceauşescu, 1970-83, Vol. 21, p. 45).

Indeed, as attested by the Romanian trade unionist Vasile Paraschiv in 1978 ('*L'itinéraire d'un syndicaliste*', 1982), the 'take-over from within' technique was applied to the trade unions as well—or rather, the 'transmission belts' were never in fact dismantled. Paraschiv's description fits the organs of 'workers' self-management', of which Daniel Nelson's work presents an extensive analysis (Nelson, 1981a, 1981b, pp. 459-60, 1981d). Instituted in 1971, 'workers' self-management' served little other purpose than that of propaganda or, occasionally, of intensifying party control over unreliable sectors (see Chapter 7). Following the unrest among the Romanian miners in the Jiul Valley in 1977, and the Polish events of the late 1970s and early 1980s, 'self-management' began to receive increasing attention as a possible pre-emptive device. Together with party-state structures, it forms the backbone of the general network of simulated change. Another illustration of the mechanism is the 1971 'abolition' of censorship. In actual fact, the layers of censorship were increased, and phased so as to cover innumerable stages of 'discussion' by different forums, some of which allegedly allow for direct participation by workers in cultural life (Shafir, 1981a, pp. 484–5).

Simulated change is not only an instrument of party dominance of the institutional system, but also one of extraction of resources from the population. In June 1982 Ceauşescu 'proposed' to translate 'participation' and 'workers' self-management' into reality by allowing workers to buy, on an allegedly voluntary basis, 30 per cent of the registered value of the fixed assets of the enterprises where they worked. Ironically enough, the idea was launched on the day Romania celebrated thirty-four years of nationalization of the major means of production which, according to Article 7 of the Constitution, *already belonged* to the workers. The scheme was in fact designed to help alleviate the economic crisis through which the country was passing, as well as to absorb the surplus purchasing power of the population (another 'lesson' from the Polish experience), which actually existed as a result of party policies which favoured heavy industry and neglected the supply of consumer goods. Western calculations indicate that the implementation of the scheme would bring the government some 2.7 times the equivalent total 1982 annual salaries (Gafton, 1982). The plan is apparently to use the new 'bonds' (or 'social parts' of the 'social fund') to stimulate productivity and profitability.[9] If precedent is any guide, the scheme is not likely to be very popular. A similar device, launched in 1973 to sell state-owned apartments to employees, ended in failure, and had to be discontinued. Yet on 23 May 1983 the party daily, *Scînteia*, reported that 'millions' had expressed interest in buying the bonds. Such 'interest', as the author was informed by several Romanian employees, is expressed typically in the form of 'organized participation': the management of each enterprise fixes the 'social part' of the salary of each employee, who is then 'free' to submit in writing his/her refusal to buy the shares.

Where do these 'innovations' place Romania in terms of her current development? In other words, what model is one to adopt to better comprehend Romania's contemporary social and political system? In a most stimulating article, Daniel Chirot advocates the use of a 'corporatist' model (Chirot, 1980). The idea is a challenging one, the more so since the national and nationalist 'organic unity' of society, implied by such an analytical framework, is rooted in the inter-war economic and political thought of Mihail Manoilescu. Similarly to Romania's current leaders, Manoilescu attempted to cope with the problem of underdevelopment, resenting his country's inferior international status, and seeking to provide a solution through economic autarky and the extension of state control over society (Schmitter, 1978). Yet the use of a corporatist model in analysing contemporary East European systems is only possible in those cases where elite perceptions of social structures and activities have evolved beyond 'transmission belt' categories. Corporatism might not imply participation in the pluralist sense of the word, but neither is it confined within the bonds of 'mobilization' Consequently, the model is possibly applicable to countries such as Hungary, Yugoslavia, 'Prague Spring' Czechoslovakia, or to some of

Solidarity's ideational stances in Poland (Pravda, 1983), but not to Romania under Ceauşescu.

Comparison with these countries at one stage or another in their post-'Khrushchev era' evolution leads to the tentative conclusion that the present stage of the Romanian system is one of 'political stagnation' (Shafir, 1984b). The term warrants explanation. In a book published in 1980, Seweryn Bialer described the Brezhnev period in the Soviet Union as one of 'political stability', while in a subsequent article he described the Soviet polity and society under Brezhnev as being in a state of 'political stagnation' (Bialer, 1980, pp. 127–225; 1983, p. 45). Are the two concepts, then, similar? According to Bialer, 'the formal logical opposite of stability is, of course, instability, not change', for 'both stable and unstable political regimes undergo political change'. Some changes, he adds 'occur without undermining the stability of a political regime'; moreover, these 'might prove to be not only incremental adjustments', but they might also bring about the transformation of 'some very essential characteristics' of the system (Bialer, 1980, p. 134). It is, however, precisely *the nature of change* which should provide one with the operational distinction between 'political stability' and 'political stagnation', and which the American writer is apparently not making.

By 'political stagnation' I understand the absence of character-defining modifications of a political regime over an extended time, as a result of either successful 'system maintenance' strategies, or the absence and/or weakness of 'dysfunctional' systemic pressures. As such, political stagnation should be regarded as merely the outcome of a regime's *ability to defend*, while political stability should be seen as resting on the regime's *ability to govern* (Hejzlar, 1982, p. 27), i.e. to mediate between and among state and societal goals. Political stability does not preclude alterations in regime–society bargained goals; political stagnation, on the other hand, knows no such process of change, because it rests on refutation of the idea of bargaining. A regime characterized by political stagnation, to use Rigby's words, 'is primarily concerned not with regulating activities, but with *directing* them' (Rigby, 1980, p. 19; emphasis in original). Under such 'goal-setting' regimes, policy making is the exclusive domain of the party. As a result, 'constitutional forms and rituals which suggest otherwise serve as a cosmetic', their 'mobilizational role' being 'transparent to all but the politically infantile' (Rigby, 1980, p. 20). Political stagnation is thus neither a state of political development, nor of political decay. Rather, it is a state of immobility,[10] for simulated change can in no way be seen as a form of social dynamism.

I am, of course, aware of the problems created by the temporal dimension in my definition of political stagnation, for, like beauty, an 'extended period of time' is in the eye of the beholder. The solution, I suggest, rests in adding a comparative dimension. In order to establish whether a political system finds itself at the point of stagnation or not, it should be seen from a comparative viewpoint, in juxtaposition to similar systems, undergoing similar or related processes, at a similar or related period of time. For political stagnation could exist over an extended period, without being in any way noticeable. It becomes blatant only in terms of comparison, i.e. at times of political change or decay in referral systems. And there can be little doubt that in comparison with Hungary, Poland or Czechoslovakia, from the 1950s onwards, the Romanian polity has been stagnant.

Assuming, however, that the basic political ethos of ruling elites in communist systems is similar, despite variations induced by local conditions and/or by the personality of their leader(s), the immediately warranted query should pertain to the causes of political stagnation *in Romania*. According to Bialer, political stability, as indeed all social concepts, treats 'relational phenomena', i.e. is 'an outcome of relations between social items, groups and institutions' (Bialer, 1980, p. 132). The same should hold true, in all probability, for political stagnation. It is, thus, the analysis of the web of such relations that will constitute the (partial) task of the following chapters.

Part II
The Political System

6   The Romanian Communist Party: Leadership, Cadres, Organization

With a contemporary political system that has persisted for nearly four decades without serious challenge one is obviously looking at a case of successful system maintenance. This applies equally to competitive and non-competitive systems. System maintenance, to be sure, can be an outcome of either system management or of system dominance. In either situation, leadership and organization play prominent roles. This is not to imply that in non-competitive one-party systems the social matrix is to be dismissed as either insignificant or of secondary importance. System maintenance implies a *relationship* between those who *maintain* and those who *form* the system, with the former being seen as both in charge and as a component, of the latter. Nor is the prominence of leadership and of organization in system maintenance to be interpreted as disregarding the actual or potential influence of extra-systemic environmental inputs, which may encourage or inhibit systemic transformation. However, whether leaderships register success as a result of organizational mediation between societal goals (political stability) or as an outcome of the absence or of the neutralization of systemic pressures (political stagnation), whether they do so by preventing the penetration of extra-systemic dysfunctional factors or, on the contrary, by encouraging penetration with the purpose of ensuring their own survival, the centrality of leadership and of organizational patterns in system maintenance is self-evident.

The ability of leaders to either induce or prevent change for the purpose of system maintenance is largely a matter of organizational capabilities, among which leadership cohesion should figure prominently. The Leninist formula of 'democratic centralism' is precisely designed to ensure this unity in the pyramid of power, as well as at its apex. It is but an irony of history that Lenin's original intention was system *transformation.* Leadership cohesion, however, is never a function of formal structures alone. Informal organizational behaviour, the cultural framework within which organizations pursue their goals, manipulation techniques employed by leaders with the purpose of ensuring self and/or organizational survival, leadership styles reflecting personality traits and, finally, the possible clash between the leader's personality and the organizational basis of his movement, are of no lesser importance in achieving, maintaining or obstructing leadership cohesion.

Leadership and organizational cohesion may partly account for system maintenance, yet they warrant explanation in themselves. This necessitates perspectives both 'from above' and 'from below'. This chapter is restricted to the former purpose. It therefore reviews the evolution of the RCP, focusing on three different, albeit interconnected, aspects: leadership *of* the party (i.e. the national leadership, by which is meant the highest level of policy-making), leadership *in* the party (the pattern of relations between national leaders and other party elites) and leadership *through* the party (the organization's cadre policy, or recruitment and promotion patterns). A separate chapter will be addressed to the question of leadership *by* the party (to the network of control and the use of governmental, mass organizations and other sectors of the official structure).

Before undertaking such a task, it should be noted that the information on which it rests is highly uneven. While evidence on national leadership is usually satisfactory, if at times inferential, data on party elites and on cadre policies suffers from substantial lacunae. Mary Ellen Fischer, the only Western analyst to have kept the RCP under a magnifying glass with complete and admirable (if not enviable) consistency, observes that secrecy regarding party matters is obsessive in Romania, with the result that 'information on the Romanian elite is consistent only in its inconsistency' (Fischer, 1980, p. 210). For this reason, political scientists who concentrate on Romanian affairs have never quite matched the performance of their colleagues who specialize in the Soviet Union, where data on party composition and evolution is less selectively disclosed. In Romania, release of information on such subjects as social or national structure, or the educational background of party members, has been irregular. Moreover, the Romanians often redefine categories in order to fit regime priorities at any given time (Fischer, 1979, pp. 9-10; Shafir, 1981a, pp. 131-2). What occasionally appear as sudden puzzling alterations in the party's structure (as discussed later) are consequently no more than yet another facet of the mechanism of simulated change. To penetrate beyond this façade is therefore a risky and not always rewarding endeavour.

Leadership Cohesion and Simulated Change

Leadership cohesion[1] is achieved by the elimination of a leader's, or a leading group's, competitors for power and/or by implementing policies of a consensus nature. The latter is often a function of the former, with the victorious faction going on to implement its policies. At first sight this pattern would seem to fit the Romanian case, where, by the end of the 1950s, Dej had succeeded in liquidating all actual or potential competitors and in forming a team loyal to him and to his line. The purge of the 'Muscovites' in 1952, Pătrăşcanu's execution in 1954, the elimination of Miron Constantinescu and Iosif Chişinevschi in the late 1950s and, finally, that of the staunchly independent C. Pîrvulescu in 1961, had left the path open for Dej to pursue policies which he had allegedly envisaged for a long time. Unless the author is quite mistaken, this is the core of the argument pursued by Stephen Fischer-Galati and by other analysts of the Romanian political scene.

Indeed, even scholars critical of Fischer-Galati's work, such as Jowitt, stress that by the time of his death in 1965, Dej was the unchallenged leader of a cohesive core and of a party cast in his own, rather simplistic and proletarian, mentality. The implicit, though unjustified, assumption, is that it was mainly through purges and other organizational means that Dej had achieved party cohesion and complexity (King, 1980, pp. 58-94).

Mary Ellen Fischer, however, demonstrates how the fourteen members of the Romanian Politbureau and CC Secretariat which Dej bequeathed his followers were of diverse ethnic, educational and social backgrounds. One third of the leading Dej group were not Romanian by birth, had had some higher education *and* had spent the war years in the Soviet Union (Fischer, 1980, pp. 212-13). Yet such differences in their formative experience proved of little use to the Soviets. For nearly five years this heterogeneous leadership had resisted Soviet pressures and even foiled attempts on the part of Khrushchev to drive a wedge between the members of the Politburo and bring about Dej's dismissal. Bodnăraş, the former agent of the Kremlin, threw his weight behind the new 'independent' line of the RCP, and refused to implement Soviet orders (Brown, 1966, pp. 67-8; Lendvai, 1970, pp. 305-6).

If homogeneity cannot explain leadership cohesion, and since there is no evidence that Dej's colleagues now feared elimination through purges, one must search elsewhere for an explanation of such remarkable unity. I am suggesting that in the case of the leading core of the Romanian party cohesion was obtained less in positive than in negative terms, and that the latter reflected 'faction anxiety' rather than fear of purge.

Leadership cohesion does not necessarily imply leadership homogeneity. It may rest on shared values and/or anxieties, which unite otherwise heterogeneous components. It is customary to assume that in competitive systems, particularly (though not solely) in multi-party coalitions, cohesion may be cultivated among leaders of different backgrounds and even of opposing outlooks, who nevertheless acknowledge a community of purpose which bridges other divisive gaps. The same, however, applies to many situations in non-competitive one-party systems. In this case, the tendency among Soviet and East European specialists has been to adopt one variant or another of the 'interest group' approach, viewing the transfer from 'monocracy' to 'oligarchy' in essentially utilitarian terms, i.e. as motivated by the urge to achieve the greatest security for the greatest number of national leaders. Without dismissing this Benthamite approach, it is necessary to emphasize that at the same time, communist leadership behaviour is also motivated by certain values, among which rejection of factionalism figures prominently.

Such rejection, of course, is common to all Leninist parties, and has been construed as an organizational principle in the concept of democratic centralism. Values, however, differ in intensity according to specific circumstances. In the case of the late Dejist leadership and its heirs, 'faction-anxiety' may have constituted the central component of an 'elite generation'. According to Bialer, an elite generation is an age-group homogeneous in its attitude *vis-à-vis* a particular life experience, which occurred at a common point in the group's development. Identification of the original causes of the social pattern reflected in a particular elite generation, Bialer indicates, has only limited relevance to the explanation of its continuity, for often elite-generational attitudes persist even after the conditions which produced the pattern have changed or disappeared. Building on Arthur L. Stinchombe's approach, Bialer emphasizes that, once established, social patterns may become self-replicating in successive periods. This is explained by the latent inbuilt ability of social institutions, including leaderships, to preserve traditions moulded around central life experiences. Through this mechanism, successive generations of leaders and elites inherit, adopt and display values similar to those of their predecessors (Bialer, 1980, pp. 99, 101).

I would like to advance the hypothesis that 'faction-anxiety' constituted the most important cohesion-generating factor among the late Dej leadership, one of the central life experiences of which had been the endless factional strife that had inhibited the organizational capabilities of the RCP ever since its birth (Fischer, 1979, p. 3). This is *not* to imply that a leader's or his group's political survival may not take precedence over such experience, and that despite its dominance in elite-generational attitudes, groups would refrain from using tactics likely to impinge on party cohesion where necessary. Rather than deny 'faction-anxiety' for this reason, however, I incline to think such survival strategies reinforce it. Having originally employed tactics for consolidation of power, Dej and the other survivors of intra-party strife must have reached the point of factional struggle saturation, the more so since the history of party schism was associated with that of Soviet domination of the RCP. The stigma of being 'agents of a foreign power' was certainly not unfamiliar to the Romanian leaders, and the outbreak of the dispute with the Soviets provided them with the opportunity of losing it, without having to bear the costs of a cognitive dissonance produced by the 'betrayal' of either organizational principles or the orthodox core of ideology (industrialization). Moreover, I suggest that 'faction anxiety' was transmitted by the late Dej leadership to its followers, and that this factor explains the remarkable leadership cohesion displayed by the RCP throughout the 1960s and the 1970s. The repeated reference in Ceaușescu's speeches[2] to factional struggles serving the interests of the Comintern and reflecting negatively on the party's national popularity are not to be taken as mere legitimization gimmicks (Ceaușescu, 1968-9, Vol. 1, pp. 357-61, 1970-83, Vol. 22, p. 524). The factional trauma of the 'founding fathers' was transmitted to their heirs.

Factional struggles and manipulation by Moscow had indeed cast their shadow on other East European parties, and 'factionalism fatigue' occasionally produced similar (if temporary) effects.[3] It should be stressed, however, that the weaker the numerical strength of a party haunted by factionalism, the stronger its impact on organizational capabilities during the formative (underground) period, and consquently the greater the 'anxiety' displayed by the victorious group after it has consolidated power at the expense of its competitors. This appears to be precisely the case with the Dej leadership, whose collective elite generational memory had been moulded by the weakness of the party in the inter-war period, and by the survival strife of the late 1940s and early 50s.

'Faction-anxiety', however, does not appear to have been capable of preventing intra-party strife elsewhere in Eastern Europe. 'Revisionist' factions have been known to appear in communist parties of similar divisive background, such as the Polish party, while numerical weakness can only partially account for the absence of a similar phenomenon in Romania. 'Revisionism', however, appears to be conditioned by the presence of an intellectual core among strategic elites, with ties to sub-national elites and channels of communication to rank-and-file and to non-party elements. Such a revisionist core should be capable of formulating demands for change in an 'elite penetrative' not Marxist jargon. This necessary, though not sufficient, condition for inducing a process of political change (Shafir, 1984a), was totally absent in Romania, where Marxist tradition was all but non-existent. Consequently, even assuming that a revisionist faction had come into existence *ex nihilo* within the national leadership, its prospects of success would probably have equalled those of an officers' corps without an army. Awareness of this situation only increased further the leadership cohesion in the Romanian Communist Party.

No leader of an East European government would be wise to rely on such cohesion-generating factors alone, however. Dej certainly did not, and his successor, Ceauşescu, adopted and 'ameliorated' his predecessor's methods in his successful bid for a personal consolidation of power. Dej's primacy had always rested on the party apparatus, which he had formally headed as First Secretary since 1944, and effectively controlled since the dismissal of the Pauker group in 1952. To achieve the position of Romania's unchallenged leader, Dej had to make full use of his political skills, behaving ruthlessly towards his enemies, relinquishing and taking over key positions as circumstances required, and promoting his own protégés in the party hierarchy. Paying lip-sevice to de-Stalinization and 'collective leadership', he gave up the position of First Secretary of the RWP from April to October 1955, but conducted the party by proxy, having entrusted the first-secretaryship to the hands of his old comrade Gheorghe Apostol, while he continued to act as Prime Minister—a position he had held since June 1952. In October 1955 he resumed the top party position, and resigned the premiership, which was taken over by his closest ally, Chivu Stoica. In March 1961 Stoica was succeeded by Ion Gheorghe Maurer, whose association with Dej dated from the early 1940s. Dej himself took over the chairmanship of the newly created Council of State in 1961, thereby combining the highest positions of party and state (Shafir, 1981b, p. 600). Last but not least, among Dej's *protégés* promoted in the hierarchy were Ceauşescu and Alexandru Drăghici, whom he sporadically checked by alternating their prominence as potential heir apparents (Jowitt, 1971, pp. 151-2n., 193). The former was entrusted with control over the party apparatus, the latter with the security forces.

Dej's cosmetic 'collective leadership', introduced in the wake of the 'New Course', thus provides the background against which simulated change was instituted in Romania at national leadership level. To grasp to what extent this change deserves to be called 'simulated', it is necessary to put it in comparative perspective. In the Soviet Union the general pattern of 'high politics' in the post-Stalin era has moved from 'monocracy' to 'oligarchy'—to be more precise, from one in which leadership cohesion was achieved through manipulation and maintained through cultivation of the leader's absolute power, combined with his lieutenants' relative insecurity, to one in which each consecutive party leader has wielded *less* individual power than his predecessor over policy making, but managed to increase power over his peers within the period of his incumbency (Brown, 1980, p. 136). This is not to indicate that political leadership in Soviet-type systems is nowadays similar, or even identical, to that exercised in competitive politics, for both leadership techniques and leadership styles are determined primarily by the scope of the arena in which 'competition' takes place. In the former systems, such competition is restricted to national, and occasionally other elite (Central Committee, Army, etc.) circles. Nevertheless, one implication of the evolution of post-Stalinist leadership in Eastern Europe has been the relative increase in 'authority building' patterns and the relative lesser prominence of 'power consolidation' techniques. Power consolidation describes a leader's skills in protecting and aggrandizing his rule via purges, patronage and manipulation of the main institutional pillars of the establishment, whereas authority building is the process by which the leader attempts to match his grip on power by demonstrating to other elites his competence and indispensability as leader (Breslauer, 1982, p. 3). Romania, however, hardly fits such a pattern. On the contrary, an initial phase of authority building, which started in 1965 and ended approximately four years later, appears to have given way to an ever-increasing extent to power consolidation. Whether such consolidation signifies security for the present leadership is a matter for further examination.

At the outset of his leadership, Ceauşescu was faced with powerful political adversaries—above all, the members of the Dejist 'old guard', who could legitimately claim both seniority and closer association with the deceased leader. Nevertheless, the main contender for power was Drăghici, who had joined the Politburo with him in 1955. At the Ninth Congress, in July 1965, it was decided to set up a commission to investigate and 'clarify the political situation of a number of party activists who were arrested or sentenced many years ago' (*Plenara*, April 1968, p. 64). Although the decision was kept secret for the time being, the results of the investigation were a foregone conclusion. Published in April 1968, and resulting, among others, in Pătrăşcanu's rehabilitation, the investigation led to Drăghici's downfall. At the same time it neutralized all Dej's other associates who had acquiesced in the former leader's 'illegalities'. This was clearly reflected in the April plenum resolution, according to which 'a heavy responsibility for proceeding to Lucreţiu Pătrăşcanu's trial without checking on the credibility of the accusations brought by the investigating organs falls on the then-members of the Political Bureau of the CC and of the RWP' (*Plenara*, April 1968, p. 70).

That Ceauşescu's colleagues in the leadership acquiesced in the setting up of the investigating commission despite its potentially damaging findings is to be explained by two main factors: first, it is more than likely that the initial stage of this process encompassed the building of a coalition headed by Ceauşescu, the main purpose of which lay in checking Drăghici's aspirations to power. As head of the security forces, Drăghici must have been perceived by Dej's successors to be far more dangerous than Ceauşescu, in what could be labelled the 'Beria syndrome'. Viewed from this angle, the Romanian leadership succession neatly fits both into Alfred G. Meyer's (1983, pp. 163-5) notion of a 'struggle *against* power' (rather than a struggle *for* power) and into Breslauer's concept of authority building. Secondly, it is also safe to assume that the demonstration of his competence and indispensability to other leaders of the party involved, as a first stage, assurances on Ceauşescu's part that the investigation would not affect them personally. It is relevant to indicate here that no major changes in personnel affected the top party leadership for quite some time after succession. This places in doubt Valery Bunce's thesis, according to which in Soviet (as well as in Western) systems, leaders enjoy greater power and authority in the earliest period of their rule than during the succeeding years[4] (Bunce, 1981, pp. 140-78).

Having once secured his colleagues' support for the move against Drăghici, Ceauşescu then proceeded to neutralize their potentially still considerable threat to his leadership.[5] This was mainly achieved through control and manipulation of Central Committee membership and of regional party secretaryships (as described later).

The April 1968 Resolution condemned Dej as personally responsible for the brutal repression of his political adversaries, thus bringing to an end a tacit campaign against Dejism that had been instituted since his death. Having rid himself of his predecessor's giant shadow, Ceauşescu could claim sole credit for the nationalist line, and could add it to the image of democratizer of a regenerated party. The 1965 decision to rename the RWP the Communist Party of Romania, counting its congresses since 1921, had already stripped Dej of the mantle of 'founding father'. On the other hand, the proclamation of Romania as a 'socialist state' (instead of the former People's Republic) opened a new 'era' associated with Ceauşescu, while simultaneously claiming for the new Socialist Republic a status equal to that of the Soviet Union (Shafir, 1981a, p. 189).

The new party statutes, adopted at the July 1965 Congress, kept democratic centralism as a leading principle (discussed later), stipulating, however, that 'collective leadership' was one of the leading axioms of the party, and that, consequently, no person should hold office in both party and state. While Ceauşescu was designated party leader, Chivu Stoica inherited Dej's position as Chairman of the Council of State, and Maurer continued to act as Prime Minister, with Apostol as his only First Deputy Premier. With the benefit of hindsight, it can now be established that the institutionalization of 'collective leadership' was the first step on the long road of simulated change at the top. The purpose of the stipulation was to weaken the power base of Ceauşescu's potential adversaries. Drăghici, for instance, was forced to give up his position as Minister of the Interior, and this proved to be the beginning of his political disgrace.

Once the rule had served its turn, the statutes were duly changed, in December 1967, making it possible for Ceauşescu to hold a number of positions in both state and party. What is striking, however, is not the commonplace of the institutionalization of power, but the lip-service which continues to be paid to the lofty principle of 'collective leadership', at a time when the cult of personality has reached grotesque proportions (see, for instance, Ceauşescu's speech in *Scînteia*, 5 August 1983). Simulated change thus appears to have raised the traditional discrepancy between *pays légal* and *pays réel* to proportions hitherto unknown in the history of Romania. Ironically enough, it was Chivu Stoica who in 1967, forced to tear himself from the top position in Ceauşescu's favour, was required to introduce a motion that the party leader should jointly hold the two foremost positions in the hierarchy. To add insult to injury, but typical of the essence of simulated change, the 'innovation' was formulated in terms suggesting that the transition to *de facto* personal rule signified *Central Committee* (i.e., widely collective) control of social and state activity (Rush, 1974, pp. 125-6). The Romanians appear to have taught their senior Soviet colleagues a lesson in the politics of simulated change, for in 1983 Chernenko would be (almost) similarly 'honoured' with proposing Andropov's candidacy to the presidency of the Supreme Soviet. It should also be recorded that Ceauşescu preceded both Brezhnev, Husák and Honecker in restoring the title of Secretary General (instead of First Secretary) to the party leader, thereby making it clear as early as July 1965 that the top party position entailed a qualitative, and not merely a quantitative, hierarchy.[6]

One of the earliest forms of simulative institutional 'innovation' was the creation of the Central Committee's Executive Committee (EC), a new intermediary body created at the Ninth Party Congress between the Central Committee and the top party leadership (*Congresul al IX-lea*, p. 739). The former Politburo was now replaced by a Standing Presidium of only seven members: Ceauşescu, Stoica, Maurer, Apostol, Alexandru Bîrlădeanu, Bodnăraş and Drăghici. The Executive Committee was composed of the members of the Standing Presidium, and by Petre Borilă, Constantin Drăgan, Alexandru Moghioroş, Niculescu-Mizil, Leonte Răutu, Gheorghe Rădulescu, Leontin Sălăjan and Ştefan Voitec, with ten other persons designated as candidate members (Iosif Banc, Maxim Berghianu, Petre Blajovici, Dumitru Coliu, Florian Dănălache, Janos Fazekas, Mihai Gere, Petre Lupu, Ilie Verdeţ and Vasile Vîlcu). It is important to note that none of the faces on the Standing Presidium were new, while the EC included only Drăgan, Niculescu-Mizil and Rădulescu as newcomers to the national leadership. It was, however, among the candidate members that one found the future reservoir of Ceauşescu's supporters. Indeed, the object of the 'innovation' introduced in 1965 appears in retrospect to have been to provide a mechanism for the advancement of Ceauşescu's protégés who could not yet make it to the topmost echelons. Displaying remarkable political skills, the new party leader built an alternative leadership in stand-by positions, without having to adopt confrontational policies and thereby provoke the wrath of his yet powerful adversaries. With the exception of Sălăjan, who died in 1966, the Standing Presidium and the EC registered no change between July 1965 and December 1967. As Mary Ellen Fischer indicates, promotion (of his supporters) rather than demotion was the pattern of personnel change at this early stage of the Ceauşescu leadership. Out of twenty-seven new members elected between 1965 and 1969 to the leading party organs, not one was demoted until April 1972 (Fischer, 1980, pp. 219-20).

The CC Secretariat, however, only partially fits into this pattern. For although this body also remained unchanged until 1967, out of its eight members elected at the Ninth Congress in July 1965, half (Manea Mănescu, Niculescu-Mizil, Vasile Patilineţ and Virgil Trofin) were people newly promoted by Ceauşescu.[7] Control of the party machine was obviously of the highest priority in the new leader's scheme for consolidating power.

By the time of the Tenth Congress, which took place in August 1969, only three members of the former Dej leadership (Ceauşescu, Prime Minister Maurer and Bodnăraş) were members of the Standing Presidium and only two additional left-overs (Răutu and Voitec) made it to the EC, now enlarged to twenty-one full and eleven candidate members. The party Secretariat (Ceauşescu, Gere, Niculescu-Mizil, Gheorghe Pană, Patilineţ, Dumitru Popescu and Trofin) was totally *'Dej-rein'* (*Congresul al X-lea*, 1969, pp. 757-8).[8] By November 1974, at the Eleventh Party Congress, Maurer had retired from political life (he was replaced as Prime Minister in March the same year by Manea Mănescu) and Bodnăraş died in 1976 (*Scînteia*, 25 January 1976). Răutu was forced to retire (*Scînteia*, 19 August 1981), following a request by members of his family to emigrate, which was deemed to be 'incompatible' with his position. Consequently, at the time of writing this, only Voitec—largely a symbolic vestige of the 1948 merger with the socialists—remains from the Dejist team, apart from Ceauşescu, of course. Born in 1918, he was the youngest member of the Dejist Politburo in 1965. By 1974 he was one of the oldest of the leadership (Fischer, 1980, p. 215).

The turnover of age-groups was but a reflection of the mechanism of power consolidation. The 'innovations' introduced by Ceauşescu turn out, in this respect, on closer scrutiny, to be strikingly familiar to the classical pattern of 'circular flow of power'. Such 'flow' is based on the hierarchy of party secretaries, who are nominally elected by provincial and local organizations, but who are, in fact, appointed by the Central Committee Secretariat. The nominees in turn implement the orders of the central apparatus, and control the selection of representatives to the higher party echelons. The party leader who controls the circular flow process is thus capable of (a) promoting his supporters to the Central Committee, and (b) ensuring the election of his own people to the higher posts (Daniels, 1971, p. 20). The process is, of course, a part of the phenomenon of political clientelism—Communist style (Willerton, 1979). The classical circular flow of power theory holds that both Stalin and Khrushchev engineered the replacement of many regional first secretaries after taking over the apparatus of the party, and that such support enabled them to neutralize political adversaries at party congresses and in the Central Committee (Hough and Fainsod, 1980, p. 281). The Ceauşescu variant of the circular flow consists in its timing: while turnover was used to control the Central Committee and promotions throughout his leadership, the process was in fact initiated *prior* to the death of his predecessor.

Ceauşescu became a Central Committee Secretary in April 1954 and was in charge of organization and cadres. In that position his influence over the apparatus in Bucharest, and through it, over the nomination of regional First Secretaries, must have been substantial. Indeed, Fischer indicates that out of the sixteen men who held that position in 1965, eleven had moved into the leading party organs by 1969, and none of them had been demoted (Fischer, 1980, pp. 222, 224). By 1967 there had been a 50 per cent turnover in the position of regional First Secretaries, but only one demotion. Seven men who held that position were promoted to either the EC, to ministerial posts, or to the CC apparatus. When, in early 1968, a territorial reorganization was carried out, replacing the former Soviet-inspired 'regions' with the historical Romanian *judeţe* (counties), the number of local party officials increased from sixteen to forty, but none of the former local 'bosses' lost their position as a result of this measure. On the contrary, four were promoted to the capital and the remainder became county party officials (Fischer, 1980, p. 224).

Another consequence of the 1967 amendment, adopted with the intention of consolidating Ceauşescu's power, was the strengthening of party control over the state apparatus at all levels of the pyramid. This included county level, where the party secretaries were to function from now on as presidents of the people's councils (local government) as well. The measure was supposedly aimed at improving efficiency. But, it also opened a new phase in the process of power consolidation for, from 1971, a 'rotation' principle requires high party dignitaries to periodically exchange positions in the central state and party apparatus. No precise rules for this rotation were ever made, but the only leaders not affected by it appear to be Ceauşescu and his wife. The principle has enabled a constant check on possible contenders for power who had advanced since 1965 and who could become too powerful in their new positions. Promotions were now replaced by rotation, with the county party position serving as one of the possible locations for alleged 'strengthening ties with the masses'. Between February 1971 and 1977 over a dozen Central Committee and EC members assumed such posts, among them many who were known to be held in high (too high?) esteem in the party hierarchy, such as Trofin or Ion Iliescu (Nelson, 1981c, pp. 226-7). While such rotations are not necessarily a definite demotion (some of those rotated returned to the capital), they seem to be arbitrary and to occur with a frequency which strengthens the hypothesis that the main purpose of the mechanism is to prevent anyone from building a fief as a potential challenge to the leader's power (Fischer, 1982, p. 33).

Ceauşescu's assumption of the office of President of the Republic (in place of the former chairmanship of the Council of State) in March 1974 opened the door to the introduction of a further 'innovation' at leadership level: the institution of the office of Presidential Counsellor. Initially an honorific title, bestowed upon those who enjoyed dangerously high prestige (such as former Foreign Minister Corneliu Mănescu), this office eventually developed into a true *locus in quo* of decision-making, being manned by officials who happen to enjoy the President's confidence, and who move from there to positions in the Secretariat, the Council of Ministers or to county party chairmanships. Well-informed sources in Bucharest have told the author that even in the highest echelons, the presidential counsellors are regarded with something of a jaundiced eye and nicknamed the '*camarilla*'.[9]

A perfect illustration of how simulated change may be exploited for radically different purposes is offered by the institutional innovation introduced in March and November/December 1974. At a Central Committee plenum held on 25-26 March it was decided to abolish the Committee's Standing Presidium, the members of which were the most influential individuals in the party, and to replace it with a Permanent Bureau. Once more, the measure was supposed to improve 'efficiency'. The Permanent Bureau was to function on the principle of *ex officio* membership, i.e. to include the Secretary General (Ceauşescu), the President of the Republic (also Ceauşescu), plus all Central Committee secretaries, the Prime Minister, and several other state and mass-organization leaders. At the Eleventh Congress, however, new party statutes were adopted (*Scînteia*, 19 December 1974), providing for changes in the structure and composition of the Permanent Bureau. According to the new provisions, the Bureau was to be appointed by the Political Executive Committee (the new name for the former Executive Committee) from among its members. Instead of keeping to the originally envisaged composition, the Political Executive Committee (PEC) nominated only five persons to the Permanent Bureau. At first sight the change may appear rational from the point of view of administrative efficiency, since a smaller forum may reach decisions more rapidly. With the benefit of hindsight, however, it may be established that the 'reform' was not dictated by considerations of efficiency. By January 1977 four new members had been promoted to the Bureau, increasing the membership to nine. At present (June 1984), the number of party officials occupying positions in this body is thirteen. It therefore appears that the evolution of the Permanent Bureau was a three-step process, aimed at the elimination of the former Standing Presidium, some of whose members might have become too influential and independent (Shafir, 1981b, p. 611).

Another facet of simulated change, the aim of which, once more, is to enforce absolute control by the party leader over the apparatus, is 'party democratization'. An interesting 'innovation' was introduced shortly before the Tenth Party Congress, abolishing the former process of election of the Central Committee, or rather altering it so as to apparently allow a greater voice to the rank and file in the election of the party's higher bodies. Whereas the county party organizations had hitherto only elected 'delegates' to party congresses, they were now given the right to make 'nominations' to those bodies, with the provision, furthermore, that the number of candidates was to exceed the number of seats available in the two relevant organs, the Central Committee and the Central Auditing Commission (*Congresul al X-lea*, pp. 134-5). Heralding the broadly similar 'simulated partici- pation' introduced in the process of elections to the Grand National Assembly and to the local people's councils in 1975 (see later), the amendment of party statutes now adopted allowed for an early screening of undesirable elements, whose demotion could from now on be attributed to the leadership's expressed wish to strengthen the influence of the rank and file over the conduct of the party's activities, thereby strengthening 'socialist democracy' (Ceauşescu, 1970-83, Vol. 4, pp. 136-7). Thus, one of the first victims of the new election mechanism was Gheorghiu-Dej's son-in-law, Gheorghe Rădoi, who did not secure nomination for election to the Central Committee. It should be pointed out, at the same time, that local party conferences cannot hinder the election of elements who enjoy the leadership's support for, according to the statutes, the party congress may also elect candidates who have *not* been proposed by lower party levels. Bearing in mind that at the Twelfth Party Congress elections took place according to 'indications' made by a special commission headed by Ceauşescu himself, 'party democratization' now appears in its true light.

Turnover in Central Committee membership even since the Tenth Congress has been extremely high (see Table 6), reaching more than 50 per cent at the Twelfth Congress in 1979:

Table 6   Central Committee Membership Turnover: CC Members
Not Re-elected to 'Higher Party Bodies'

	Full CC members	%	Alternate CC members	%	Total members	%
1969 (July)	24	14.5	34	28.3	58	20.3
1974 (November)	28	13.7	125	80.1	153	42.4
1979 (November)	88	35.9	133	82.0	221	54.0

The significant jump in these figures, occuring in 1974, also reflected the leadership's determination to promote cadres who combined the technical skills needed for the management of the 'Multilaterally developed socialist society' with a display of 'revolutionary mentality', a requirement hardly met by members of local elites before. At the same time, the turnover was to allow for better representation of young cadres and of women (discussed later). In order to enforce a July 1972 National Party Conference decision regarding the periodical 'rotation' of party cadres (*Scînteia*, 23 July 1972), criteria were adopted in July 1974 according to which, during elections, party bodies should take the necessary measures to ensure that not less than one-third of the members of the bureaux of local organizations and of party committees, including the CC, were freshly promoted cadres (*Scînteia*, 30 July 1974). This was also supposed to be part of the drive for 'party democratization'. The turnover in Central Committee membership in 1979, however, considerably exceeded this requirement, thus indicating that the mechanism is at least partially employed for the purpose of either checking the power of suspected uncontrollable elements and/or for the promotion of those who enjoy the confidence of the 'ruling family'.

It was certainly not accidental that three of those promoted to the Permanent Bureau in January 1977 were relatives of Ceauşescu: his wife Elena, his brother-in-law Verdeţ and Corneliu Burtică, who is reportedly (*New York Times*, 30 May 1982) a nephew of the President. Another brother-in-law, Manea Mănescu, had been a member of the Bureau since its establishment, and was Prime Minister between March 1974 and March 1979, when he resigned for health reasons. He was replaced by Verdeţ, who held the position until 1982.

Mrs Ceauşescu[10] is nowadays virtually the second highest Romanian official. In addition to her membership of the Bureau of the PEC (she joined the Bucharest Municipal Party Committee in 1968, was elected a full CC member in 1972 and became an EC member in June 1973), Elena Ceauşescu is a member of the Grand National Assembly and, as a trained chemist, she became Chairwoman of the National Council of Science and Technology in 1979, a position with ministerial status which she still holds in 1984. Although her academic credentials appear to be somewhat obscure,[11] the Romanian press constantly refer to her as Academician-Doctor-Engineer, for, among other things, she is also a member of the Technical Sciences section of the Romanian Academy. In 1980 her ministerial status was raised, and the President's 'revolutionary companion' became one of the three First Deputy Prime Ministers in the Romanian government. What appears to be far more important, in January 1979, she became Chairwoman of the CC Commission for State and Party Cadres, a position from which she can watch over the security of what is commonly referred to in Romania as the 'Ceauşescu dynasty'.[12]

Romania's first family appears to have had a direct impact on the social structure of the party. At the CC plenum that elected Elena Ceauşescu to membership on the EC, her husband emphasized the role played by women in Romanian society and economy, adding that the structure of the party had not hitherto satisfactorily reflected the proportion of women (about 51 per cent) and their contribution to social life (Ceauşescu, 1970-83, Vol. 9, pp. 646-53). At that time women accounted for nearly 24 per cent of party membership (*Scînteia*, 22 June 1973). By 1980 the figure had risen to nearly 29 per cent (*Scînteia*, 28 March 1981), and at the CC plenum which took place in March 1981, the party leader set the target of 34-35 per cent for the Thirteenth Congress (Ceauşescu, 1970-83, Vol. 21, p. 506). Yet in 1983, the latest year for which figures are available, the proportion of women in the party was just 31.61 per cent (*Scînteia*, 27 March 1984). Representation in the Central Committee (full and candidate members) had risen from 4 per cent in the body elected at the Tenth Party Congress in 1969 to 25 per cent at the Twelfth Congress in 1979 (Fischer, 1983b). By mid-1984 there were three women (Elena Ceauşescu, Lina Ciobanu and Alexandrina Găinuşe) on the party's Political Executive Committee with full membership status, but only Elena Ceauşescu was a member of the Permanent Bureau. Three other women (Suzana Gâdea, Ana Mureşan and Elena Nae) were alternate members of the PEC, and Lina Ciobanu was nominated to the Party Secretariat in 1984. In May 1984, out of forty-nine ministers or executives with ministerial rank, there were four women. These promotions do not necessarily reflect an improvement in the social status of women in Romania (see Chapter 9), although, according to the indications of the PEC issued in June 1983, by 1985 women should constitute 'over 30 per cent' of leading cadres in industry and agriculture, thereby more than doubling the present proportion of 14.4 per cent (*Scînteia*, 22 June 1983).

Approximately at the same time as the party leader began to emphasize the need for better representation of women in the RCP, the issue of 'party rejuvenation' began to be raised as well, although, for reasons discussed below, Ceauşescu's personal attitude towards this problem appears to be more ambivalent. Just as Elena Ceauşescu's promotion coincided with the seemingly 'affirmative action' directed towards recruitment of women into the party (Fischer, 1983b), so the promotion of younger cadres appears to be linked with the rising star of the family, Nicu Ceauşescu, one of the 'steering couple's' three children. Born in 1950, Nicu Ceauşescu began his political career in 1973, when he apparently inherited from his sister, Elena Zoe Ceauşescu, the position of Vice-Chairman of the Romanian Communist Students' Association. During that year he began accompanying his father on trips abroad, and eventually headed several Romanian delegations on official visits of his own. In 1974 he was elected a member of the Council of the Front of Socialist Unity where he is now a member of the Executive Bureau. A year later he became a member of the Union of Communist Youth's Central Committee, then one of its secretaries, as well as a member of the organization's Bureau. On 10 December 1983 the young Ceauşescu was 'elected' First Secretary of the Union, a position which bestows on him ministerial status as well. Previously, at the Twelfth Party Congress in 1979, he had become a candidate member of the party's Central Committee, and was promoted to full membership at the National Party Conference of December 1982. Like his parents and several other members of the family, he has been a deputy in the Grand National Assembly since 1980, and was even elevated to the post of Secretary in the Romanian parliament. He is also on the National Council of the Working People (author's files). On 13 May 1983 *Scînteia* announced that Nicu Ceauşescu had been awarded the Order of Labour, First Class, by presidential decree. Like his mother, Dr Nicu Ceauşescu is also a 'scientist of international reputation', and the author of several volumes on nuclear physics (*Scînteia tineretului*, 19 February 1983; *Scînteia*, 25 June 1983).

Alongside Nicu Ceauşescu, several other members of the 'clan' were decorated on the same occasion. Elena Zoe Ceauşescu, who is head of the section for mathematics at the National Institute for Scientific Creation, was awarded the same medal as her brother (but Second Class!), while the third child, Valentin, who is Senior Research Associate and scientific secretary at the Bucharest Institute of Physics and Nuclear Energy, was honoured with the Order for Scientific Merits, Second Class. One of the President's sisters, a school inspector in Ceaușescu's native county, was also awarded the Order of Labour, First Class.

It is almost impossible to provide a complete list of Ceaușescu kin promoted through the framework of family power consolidation. Among the more prominent figures, however, are Gheorghe Petrescu, Elena Ceaușescu's brother, who has been a Deputy Prime Minister since 1982, as well as Chairman of the Section for Transportation and Communication of the Supreme Council for Economic and Social Development, a body apparently particularly fortunate to have so many members of the family in its leading positions; Nicolae A. Ceaușescu, a brother of the party leader, who since 1983 has held the rank of Lieutenant General in the Ministry of the Interior; Ilie Ceaușescu, yet another brother, appointed during the same year Deputy Minister of Defence and Head of the Higher Political Council of the Romanian Army (*Buletinul oficial*, 20 April 1983), after having previously risen in the field of official historiography, and better known in the west as Dr Ilie Ceaușescu, a specialist in military history; and Ioan Ceaușescu, yet another brother, who is Vice-Chairman of the State Planning Commission, and since 1983 also Vice-Chairman of the Council of Forestry (Socor, 1983a).

However, the Romanian economic fiasco of the early 1980s (see Chapter 8), accompanied, as it was, by the endemic personal corruption of party and state officialdom, affected even the President's family. Corneliu Burtică, whose latest position had been that of Minister of Foreign Trade and International Economic Co-operation, was first demoted to a county party chairmanship, and eventually expelled from the Central Committee and from the PEC (*Scînteia*, 22 May 1982; 9 October 1982). Brother-in-law Ilie Verdeț was replaced as Prime Minister by Constantin Dăscălescu, but unlike Burtică he was first designated Vice-Chairman of the Council of State and was later nominated Secretary of the CC (*Scînteia*, 22 May 1982; 9 October 1982). By mid-1983 his positions included membership of the PEC and its Permanent Bureau, the secretaryship of the Central Committee and the chairmanship of the Central Council of Workers' Control of Economic and Social Activities.

Burtică's sacrifice and Verdeț's partial and temporary eclipse were, however, immediately balanced by Petrescu's nomination to the first deputyship in the government, as well as by the comeback of the other brother-in-law, Manea Mănescu who, in October 1982, took over Verdeț's position as Vice-Chairman of the Council of State, and was eventually re-appointed a full CC member in December (*Scînteia*, 19 December 1982) and a member of the PEC early in 1983 (*Scînteia*, 25 March 1983). Even so, the demotions of 1982 were a shrewd move, once more demonstrating that Ceaușescu's skills as a political manœuvrer are quite remarkable. By taking action against his own kin, the President wished to demonstrate, as he put it in a speech delivered at the conclusion of the CC plenum, that 'no one can be allowed to encroach upon the law' (*Scînteia*, 22 May 1982), thereby reinforcing his own righteous image as an impartial and Draconic ruler, cast in a contemporary reincarnation of the national hero, Vlad the Impaler. By so doing, he was shifting blame away, not only from himself, but also from the party, for it was certainly no coincidence that the plenum insisted on the responsibility of the *state* in implementing the (infallibly correct) policies of the party (see, for instance, the first speech delivered by Dăscălescu as Premier, in *Scînteia*, 22 May 1982). Indeed, it was in their capacity as state, rather than party officials, that Burtică, Verdeţ and other ministers and officials of lesser rank had been sanctioned throughout the early 1980s.

Promotion of family members in the hierarchy is certainly not a new phenomenon in Romania, nor is it one restricted to that country. Gheorghe Rădoi, Dej's son-in-law, became a member of the government under the previous party First Secretary. China under Mao, Albania, Bulgaria, Czechoslovakia, Cuba and even East Germany have witnessed wives, brothers, daughters and sons-in-laws climbing the political ladder, and often losing their positions after the death or demotion of their relatives (Prifti, 1978, pp. 100-1; Pano, 1982, p. 212; Zagoria, 1982; Bell, 1982, p. 228; Rush, 1974, p. 49; Lewytzkyj & Stonynowski, 1978, pp. 224, 644). The Soviet Union itself has not been immune to nepotism: Stalin's daughter Svetlana married the son of A. Zhdanov, who was a candidate for the *Vozh'd*'s mantle before his death in 1948; Alexei Adzhubei, Editor-in-chief of *Izvestia* and husband of Rada (neé Khruscheva) was considered a kind of unofficial Minister of Foreign Affairs; Leonid Brezhnev's son Yuri was Deputy Minister of Foreign Trade when his father died (Rush, 1974, p. 49; Hodnett, 1981, p. 91; McCauley, 1983, p. 32). Finally, Yuri Andropov's death found his son representing the Soviet Union as a diplomat in Sweden. But it is apparently the example of North Korea, where Kim Chong-il is being groomed to hereditary succession (Park, 1982) that Ceauşescu became fascinated with, while on a visit to that country in 1971 (Jowitt, 1974b, pp. 133-5).

The phenomenon of 'party familialization' is not easily accounted for. It appears to be connected with both a continuation of behavioural patterns typical of scarcity-conditioned peasant societies and with the monopolist ethos of Leninist regimes. Z. Bauman has argued that patronage is a way of life for peasant societies, and that the probability of its occurrence or persistence in environments with this tradition is particularly high (Bauman, 1979, p. 184). Jowitt, who first coined the term 'party familialization', indicates that in such societies the 'corporate family' becomes a basic self-defensive unit. His analysis is partially based on Foster's notion of 'limited good'. According to Foster, the image of limited good, typical of peasant societies, perceives the 'goods' as existing in limited amounts which cannot be increased, from which it follows that '*an individual or a family can improve a position only at the expense of others*'. Furthermore, this image implies that 'each minimal social unit (often the nuclear family, and, in many situations, a single individual) sees itself in perpetual, unrelenting struggle with its fellows for possession of or control over what it considers to be its share of scarce values' (Foster, 1967, pp. 305, 311; emphasis in the original). Party familialization could thus be seen as the epitome of patronage induced by defensive postures, in societies where one's sense of security is enhanced through the distribution of 'goods' to people whom one knows and trusts, and who, in turn, are expected to watch over the common 'family courtyard'. With the exception of Czechoslovakia and East Germany, instances of nepotism such as those described in the previous paragraph, seem indeed, to have occurred in societies of a more or less peasant character.[13]

Such societies may have more in common than meets the eye with non-communist communities, where 'familialization' is known to have occurred in the political structure (Taiwan, the Philippines, Argentine, Egypt, Syria, etc.). Nevertheless, both Bauman and Jowitt indicate that latent or actual peasant mentalities are reinforced by the communist organizational matrix of social and political life. According to the second author, communist-type forms of 'familialism' are related to both the routinization of the party and to the rationalization of society.[14] Unlike in the West, where the earlier 'status society' has been replaced by 'the individual entrepreneur and citizen, acting in the market of the public order', in communist countries 'status society' was replaced by a 'neo-traditionalist' society, which involves 'the deliberate pre-emption by the party of any political arena or role not coterminous with its own organisation and membership'. At societal level, this results in a self-defensive reaction, with non-party elites orientating themselves 'to achievement norms, calculable rules, and the nuclear family as the locus of affection and individual effort'. At party level, on the other hand, it generates 'intermarriage . . . and the development of a "right to rule" mentality within elite families' (Jowitt, 1978a, pp. 69-71).

Ever since the early 1970s Romanian leadership cohesion seems to be anchored in a continuum, one end of which is party pre-emption of the political arena, the other the pre-emption of the party by the Ceauşescus. Simulated change is employed to the same effect, for numerous combined party-state bodies (the backbone of 'political innovation' in the 'Ceauşescu era') are headed by members of the leader's 'extended family': the Leninist representation of society's 'real interests' by the party appears to have evolved into the embodiment of these interests by 'the family', *via* the party. This, however, is not so much a matter of 'routinization of charisma' to which Jowitt refers in an article published in 1983, as of manipulated 'charismatization of routine'.

Such manipulated charismatization (a *contradictio in adjectio* if ever there was one) finds its blatant expression in the 'cult of personality' which has been known to plague the Romanian public arena from the late sixties onwards, making the party leader into a demi-god adored by his nation, and indeed by the 'peace-loving' world at large. Among Ceauşescu's official titles are counted those of Secretary General of the RCP, President of the Republic and of the Council of State, Chairman of the Front of Socialist Unity and Democracy, Chairman of the Supreme Council for Economic and Social Development, Chairman of the National Defence Council and thus also Supreme Commander of the Armed

Forces, President of the National Council of Working People, and many others, among them Honorary President of the Academy for Social and Political Sciences (see Table 11, Chapter 7). The cult has reached paroxysmal dimensions, for Nicolae Ceauşescu is not only supposed to be the most important living Marxist thinker, nor is he merely the personal reincarnation of the national struggle for independence, but he is also the only hope left to a world maddened by the arms race (Tismăneanu, 1983, p. 257). The leviathan volume *Homage to Comrade Ceauşescu* (*Omagiu*, 1973), published on the occasion of the leader's fifty-fifth birthday, might have taught even Stalin a lesson in public adulation.

The ridiculous dimensions of these displays of paganism—Marxist style—have been described in detail by Anelie Maier and others, and the functions of the cult analysed by Mary Ellen Fischer and Trond Gilberg (Maier, 1980, 1983a, 1983b; Shafir, 1983b, pp. 418-19; Fischer, 1981; Gilberg, 1974a, 1979, pp. 315-19, 1981b, pp. 148-53). Riding on the back of an ever-functional nationalism, the Romanian leader manipulated himself into the position of idol of his people. Owing to positions adopted on occasions such as the May 1966 speech delivered on the occasion of the party's anniversary (see Chapter 3), and the denunciation of the 1968 invasion of Czechoslovakia by Warsaw Pact forces, as well as to the not yet fully transparent aspects of simulated change introduced between 1965 and 1969, his popularity seemed to be genuine. By the late seventies, however, he was indulging in the creation of artificial crisis situations[15] (such as the over-dramatized and widely publicized dispute with the Warsaw Pact over military budget increases) in order to safeguard the image of the irreplaceable *defensor nationis*.

The manipulative character of the cult of personality notwithstanding, additional factors probably contribute to its proportions. At the outset of his rule, Ceauşescu acted in what Korbonski terms the manner of 'a traditional Balkan autocratic, yet benevolent ruler' (Korbonski, 1976, p. 13). A similar 'paternal orientalism' was also characteristic of Dej's attitudes towards leadership, although his paternalism was limited to his working-class constituency (Jowitt, 1971, p. 171). Some five years after his nomination as Secretary General, however, Ceauşescu's leadership style had obviously changed. He had become the 'leader, visionary, philosopher, apostle, father saviour, synthesis of Latin genius, personification of Daco-Roman tradition, and superman of dizzying simplicity'. These titles, and many more, are nowadays bestowed upon Ceauşescu. The sentence just quoted, however, is not from one of the thousands of articles glorifying him. It is just Eugen Weber's description of an introduction to a volume of speeches by Romania's wartime leader, Marshal Ion Antonescu (Weber, 1966, p. 567). Like Antonescu, Ceauşescu is his country's beloved *Conducător* (leader). Both men did more than merely reflect traditionally based authoritarianism when they allowed and encouraged adulation. In all likelihood it was also a matter of personal inclination.

The personality factor, indeed, is forever likely to remain the 'black box' of political leadership analysis. Yet leadership styles are influenced, and leaders often make choices, on the basis of personal inclination. Leaders opt for different solutions according to their differing personalities.[16] One would be well advised to heed Bialer's observation that 'the man is as important as the context in which he acts', and that although 'molded by his bureaucratic environment', the political leader in Soviet-type systems 'at the same tie molds his environment in accordance with his personality, his vision and his style' (Bialer, 1983, p. 46). As indicated by Korbonski (1976, p. 20), the importance of the personality factor means 'that we should try to find out as much as possible about individual leaders'. Indeed. But as long as secrecy continues to remain a systemic feature of communist systems (Jowitt, 1983, p. 282), our chances of success are hardly encouraging. It is doubtful whether we shall ever know why Ceauşescu (or Antonescu) deviated from the pattern of Balkan paternal orientalism into that of leader-worship. Ceauşescu might have started the process of self-adulation as part of his many-faceted manipulation of the consolidation of power. He may have cynically consented to national image-making manipulations such as the official presidential portrait in which he holds a sceptre and is graced by other paraphernalia of power. He ended, however, by taking his 'imperial role' seriously. In an article on the communist theory of leadership, Alfred G. Meyer reminds us of Marx's words on Louis Bonaparte:

> Only when he eliminates his solemn opponent, when he himself now takes his imperial role seriously, and under the Napoleonic mask imagines that he is the real Napoleon, does he become the victim of his own conception of the world, the serious buffoon who no longer takes world history for a comedy, but his comedy for world history [*The 18th Brumaire of Louis Bonaparte*, as quoted in Meyer, 1970, p. 7].

The 'cult' in its present form may thus be said to have escaped the control of those whom it should 'cultivate'. It may no longer be Ceauşescu who manipulates the symbols of power, but rather the other way round. In the long run this possibility may impinge on both leadership cohesiveness and on party unity, the Secretary General's remarkable political skills notwithstanding. In two verified instances, and at least on one occasion where evidence is circumstantial, forces in or near the centre of power have attempted to challenge Ceauşescu's infallibility.

At the Twelfth Congress, in 1979 (Moore, 1979), a veteran party figure, Constantin Pîrvulescu, aged 84, protested against not having been granted permission to speak. Once given the floor by Ceauşescu personally, he proceeded to accuse the Secretary General of putting personal interests above those of the country. In an unprecedented gesture of defiance, Pîrvulescu declared he would not vote for Ceauşescu's re-election. However, he was not to be allowed to pursue his 'heresy'. In a move of doubtful legality, the delegates decided to remove his credentials, and Ceauşescu's unanimous election was once more ensured. Although Pîrvulescu's intervention is to be found nowhere in the published proceedings of the meeting, the offical Romanian news agency (apparently aware that some Western journalists had picked up information on the incident) was forced to issue a statement which mentioned the 'deep indignation' of the delegates. The statement also quoted Ceauşescu's rebuttal, where Pîrvulescu was called an 'instigator' and 'alien to the country', thus hinting that the former Politburo member's attack on Ceauşescu had been inspired by Moscow. Once more posing as the embodiment of Romanian authenticity, the party leader stated that his accuser was 'probably longing for the time when the fate of the party and of the people were not decided here but elsewhere' (*Agerpres*, 23 November 1979).

There is very little ground on which the accusations could be substantiated. Pîrvulescu could hardly be called a 'Muscovite' for, although he had spent the war in the Soviet Union, he had previously (in 1934) been imprisoned together with Dej and the rest of the 'home communists' in Romania. Moreover, as Chairman of the Party Control Commission, he played a major role in the purge of the Pauker group and was apparently ousted by Dej not because he had supported the Chişinevschi-Constantinescu faction, as it was alleged in 1961, but rather because he was—and apparently remained—a rare specimen of the independent 'true believer'. There is also very little likelihood that Moscow would bet on such 'old horses' as Pîrvulescu to initiate an anti-Ceauşescu move in the Romanian party. Be that as it may, after the Twelfth Congress Pîrvulescu disappeared from public view, and rumour has it that he either died or was consigned to a psychiatric institution.

A similar fate awaited Ceauşescu's other major challenger, Virgil Trofin, who is reported to have committed suicide in 1982 (Bacon, 1983, p. 327). One of the more capable party functionaries who rose to prominence under Ceauşescu, Trofin was at one time head of the CC's Cadre and Organization Department. As with many other former Ceauşescu protégés, he was eventually subjected to the 'rotation of cadres' mechanism, occupying different positions, his last post being that of Minister of Mines, Oil and Geology, a portfolio to which he was appointed in December 1979. Following repeated manifestations of unrest among miners, as well as the non-fulfilment of energy targets, which were accompanied by the common practice of reporting more coal than actually extracted (Ceauşescu, 1970-83, Vol. 23, pp. 53, 89), the party leader attempted to shift the blame to his deputies. He therefore 'reorganized' the ministry headed by Trofin, who was removed from office and appointed Chairman of the Central Council of Artisans' Co-operatives. Had he sagely followed the practice of taking the blame upon himself and paying some self-critical lip-service, it is safe to assume that Trofin would have suffered no further damage, for the September 1981 ministerial 'reorganization' left his membership of the PEC untouched (*Scînteia*, 8 September 1981). At a joint plenum of the CC and the Supreme Council for Economic and Social Development held on 25-26 November, however, Trofin apparently refused to comply with the practice and absolve Ceauşescu himself of responsibility (*Scînteia*, 27 November 1981). Consequently, he was expelled from the Central Committee, losing his seat in the Grand National Assembly as well.

In early 1983 there were rumours in the Western press concerning an alleged abortive military coup against Ceauşescu (*The Times* and *Süddeutsche Zeitung*, 7 February 1983). Although these could not be substantiated, the promotion of the party leader's two brothers in the Ministry of Interior and the Ministry of Defence, and the demotion of a number of generals which occurred soon afterwards, might be taken as an indication of the 'ruling family's' reaction to some threat emanating from the officer corps. Should this eventually turn out to have been the case, it should be seen as one of the most serious challenges ever faced by the Romanian leadership, for, unlike the Şerb case in 1972 (Bacon, 1978, pp. 170–1), it appears to have been triggered by discontent among military professionals and not by Soviet machinations. The military as a group have clearly been courted by the Romanian leadership, and their representation in the Central Committee rose from 3 to nearly 5 per cent of full members, and from 3 to $5\frac{1}{2}$ per cent of candidate members between the Eleventh and the Twelfth Congress (Bacon, 1978, p. 168; author's calculations). Yet the autonomous foreign policy pursued by Ceauşescu resulted in, among other things, delay in the modernization of the army, due to Soviet reluctance to provide the Romanians with advanced military technology and equipment. Combined with the doctrine of the 'people's war', which is promoted by the leadership and which must result in the decline of professional military prestige, together with the employment of the army in construction and harvesting jobs, these policies might have produced a sense of injury among what is possibly the one institution maintaining some degree of professional autonomy in present-day Romania (Moore, 1983).

However, it is not very likely that such a coup could (or would) be envisaged without at least some tacit support from other party elites. It is at this point that the focus of attention should turn from leadership to organizational cohesion.

Organizational Cohesion: Cadre Policies and Sub-National Elites

In any political system goals are set according to priorities determined by relatively restricted circles. These circles constitute the apex of one or more elitist structures, the capabilities of which, as observed, are significantly influenced by leadership cohesion. Even the most cohesive leadership, however, is unlikely to achieve its purpose unless it can count on consensual, manipulated or enforced *organizational* cohesion, i.e. on cadres and on local elites on whom the implementation of leadership-designated strategies depends. Organizational cohesion is a function of organizational *principles*, which reflect value-systems, and of organizational *adaptability*, which at times requires alterations in the pattern of cadre recruitment and promotion, in order to facilitate enrolment and advancement of those elements most suitable to implement the tasks of the day. Organizational principles, nevertheless, may constitute an impediment to organizational adaptability, and in those communist systems which had left behind the phases of 'transformation' and 'consolidation', this clash creates what is commonly known as the conflict between 'red' and 'expert'. In Richard Lowenthal's view, this conflict is the outcome of two conflicting tendencies in the leadership, one striving to 'institu-tionalize' revolution, the other to put society on the path of modernization (Lowenthal, 1970, 1983). Lowenthal's approach belongs to what I am tempted to label the 'optimist' developmental school, for he appears to be persuaded that the party's organizational principles will eventually have to give in to the requirements of modernization. 'Development' is to overcome 'utopia'.

Although the RCP's physiognomy underwent significant changes as a result of organizational adaptability requirements, there is at present no indication that its leadership envisages basic alterations in the party's organizational principles. To what extent the party's cadre policies are likely to generate genuine change in the future must, of course, remain a matter for speculation. For the time being, the Ceauşescu leadership has attempted to cope with the dilemma of 'red' versus 'expert' by both having their cake and eating it, i.e. by creating cadres which are ideally 'red' as well as 'expert'. Simulated change, however, is discernible in these tactics too, for the necessity to promote 'suitable' elements to responsible party positions has also been exploited for the purpose of consolidating personal power.

The present statutes of the RCP were adopted at the Ninth Congress (1965) and have been amended on different occasions. Their preamble defines the RCP as the 'vanguard detachment of the working class, leader of the entire working people in the struggle for building socialism and communism, the leading political force in the Socialist Republic of Romania'. Article 14 enshrines democratic centralism as the 'fundamental principle of the party's organizational structure and activity', with minorities unconditionally bound to accept and implement the decisions of the majority. This principle is reinforced by further riders, such as Article 2, according to which the existence of factions is strictly forbidden—factional activity constituting a 'crime against the party' (*Congresul al XII-lea*, pp. 851, 856).

The primary party level is the basic cell, the general assembly of which elects a bureau. In institutions, factories or agricultural co-operatives where more than one cell ('basic organization') functions, the General Assembly elects a party committee. In December 1983 the RCP had 69,792 cells (*Scînteia*, 27 March 1984).

The RCP is organized according to territorial subdivisions, which are superior to party structures in lieu of production. These include rural, city, municipal and county organizations, the general assembly (or conference) of which elect a party committee as their 'executive organ'. According to the statutes, the highest party organ is the Congress, which meets every five years. Extraordinary congresses may be convened on the initiative of the Central Committee or at the request of a third of the party members.

The Congress elects the CC and the Secretary General, as well as the Central Revision Commission. The Central Committee nominally directs all party activity between congresses. It holds plenary sessions at least every four months. When, between congresses, it considers it necessary to debate important matters of policy, it may convene a National Party Conference. The Central Committee elects the PEC and the Secretariat, and organizes the Central Party College. The PEC designates from among its members the Permanent Bureau, headed by the

Secretary General. Clearly, this organizational structure faithfully reflects the Leninist principles of party organization. Nevertheless, throughout the period 1965-83, the mechanism of representation in the Central Committee (undoubtedly one of the most important levels of sub-national elite promotion and representation) has been subjected to several 'innovations', the institutionalization of which was an attempt to bridge the changing composition of the RCP (itself the outcome of regime-designated strategies of development) and the unchanged nature of the organizational principle and of centralized and personalized leadership patterns.

The most striking feature of the Romanian party rests perhaps in its size. The organization is now approaching the landmark of 3.5 million members, a figure all the more gigantic since, on the eve of the take-over, it had counted less than a thousand adherents. Proportionally, it is now the largest ruling party in Eastern Europe (see Table 7). At the end of 1982, the RCP included over 21 per cent of the adult population and 32.32 per cent of the workforce (*Scînteia*, 27 March 1984).

Table 7   Communist Party Membership in Eastern Europe:
Percentage of Estimated Total Population

	1960	1965	1970	1975	1980	1982
Albania	*	*	3.6	4.2	3.7	5.2
Bulgaria	*	*	*	*	9.2	9.2
Czechoslovakia	11.4	11.9	8.6	*	9.9	10.3
GDR	*	*	*	11.3	12.7	13.1
Hungary	*	5.3	6.4	7.2	7.5	7.5
Poland	3.9	5.6	7.1	6.9	8.5	6.8
Romania	4.5	7.6	9.8	12.1	13.7	14.4
USSR	4.1	5.1	5.9	6.0	6.4	6.5
Yugoslavia	5.5	5.2	5.0	5.7	8.9	9.6

Sources: For Romanian absolute party membership figures see Table 8. Proportionate membership calculated from Republica Socialistă România. Direcţia centrală de statistică, 1980, pp. 55; 1981, p. 45; 1982, p. 12. For other countries: 1960-75 Shoup, 1981, pp. 82-5; 1980: calculated from Staar, 1981, p. 91; 1982: calculated from Wesson, 1983, p. 98.

* No figures available.

The numerical growth of the Romanian party, as well as the social composition of its membership as officially disclosed, provide a true mirror of leadership priorities (see Table 8). Between 1944 and 1948 the party registered a rapid increase in membership. This period was followed by one of extensive purges, during which some 465,000 members, or 44 per cent of the total, were expelled from the organization (King, 1980, p. 73). The pattern was by no means unique to Romania, being inspired by Moscow's binding instructions to the East European parties. Eventually, the 'home communists', headed by Dej, would accuse the Pauker group of having encouraged undifferentiated recruitment of undesirable elements, but, as Robert R. King convincingly demonstrates, it is highly unlikely that the Dejist team had opposed the admission of Iron Guardists and other opportunists and careerists, whose 'services' were probably irreplaceable at a time when

Table 8   Membership and Social Composition of the RCP, 1944-1983

	Total membership	Workers %	Peasants %	Intellectuals/ functionaries %
1944	less than 1,000	*	*	*
Feb. 1948	1,060,000	39	*	*
May 1950	720,000	42	*	*
Dec. 1955	595,398	42.6	*	*
June 1960	834,600	51.0	33.5	approx. 11.0
Apr. 1962	919,873	*	*	*
July 1965	1,450,000	44.0	34.0	approx. 10.0
Aug. 1969	1,924,000	43.0	28.0	23.0
Dec. 1970	2,089,085	44.0	25.0	*
Dec. 1971	2,194,627	45.4	24.3	*
Dec. 1972	2,281,372	46.4	23.0	18.8
Dec. 1973	2,386,819	*	*	*
Dec. 1974	2,500,000	nearly 50.0	over 20.0	22
Dec. 1975	2,577,434	nearly 50.0	over 20.0	22
Dec. 1976	2,655,000	*	*	*
Dec. 1977	2,747,110	*	*	*
Dec. 1978	2,842,064	52.6	*	*
Nov. 1979	2,930,000	nearly 54.0	nearly 18.0	29.0
Dec. 1980	3,044,336	54.6	*	*
Dec. 1981	3,150,812	55.1	*	*
Dec. 1982	3,262,125	55.6	15.8	20.8
Dec. 1983	3,370,343	55.7	15.7	20.6

Source: 1944—Grigorian, 1950, p. 14; 1948—*Scînteia*, 13 December 1961; 1950—King, 1980, pp. 64-5; 1955 and 1960—Gheorghiu-Dej, 1961, p. 166; 1962—*Scînteia*, 17 April 1965; 1965—*Congresul al IX-lea*, pp. 71-2; 1969—*Congresul al X-lea*, pp. 127-8; 1970—*Scînteia*, 17 February 1971; 1971—*Scînteia*, 25 April 1972; 1972—*Scînteia*, 22 June 1973; 1973—*Scînteia*, 3 April 1974; 1974—*Scînteia*, 25 July 1975; 1975—*Scînteia*, 24 April 1976; 1976—*Scînteia*, 7 April 1977; 1977—*Scînteia*, 24 March 1978; 1978—*Scînteia*, 30 March 1979; 1979—*Congresul al XII-lea*, pp. 59-60; 1980—*Scînteia*, 28 March 1981; 1982—*Scînteia*, 31 March 1983; 1983—*Scînteia*, 27 March 1984.

* No figures available.

the RCP had yet to build its own trained cadres. It is significant, in this sense, that when the purge of the Pauker group was initiated in 1952, the accusations made no mention of the part played by her in the affair, and that Miron Constantinescu, who in 1961 was accused of having followed Pauker's instructions concerning recruitment, remained in the leadership until that year (King, 1980, pp. 66-7).

Recruitment of new members was initiated again in 1955, but the criteria for admission were stringent, with clear preference given to 'working-class' elements. The real leap in party growth-rate is to be found in the early sixties, i.e. in the period *preceding* Ceauşescu's advent to the leadership. As Table 9 clearly indicates, the most impressive average annual increase obtained between April 1962 and December 1964, i.e. precisely in the years when, faced with the growing conflict with the Soviet Union, the RCP had to abandon its earlier policies of 'primitive accumulation of legitimacy' and search for grass-roots support in the population. A plenum of the Central Committee in April 1962 simplified admission categories, replacing the former system of promotion from candidate to full party membership, which had strongly favoured workers, with a simpler process.

Table 9   Increase in Party Membership, 1955-1982

Time period	Total increase %	Average annual increase %
December 1955-June 1960	40.0	8.8
June 1960-April 1962	10.0	5.0
April 1962-December 1964	50.0	20.0
July 1965-August 1969	32.7	8.1
August 1969-November 1974	28.8	5.7
November 1974-November 1979	18.1	3.6
November 1979-December 1983	15.2	3.8

Sources: 1955-1964—Fischer, 1979, p. 23; July 1965 to December 1983—calculated from *Congresul al IX-lea*, p. 71; Ceauşescu, 1970-83, Vol. 4, p. 315; *Congresul al XII-lea*, p. 59; *Scînteia*, 27 March 1984.

Among other things, the new system shortened the period of candidacy from two years to one, or to eighteen months, in some cases, and for certain categories it even dispensed with the probationary period altogether. Even more important, perhaps, was a provision facilitating admission of elements that had been active in 'bourgeois' or in 'other' (i.e. Social Democrat) parties before 1948 (*Scînteia*, 17 May 1962).

Apart from the obvious need to acquire legitimacy in the population at large, the relaxation of admission requirements clearly stemmed from the leadership's perceived need to enrol the support of both 'technical' and 'creative' intelligentsias. The former were clearly needed in the planned process of intensified development, while the latter's deep attachment to national values, hitherto perceived as incompatible with the party's ethos, was now to become 'functional' in the moulding of the new formula, according to which the RCP is the embodiment of national traditions.

At the Tenth Congress in 1965, categories for admission were abolished altogether,[17] as was the requirement for the probationary candidacy. Furthermore, membership of Social Democrat parties was now recognized for party seniority purposes (*Scînteia*, 3 June 1965; *Congresul al IX-lea*, p. 340), a significant amendment considering that before the war most intellectuals with leftist inclinations had opted for identification with organizations untainted with the stigma of 'foreign agent'.

Although the party's policies (now combining pride in autarkic industrialization and achievement with a return to values previously disavowed) certainly struck a responsive cord among targeted categories for recruitment, the official statistics concerning the party's social composition are to be taken with more than a pinch of salt. As already indicated, such information, more than providing an accurate image of the party itself, reflects above all, regime priorities at a given point in time. For example, in his report to the Third RWP (Eighth RCP) Congress in June 1960, Gheorghiu-Dej stated that the number of intellectuals in the party stood at 93,000, i.e. at approximately 11 per cent of total membership (Gheorghiu-Dej, 1961, pp. 166-7). At the next congress, in 1965, following Dej's death, the number of intellectuals was said to be 145,000, i.e. some 10 per cent of total membership—yet at the same time to have 'more than doubled' since the last congress (Ceauşescu, 1968-9, Vol. 1, p. 65). Obviously, something strange must have happened to the 'intellectuals' on the road to the supreme party forum headed by the new leader. By the time of the Tenth Congress, in August 1969, the proportion of intellectuals had jumped to not less than 23 per cent, yet by December 1972, when the leadership was obviously displeased with its intellectuals (following the so-called 'mini-cultural revolution'), less than 19 per cent of members were put in this category. In November 1979 a record 29 per cent were 'intellectualized', but two years later, in December 1981, the proportion of this category had once more diminished to less than 21 per cent.

Whatever the reasons for these official zig-zags, the stable feature of the RCP ever since the outbreak of the conflict with the Soviet Union remains a constant overall growth in party membership. Although the average annual increase in party growth diminished in the last decade, Romanian recruitment strategies ignored beyond doubt what has been termed 'the dilemma of party saturation' (Hammer, 1971; Hough, 1977, pp. 125-39; Miller, 1982). Such 'saturation', as convincingly demonstrated by Hough for the Soviet Union, is best comprehended when calculating the proportion of party members within the total active population and among those who are in the '25-plus' age bracket.[18] In Romania's case, this produces the picture as shown in Table 10.

The RCP may have generated these mammoth dimensions in the quest to project an image of widespread support for its policies, which was directed at both foreign (Soviet) and domestic audiences. To a certain extent, the image was genuine, particularly in its nationalist implications, and probably remained so well into the early seventies. By that time, the leadership's determination to stick to its basic organizational principles and to implement them in practice, generated an ideological campaign, the basic features of which essentially aimed at reinforcing

Table 10   Party Saturation in the RCP

	% Total estimated population	% Population over 25	% Total active population
1960	4.5	*	8.7
1965	7.6	13.0	14.9
1970	9.8	*	21.1
1975	12.1	20.9	25.3
1980	13.7	23.2	29.4
1981	14.0	23.7	30.3
1982	14.4	*	31.0

Sources: Calculated from Table 7 and from Republica Socialistă România. Direcţia Centrală de Statistică, 1966, p. 72; 1976, p. 15; 1980, p. 55; 1981, pp. 20-21; *Scînteia*, 25 March 1983, 27 April 1983.
* No figures available

the party's leading role in society. Instead of encroaching on the policies of 'party saturation', i.e. in restoring the vanguard-like image to the RCP and restricting admission policies, however, the new line emphasized 'take-over from within' tactics, which necessitate, once more, the numerical growth of cadres.

The RCP thus finds itself in an apparently self-defeating situation. On one hand, ideological primacy, combined with 'take-over from within' tactics, call for a rise in the quality of 'revolutionary consciousness', which explains measures such as the code of 'communist ethics', adopted in 1972, and repeated campaigns for improving party education of members. By August 1983 over 200,000 party members had 'graduated' from party schools (Ceauşescu in *Scînteia*, 5 August 1983). For similar reasons, party ranks must occasionally be 'cleansed' of elements which prove 'unworthy of the communist title'. On the other hand, 'take-over from within' tactics cannot possibly be pursued under the 'vanguardship' formula. A CC Plenum of March 1979, for example, decided to proceed to a 'revision of party documents' (*Scînteia*, 30 March 1979), but in practice the measure affected only 30,210 members, i.e. less than 1 per cent of the total (*Scînteia*, 31 March 1983).

A distinction should be made between 'party teaching' (*învăţămîntul de partid*) and 'party higher education'. The former has no other purpose than to improve the 'political level' of RCP members, so as to transform them into 'living examples' of communist morality—and above all of efficiency in production. In other words, grass-roots membership should ideally be motivated by the ideological incentive. The results, however, have failed to serve the purpose, and at a session of the PEC in February 1982, the decision was adopted to reorganize party teaching, putting it in closer contact with the Central Committee apparatus. According to the new scheme, a group of propagandists made up of CC members, of members of the Central Revision Commission and of the Central Party Collegium, as well as of officials who occupy high positions in party, state and mass organizations, has been constituted at Central Committee level. Each county is to be visited by three or four such 'propagandists', who are to spend up to four days there every month, training and preparing 'propagandists' at local level in the area. In their turn, these party activists are to take charge of the commissions of propagandists and agitators, which have been set up in all enterprises and institutions, comprising between nine and fifteen members. The new commissions replaced the former 'commissions for party teaching', the activities of which have obviously been judged unsatisfactory (*Munca de partid*, No. 3, 1982).

Apart from the burden and boredom which 'party teaching' inflicts on members forced to attend classes after working hours, an additional reason for its failure might rest in the poor level of schooling among significant segments of the rank and file. While official statistics occasionally emphasize the growth in the proportion of members with academic training, only seldom are figures published from which an overall perspective of the level of education of party members can be obtained. The latest date on which this was carried out was March 1981, when *Scînteia* published statistics on the composition of the RCP in the preceding year. According to these figures, out of a total of 3,044,336 members, 343,042 (11.26 per cent) had a university degree or its equivalent, 465,504 (15.29 per cent) were graduates of high schools and 806,624 (26.49 per cent) had attended technical and professional schools. This leaves nearly 47 per cent of the membership with elementary or uncompleted high-school education. Since only a year earlier 29 per cent of members had been designated as 'intellectuals', it obviously follows (once more) that categorization of occupational status is extremely unreliable. Often in the past, 'functionaries' had been defined as 'intellectuals'. This is liable to present an extremely distorted picture, as one can learn from a decision adopted in 1974, according to which recruitment of new members from among the 'functionaries' was to be conditioned in future by their having obtained a university degree (*Scînteia*, 25 July 1975). According to the same decision, admission into the party for all other occupational categories should have been limited to those who completed seven or eight years of schooling at least, with four years allowed in exceptional cases. Younger members were to be encouraged to attend evening and other forms of elementary schooling, with the purpose of completing a minimum of eight years' learning. Five years later, as the statistics for 1980 demonstrated, the situation had not improved to any great extent.

The co-option of intellectuals to sub-national elite level in the sixties was thus partially due to the absence of trustworthy professionals in the party. Those co-opted consisted of what Daniel Nelson accurately designates as 'the needed'. They remained subject to control via the '*nomenklatura* system', i.e. the organizational principles of the party were never subjected to revision (Nelson, 1980, pp. 110-20). By the end of the sixties over a quarter of the members of the Romanian Academy and of holders of doctorates, some 46 per cent of engineers and over half of the teachers had joined the party (*Scînteia*, 20 March 1970). But the policies of massive co-option of technocrats apparently made the more orthodox group in the leadership, headed by Ceauşescu himself, anxious lest the party's basic values should eventually become endangered by 'narrow professionalism'. The July 1971 'Theses' (the so-called mini-cultural revolution) with their insistence on the necessity for 'moulding socialist consciousness', were designated to impair such developments, as well as to bring under control minorities among the creative intelligentsia which attempted to push well beyond party-designated limitations on the freedom of expression (Shafir, 1981a, pp. 279-356). Premier Maurer, one of the few national leaders with an independent standing, apparently dissented from the renewed tendency to ideologization, and failed to join the chorus of those who expressed enthusiastic support. But Maurer's strength in the party had never been great, and leadership cohesion was not broken, the more so since three years later he would resign for reasons of health.

The Ceauşescu solution to the dilemma of 'red' versus 'expert' consisted of reforming 'party higher education', so as to produce individuals with satisfactory professional qualifications, who at the same time would be imbued with the 'right' ideological values. To this purpose, the Ştefan Gheorghiu Academy for Social and Political Education (set up in 1946), was reorganized in 1971 (*Scînteia*, 3 October 1971), being divided into two main faculties, one in charge of 'scientific management', the other dealing with party and mass organization propaganda matters (Shafir, 1981a, p. 489). The Academy's courses can last up to four years, and attendance is regarded by many activists as likely to considerably help their careers (Nelson, 1980, p. 121).

The necessity to combine managerial and ideological skills was institutionalized in July 1974, when a CC plenum adopted a resolution concerning the criteria of election of party members to positions on central and local party bodies (*Scînteia*, 30 July 1974). These criteria are a combined attempt to cope with the 'red' versus 'expert' dilemma, and with the generational problem,[19] which apparently made younger cadres resentful of their meagre prospects for advancement in the hierarchy. They are based on three main requirements, which change according to the envisaged level of the position to be filled: party seniority, experience in previous party work, and party education. For example, while in order to be elected a member of the Central Committee or of the Central Auditing Commission, a candidate must have been a party member for at least twelve years, to have had at least six years' experience in other party assignments, and to have completed advanced studies, the requirements diminish in stringency as one descends the hierarchical ladder (Radio Free Europe Research, Situation Report, Rumania, 27-28 August 1974). Since the provisions conditioned election to local and national party bodies on a minimum seniority ranging from four to eight years' membership, it was decided to cut seniority requirements in half for members with 'responsible positions' in the Union of Communist Youth and in the Communist Students' Union, and the party statutes were amended in this spirit.

The problem of party rejuvenation had been raised at the Eleventh Congress by Petre Blajovici, who proposed an amendment establishing an age limit for candidates to central party bodies. Such an amendment, however, might have eventually affected Ceauşescu personally. A Western observer present at the Congress attests that the motion stirred animation among the delegates, and that Ceauşescu rejected it by joking about variations in the capabilities of individuals during the ageing process (Fischer, 1979, pp. 14–15). The motion must have placed the party leader in a classic state of cognitive dissonance, for ever since 1972, in attempting to promote his wife and son, he had often emphasized the necessity to promote women and younger cadres. Eventually, at the Eleventh Congress, the party statutes were so amended as to provide for the 'promotion of younger cadres, suitable from all points of view, alongside cadres with rich experience' (*Congresul al XII-lea*, p. 856), a formula ambiguous enough to be rendered meaningless.

Neither of the two aims pursued by the July 1974 decision have been satisfactorily fulfilled. In early August 1983, in a major speech delivered in Mangalia, Ceauşescu obliquely admitted that a spirit of dissatisfaction could be discerned among the generations, and that a generational struggle might now be under way in the RCP. The older generation, he stated, often displayed 'prejudice', considering that younger cadres should 'still wait and gain experience'. It forgot that shortly after 23 August 1944, when many of the present aged cadres were under thirty, young people had held 'positions of high responsibility'. On the other hand, the younger generation 'unjustly' considered that 'elderly, experienced cadres should be removed', manifested 'impatience' and forgot that society should ensure a 'blend' of 'experience, age and wisdom' with 'youthful revolutionary enthusiasm' (*Scînteia*, 5 August 1983).

The generation gap may thus be said to affect the party's organizational cohesion. The cohesion, furthermore, appears to be further weakened by the leadership's failure to achieve the envisaged blend of 'manager' and 'ideologue'. In the same speech, Ceauşescu admitted that some cadres regard the Ştefan Gheorghiu Academy or other forms of party higher education as an easy way of acquiring a university degree, while others fail to display the right revolutionary spirit and become mere 'technocrats', which is deemed to 'constitute a great danger for a revolutionary party'.

Far more importantly, Ceauşescu's speech in Mangalia revealed resistance among party activists to his policy of 'rotating cadres', and that 'leading cadres' even dare to 'argue whether or not to fulfil a task, whether or not to acquiesce in leaving a certain county'. Such an attitude, he stated, was tantamount to 'viewing the party and state work as if these were some form of [private] property, as if they were a bailiwick from which one refuses to part'.

How far up the hierarchical ladder such resistance goes must remain a matter for speculation, but Trofin's case would seem to indicate that Ceauşescu's techniques of consolidating power, accompanied as they are by failures in 'building authority', not only no longer make him appear in the eyes of the national and sub-national leadership 'competent' or 'indispensable', but he may come very close to being regarded as a threat to personal security, since cadres expect the blame for failure in policy to be put on their shoulders. During 1982 not less than fourteen out of forty-one county party secretaries, mostly young, and apparently with some expertise, lost their positions (Bacon, 1983, p. 327). It is against this background that one should judge the (albeit unconfirmed) reports concerning the abortive military coup of early 1983, bearing in mind that 'faction anxiety' may no longer play the part it used to among the previous 'generational elite', as well as that it may have given way to anxieties concerning personal security.

Western specialists in Romanian affairs, such as Mary Ellen Fischer (1981, pp. 123-4; 1982, pp. 23-4) have indicated that one could easily draw parallels between the Khrushchev and the Ceauşescu tactics of consolidating power. Like Khrushchev, Ceauşescu denounced the 'abuses' of his predecessor in order to neutralize, and eventually bring about the dismissal of actual or potential political adversaries. The similarities, however, do not stop here. A pronounced tendency to 'solve' problems through grandiose projects and 'campaigns' which prove unfeasible, combined with personal interference and directives in all fields of activity, have been known to be just as characteristic of Ceauşescu's style of leadership as they were of Khrushchev's—and more so. The two leaders, furthermore, seem to share a 'storming mentality' *vis-à-vis* heavy industry priorities, which, as Breslauer writes when analysing the Khrushchev era, calls for 'intensified pressure on workers and peasants in order to increase discipline, productivity, collectivism', and for 'sharply expanded party and mass intervention in managerial affairs' (Breslauer, 1982, pp. 279-80). Like Khrushchev, Ceauşescu chose to ignore the 'dilemma of party growth'.

To these analogies, a future historian might yet add a further note. For it should not be forgotten that what finally brought about Khrushchev's dismissal were practices such as rotation in office and its 'institutionalization' in 1961, which provided for the 'systemic renewal' of cadres (Hodnett, 1981, p. 88; Baker, 1982, p. 46). Ceauşescu, who instituted a similar process, appears to ignore, just as his Soviet counterpart did, that political clientelism is a *two-way* relationship. And if Khrushchev was accused, following his fall, of having set up a cabinet of friends and relatives, one wonders how the resolution of the Romanian Central Committee would read.

For the time being, and given the dominance of the instruments of power through 'familialization', this possibility appears remote. Yet, as observed earlier, there are indications that the present leadership might be less immune to upheaval than it seemed a few years ago. On the other hand, and if Soviet experience is to serve as a yardstick, Romania's way out of political stagnation can hardly consist in instituting a policy of 'trust in the cadres'.

7 Leadership by the Party: Governmental Structure and Mass Organizations

As already observed, the mechanism for party supervision at all levels is to be ensured in the 'Multilaterally developed socialist society' by 'take-over from within', i.e. on one hand by the 'blending' of party and state organs, and on the other by the simulative device of 'participation' through mass organizations or other structures in which the party dominates. This chapter reviews the basic structure of the Romanian government, emphasizing the prominence of the RCP in the system.

Government

The Constitution

According to the Constitution adopted in 1965 and only slightly amended since, Romania is a socialist republic and a 'sovereign, independent and unitary state of workers from town and village'. The Constitution's first article specifies the country's territory to be 'inalienable and indivisible', whereas the second article stipulates that 'the whole power' belongs 'to the people, free and master of its own fate', and is based on the alliance of all classes, regardless of nationality. It is, however, the third article of the Romanian document which includes the most important constitutional provision, i.e. the stipulation that the leading political force in the entire country is the Romanian Communist Party (*Constituţia*, 1969, p. 3).

The Grand National Assembly

Article 4 of the Constitution declares that the people exercise their sovereign right to power through the Grand National Assembly (GNA—Marea Adunare Naţională) and through the people's councils. The GNA is defined as the 'supreme organ of state power'.

The GNA is elected for a term of five years. It meets in session twice a year and in extraordinary meetings, convened on the initiative of the Council of State, of the Bureau of the GNA, or, theoretically of at least a third of the total number of deputies, whenever necessary. Between sessions, the work of the Romanian parliament is carried out by the Council of State and by the GNA commissions, the activity of which is co-ordinated by the Bureau, composed of a President and four Vice-Presidents. Since July 1974 the President of the Grand National Assembly has been Nicolae Giosan. There are at present nine standing commissions in the Romanian parliament. Their functions and responsibilities have been substantially increased during the Ceauşescu period.

The prerogative of initiating legislation belongs to the party's Central

Committee, a provision which virtually makes the designation of the GNA as the supreme organ of state power superfluous, but one which is fully in line with the leading role ascribed to the RCP by the Constitution. Legislative initiative may also be taken by the Council of Ministers, by the National Council of the Front of Socialist Unity and Democracy, by the house's permanent commissions and by at least thirty-five deputies (Alberti, 1979, pp. 115, 128). Moreover, the party's domination of the GNA is also ensured by the massive presence of Central Committee members in the Assembly. At the 1980 elections no fewer than 171 full or candidate Central Committee members (46.34 per cent of all deputies) were elected to the GNA.[1]

The pseudo-participatory nature of simulated change affected the Romanian electoral system, beginning with the 1975 elections to the GNA and to the people's councils (Fischer, 1977b; Nelson, 1982b; King, 1980, pp. 113-15). Until 1974 elections to the Assembly and to the organs of local government were based on the Soviet model, i.e. one candidate for each seat. Since 1975, however, Romania has moved closer to the Polish (1957, 1961, and 1984), the Hungarian and the Yugoslav models, albeit with significant differences. In a resolution adopted at the National Conference of the RCP in July 1972 it was stated that in view of 'the necessity of an ever broader participation of the people in the country's management', measures should be taken to ensure that 'in future, there should be more [than one] nomination for one deputy seat in the Grand National Assembly or in the people's councils' (*National Conference*, 1972, pp. 72-3). The spirit of this provision was first translated into practice in 1975, and again in 1980. In 1975 two candidates competed in 139 out of the 349 constituencies, while in 1980 the 369 parliamentary seats were subject to 'multiple candidacy' elections in 190 electoral 'circumscriptions', of which 151 offered a choice between two runners and 39 gave voters the choice of three candidates.

However, as Robert R. King rightly observes, the introduction of multiple candidacies was at no point intended to offer the electorate a choice of political platforms (King, 1980, p. 113). It was merely a step in the direction of offering a limited measure of choice between individuals. Not only is the voter not allowed to choose between several candidates when his district 'elects' an important party or state official, but, what is equally important, even in those cases where an alternative is being offered, party supervision is omnipresent. In order to become a candidate, one must acquire the endorsement of the Front of Socialist Unity and Democracy, which in 1968 replaced the defunct Democratic Front (see later). In practice, this means that the 'unique list' system remains in force, and 'democratization' amounts to more of the same, for, as indicated in a volume sponsored by the RCP and published in Italy, affiliation to the Front means that the candidate's programme is identical to that of his opponents, and must express 'the guidelines established in the party congress convened in the year preceding the general election' (Alberti, 1979, p. 113).

The '*nomenklatura*' system functions as a check on the nomination of any candidates unacceptable to the party (Nelson, 1980, pp. 111-12), the more so since, following the introduction of multiple candidacies, the party secretary in each locality also became local chairperson of the Front, while the personnel of the Executive Bureaux of the Front's territorial units were amalgamated with that of the party's and the people's councils' bureaux (Nelson, 1982b, p. 87).

Simulated change, moreover, is also to be discerned in the 'choice' offered to the electorate. First, unlike Western systems, where 'choosing' involves rejection, Romanian electors may cast their votes for each of the two or three candidates; this device virtually ensures all nominees of a majority, electing to the GNA the candidate with the fewest negative votes. The rationale of the system, in all probability, is to be sought in the direct or indirect sponsorship by the party of all would-be deputies. It might appear as a vote of no confidence in the party itself, were a party-endorsed candidate to be considered unsuitable by a majority of the electorate. Second, since the GNA is supposed to be a true mirror of all social categories, a 'quota' system is obviously at work, with opposing candidates coming from strikingly similar backgrounds in so far as occupation, education, age, sex and ethnic nationality are concerned.

The Council of State

While in most other East European countries it is customary for parliamentary functions to be delegated, between sessions, to a presidium elected from among the deputies, in Romania this role has belonged since 1961 to the Council of State. Articles 62-69 of the Constitution list the Council's main functions, which are divided into permanent functions, and those exercised in the intervals between the meetings of the GNA. The former include the establishment of election dates for the Grand National Assembly and for the people's councils, nomination and revocation of administration officials who are not members of the Council of Ministers, establishment of military ranks, the setting up of decorations and of honorary titles, ratification and rejection of international treaties, except those which fall within the competence of the GNA, etc. The Council of State is elected by the GNA from among its members for the entire term of the legislature. It is composed of the President of State, six Vice-Presidents of the Council and seven-teen members (1982). The Council's prerogatives were substantially reduced with the creation, in 1974, of the office of the President of the Republic.

The President of the Republic

Although Ceaușescu has effectively acted as State President ever since his election to the presidency of the Council of State in 1967, the creation of the office of President of the Socialist Republic of Romania was the institutionalization of the personality cult. Rule by presidential decree has become common practice in recent years. Ceaușescu's prerogatives are considerable, for the Constitution does not require him to submit his decisions for the approval of any state authority.

The President is elected on the recommendation of the Central Committee of the RCP and on that of the Front of Socialist Unity and Democracy by a two-thirds majority of GNA deputies, for the entire legislative period of the Assembly.

The head of State is also ex-officio President of the Council of State, Supreme Commander of the Armed Forces and President of the Defence Council. If necessary, he may also preside over the meetings of the Council of Ministers. He appoints and revokes, allegedly on the recommendation of the government, the Vice-Presidents of the Council of Ministers, the ministers and presidents of other institutions belonging to the same council, as well as leaders of state bodies which do not form part of the official structure of government. When the GNA is not convened in plenary session, i.e. most of the year, it is, once more, the President who appoints the President of the Supreme Court and the General Prosecutor, a prerogative he may exercise in the appointment of members of the Supreme Court even when parliament conducts its bi-annual debates (Alberti, 1979, p. 116).

The Council of Ministers

The Council of Ministers (the Government) is elected by the GNA for the whole parliamentary term and is collectively responsible to it. Its composition is recommended by the Central Committee and the National Council of the Front of Socialist Unity and Democracy. During recent years government reshuffles have occurred with increasing frequency.

From the structural point of view, there are three categories of membership of the Romanian government. The first, including members nominated by the GNA, is composed of the Prime Minister, his First Deputies, Deputy Prime Ministers and Secretaries of State. The second category is made up of leaders of public and administrative organizations whom special legislation designates as members of the government. Finally, a third category comprises the chairpersons of a number of mass organizations who belong ex officio to the forum.

Representation of the latter two categories in the Council of Ministers is supposed to constitute an example of democratization and participation. In reality, it is but one more example of both party domination and party familialization, for many of the organizations allegedly representing broad social interests are either joint party-state bodies or mass organizations, headed by prominent members of the party leadership and/or the Ceauşescu family.[2] The Romanian mechanism of simulated change thus legitimizes the holding of multiple positions in state and party structures. Not only is such 'blending' no longer said to be a 'deviation' from the principles of 'collective leadership', but it supposedly epitomizes the party's constant consultation with all strata of society.

The structure of the government is therefore a clear illustration of the institutionalized discrepancy between form and content. The Central Council of Workers' Control of Economic and Social Activity, for example, is yet one more instrument of *party control* over the production process. This is obliquely admitted in a propaganda publication of the RCP, according to which the party's branch organizations 'have the right to check up the activity developed in the administrative leadership of production and trade enterprises, of agricultural production co-operatives, of research and design institutes, schools and universities'. The party is said to exercise such control 'by mixed control brigades, led by party bodies in whom [*sic*] some specialists participate', with the findings then 'discussed with the workers' and with 'efficient conclusions drawn for improving the work' (Alberti, 1979, p. 123).

Table 11   State or Joint Party-State Positions Held by Members of the Permanent Bureau (Early 1984)

Nicolae Ceauşescu	President of the Republic
	President, Council of State
	Chairman, National Defence Council*
	Chairman, Supreme Council for Economic and Social Development
	President, National Council of Working People*
	Chairman, Front of Socialist Unity and Democracy†
Elena Ceauşescu	First Deputy Prime Minister
	Chairwoman, National Council for Science and Technology*
	Chairwoman, Commission for Standardization of the Economy*
Constantin Dăscălescu	Prime Minister
	Member of Defence Council*
	First Vice-President, National Council of Working People*
Ştefan Andrei	Minister of Foreign Affairs
	Member of Defence Council*
Iosif Banc	Vice President, National Council of Working People*
	Vice Chairman, Commission for Standardization of the Economy*
	Chairman of section, Supreme Council for Economic and Social Development*
Emil Bobu	Chairman, Council of Economic and Social Organization*
	Chairman of section, Supreme Council for Economic and Social Development*
Virgil Cazacu	Chairman of section, Supreme Council for Economic and Social Development*
Nicolae Constantin	Vice Chairman, Supreme Council for Economic and Social Development*
	Chairman, Central Council of the General Confederation of Trade Unions†
Petru Enache	Vice President, Council of State

Table 11 (*Cont.*)

Gheorghe Oprea	First Deputy Prime Minister Vice Chairman, Supreme Council for Economic and Social Development* Vice President, National Council of Working People* First Vice Chairman, Commission for Standardization of the Economy*
Ion Pățan	Minister of Light Industry Vice Chairman, Commission for Standardization of the Economy*
Gheorghe Rădulescu	Vice President, Council of State Vice Chairman, Supreme Council for Economic and Social Development*
Ilie Verdeț	Vice Chairman, Supreme Council for Economic and Social Development* Chairman, Central Council of Workers' Control of Economic and Social Activity*

* Joint party-state organization   † Mass organization

Mass Organizations

As shown in Chapter 5, 'organized participation' forms the backbone of simulated change in the party's strategy regarding mass organizations. It is mainly through these bodies that the 'containment' function is fulfilled at the present stage of development. Among others, this is attested by official or semi-official pronouncements concerning the character of these structures and their role in moulding man in the 'multilaterally developed socialist society'. Although 'public' and mass organizations are supposed to have undergone, and even to have '*caused*' what are labelled 'important qualitative transformations' reflecting the 'dynamic process of socialist democracy', (Boboş & Deleanu, 1979, p. 187; emphasis mine), the 'transmission belt' concept clearly remains one of the regime's systemic features, even if the concept itself is publicly decried nowadays.

'Dynamism' notwithstanding, it is stated that the 'first and most fundamental feature' of the democratization process is 'the assertion of the leading role of the Romanian Communist Party, both in the general system of democracy and in relation to the pecific area of public organizations'. Consequently, it is the party which sets '*specific tasks*' for each of these bodies, 'according to their nature and the specific object of their activity'. Such organizations, furthermore, supposedly exercise their autonomy in society through an '*enhanced ideologic and educational task*', thereby increasing their members' 'militant and revolutionary responsibility toward their duties' (Boboş & Deleanu, 1979, pp. 187-8; emphasis in original).

The Front of Socialist Unity and Democracy is the largest mass organization, constituting in fact, a kind of umbrella structure covering both party and public and mass organizations. Its activities are directed by a National Council, defined as a 'widely representative body' (Alberti, 1979, p. 127), headed by an Executive Bureau whose president, as already mentioned, is Ceauşescu himself. Locally, it is the party secretary who heads the district, municipal, town and communal councils of the Front. Apart from the RCP, among its members are the General Trade Union Confederation (GTUC) (the trade unions), the Union of Communist Youth, the Councils of Working People of the Co-Inhabiting Nationalities, the National Council of Women and the National Union of Agricultural Production Co-operatives.

The Romanian trade unions are defined as 'professional organizations, uniting all the working people . . . in their double capacity as owners of the production means and as producers of material and spiritual goods'. They are said to be 'constituted by the workers' free adhesion' (Alberti, 1979, p. 124). The unions are supposed to make up a forum for 'large manifestation of workers' democracy, of syndicate autonomy' (Academia Ştefan Gheorghiu, 1975, p. 609), but such autonomy does not preclude the official definition of their tasks in terms such as those contained in Section 165 (1) of the Labour Code, according to which the trade unions 'mobilize the masses for implementing the programme of the Romanian Communist Party . . . and to this end carry on sustained activities for raising labour productivity, improving the quality of production . . . promoting strict discipline in production and the fulfillment of each worker on the staff of his obligations' (quoted in Karatnycky, Motyl & Sturmthal, 1980, p. 81). The worth of autonomy was perhaps best illustrated in the period 1977–81, when the Chairman of the General Trade Union Confederation also served as Minister of Labour in the government, a practice discontinued under the impact of events in Poland.

The Romanian trade unions are organized in line with the field of production rather than according to craft or trade. They are set up according to the place of work in productive units, or according to industrial branches. Collective farm workers are not permitted to joint the GTUC, in violation of Convention 11 of the International Labour Organisation, which Romania has ratified (Karatnycky, Motyl & Sturmthal, 1980, p. 78). The right to strike is nowhere mentioned in Romanian legislation.

The unions are united in the GTUC, the supreme body of which is the congress, which is convened every five years. Between congresses, the GTUC is headed by a Central Council, which 'elects' from among its members an Executive Committee, a Chairman, Vice-Chairmen and Secretaries. The Executive Committee controls all union activity between plenums. Consequently, one finds a Soviet-type system of single union 'representation'. Section 164 of the Labour Code makes no mention of union activity outside the framework of the GTUC. In 1979 this aspect was noted by the International Labour Organization, which expressed the hope that Romania would in future allow syndicate activity 'in complete independence from the General Trade Union Confederation', since 'trade union unity imposed by law' contravened 'the principle of formation by workers of organizations of their own choice' (quoted in Karatnycky, Motyl, & Sturmthal, 1980, p. 79). An attempt to set up independent trade unions during that year was quickly and ruthlessly suppressed by the regime (see Chapter 9).

Trade unions are supposed to play a prominent part in 'workers' self-management'[3], which in reality they do by exercising party control over employees, rather than by promoting the interests of workers. Organizationally, workers' self-management is supposed to include three stages (Ceterchi, 1979, pp. 120-1):

(a) The General Assembly, comprising all the employees of the unit, which is convened twice a year and allegedly debates and approves the plan and the budget and annually supervises the unit's management, approves appointments and dismissals and, above all, ensures exemplary fulfilment of the plan, through penalities if necessary;
(b) The Working People's Council, which represents collective management between the General Assemblies and is composed of managerial staff and at least 30 per cent elected workers;
(c) day-to-day management, which is exercised by the Executive Bureau of the Council, presided over by the unit's Managing Director and including other members of the managerial staff.

The General Assembly is presided over by the Chairman of the Trade Union Committee, who, however, 'happens' always to be an active and prominent member of the party as well. The trade union head is also Vice-Chairman of the Workers' Council, which, to prevent all surprise, is always presided over by the secretary of the party organization. Party activists, alongside members in this unofficial party capacity, make up the bulk of the Council members, for the *nomenklatura* system, which ensures occupation of responsible managerial positions by the politically reliable, is not absent from this structure either (Shafir, 1982).

Even so, it seems that the Romanian leadership is reluctant to let either the General Assemblies or the trade unions supervising them have too much autonomy. At the Second Congress of the Working People's Councils, in June 1981, Ceauşescu bestowed on the assemblies rights of veto over appointments and dismissal of managers. The PEC, however, decided on 8 February 1982 that, prior to General Assembly meetings in which the confirmation of managers is to be discussed, the party organization of the enterprise must hold a separate meeting and establish its position *vis-à-vis* the candidate. Side by side with this measure, the CC monthly *Munca de partid* disclosed in March that jurisdiction over the Council of Workers' Control of Economic and Social Activity was to pass from the trade unions to direct subordination to the party committee of the industrial units, with the deputy party secretary in charge of economic problems acting as its chairman. In June 1983 even the largely fictitious right of employee control of management was abolished (*Scînteia*, 2 July 1983). Managers are no longer appointed by the General Assembly. Rather, on nomination, they are to sign pledges of 'strict observance of party and state laws' and merely 'report' to the General Assembly on their activity (*Buletinul oficial*, 9 July 1983).

These individual commitments of managers are part of a new 'remuneration' system, introduced in September 1983. The new system turns 'self-management' and the accompanying principle of enterprise 'self-financing' into instruments for extracting resources from the population—an aspect already mentioned in Chapter 5. This additional facet of simulated change was presented by the regime as opening up new possibilities for wage increases (*Scînteia*, 7 September 1983). In fact, it did away with the previous system of a guaranteed minimum salary, replacing it with a new structure of 'individual' and 'collective' contracts, in which the monthly income is dependent on both individual and team productivity. In addition, the new system allows for deployment of the labour force and virtually abolishes job security, while conserving all the familiar features of a centrally planned economy. 'Self-financing' is not accompanied by any genuine decentralization and/or enterprise independence, and places the entire burden of the revitalization of the economy on the shoulders of the employees (Berindei & Colas, 1984b). Although the Labour Code states that trade union organizations are supposed to 'defend the rights of their members under labour legislation' (quoted in Karatnycky, Motyl & Sturmthal, p. 81), they are not known to have protested this measure.

Among the other important mass organizations are the Union of Communist Youth (UCY), the Union of Communist Students' Association and the Women's National Council. UCY organizations are set up on principles identical to those of the RCP, and their organizational set-up is likewise similar. The supreme body of the UCY is its congress, convened every five years. The congress elects the Central Committee, which, in turn, chooses from among its members the Bureau and the Secretariat. The First Secretary of the UCY (Nicu Ceauşescu) serves *ex officio* in the government as Minister for Youth Problems. The principle of 'blending' party, state and mass organizational activities is thereby fully translated into practice.

The specific form of UCY activity in higher educational establishments is the Union of Communist Students' Associations. These are said to 'contribute to the improvement and modernization of the training and educational process through their representatives on professional boards and university senates', while also carrying out 'a constant activity aimed at increasing the students' responsibility and enhancing their political and ideological awareness' (Boboş & Deleanu, 1979, p. 179).

The Women's National Council, as with all other mass organizations, is supposed to 'mobilize' its members 'in view of achieving the party's home and foreign policy, of fulfilling in all fields the targets set up for building socialism' (Alberti, 1979, p. 126). It is organized on a territorial basis and it holds congresses at five-yearly intervals.

Apart from these structures, there is a plethora of pseudo-participatory activity taking place within different structures, the status of which is seldom very clear. Some of them appear to belong to joint party-state bodies, others are defined as 'public organizations', and the remainder affect virtually all societal levers. Such forums are defined as 'a most important step for the further development of democracy'. Among them, mention should be made of forums such as the Congress of the County People's Councils and Chairmen (convened every five years), the Conference of Chairmen of the People's Councils (held at similar intervals) and the County Conferences of the People's Councils, which precede the 'debates' of the aforementioned bodies (Ceterchi, 1979, pp. 117, 121). These gatherings are rubber-stamp meetings, where party sub-national elites talk to themselves and/or are addressed by the Secretary General.

Local Government

When not required to attend such forums, those in charge of running the people's councils attempt to implement the (often contradictory) directives of the centre at local level. The people's councils are the Romanian version of local government. They function according to the principles of 'double responsibility' and 'double subordination', which are a reflection of democratic centralist organizational credo. The people's councils are supposed to illustrate local autonomy, and are elected at intervals of two-and-a-half years by the citizens of the respective territorial-administrative units—counties, towns (or municipalities) and communes. Since January 1981 territorial-administrative units comprise forty counties and one municipality (Bucharest). In 1982 there were 237 towns and 2,705 communes (Republica Socialistă România. Direcția Centrală de Statistică, 1982, p. 10).

Although the councils are described as 'state bodies with full powers in their respective territory', they are hierarchically subordinate, with communal councils (usually encompassing several villages) forming the lowest unit and county councils the highest. Formally, at the top of this pyramid, are the GNA and the Council of State. This hierarchy supposedly 'does not in the least prejudice' their autonomous character, since 'the territorial-administrative units within which they act are comprised in one another, so that the electoral basis of the inferior hierarchical body, represents a minority as compared to the electoral basis of the superior hierarchical body' (Alberti, 1979, p. 118).

'Dual responsibility' means that the councils are responsible to both their own electorate and to the central administration. In every county there are local ministerial 'sections', subordinated to the local council (in form) and to Bucharest (in practice). These are known as the 'specialized local bodies of state administration'.

Although they are called local organs of *state* power, the people's councils (as with all other formal structures) are controlled by the party. In the wake of Ceaușescu's institutionalization of personal power, party and state functions were also 'blended' at the level of local government, with the local party First Secretary fulfilling, since 1968, the function of people's council chairman. On the other hand, the administrative re-organization of the territory implemented in that year might have strengthened not only the party as the dominant organization in society, but also Ceauşescu as the dominant personality in the party. As Daniel N. Nelson remarks, apart from appealing to national sentiment, the abolition of the Soviet-inspired 'regions' and the return to the historical '*judeţe*' made each of the (originally thirty-nine) local party bosses less independent and more vulnerable to directives from the centre than the former sixteen regional First Secretaries (Nelson, 1981c, p. 213).

As already observed, such 'quantitative' accumulation would eventually be accompanied by the 'qualititative' practice of 'rotating cadres', with county party First Secretaryship transformed into one of the main units affected by the mechanism. Furthermore, local government has not been immune to the phenomenon of party familialization: the First Secretary of the party committee in Ceauşescu's native '*judeţ*', Olt, is his brother-in-law Vasile Bărbulescu.

People's council deputies meet in session only four times a year. They elect from among their members permanent commissions, organized according to the main branches and fields of activity (Article 82 of the Constitution; Alberti, 1979, p. 118). At their first session they also elect an Executive Committee, its Chairman (the local party First Secretary), First Vice-Chairman, Vice-Chairmen (Article 90 of the Constitution) and a Secretary, who is appointed from the state bureaucracy but is always a loyal party member (Nelson, 1980, p. 38). However, since the Executive Committee meets only once a month for a few hours, day-to-day local government affairs are obviously not conducted by this body, but rather by its Standing Bureau (Nelson, 1980, p. 39). Up to 1979 the Standing Bureau was chaired by the First Secretary of the party, but in December of that year the GNA modified the situation, placing the position in the hands of his deputy (*Scînteia*, 15 December 1979). This amendment did not necessarily curtail the powers of the First Secretary. Rather, since more and more responsibilities were now beginning to be placed on the county people's councils, it was apparently intended to relieve the highest party representative of daily administrative duties—and possibly personal responsibility (the Vice-Chairman of the council is usually a *local* party personality).

The responsibilities of local government were indeed increased as a result of the introduction of the New Economic and Financial Mechanism (NEFM), the gradual application of which began in January 1979. The mechanism is supposed to function on the principles of 'self-financing' and 'self-management', but on closer scrutiny it appears that only the first of these two principles is pursued by the leadership. In an attempt to cope with a disastrous economic situation, an amendment was passed in late 1980 to the law concerning the organization and operation of the people's councils, according to which localities were to 'manage their labour and material resources'. In so doing, however, local government must take into consideration 'the provisions of the unified national plan of economic development', a task obliging them to 'organize, guide and check on the implementation of the plan targets by all economic units in their own territories, irrespective of those units' formal place in the nationwide network of organization'. In other words, while the people's councils are to be held responsible for the implementation of plan directives and for recruitment of resources, they have no say of their own in the planning process.[4]

Managing 'labour and material resources' on their own turned out to mean that local government authorities were to achieve food self-sufficiency autarkically. Simulated change was once more at work, for under the guise of 'self-management', responsibility for guaranteeing food supplies was shifted on to the shoulders of local authorities—and via them, on to those of the population at large. People living in villages and towns, and those owning agricultural land, were to be required not only to satisfy their own needs, but also to deliver to the 'state fund' surplus agricultural products (*Buletinul oficial*, 25 December 1980).

The 'state fund' itself was to be set up by the counties, but managed by the centre. Counties capable of over-fulfilling their plan receive from the 'fund' additional goods for the purpose of improving local supplies, but those which cannot do so are to be penalized by receiving a proportionately smaller quantity than that provided for in the all-country plan, which covers certain basic needs. This is called 'self-sufficiency' and it supposedly brings 'self-management' to a higher stage of development. As always, however, it is the party apparatus which is expected to control every possible fact of the implementation of the new scheme (Ceauşescu, 1970-83, Vol. 18, p. 665).

By 1982 only 58 per cent of the budget of the people's councils came from their own funds, and in the following year this figure dropped to 39.6 per cent (A. G., 1982; Gafton, 1983). It is also quite probable that the requirement to proceed to intensified cultivation of all agricultural land will affect the 'systematization' programme adopted by the RCP Conference in July 1972, which was aimed to bring about the gradual disappearance of differences between town and countryside. It is, indeed, hardly likely that schemes such as the former, the basic premiss of which rested on village urbanization, could fit into the requirements of the 1981 dispositions. Such shifts, nevertheless, have become rather familiar in contemporary Romania, where the inefficiency of the party apparatus combines with 'harebrained' schemes arising from the cult of personality to produce one grand failure of a 'solution' after the other.

Part III
The Economy

8 Simulated Change and the Economic System

In late 1981 Romania followed Poland to become CMEA's second member forced to request re-scheduling of its foreign debts in hard currency. The crisis was partially the outcome of natural calamities, such as the earthquake of March 1977, which incapacitated for some time important industrial bases, and the poor weather conditions of 1980 and 1981. These natural disasters affected the costs of current output and of investment planning and upset the foreign trade balance, since the latter had been geared to a considerable extent towards exports of agricultural products to Western and other markets, in an attempt to reduce the burden of debt acquired during rapid industrial modernization.

Such immediate causes, however, were but the finishing touches to the country's economic malady. The origins of Romania's economic plight should be sought in the strategies pursued during the phase of 'extensive' development, in the policies of autarkic nationalist 'economic independence' adopted in the early 1960s and, above all, in the leadership's unaltered adherence to centralization of planning and to high rates of investment in heavy industry at the expense of current consumption. Paraphrasing T. H. Rigby (1972, p. 23), it could be stated that Romania's economic problems in the late 1970s and early 1980s derived from the orthodox political-economic mentality of a leadership incapable of pursuing measures conducive to a 'second' industrial revolution, because that leadership had 'overlearnt' the task of implementing the first economic breakthrough, the core of which rested in mobilizational tactics geared towards high growth rates.

Between 1950 and 1977 Romania maintained one of the highest growth rates in the world. Industrial output grew at an annual rate of about 12.9 per cent, industrial investment averaged 13 per cent per annum, while the industrial labour force grew at the rate of 5 per cent yearly, with labour productivity averaging a growth of nearly 8 per cent. The proportion of national income allocated to investments grew from 17.6 per cent in the period 1951-55 to 34.1 per cent in the 1971-75 Five-Year Plan and to 36.3 per cent in 1976-80. Such typical policies as 'extensive' growth were also reflected in the distribution of total investments, with 'Group A' in industry getting the lion's share (see Table 12). Another direct consequence of these strategies was that national income growth (averaging 9.3 per cent between 1951 and 1980) did not come to be fully reflected in the growth of real wages, the growth rate of which was only 4.9 per cent during the same period. Supplemented by the social wage, this resulted in a

Table 12   Investment Patterns by Sector of the Economy, 1951–1982

%

	1951–55*	1956–60*	1961–65*	1966–70†	1971–75†	1976–80‡	1981§	1982¶
Industry	53.7	44.9	46.4	49.9	50.5	49.2	50.7	46.4
Group A	46.7	39.1	41.4	42.3	42.1	42.0	43.1	NA
Group B	7.0	5.7	5.0	7.6	8.3	7.1	7.5	NA
Construction	3.6	2.4	3.3	3.8	4.7	5.9	3.4	3.6
Agriculture & forestry	11.3	17.2	19.3	16.0	14.4	13.7	15.7	13.3
Transportation & communications	10.3	8.1	8.7	10.2	10.1	10.6	9.9	13.5
Housing	10.1	15.6	11.5	9.4	9.2	10.2	11.2	12.9

* 1959 prices   † 1963 prices   ‡ 1st January 1977 prices   § 1981 prices   ¶ 1982 prices
Sources: Calculated from Republica Socialistă România. Direcția Centrală de Statistică, 1982; Jackson, 1983.

growth rate of 5.3 per cent per annum in real income per head (Smith, 1980, p. 36; Republica Socialistă România. Direcţia Centrală de Statistică, 1981, p. 36).

For a very long time the chief victim of these policies typical of 'primitive socialist accumulation' was agriculture. In 1950 it was contributing nearly 40 per cent of GNP, yet only 11.1 per cent of total national investment (not including forestry) was directed towards this sector (Cole, 1981, p. 99). Together with forestry, investments during the first Five-Year Plan amounted to 11.3 per cent of the total. By the end of the 1976-80 period, the industrial sector was still benefiting from investments which were three-and-a-half times larger than those directed towards agriculture and forestry (see Table 12). Gross agricultural output, which measures the potential delivery increases for food supplies and exports, registered an annual growth of 5.5 per cent for the first two Five-Year Plans, but decreased to 2.2 per cent in the following two five-year periods (Jackson, 1981a, p. 259), probably reflecting peasant resentment at the 'completion of agricultural socialization' in 1962. It rose again, to 4.7 per cent in the period 1971-75, and to 4.9 per cent during the next Five-Year Plan (Jackson, 1981b, p. 247; U.N. 1983, p. 127), possibly as a result of relatively higher investments in this sector in the 1960s, as well as of a series of reforms passed in the 1970s which were aimed at improving the peasant's lot. These reforms included, among others, the institution of the so-called 'global accord' system, which allowed individuals and groups to sign contracts with collective farms to work in exchange for share-cropping or at piece-rate wages, permission to families which satisfied certain conditions to cultivate more land privately than before, and a guaranteed income for the peasantry, as well as opportunities for more adequate pensions, paid vacations and some social benefits (Chirot, 1978, pp. 483-4; Jackson, 1977, p. 935). Income differentials between the agricultural and the industrial sector, nonetheless, remained substantial (Jackson, 1977, p. 934-5).

By the mid-1970s it was becoming clear that Romanian economic performance was slowing down. Net Material Product (NMP), i.e. the 'national income produced', which equals the social product minus 'material expenditures' and the balance of imports over exports, slowed down from an average annual growth rate of 11.3 per cent in 1971-5 to one of 7.3 per cent in 1976-80. Although the 1981-85 Five-Year Plan provided for an average growth of 7.1 per cent in the NMP, performance in the years 1981-83 (2.2, 2.6 and 3.4 per cent respectively) was well below target (see Table 13). Calculations in terms of gross national product (GNP), reconstructed by Thad Alton and his associates, which include the services sector and give greater weight to the farm sector, indicate a similar trend. According to these figures, the rate of growth of total GNP for 1965-70 was 4.6 per cent, rising to 6.2 per cent in 1970-75; it witnessed a sharp decline (3.9 per cent) in 1975-80 and registered a *negative* performance of −1.6 per cent in 1980. A slow recovery (0.6 per cent) in 1981 was followed by a slightly better (2.7 per cent) performance in 1982 (Alton *et al.*, 1983, p. 24).

As indicated in Chapter 5, Romania's autarkic nationalist economic policies

Table 13   Planned and Achieved NMP Growth, 1971-85

	Planned	Achieved
1971-75	9-10	11.3
1976-80	10.0-11.0	7.3
1981	7.0	2.2
1982	5.5	2.6
1983	5.0	3.4
1981-85	7.6	—

Sources: Jackson, 1981b, p. 247; U.N., 1983, p. 104; *Scînteia*, 29 January 1984.

were generated by the Stalinist orthodoxy of industrialization at all costs. With the Soviets unwilling to foot the bill for its policies, Bucharest not only altered its foreign trade patterns, but also turned to the West for credit facilities. Borrowing in the West was based on unrealistic estimates of their ability to repay through exports, which disregarded both the poor quality of Romanian products and trade barriers. For their part, Western financial circles appeared to be surprisingly unconcerned about Romania's credit-worthiness (Jackson, 1983, p. 32). This attitude was due at least in part to the fact that until 1980 Romania's debt services ratio was among the lowest in CMEA.[1] Poor performance in agriculture, which had a negative impact on exports, combined with the influence of the Polish developments, contributed to the revaluation of Western estimates of Romanian economic performance. Above all, the revaluation was due to the country's balance of trade deficit, which had its roots in the increasing needs of energy-intensive industries developed during the last two decades, in wasteful energy consumption patterns (Romania uses two to four times as much energy per dollar of domestic NMP as some advanced countries)[2] and in the rise of the price in crude oil on the international market.

Between 1973 and 1978 Romania's oil refining capacity had been increased from 18.5 million to 25.4 million tons. While up to 1975 the country had still been exporting a small quantity of crude oil, from 1976 onwards it was forced to begin importing ever-increasing amounts. Since 1977, domestic production of crude oil has constantly failed to reach (unrealistically high) targets (see Table 14). Although the launching of the increased refining capacity had coincided with the 1973-74 rise in international oil prices, the initial results were not disturbing, since they were accompanied by a parallel increase in oil product prices. The 1978 price saltation on the international petroleum market was another matter, however, and Bucharest soon found itself faced with a trade deficit of worrying proportions (see Table 15) and incapable of satisfying both domestic and export demands. Consequently, by 1981, Romania was faced with having nearly a third of its refining capacity idle (Luftman, 1982).

Table 14   Romanian Oil Production and Imports, 1975-1983
(in million tons)

	1975	1976	1977	1978	1979	1980	1981	1982	1983
Planned production of crude	14.6	14.7	14.9	15.1	14.8	15.0	12.6	12.5	13.5
Actual production of crude	14.6	14.7	14.7	13.7	12.3	11.5	11.6	11.7	11.6
Imports	5.0	8.4	8.8	12.9	14.2	15.9	12.9	NA	NA

Sources: Luftman, 1982; Jackson, 1983, p. 43; Republica Socialistă România, Direcţia Centrală de Statistică, 1981, pp. 556-7, 1982, p. 271; *Scînteia*, 11 February 1982, 29 January 1984.

These disturbing developments were further intensified by the Iranian revolution and by the war in the Gulf. Since the Soviet Union was unwilling to supply Romania with crude oil under the same favourable terms from which Moscow's other CMEA partners benefit,[3] unless Bucharest paid the political price, Romania began to devote increasing attention in the 1970s to developing trade with the Lesser Developed Countries (LDCs). This shift (illustrated in Table 5 for the years 1960-80) led to an increase in the share of the LDCs in Romania's foreign trade, from a mere 8.2 per cent in 1970 to 25.2 per cent in 1980. According to Romanian sources (*Revista economică*, No. 42, 22 October 1982 and No. 45, 12 November 1982), by 1981 this share had increased to nearly 29 per cent, slightly below the one-third target set by the 1980 plan.

The LDCs, as Robert R. King indicates, initially appeared to be ideal trade partners, for their quality requirements and the problems of marketing were less severe than those in the West, and long-term agreements could provide a solution to Romanian needs for importing raw materials (King, 1978b, p. 878). In addition, it was hoped to use these countries as a means of avoiding Western technology export bans (Lawson, 1983, p. 364), penetrating West European and North American markets via the back door. It is highly relevant that, by 1980, some 85 per cent of Romania's contacts with the countries of 'the South' were based on 'joint company' ventures, which in most cases were either related to the extracting industries or to oil refining[4] (Radu, 1981, p. 253). In an effort to stimulate exports and ensure supply of raw materials, Romania gradually became Eastern Europe's second (after the USSR) aid donor to the LDCs (Linden, 1983, pp. 55-6; Kanet, 1983, pp. 244-6).

Such aid, however, does not consist of loans or grants, but rather of reimbursable investments, thus hardly qualifying for the terminology Bucharest employs for propaganda purposes (Radu, 1981, p. 256). Payment is expected from the joint projects' output 'in the products resulting from the co-operation activities [and] in other goods agreed upon, particularly raw materials, or in convertible currency' (*Romanian Foreign Trade*, No. 3, 1981, as quoted in Lawson, 1983,

p. 364). Moreover, Romania's specialists working in the LDCs must be partially paid in hard currency (Radu, 1981, p. 257).

The shrewdest Romanian step taken towards intensifying contacts with the Third World was the official proclamation of the country as a 'socialist developing' (rather than developed) state at the National Party Conference in 1972.[5] According to Ceauşescu's pronouncements at this forum, Romania could count itself among the advanced countries in so far as the social order was concerned, but lagged behind in national income, in the ratio of population employed in agriculture versus industry and in 'other factors' (Ceauşescu, 1970-83, Vol. 7, p. 547). The official line, adopted at the Twelfth Congress, holds that Romania should reach the status of a 'middle level developed country' by 1985, proceeding to attain economic maturity some time in the last decade of this century (*Congresul al XII-lea*, pp. 723-9). In view of economic difficulties in recent years, however, it is more than likely that this time-table will have to be revised. As Colin W. Lawson indicates, no one believes that Romania is as developed as most industrial market (or, for that matter, some planned) economies, but on the other hand, there is little evidence that the country is a less-developed one in the normally accepted sense of the term. Official Romanian statistics supplied to the United Nations appear to have been subject to manipulation, in order to overemphasize the country's underdevelopment (Lawson, 1983, pp. 369-70).

Such manipulation is at first sight puzzling, in view of official pronouncements concerning the country's economic (as well as other) achievements under the leadership of the RCP. Contradictory as they undoubtedly remain, these statements were motivated by endeavours to diversify trade, and, above all, to enjoy the benefits extended to LDCs by the advanced countries and by UN agencies and to gain access to energy and other raw materials. In addition, the claim to 'developing' status served the purposes of the regime in demanding further sacrifices from the population very well. In this sense, the country's self-proclaimed developing status is a part of the rhetorics of simulated change, for it implies 'participation' in the party-directed common effort to put Romania on the path of economic prosperity and national independence.

In pursuit of these aims, Romania joined GATT in 1971 and became the first CMEA country to gain membership in the IMF in 1972, while in 1976 she gained admission to the 'Group of 77'. Consequently, she was to benefit from 1974 onwards from the developed countries' system of general preferences, the most important aspect of which was the signing of an agreement with the Common Market. Bucharest thus became the first Comecon member to come to terms with the existence of the Common Market as an institution, and although trade barriers were by no means overcome to the extent that the Romanians had envisaged, the agreement opened the door for further Romanian-EEC relations. In 1980, for example, Romanian export quotas to the Common Market were increased by roughly 50 per cent. Romanian trade with the EEC registered a surplus of US$59m in 1980, $151m in 1981 and $710m in 1982.

Impressive as these figures are, it should be remembered that they reflect

Table 15 Romania's Foreign Trade Balance With Presumed LDC Oil Suppliers*
(million devisa lei)

	1965	1970	1975	1976	1977	1978	1979	1980	1981[†]
Algeria	+5.2	+25.4	−51.2	+197.4	+374.3	+64.9	−12.4	−144.6	+770.9
Iraq	+15.9	+3.3	+290.3	−699.1	−953.9	−1815.8	−3860.6	−3445.0	+9134.2
Iran	+0.3	+52.0	−79.7	−578.0	−412.8	−264.5	−1038.0	−2000.1	−5440.3
Kuwait	+6.1	+21.2	−280.0	−206.1	−352.7	−105.1	+78.4	−585.1	−2420.3
Libya	+19.0	+87.2	+230.7	−141.8	+211.4	−441.3	−805.3	−1360.4	−1719.8
Nigeria	†	+16.3	+54.7	+30.5	+120.1	+1.8	−324.1	−1239.3	−2364.4
Saudi Arabia	+6.1	+9.1	+40.3	+87.5	105.5	+86.5	+177.1	−606.7	−5715.9
Total trade balance	+146.5	−655.9	−1.6	+210.6	−195.4	−5797.6	−5325.4	−8043.3	+3031.5

* In most cases Romania does not disclose the identity of countries from which it imports oil.
† Less than 0.1 per cent.
¶ Figures for 1981 in million lei.
Sources: Republica Socialistă România. Direcţia Centrală de Statistică, 1981, pp. 526–39, 256–62, 1982.

Romania's financial and domestic consumption crisis, for Bucharest's endeavours to reduce hard currency debts resulted in massive reductions of imports from Western countries, partially reflecting Romanian inability to increase exports to market economies. While in 1980 imports from these countries had grown by 4 per cent and exports had registered an increase of 6 per cent, in 1981 there was a reduction of 22 per cent in imports (and no change in export figures), and in 1982 imports were cut by 43 per cent and exports diminished by some 26 per cent. A similar trend was discernible in UN estimated figures for 1983. Such drastic cuts in imports led to a slow-down in the introduction of modern tech-nologies and in the modernization of old industrial facilities, and were likely to hinder, rather than benefit, the country's future economic development (Maier, 1983c).

Romania's courtship of the Third World determined Bucharest to adopt postures favouring the establishment of a New International Economic Order (NIEO), in strong contrast to the positions displayed by other members of CMEA, who accept the Soviet approach, declining any moral obligation to aid the LDCs and shifting the blame for the state of LDC economies on the West alone. In the speech delivered at the Eleventh Party Congress in November 1974, Ceauşescu dealt with the problem of the NIEO at length, underpinning it with the long-established Romanian principles of sovereignty, independence and non-interfer-ence in internal affairs (Ceauşescu, 1970-83, Vol. 11, pp. 36-9). This position has often been reiterated (e.g. Gheorghiu, 1983a, Bodgan, 1983), underlining purposes which may, however, be suspected of attempting to serve interests other than mere support of 'the South'. For example, Romania's failure to distinguish between socialist and capitalist industrial states in their duty to aid the LDCs appears to be strikingly consonant with Bucharest's demands that CMEA indus-trialized countries extend intensive aid and advantageous conditions to the less developed members of the organization, and with the position that integration within Comecon would become possible only if and when all members had reached a similar level of development (*Scînteia*, 4 August 1978, 19 June 1980). Similarly, the suggestion made by the former Deputy Prime Minister Corneliu Burtică at the UN Special Session on the NIEO, advocating 'moratoriums or postponement of payments without interest over 15-20 year periods' certainly reflected more than disinterested support of the Third World (*Romanian Foreign Trade*, No. 4, 1980, as quoted in Lawson, 1983, p. 368).

As Table 5 illustrates, the Romanian decision to develop ties with the LDCs paid off until about 1975, when Bucharest was still registering a significant surplus in its balance of trade with the developing economies. This situation, however, changed after 1976. According to official Romanian data (*Revista economică*, No. 54, 12 November 1982), while commercial exchanges with the LDCs in the years 1971-75 produced a favourable balance of 483m roubles, they registered a deficit of 713m roubles in the period 1976-80. It is true that this deficit was part of Romania's unfavourable balance of trade with all the countries of the world, which for the second half of the decade stood at 2,362m roubles.

However, it is also true that the LDCs had by then ceased to be the profitable partner they had been in the past. An increasingly important role in causing this deficit is to be attributed to oil imports. In fact, by 1980, nearly 77 per cent of Romania's total trade with its petroleum suppliers (including the Soviet Union and China) was represented by imports. At the end of 1981, at a CC plenary session, Ceauşescu disclosed that over 80 per cent of Romanian petroleum imports came 'from developing countries, particularly from friendly Arab countries' (Ceauşescu, 1970-83, Vol. 23, pp. 66-7).

On this occasion he revealed that Romanian delegates at CMEA, including premiers who participated at CMEA Council meetings, had failed to convince their partners of the urgency of Romanian energy needs, and that Romanian insistence on a meeting at the highest level to deal with these aspects had been dismissed, allegedly because the communist parties ruling in Eastern Europe had 'other preoccupations'. A Comecon summit meeting was finally held in Moscow in June 1984, but it is doubtful whether Romanian demands to enjoy the same privileges as those benefiting other members of CMEA in energy supplies from the Soviet Union were now satisfied. The Soviets appear to understand too well Bucharest's desire to have their cake and eat it, i.e. the RCP's insistence on its prerogative to remain the final arbiter of Romania's economic and foreign policy. Indeed, although in the 1970s Romania had shown signs of overcoming her initial reluctance to join CMEA-sponsored multinational projects (Laux, 1981, p. 115), Bucharest remains as adamant in rejecting supranational planning as it was in the early 1960s, when the dispute with the Soviets developed around precisely this issue. Acceptance of the need for better 'co-ordination' of planning does not signify in Bucharest what it signifies in Moscow. An article in the RCP's theoretical monthly *Era socialistă* in early 1983 (Badrus, 1983, p. 23), for example, while insisting on the need for 'co-ordination', stressed at the same time the validity of 'the principles of full equality of rights, non-interference in internal affairs, mutual advantage', indicating that CMEA's future activity must continue to take into consideration that each communist party is sovereign in deter-mining its 'national economic activity'. Respect for these principles, according to the rather allusive Romanian terminology, is what differentiates Comecon activity from that of 'capitalist integrationist organs'. Moreover, intensification of collaboration within CMEA, according to the Romanian line, should enhance, rather than hinder, 'the socialist countries' participation in the inter-national division of labour' (Totu, 1984). In plain language, this indicates Romanian reluctance to pursue a policy of international economic isolation.

Nevertheless, the negative balance of payments with oil-producing LDCs has determined Bucharest to call for CMEA 'self-reliance' on energy and raw material sources, a position somewhat contradictory to the advocacy of continued international collaboration. According to Ioan V. Totu, in an article published in *Revista economică* in 1984, for example, 'CMEA country-members are in a position to satisfy their needs . . . giving up costly hard-currency imports from third countries'. Romania, the author stressed, was particularly interested in solving her energy requirements, adding that deliveries of fuel to Bucharest could be compensated for by exports of machinery, tools and know-how, and by participation in the joint exploitation of raw material sources (Totu, 1984).

The Soviets, however, show little inclination to oblige. In 1979 Romania imported for the first time 400,000 tons of Soviet crude (Luftman, 1982) and in the following year Ceauşescu disclosed that 1,496,000 tons had been imported from the USSR, alongside 777,000 tons from China (Ceauşescu, 1970-83, Vol. 21, p. 35). These constituted only some 10 per cent of Romanian petroleum imports. There is some disagreement among Western specialists concerning quantities imported in 1981. According to one source (Luftman, 1982), imports from the Soviet Union amounted to 1.3 million tons, representing some 7 per cent of the total crude imported into Romania. Another source, on the other hand (Wharton Econometric Forecasting Associates, 1983), has calculated from Soviet sources that exports of crude to Romania in 1981 amounted to 2,700,000 tons. Be that as it may, by 1982, imports of crude from the USSR diminished in value from 523.6 to an insignificant 66.3m roubles (Măgereanu, 1984), i.e. to some 230,000 tons (Wharton Econometric Forecasting Associates, 1983).

What is more important, even these small quantities are not imported under the same trade terms as those enjoyed by other CMEA members, who up to 1984 only had to pay world-market prices for quantities exceeding established agreements. In an article published in *Revista economică* in February 1984 it was revealed that Soviet deliveries of crude to Romania are not included in the trade protocols between the two countries, being rather made 'in the context of operations connected with discounting in convertible currency'. In other words, Bucharest has to pay for these deliveries either in hard currency, with the price based on the world market, or in 'goods of high economic value, mainly food products'. An agreement concluded for 1983, the article disclosed, stipulated delivery of 'a certain amount of crude' under 'conditions similar to previous years'. Yet it was also revealed that, in 1983, it was the second, rather than the first form of payment that was to be applied (Măgereanu, 1984).

Although no figures are available for Soviet deliveries of oil in 1983, this may partly explain the shift registered in Romanian foreign trade turnover. At the end of 1983 the share of communist countries in Romania's trade had risen from 40.5 per cent in 1980 (see Table 5) to some 53 per cent (*Scînteia*, 29 January 1984). About half of this trade was accounted for by the USSR, with petroleum deliveries most likely sharing a large proportion of imports.The Soviet Union handles a fifth of Romania's total foreign trade (Gafton, 1984). Apart from oil imports, the explanation for such a shift probably rests in the possibility of conducting trade on a barter basis (an important consideration in view of Romania's hard currency debts) and in the improvement of the structure of Romanian exports (including machinery, chemicals and industrial consumption goods) (Totu, 1984).

Drastic measures aimed at reducing the country's foreign debt brought about a considerable drop in Romanian foreign trade, with most efforts geared at cutting imports to minimal requirements. 'We must understand', Ceauşescu stated in 1980 'that we cannot consume more than we produce (*Scînteia*, 1 June 1980). Consequently, instead of a 'planned' increase in foreign trade of 20.8 per cent from 1981 to 1983, Romania's commercial exchange with foreign partners actually decreased by 14.5 per cent in this period (*Scînteia*, 18 October 1980, 28 November 1981, 10 December 1982, 9 February 1983 and 29 January 1984). Imports were cut by 26.6 per cent. According to Western sources (Jackson, 1983, p. 41), in 1981 net exports were increased by $1762m, some 60 per cent of which came from increased net exports of machinery and equipment, with 26 per cent resulting from net exports (i.e. reducing the deficit) of petroleum products. In 1981, it was estimated in the West, Romania had managed to register a trade surplus of some $300m and in 1982 this jumped to $1,600m. (*International Herald Tribune*, 26 December 1983). On 29 January 1984 the party daily *Scînteia* reported that the surplus for 1983 stood at $2,418m. In 1982 (*Scînteia*, 17 December 1982) Ceauşescu was making the optimistic claim that by 1990 Romania's foreign debt would be completely cleared. In 1983, however, he merely called for a reduction in the foreign debt of 25 per cent by the end of 1984, without referring to any long-term schedule (Maier, 1983c).

To achieve these aims, the RCP introduced a series of austerity measures which affected standards of living, lowering them to levels unmatched since the famine of the post-war period. In 1981, bread rationing was re-introduced after twenty-seven years and measures were taken to limit consumption and storage (officially called 'hoarding') of basic foodstuffs, such as edible oil, sugar, flour, rice, coffee and corn. As already mentioned in Chapter 7, the people's councils were supposed to ensure local food self-sufficiency, which basically meant that non-residents (mainly commuting peasants) could no longer buy food in town. To make matters worse, in 1984 the authorities announced a new programme, which compelled every farmstead to produce strictly specified minimum quotas of agricultural products, according to the plan set by the local authorities (*Scînteia*, 17-19 January 1984). Non-compliance with the provisions established by the 'contract' can involve loss of the use of private plots or, in the case of individual peasants, transfer of these plots to the 'co-operative' or to state ownership. Furthermore, product prices are established by the state, and only those peasants who have met their contractual obligations are allowed to sell surplus products on the open market (Gafton and Moore, 1984). What is more important, prices of goods sold on the open market are set by the state.[6] Returning to classical Stalinist principles, the government daily *România liberă* said, on 4 April 1983, that in a socialist economy prices cannot be left to market fluctuations, while Ceauşescu emphasized that the peasantry, who benefit from fixed prices of industrial products and some foods, must reciprocate by selling their products at prices set by the state (*Scînteia*, 20 March 1983). These measures affected incentives to sell products on the market, with the effect that, whenever possible, large numbers of city dwellers go into the countryside, where food products are (illegally) sold by peasant entrepreneurs, sometimes in exchange for goods whose access by countrypeople has been made difficult by the 1981 decrees (Bacon, 1983, p. 329; Jackson, 1983, p. 58). Ceauşescu's 'multilaterally developed socialist society' appears to have evolved into a medieval-style economy.

What must be more irritating than the measures themselves are the rhetorics of simulated change which accompany each presidential or State Council decree announcing further sacrifices. In early 1983, for example, Ceauşescu stated 'We should not fear that some peasants become rich' (Scînteia, 29 January 1983); the programme launched a year later was presented as if it implied abolition of the system of compulsory quotas for the state, with the extension of incentives to the agricultural sector, within the framework of the NEFM. Likewise, in July 1982, the Romanian media released a programme for a 'scientific diet', allegedly aimed at ensuring that Romanians consume fewer calories and healthier food (Scînteia, 14 July 1982). In interviews with West German newspapers (Scînteia, 27 and 29 October 1981), Ceauşescu complained that his countrymen ate too much and gained too much weight!

In February 1982 prices of 220 different foods rose by an average of 35 per cent (Scînteia, 15 February 1982), the highest one-off price increase since the end of the war. Although the decision was accompanied by modest wage increases, Western diplomats in Bucharest reported that the actual increase in prices was twice as high (P. G., 1982). The population's purchasing power in 1982 was eroded by at least 8.8 per cent.[7] The proportion of the family budget spent on food in Romania, according to UN statistics released for that year, was higher than anywhere else in the Comecon countries (Jackson, 1983, p. 53).

The energy crisis (intensified by the continuous failure to achieve planned targets in coal production) brought about several rounds of price increases. In June and July 1979 prices for gasoline, electricity, natural gas and heating fuel rose twice within a six-week period (Buletinul oficial, 31 July 1979). In June 1982 electricity prices rose again by some 30 per cent while domestic heating fuel went up by an average of 300 per cent (Scînteia, 30 June 1982). These steps were accompanied by restrictions on the amount of fuel and electric power distributed to the public, enacted in late January 1982, which were reduced by a further half in November 1983 (Scînteia, 28 January 1982, 25 November 1983). Although private consumption amounts to only 7 per cent of the national total, it was mainly the population who were required to bear the burden, possibly because a 20 per cent cut in energy consumption, introduced in 1979, had caused costly damage to industry.[8] The authorities now decided to forbid use of refrigerators, vacuum cleaners and other household appliances, urging the population to store food outside during winter time, to refrain from using elevators and central heating, and so on. Street lighting, which had already been reduced in 1979, was cut off altogether in the countryside, while in cities only the main streets are (poorly) lit. Inspection teams were set up, and stiff penalties are applied to those caught infringing the regulations.[9] Yet official propaganda often makes reference to Ceauşescu's rule as 'the years of light'.

No personal responsibility for this state of affairs is anywhere acknowledged by Ceauşescu, although some of his harebrained schemes appear to have contributed directly to economic deterioration. Blame is shifted instead either on to 'hoarders' or on to subordinates, who allegedly fail to implement the leadership's directives. According to the Romanian party leader:

> Our programmes and decisions are clear, we have an accurate general line of activity in all sectors; what is now decisive are the organizational, political and educational measures for achieving them. No matter how accurate a general line can be, regardless of the accuracy of our programmes and plans, they remain mere plans, mere documents, if one does not act responsibly, and if measures are not taken for their implementation in [daily] life ... Unfortunately, we must say that particularly in this field we have serious shortcomings [*Scînteia*, 5 August 1983].

The case of Virgil Trofin (see Chapter 6), who was blamed for having in fact implemented Ceauşescu's directives on coal extraction, provides but one of the many instances where the leader's subordinates were required to submit to the Secretary General's undisputable rule. Lesser officials, too, are often dismissed for similar reasons. For example, following an 'inspection' of Bucharest's markets, Ceauşescu dismissed 'on the spot' the Deputy Minister of Agriculture, the First Vice-chairman and the Vice-chairman of the Executive Committee of the municipal people's council (*Scînteia*, 4 October 1982).

Foreign elements are also supposed to share in the blame. On 10 July 1981, for example, *Scînteia* complained about 'the exploitative character of credits' and in September the party leader himself defined Western interest rates as a 'new form of exploitation', calling for 'putting an end to imperialist plundering' (Ceauşescu, 1970–83, Vol. 22, p. 435). In a conference published by the theoretical monthly *Era socialistă* (No. 1, 10 January 1983), one of the participants complained that:

> Hundreds of millions of people from numerous countries ... make efforts, sometimes considerable ones, to produce goods and services for making their lives easier and more comfortable; but the intrigues of politics and the financial and banking mechanisms led to the destruction of their expectations and aspirations. Through discriminating policies, through the money market and high interest rates, the people's income and, what is truly tragic, that of entire nations, is purloined and routed to a financial and banking oligarchy.

Such complaints, however, did not hinder the Romanian authorities from using the IMF's services in order to re-schedule foreign debts.[10] The IMF rescue operation of 1982 was conditioned by a series of reforms such as cutting back on imports, increasing efficiency in agriculture to avoid dependence on agricultural exports, a wage-price stabilization scheme, as well as overcoming xenophobic suspicion and making economic statistics available to Western financial circles.

These reforms, together with others, were to become part of the NEFM. This does not imply, as Romanian officials attempted to claim in private discussion with this author, that the blame for the harsh economic conditions prevailing in Romania in the 1980s is to be laid at the door of the IMF.

The reforms were long overdue and could be seen as the continuation of a number of organizational economic measures dating as far back as the end of 1967. However, while production and marketing costs are taken into consideration, with their burden on the standard of living, decentralization remains limited to policy implementation and the party maintains its unchallenged role of planner and supervisor.

The NEFM is a belated and revised version of measures adopted by the RCP in December 1967 (Shafir, 1981b, pp. 622-4). By that time, Romania was the last member of Comecon to adopt a programme of economic reform. The core of the 1967 programme (Spigler, 1973; Gumpel, 1977; Smith, 1980 and 1981) consisted in establishing a new, intermediary level between economic ministries and enterprises, a device similar to the three-tier system introduced in the Soviet Union, East Germany, Bulgaria and Poland. The industrial 'centrals', as they are known in their Romanian version, came into being in 1969. They were conceived as 'autonomous economic units' (*Directivele*, 1967), formed by a number of enterprises combined through vertical and horizontal integration (Smith, 1980, p. 38). The 'democratic centralist' principle in economic organization, however, was not abolished, for the centrals were still subject to central planning directives and one of their main functions was that of ensuring plan fulfilment. They were to draw up plans for the enterprises, to allocate materials and investment funds, to supervise selling of output and to be in charge of the redistribution of profits among their component units (Bornstein, 1977, p. 14). Since the directives stipulated that the centrals were to be provided with 'material and money resources, operating on the principle of self-administration', an increased role was envisaged for prices, financing and credit levers.

Enterprises were to be allowed to retain part of their profits, which they could use as payment either for incentives or for financing investments. Yet it was difficult to see how these units could fulfil the criterion of profitability as long as no real reform of the price system or market mechanism was envisaged. An accurate description of this bogus 'decentralization' is provided by Allan H. Smith, who indicates that the 'crucial inconsistency of the Directives was the unwillingness to give up detailed centralized control, while simultaneously proposing greater autonomy for economic units to stimulate production efficiency'. Decentralization, in other words, was mainly 'administrative' (Bornstein, 1977, p. 109). While enterprises were instructed to borrow from banks, to modernize plant and to cover unused reserves, such activities were to be 'incorporated in compulsory indicators (including profits), with monetary sanctions to be imposed at all levels of the economic hierarchy for their non-fulfilment' (Smith, 1980, pp. 39-40).

The implementation of these directives was postponed by over a year. By autumn 1969, when some two hundred centrals were finally set up, their functioning had little in common with the original stipulations. Instead of acting as 'autonomous units' they became 'executants of the ministries' programmes'

(Spigler, 1973, p. 60-1). Analysing the Romanian industrial management system on the basis of interviews conducted with managers, D. Granick concluded that target plans for the centrals were often changed by ministries, and that the role of enterprise managers consisted in mere improvement of technical efficiency. Economic decisions were 'taken in ministries or higher bodies or . . . not taken at all' (Granick, 1975, pp. 127-8).

Eventually, Ceauşescu would lay the blame for this state of affairs at the door of the state apparatus. In a speech delivered at the CC plenum of March 1978, he stated that measures designed to improve the economic system had been devised as far back as 1974, but their implementation had been hindered by those entrusted with the experiment. These persons, the Secretary General said, were removed for having resisted the implementation of the party's decisions (Ceauşescu, 1970-83, Vol. 15, pp. 590-1). That in the late 1960s state officials might still have been in a position to resists encroachments on their powers is entirely possible. That Ceauşescu, whose power base rested in the party, would pose as a champion of reform is, again, quite consonant with his tactics of power consolidation. By 1974, however, he had already achieved unchallenged primacy, and, consequently, his statement of March 1978 was hardly plausible.

What actually occurred in the early 1970s was a reflection of the mobilizational ethos of the party and its Secretary General, with Ceauşescu now freed from the necessity to recruit support. Once ambiguous declarations of policy-intent were no longer imperative, the party leader initiated a campaign to fulfil the 1971-75 plan in four-and-a-half years. Targets were increased twice during the decade, in 1972 and in 1977. By 1974, at the time of the Eleventh Congress, investment rates in heavy industry were raised to 39 per cent of the national income (28 per cent in 1969). The 1976-80 plan provided for an increase in investments to an *annual* rise of 12.7 per cent, i.e. 1.2 per cent above 1970-75 (Spechler, 1983, p. 37).

These policies called for recentralization. The number of industrial centrals was reduced to 102 by 1974, thereby facilitating closer control by ministries.[11] The number of industrial enterprises and of locally (as opposed to centrally) subordinated units was also reduced. In 1973, and again in 1975, the authorities cut the number of organizations which, according to late 1960s legislation, had been permitted to negotiate foreign trade contracts, returning a substantial number of these enterprises to the jurisdiction of the Ministry of Foreign Trade. Finally, the plan for 1974 stipulated an increase in centrally allocated products (180 in 1973 versus 720 in the subsequent year), elimination of 'decentralized' investments as well as of 'departmental' imports (i.e. imports not specifically approved by a central body), and designated a single agency for each type of imported product (Jackson, 1977, p. 891).

A second phase in the implementation of economic change can be dated 1973. Perhaps the most significant innovation of this phase was one that failed, namely the attempt to replace gross output as a main indicator by 'net output', which is a measure of value-added production, including additions and inventories. This indicator, together with one measuring the output of finished goods (commodity production) in physical units, was eventually introduced within the framework of the NEFM, after 1978 (Jackson, 1983, pp. 66-7). Far from signifying relinquishment of party control over the economy, the 1973-78 phase saw the implementation of 'take-over from within tactics' in the form of the blending of the party and state apparatus in charge of the economy. Its symbol was the 'Unitary National Socio-Economic Plan', which was accompanied by a reorganization of ministries, centrals and enterprises, geared to concentrate production at enterprise, as well as at central, level. These measures, as Smith (1980, p. 41) writes, were adopted and accompanied by an incomprehensible number of administrative shake-ups, which both reflected the Secretary General's personal predilections for organizational change, and strengthened his personal power, now exercised more and more through his extended family. The Supreme Council of Social and Economic Development, chaired by Ceauşescu, became the main policy-making and supervisory body, taking over some of the functions of the State Planning Committee.

Democratic centralism as the key organizational principle for the control of the economy found authoritative enunciation in the declarations of Manea Mănescu and Ceauşescu himself. Speaking as Chairman of the State Planning Committee in 1973, the future head of government indicated that the Single National Plan must include even the smallest sector of the economy, adding that the reforms implemented since 1969 did not consist of mere decentralization of decision-making. Such alleged decentralization was supposed to 'ensure simultaneously an *increased* role for the plan in guiding socio-economic processes ... according to the principles of democratic socialism'. Centrals and enterprises, he added, could make decisions only after these had been 'comprehensively discussed by the party and state managing bodies' (quoted in Smith, 1980, pp. 41-2). In turn, Ceauşescu declared, on 2 July 1974:

> To give everyone the freedom of spending our society's money on whatever, and however, it might strike one's mind—this is not possible. We have a planned economy. The slogan of autonomy cannot be employed for giving everyone the right to spend money as he likes. There is *full freedom of initiative in implementing the plan* ... Let us understand this well: in investments, all growth must be included in the quinquennium or, for things of more minor a nature, occurring en route, in the yearly plan. *Nobody has the right to build what is not provided for by the plan* ... We cannot allow anarchy in this field [Ceauşescu, 1970-83, Vol. 10, p. 453. Emphasis mine].

This is yet another typical case of pseudo-participation, with the role of centrals and enterprises limited to policy implementation. These bodies, and the organs of workers' self-management in their earliest version, were to take part in discussions of target plans before these were approved by the central authorities, but the prerogative of plan formulation rested with the centre and was binding upon all subordinate units.

The 'autonomy' of the centrals, as it turns out, consisted in being 'plan titulars', i.e. in receiving a considerable number of plan indicators, allocating them to component enterprises, and supervising plan fulfilment. As for the organs of workers' self-management, their subordination to the party has been discussed elsewhere in this study (Chapter 6). Similarly to the Soviet concept of *khozraschyot*, on the other hand, the centrals were to operate as self-financing units, i.e. to cover costs from their own revenues. In addition, they were to take upon themselves a larger share in the financing of social services, thereby freeing the state budget of some of its burden (Smith, 1981, pp. 70-1). In what appears to have been an earlier version of the NEFM, the party made use of a plethora of reformist terminology ('decentralization', 'self-finance', 'self-management'), but in practice it reserved for itself central planning while offloading responsibility for local enterprise self-sufficiency. This kind of terminology was geared towards both domestic and foreign (Western) support, suggesting a movement in the direction of genuine change. As Smith accurately perceives (1980, p. 35, 1981, p. 74), it raised associations with the Yugoslav, Hungarian and 1968 Czechoslovak systems. However, the similarity was merely semantic. The tradition of 'forms without content' was kept intact.

Officially announced in March 1978 and implemented gradually since 1979, the NEFM[12] is based on the same principles as before: self-finance, self-management and workers' self-management, with the caveat that the latter two remain as far from reality as before. Self-finance has been extended to all economic units (including the agricultural sector and local government), with the purpose of increasing awareness as to the economic value of their incomes and expenditure (Jackson, 1983, p. 65). Of particular importance are costs of imports, and Ceauşescu stated bluntly (*Scînteia*, 1 June 1980) that no enterprise is to be allowed to import a greater value of goods to be paid in foreign currency than it manages to export to foreign markets.[13] Cost reductions and profitability are to be achieved by using 'net output' and 'commodity production' as indicators, and by linking material incentives directly to profits. In practice, this means that overhead costs, such as investments, research and development but, above all, an increasing proportion of the social wage, are no longer provided for from the state budget.

For this purpose, a distinction is made between planned and above-plan profits. The former are divided between payments to the state, payments to banks and the enterprises' own funds, of which there are six: the fund for economic development, for working capital, for housing construction and for other investments of a social nature, one for social actions and, finally, the fund for participation in profits. Where above-plan profits are achieved as a result of exports, an additional bonus of up to 10 per cent is directed to the fund for profit-sharing, in proportion to the degree of over-fulfilment. The state budget, however, receives at least 35 per cent of such profits, and the law provides for additional payments to the state. Enterprise funds are mainly dependent on *above-plan profits*, which means that mere fulfilment of the plan can equal close to zero profit-sharing. When such profits are achieved, on the other hand, they can be directed to the profit-sharing fund in limited amounts only (Smith, 1981, p. 79).

According to this design, surplus income over expenditure should provide both fixed and working capital for the enterprise and funds for the state budget. Banks are to play a greater role in supervising achievements of planned targets, with financial penalties imposed for mismanagement of resources and of capital. Investments, however, remain centrally determined, as indeed do plan indicators. Ceauşescu's statement of June 1980 that self-management should not be understood 'as each and everyone's right to engage and spend financial and human means, and to start activities, as he thinks fit' (quoted in Smith, 1981, p. 75) bears a familiar note of *plus ça change.*

Consequently, in drawing up revenue and expenditure plans, all economic units must take into consideration three factors: compulsory payments to the state, return of loans, and funds for bonuses and social expenditures. The latter, however, come last, priority being given to the state and to the banks even in cases where the unit did not fulfil planned targets. Where the enterprise's profits are insufficient for making payments, loans are to be provided at penalizing interest rates, for a period not exceeding three months. If after three months the enterprise still fails to secure expenditure funds, it must revise costs and cut staff accordingly. Should this also fail, the ministry is entitled to authorize special supervision (*Buletinul oficial*, 13 July 1979). The Secretary General repeatedly insisted that inefficient enterprises should close down (Ceauşescu, 1970-83, Vol. 10, p. 211; *Scînteia*, 14 June 1980). However, since political criteria continue to be applied to the economy, no such steps have been reported up to the present. In December 1980 the party leader complained that subsidies in the extractive industries had risen in recent years (Ceauşescu, 1970-83, Vol. 21, pp. 201-2). Nevertheless, according to official Romanian sources, the authorities succeeded in cutting operating subsidies to enterprises from 20 per cent in the 1980 budget to 6 per cent in 1982. The share of fixed capital financed from the state budget was 55 per cent in 1979, 45 per cent in 1981 and 50 per cent in 1982 (Jackson, 1983, p. 71).

The most striking feature of the NEFM, in any case, seems to be the penalizing of the populace, dressed up as an incentive. For example, failure to meet output targets triggers a reduction of 1 per cent in the profit participation fund for every percentage point of underfulfilment, up to a maximum of 25 per cent. The enterprise's other funds, including housing, are similarly affected. The full severity of the scheme comes to light when bearing in mind the new 'remuneration' system adopted in September 1983 and now applied to all economic sectors. As discussed briefly in the previous chapter, this new piece-rate system abolished the earlier guarantee of a monthly income equal to an employee's 80 per cent of regular pay, while at the same time doing away with an earlier provision, according to which any supplementary income earned by overfulfilment of plan targets was to be limited to 20 per cent of his regular salary (*Buletinul oficial*, 1 November 1974). Whereas on paper a worker can now have an unlimited income, in practice this means that his earnings depend on centrally-defined individual norms (known as the 'direct individual contract') as well as on the fulfilment of the plan by his enterprise (the 'collective contract'). Moreover, the new regulations require any new employees to sign a contract binding them to work in the enterprise for at least five years. During this probationary period, the employee receives only half of the funds deriving from the profits of the enterprise, with the other half deposited in a bank (without interest) and only released if he has not left the job in the meantime. Should the employee leave his work place, he forfeits not only the deposited money, but also the years counting towards his pension rights. On top of this, the authorities are entitled to transfer the entire personnel of an enterprise, either temporarily or for a longer period, with no assistance stipulated for the period of unemployment generated by the redeployment of the workforce (*Buletinul oficial*, 10 September, 13 September, 17 September and 5 October 1983).

Simulated change continues to affect the agricultural sector as well. In a speech delivered in early 1981, Ceauşescu surprisingly admitted that:

> In the light of the experience of socialist construction in our country, it appears now very evident that the thesis of priority of industrialization to the detriment of the development and modernization of agriculture brought, in fact, neglect of the importance of the growth of agricultural production. Application of this orientation determined disproportions in general economic social-development and influenced negatively the people's standard of living. At the same time, it must be said that the general practice of socialist edification demonstrates that underestimation of placing agriculture on the foundations of socialist relations of production generates serious contradictions in social life, harms the cause of building socialism and communism. Our country's theoretical and practical experience as well as the experience of other countries in agrarian policies . . . emphasizes the necessity of giving agriculture an outstanding role, for the harmonious development of the national economy and raising the people's living standards, for the consolidation of national independence [Ceauşescu, 1970–83, Vol. 21, p. 408].

Furthermore, in his opening address to the National Party Conference of December 1982, the Secretary General suggested a better allocation of the national income between the development and the consumption funds, without indicating, however, what such a switch would entail (*Scînteia*, 17 December 1982). Only six months earlier he had castigated 'some theorists and economists abroad' who 'propagate that Romania was wrong in paying so much attention to the development of its production forces, *of socialist industry in particular*', specifying that a higher consumption rate could result in 'loss of independence and sovereignty' (Ceauşescu, 1982, p. 9. Emphasis mine). Investments in agriculture were indeed increased in the 1983 plan (*Scînteia*, 10 December 1982), but mainly at the expense of those in scientific research, education, culture and other related areas.

The 'agricultural revolution', as Ceauşescu himself named his call for a change in development priorities, failed to produce the expected results, partly because of the quality of manpower in the countryside (see Chapter 9), but mainly because it did not entail any real change in the party's mobilization policies. The extension of the NEFM to the agricultural sector virtually abolished the guaranteed minimum income for 'collectivized' peasantry, legislated for in 1970 (*Scînteia*, 25 December 1970) and instituted in 1971, for, according to a change introduced in the status of 'socialist' agricultural organizations (state farms and the APC—Agricultural Production Co-operatives), this minimum income became contingent on plan fulfilment (*Buletinul oficial*, 28 March 1983). 'Without production', the Secretary General stipulated, 'no one can be entitled to receive a minimum income . . . Income must not be linked to the number of working days,[14] but to productivity' (*Scînteia*, 10 January 1981). None the less, according to the remuneration system in agriculture established by decree of the Council of State (*Scînteia*, 24 January 1982), the co-operative farmer is required to work a minimum of three hundred days a year. When there is no work to be done in his own APC, he may be transferred to areas where there is a shortage of agricultural workers, or be employed in peripheral work in the services or in local small industry. The authorities may also send him to construction sites, to lumber units or to other work. The 'agricultural revolution' decreed by Ceauşescu thus appears to be revolutionary indeed—but it is a revolution of the Stalinist type. As a result of such measures, production in both agriculture and the food industry in 1983 fell below planned targets, with agricultural output failing to reach even the 1982 target (*Scînteia*, 10 December 1982, 29 January 1984).

Short of the unlikely radical re-orientation of strategies, the prospects for the Romanian economy and for the population's standard of living do not look very bright. The introduction of a reduced working week, first announced by Ceauşescu at the National Party Conference in 1972 (Ceauşescu, 1970-83, Vol. 7, p. 495), has been postponed several times[15] and is likely to be delayed again. Despite efforts to cope with the energy problem, including the purchase of nuclear reactors from Canada and the development of alternative sources, such as bio-gas, thermal, water, wind or solar energy, it is not very likely that Romania will achieve energy independence by 1990, as decreed in the guidelines established at the Twelfth Party Congress. The Soviet Union will presumably continue to refuse to supply Bucharest with cheap crude, the more so since some Romanian development projects, such as the Danube-Black Sea Canal, inaugurated in 1984, might encroach on Soviet interests. But above all, Romania's economy will continue to suffer as a consequence of being the most centralized, least flexible system in Soviet-influenced Eastern Europe (Anderson, 1983, p. 226).

Part IV
The Social Structure and
Its Political Consequences

9 Autonomy, Conformity and Political Stagnation: A Socio-Historical Perspective of Contemporary Romanian Society

In Lieu of Introduction: The Party and the Bedroom— or Domination and Response

A famous Soviet joke has it that all double beds in the USSR are to be replaced by beds for triple occupancy which will carry the inscription *Lenin s nami* (Lenin is with us). The joke, of course, attests to party invasion of any and all forms of privacy. In Romania, however, this joke has come very close to literal implementation through the policies of enforced demographic growth pursued by the RCP since 1966.

Faced with a record post-war growth rate of 6.0 per thousand inhabitants in 1965, the party made abortions illegal and divorce very difficult (*Buletinul oficial*, 1 and 8 October 1966), forbade the use of contraceptives and increased taxes on childless couples. Initially, these measures proved successful, for natural increase (births minus deaths) rose from 6.1 per thousand in 1966 to 18.1 per thousand in the following year. Soon, however, the population resorted to traditional ways of coping with this problem (as well as to illegal abortions and the use of contraceptives smuggled from abroad) and natural increase once again showed a constant decline (see Table 16).

The measures taken by the leadership in 1966 are to be attributed to its nationalist postures, but also to the dangers faced by the Romanian economy in view of a potential labour shortage (Jackson, 1977, p. 932; Fischer, 1983b). This potential shortage was particularly blatant in urban areas and in the industrial sector, in strong contrast to rural areas and the agricultural sector, where the opposite trend was beginning to emerge (see later). Consequently, in June 1973, at a CC plenum, Ceauşescu indicated that since women represented 51 per cent of the total population, a process of socialist construction could not be conceived without their active participation 'in the totality of social life' (Ceauşescu, 1970-83, Vol. 8, p. 646). The resolution of the forum called for more widespread employment of women and their promotion to responsible positions in the party, as well as in administration and all other branches of the economy (*Scînteia*, 20 June 1973).

The directives were seemingly implemented, for the proportion of women in

Table 16   Natural Growth of Population, per Thousand Inhabitants, 1965–1983

	Live births	Natural increase (births minus deaths)
1965	14.6	6.0
1966	14.3	6.1
1967	27.4	18.1
1968	26.7	17.1
1969	23.3	13.2
1970	21.1	11.6
1975	19.7	10.4
1980	18.0	7.6
1983	14.3	2.9

Source: Republica Socialistă România. Direcţia Centrală de Statistică, 1982, p. 23; *Scînteia*, 3 March 1984.

the RCP rose from 23.78 per cent in 1972 to 28.71 per cent in 1980 and 31.61 per cent in 1983 (*Scînteia*, 22 June 1973, 28 March 1981, 27 March 1984), although this figure is well under the target of 34–35 per cent set by Ceauşescu in March 1981 for the forthcoming Thirteenth RCP Congress (Ceauşescu, 1970–83, Vol. 21, p. 506). Central Committee female membership (full and candidate) rose from 9 to 25 per cent between 1974 and 1979, while in the GNA the proportion of women deputies more than doubled from the 1975 to the 1980 elections (14.3 and 32.5 per cent respectively) (Fischer, 1983b).

Yet these figures hardly attest to real participation and responsibility for women in Romanian society. As indicated in Chapter 6, less than 15 per cent of leading positions in industry and agriculture were occupied by women in 1983. What is more, Mary Ellen Fischer demonstrated convincingly (1983b) that promotion in the party's leading organs or to deputyship in the GNA is on a strictly imposed 'quota' basis, that it varies inversely with the power of the political body or position, and that women are concentrated in those sectors where they are assumed to have special competence (health, education, light industry, consumer goods), leaving the management of society's 'serious' affairs in male hands.

The most blatant contradiction between declarations of intent and reality, however, stems from the fact that while women are expected to contribute fully to the process of 'socialist edification' by being recruited into the workforce, facilities promoting equality between the sexes have been *deteriorating*. Consequently, the 'triple burden of job, home and children makes it impossible for most Romanian women to devote the time and attention to their careers that would be necessary for promotion to the top of the economic and political ladder'. Yet Ceauşescu 'wants women to participate more fully in the economy and to produce more children, goals which are contradictory, unless a reorientation of sex roles does occur' (Fischer, 1983b).

Indeed, it is highly improbable that measures such as the interdiction on use of household appliances, not to mention food shortages, are likely to promote enthusiasm for enlarging families (though power shortages might eventually help!). In 1983, when economic hardship had reached proportions affecting all strata of the population, natural increase registered a steep decline, dropping from 7.8 per thousand inhabitants to a mere 2.9. In response, the party's PEC announced a new series of measures, introducing even stricter controls and stiffer penalties. In March 1984 taxes on couples who proved recalcitrant in following the Secretary General's appeal to fulfil their patriotic duty to breed (*Scînteia*, 8 March 1984) were raised once more. At the same time, party bodies were instructed to 'increase controls . . . for improving the supervision of pregnant women' (*Scînteia*, 3 March 1984). 'Nothing that happens in society', the RCP daily candidly explained, 'can be excluded from preoccupation of the party'. In turn, Ceauşescu instructed the party organs 'to understand that fulfilment of their leading role requires increasing the responsibility *vis-à-vis* the accomplishment of demographic policy too', for this was deemed to constitute 'one of the fundamental problems in the activity of our party and state' (*Scînteia*, 8 March 1984). An officially proclaimed declaration of intent of 'take-over from within' was thus acquiring a somewhat unexpected character. The party's omniscience was to be extended to the bedroom, as well as into the gynaecologist's office.

There is an obvious difference between the excellent analysis of the status of women in contemporary Romania provided by Mary Ellen Fischer and the insights revealed by George Stănică, a former Romanian journalist now working in London. Yet the difference is more one of perspective than of substance. Although most Romanian women work just as hard as men do, Stănică writes, they get extremely little help from their husbands who, still in the Oriental tradition, regard jobs such as cleaning, shopping, cooking and child-rearing as essentially female duties. Attitudes towards women, according to this interpretation, are still 'in the tradition of the Ottoman Empire, which imposed its ethos over long centuries of domination' (*The Guardian*, 3 April 1984). A strange symbiosis between party-promoted simulated change and the persistence of traditional values thus appears to leave its mark on one of the most significant aspects of society.

Congruence between Leninist party norms and traditional components of the political culture, as demonstrated by Jowitt (1974a), can be extended over many additional aspects of social life in Eastern Europe. On the other hand, it is no less true that in some countries in the area 'official' and 'dominant' political cultures (or elements thereof) may clash. And precisely because of such differences, the comparative study of state-society relations in Leninist systems is a challenging, if somewhat slippery, enterprise.

In a paper delivered at an international conference, Ole Nørgaard and Steven Sampson[1] concluded that, despite many similarities, one should not expect Romania to become 'the next Poland'. Although the two countries share economic difficulties, such as low productivity in industry and agriculture, shortages of consumer goods and a heavy foreign debt, although they are both ruled by parties led by powerful leaders (Jaruzelski and Ceaușescu) who do not allow any measure of institutional criticism, and though both states have lost territory to the Soviet Union and their population is traditionally anti-Russian, there is little indication that Romania's rulers are likely to be faced with a Solidarity-like mass movement in the foreseeable future (Nørgaard & Sampson, 1982). Among the reasons for this, Nørgaard and Sampson list such points as the benefits of legitimization derived by the regime from the industrialization-nationalism equation; access to consumer goods despite shortages, due to working-class 'connections to the countryside', where many city-dwellers from among the proletariat are said to be still able to 'obtain the necessary foodstuffs from family and friends'; party legitimacy generated by general anti-Soviet stances, to the extent that 'many Romanians believe that tensions among the Hungarian minority and even certain factory disturbances (e.g. sabotage) are the result of Soviet intrigues'; the absence of an alternative centre of power, and, in particular, of an independent Church; the lack of experience and the fragmentation of a working class divided by nationality differences and lacking support of intellectuals; and finally, a series of 'subjective factors', ranging from the population's low level of expectation to the Romanian's 'traditional ability to "get by" with the help of family, friends and connections'. The latter is said to generate a tendency to solve problems on an individual, rather than a collective basis, regarding others 'as competitors for scarce resources rather than as possible allies'.[2] In a similar manner, George Schöpflin argues that although the working class in Romania 'has the most cause to follow the Poles . . . there is little evidence that the Romanian workers had reached the level of cohesion where they would form organizations and pursue sustained action against the authorities'. The reasons, according to Schöpflin, 'lie in the general backwardness of Romania—the country with the lowest standard of living in Comecon—and the immaturity of the working class', for the bulk of the proletariat is made up of 'ex-peasants, not long away from much worse drudgery on the land, and thus satisfied with the meager improvement in conditions represented by urban life' (Schöpflin, 1983a, p. 129).

There is very little in these arguments that I would question, although Nørgaard and Sampson underestimate some components of the political culture (see later) and, in my opinion, overestimate the average Romanian's success in 'getting by' in the face of economic hardship. On the contrary, it seems to me that, if anything, the insights of the three scholars need to be further explored and expanded. However, their analysis might gain if the subject were approached from a different (or rather additional) perspective, namely that of propensities towards autonomy versus conformity in Romanian society.

Commenting on 'the pronounced tendency' of journalists and scholars to 'dwell on difficulties, troubles and unresolved issues' in the Soviet Union, Seweryn Bialer writes that virtually every possible aspect of social life has been described as a 'problem'. The economy, nationalities, technological lag, and many other aspects, are assumed to be 'problematic', not to mention the 'problem' of dissent, which is sometimes presented as if it constituted 'the overwhelming fact of life', one that 'decisively shapes internal politics and policies'. All these aspects of life, the American scholar adds, are truly 'problems', are 'points of genuine and recognized vulnerability and potential crises'. However, 'what has been most surprising . . . is not the presence of these genuine problems, but rather that they did not create any semblance of a systemic crisis, whether separately or in combination' (Bialer, 1980, p. 141). On one hand, the political order has exhibited the ability to 'prevent the translation of instability conditions in other social spheres into factors of *political instability*' (Bialer, 1980, p. 139. Emphasis mine); on the other hand, one can observe 'a degree of political apathy in society, an element of apoliticization', which 'is not undesirable *from the systemic point of view*' (Bialer, 1980, p. 166; emphasis in original).

Although he insists on describing this situation as one of 'political stability', Bailer's is nothing but a statement of the failure of scholars to analyse the roots of political stagnation. *Mutatis mutandis*, this applies not only to Soviet, but also to contemporary analyses of Romanian affairs.

Scholars writing on Romania are naturally inclined to seek parallels with other East European systems—by no means a 'sinful' enterprise. Even in the pages of this book simulated change has been described as a systemic trait, common to all communist regimes. This does not necessarily indicate the absence of an impetus for political change in Eastern Europe. But in those countries where such impetus has not been confined to mere rhetoric, political change was short-lived, if only because Soviet tanks are not in the habit of failing where the hard core of a party occasionally stumbles. And 'normalization' has meant, among other things, a return to tactics of simulated change. It has restored to the foreground political figures who, though bent on 'suppressing the aspirations of society which had emerged during a period of weakened party control' (Schöpflin, 1982b, p. 149), none the less continue to employ some reformist jargon. The jargon, to be sure, usually attests to leadership awareness of societal aspirations. The absence of genuine implementation, on the other hand, attests to generic limitations. Even in such countries as Hungary, where an originally Soviet-imposed leadership eventually instituted economic and political reforms, these were much constrained by both the strength of domestic conservatism and by the Soviet shadow (Schöpflin, 1982a). Scholarly awareness of interludes of weakened party domination of society in some East European systems generated a search for signs of similar developments elsewhere, including Romania.

However, such pursuit fails to make the necessary distinction between the common systemic trait of simulated change and the system-particularistic one of political stagnation. The latter, i.e. a regime's 'ability to defend' generated by successful 'system-maintenance' strategies or by the weakness of 'dysfunctional' systemic pressures, may vary from one communist country to another. As pointed out in the concluding remarks to Chapter 5, the assumption of similarity in the basic political ethos of ruling elites does not preclude variations in the measure of success met in endeavours to preserve party monopoly. Being a relational phenomenon, political stagnation is a function of more than one variable. It is related not only to leadership aspirations, but also to the web of intra-social, as well as state-societal relations. To put it slightly differently: while everywhere in Eastern Europe the party has had moments when it attempted to enter the bedroom, in some instances it found out to its amazement that the occupants were absent, and in other cases it discovered that the door was locked and had to be forced.

Until now, Romania has never had to be 'normalized'. Leadership cohesion, although lately displaying some indication of deterioration, provides part of the explanation. Yet Romanian 'normalcy' is probably due, to a similar, and possibly greater, extent, to the weakness of societal aspirations to autonomy.[3] It is precisely group or individual autonomy,[4] as values to which a significant proportion of the population attach primacy, that generates (or provides support for) the impetus for attempted political change in Eastern Europe and which, if this analysis is correct, has been traditionally weak in Romania, as indeed in the Soviet Union (Friedgut, 1975; Feifer, 1975). Territorial autonomy, on the other hand, is an issue confined to the problem of the national minorities and, what is more, one that in Romania contributes to division, rather than to cementation, among potential agents of innovation.

It is the purpose of this chapter to examine political stagnation from a perspective of continuity and change in the social structure, in values, and in their derivative behavioural implications for state (party)-society relations. My intention is to demonstrate that the dominance of norms not congruent to the existence of enclaves or of forces outside the direct impact of the centre, together with other components of the political culture cunningly employed (such as nationalism), combine to reinforce the party's self-attributed 'leading role', and are generally conducive to conformity. Acquiescence and/or consent, rather than dissent, appear to be the response of society to party domination, although instances of resistance may herald the birth of future societal turmoil.

Autonomy and Conformity in Historical Romania

As mentioned in Chapter 1, state and society in pre-communist Romania were widely divergent, yet the pattern of relationships between rulers and ruled remained unaffected by the modernization process until the beginning of this century. Urbanization and its related growth of a middle class were slow and affected only an insignificant proportion of people. Industrialization proceeded at a similarly moderate rate, and the working class was rather insignificant both in number and as a social movement. Romanian society, in short, was very much the typical *Agrargesellschaft*, hindering the development of attitudes conducive to individual and group autonomy, or to political activism.

The most significant schism between rulers and ruled occurred at the outset of the sixteenth century. A change in trade patterns, resulting in loss of revenue for the state(s)[5], as well as a considerable rise in the Ottoman tribute, led to the enserfment of large sections of the peasantry. Serf and *rumân* (Romanian) became synonymous in the Wallach idiom. In Moldavia the serfs were called *vecin* (neighbour), attesting to the sheer number of serfs (Chirot, 1976, p. 48). Traditional bonds of loyalty between local nobility and peasantry were now destroyed, never really to be re-tied.

A considerable proportion of the peasantry, however, managed to escape enserfment, and belonged to the special category of 'free peasants'. The free peasants cultivated the land in communal villages, the vestiges of some of which have lasted as late as the early part of this century. One should beware, however, of associating them with traditions of autonomy, and even more of attributing such values to the consequences of communal management. Communal forms of property ownership are not necessarily conducive to group autonomy, and they are probably obstructive to individual autonomy. In fact, the two might be entirely separate. In Romania, where many nobles had seized villages for tax-collecting purposes only and never intended to cultivate the land themselves, communal farming had persisted for a long time after the loss of village freedom, since it was suitable to the agri-pastoral techniques still employed (Stahl, 1969; Chirot, 1976, pp. 50-1, 70, 78, 103).

On the other hand, communal traditions might contribute to the diminution of individual entrepreneurship. Constantin Rădulescu-Motru, an early Romanian sociologist, wrote that the Romanian peasants showed 'no spirit of initiative in business and very little feeling for social and political independence'. They were ruled by 'the tradition of collective effort', with each villager doing 'what he thinks the others would do' (Rădulescu-Motru, 1937, pp. 5-6). As he put it in a book published earlier, the peasant believed 'that what the rest of the [surrounding] world does is the only rule for a sane person to abide by' (Rădulescu-Motru, 1936, p. 113). Such attitudes are hardly consonant with those attributed to the population by Nørgaard and Sampson, who claim that *individualism* makes it difficult for the Romanians 'to mobilize for long-term, societal goals'.

This tendency to conformism, or as Rădulescu-Motru called it, 'collectivism', was supposed to be accompanied by a 'pronounced mystical character', which the sociologist, rather mistakenly, took for a national, specifically Romanian singularity. But conformism and mystic tendencies have been proven to be characteristic of many other peasant societies. Not only do they seem to go hand in hand, but a degree of consonance appears to exist between such traits and a fatalistic attitude towards life; such attitudes, however, also bear heavily on behavioural reactions toward authority which is perceived as 'unfriendly'. In a study devoted to the impact of the modernization process on peasants, Everett M. Rogers discovered that fatalism defined as 'the degree to which an individual perceives his lack of ability to control his future' was widespread among members of peasant societies. Such individuals 'believe that the events of their lives are pre-ordained and determined by fate or supernatural forces. Their attitudes toward self-control of future events involve passivity, pessimism, acceptance, endurance, pliancy and evasion'. Since 'peasants have a relatively low degree of mastery over their natural and social environment', Rogers indicates, a 'fatalistic outlook reflects psychological adaptation to a harsh environment' (Rogers, 1969, pp. 273-4). And in a culture 'in which men's orientation toward nature is essentially one of fatalism and resignation', as Sidney Verba remarks (1965, p. 522), 'their orientation toward government is likely to be much the same'. By the mid-twentieth century, the Romanian poet and philosopher Lucian Blaga was raising these orientations to the rank of national virtue,[6] in a Spengler-influenced theory which accounted for national survival through an existential union with nature, which ignored the temporality of hostile historical developments (Blaga, 1969, pp. 119-31).

The pattern of tax-conditioned external independence, combined with internal conformity, typical of the communal village, and later of larger sections of the Romanian peasantry, was reproduced at state level, for the Turks never ruled the Romanian principalities directly. Unlike the situation in the neighbouring Balkan countries, Ottoman rule was 'indirect', i.e. with a native elite running affairs for the metropole or (under the phanariots), a non-native, non-metropolitan elite squeezing the country's resources for the centre and for its own benefit (Chirot, 1976, pp. 62-3).

This form of rule had several consequences. First, the struggle for national liberation in nineteenth-century Moldavia and Wallachia was not accompanied by one against the landowners. Unlike the *pashas* in Bulgaria and in parts of modern Yugoslavia, the Romanian *boyars* were native to the country (Chirot, 1976, p. 63). Social reform was not what their offspring, who led this struggle after first coming into contact with liberal ideas in Paris and elsewhere in the West (Fischer-Galati, 1971), were most eager to implement. Descent from the 'generation of 1848', on the other hand, left a deeply nationalist imprint on the Romanian intelligentsia, which, in a manner not dissimilar to contemporary Third World countries, sees itself as political parent and guardian of the national ethos. The behavioural implication of this close identification with the community, on the other hand, is hardly conducive to the primacy of individualistic or autonomous values. Devotion to the national communitarian cause took precedence over class and other sectional interests.

A second consequence of the pattern of indirect rule, particularly of that enforced during the phanariot period, was, however, somewhat disconsonant with national values. Turkish rule in general, and phanariotism in particular, were hardly conducive to the development of a Weberian-type bureaucracy. Rulers and ruled alike viewed the state as primarily an instrument for fulfilling their needs (Chirot, 1976, pp. 85-6, 99, 104-5; János, 1978, pp. 92-4, 106). If cognitive dissonance with national interests was ever produced, one may speculate, its magnitude was probably diminished to very bearable proportions by another Ottoman tradition—that which encouraged a bombastic externalization of political allegiance without expecting an accompanying internalization of values.

Both nationalism and dissimulation were also separately reinforced by values stemming from the dominant religion, although in as much as the issues of autonomy and conformity are concerned, political behaviour based in religion had further consequences. In strong contrast to other East European countries, and above all to Poland, where the Church has long constituted a potential nucleus of separate political allegiance (Szajkowski, 1983), the Romanian Church, as indeed her Eastern sisters (Golan, 1975, p. 24), has been traditionally subservient to central political authority.

Although an active and important contributor to the process of nation-building and state-building, the Church claimed neither political primacy nor parity with 'Caesar'. In the 1920s and 1930s relations between Church and state were somewhat tense, but these did not stem from ecclesiastical endeavours to assume a political role *at the expense of* local authority. Rather, claiming to embody the spiritual unity of the nation, the Orthodox Church struggled against such measures as the Concordat with the Vatican (1927), i.e. it fought the creation of potential islands of autonomy outside the jurisdiction of what was seen to be an unbreakable bond between the nation and its faith (Durandin, 1983). In 1925, under Patriach Miron Cristea, the Romanian Orthodox Church became auto-cephalous, and this only helped to increase its identification with the Romanian nation and its political institutions. The country, as a Romanian church historian proudly put it (Ursul, 1982, p. 240), became 'a full *master* of its own Church' (emphasis mine). And although Cristea was to serve as Prime Minister between February 1937 and March 1939 (Rothchild, 1979, pp. 311-13), he was obviously only a figurehead manipulated by the politicians. The Romanian Orthodox Church, Rădulescu-Motru wrote, 'let itself be dominated by the interests of the state. Her great glorious title has always been to have served . . . the Romanian nation' (Rădulescu-Motro, 1936, p. 130). Similarly, Nichifor Crainic, a leading right-wing poet, stressed in 1944 that the Orthodox faith in Romania never had, and never could have, politics separate from those of the state (Micu, 1975, pp. 226-7).

Church ritual, with its emphasis on ceremony and externalization, may have contributed in yet another sense to outward political conformity, for, if declarative displays were not often accompanied by equivalent behaviour in the Ottoman-influenced states, neither were they really expected to be so by Byzantine pomp. At the turn of the century Rădulescu-Motru noted that the Eastern churches place more emphasis on ritual than those in the West, a point later emphasized by A. Harnak (Rădulescu-Motru, 1904, p. 107: Jowitt, 1974a, p. 1185). The ethnologist D. Drăghicescu remarked in 1907 that the intellectual, 'metaphysical aspect of Christianity' was unknown to the local peasant, for whom 'the cornerstone of religious practice rests in the cult of the ritual, that is to say, the fulfilment of all forms and formulations' (quoted in Ornea, 1980, pp. 431-2). Moreover, as Rădulescu-Motru observes, it is the community, not the individual, which is central in Eastern church rites, again a factor hardly conducive to autonomy.

Neither mores nor social development, consequently, were fertile to the growth of group or personal autonomy among pre-communist Romania's ethnic majority. Territorial autonomy only became a relevant issue in the wake of the First World War. Immediately following the establishment of 'Greater Romania', the newly-acquired provinces of Transylvania, Bessarabia and Bukovina were to be granted autonomous status, reflecting their specific character. Nevertheless, the autonomous Ruling Council of Transylvania, and the quasi-autonomous administrative directorates of Bessarabia and Bukovina, lasted less than two years. In April 1920 General Alexandru Averescu, the Romanian Prime Minister, simply issued a decree dissolving all three bodies, and although a few politicians in the provinces resigned in protest, they were soon co-opted by the centre, and the issue was closed and forgotten (Roberts, 1969, pp. 33-7; Shapiro, 1981, p. 24).

The arrangement initially envisaged for territorial autonomy, it should be noted, was not intended to solve the problem of national minorities, the proportion of which was high in all three territories. Yet it is precisely among this population that state-society relations were differently conceived, due to historical development and specificity. To be more precise, whereas most of 'Greater Romania's' ethnic minorities residing in Bessarabia shared with the majority the consequences of underdevelopment and of an authoritarian system of government, the Hungarian population of Transylvania and the German population residing in that province and in Bukovina benefited from a long tradition of self-rule and institutions created for this purpose, as well as from a higher level of social mobility and economic development.

The so-called 'Union of Three Nations' (*Unio trium nationum Transsylvaniæ*), concluded in 1437 and reaffirmed in 1542, had established domination of the Hungarian, Szekler and Saxon nobles over the province, at the expense of their own, as well as the Romanian serf peasantry. As such, the pact, which remained the basis for state administration for many centuries, should neither be regarded as reflecting 'nationalities' in the modern sense of the word, nor as being in any way democratic. Yet each in its own way, the Hungarian and German populations eventually managed to establish representative institutions and a considerable measure of self-government. This was reinforced by the recognition of religious diversity in Transylvania—once more at the expense of the Romanians—for after the Reformation, the churches of the three dominant nations were officially recognized. The Hungarians are Roman Catholic, Reformed (Calvinist) and Unitarian, with a small group belonging to the Lutheran Church, while the Germans are Lutheran and Roman Catholic. These divisions sometimes—but not always—reflect separation into ethnographically and historically distinguishable groups. The German Saxons, for instance, are Lutherans whose ancestors first came to Transylvania in the twelfth century, at the invitation of the Hungarian King Géza II; the German Swabians, on the other hand, only immigrated in the eighteenth century, and by and large are Roman Catholic. The Szeklers speak a slightly different dialect—one regarded in Budapest as the purest and most attractive form of Hungarian—and most of them belong to the Calvinist or Unitarian churches. Settled in the bend of the Carpathian mountains by Hungary's kings to protect the eastern border, they enjoyed a certain measure of autonomy and were not serfs. Another group of ethnic Hungarians are the (mostly Roman Catholic) Csángós, but they migrated from Transylvania in the twelfth or thirteenth century, settling in Moldavia and Bukovina, and had to cope with a rather different socio-political environment (Schöpflin, 1978, pp. 6-7, Illyés, 1982, pp. 10-14).

Autonomous Saxon tradition[7] encompasses, above all, group distinction. Individual autonomy was less cherished as a virtue and to the extent that it emerged, it was more the outcome of the modernization process than of encouragement by the established code. The latter, on the contrary, provided for an intricate set of rules aimed at the conservation of group solidarity, if need be at the expense of individual affirmation—the *Zusammenhalten*. In 1224 the Hungarian King Endre II granted territorial, political and religious autonomy to the Saxons and in 1486 Matthias Corvinus extended these privileges, establishing the basis for the so-called 'University of the Saxon Nation' (*Sächsische Nation-universität*), a collective representative body. The 'University' extended its authority over the administration of justice, management of the economy and the enunciation of internal regulations. It elected a *Graf*, who represented the community in Parliament. The *Graf* was supported by a Saxon Assembly (*Sachsentag*), in an advisory as well as executive capacity (McArthur, 1976, p. 351; Illyés, 1982, p. 13). The Saxons consciously copied German institutions and sent their children to German universities. It is highly relevant that the Reformation itself was brought to the *Sachsenboden* by a local son, Johannes Honterus, who studied at the University of Basel. The Autonomous Lutheran Church, estab-lished in the mid-sixteenth century, became the central institution around which Saxon local life revolved. It dominated society in the countryside to the extent that 'the community of the faithful and Saxon society became synonymous' (McArthur, 1976, p. 352). Of primary importance was ecclesiastical control over education, which was funded by the *Nationuniversität* and by local church taxes. Owing to these self-supporting institutions, in the nineteenth century the Saxons were in a much better position than the Romanian inhabitants of Transylvania to resist pressures for Magyarization through the educational system. In 1919, following the collapse of Austro-Hungary, the Saxon Diet voted for Transyl-vania's unification with Romania, but soon after this the community suffered two heavy blows, one as a result of the land reform of 1921, in which the *Nation-universität* lost the majority of its property (as did other churches of the national minorities: see Illyés, 1982, p. 218), the other following a government disposition to ensure Romanian ethnics shared local government responsibility in mixed Saxon-Romanian villages. Although in the latter case traditions of separate self-government were somewhat shattered, the Saxons still retained effective control of the village due to superior economic positions and organizational experience (McArthur, 1976, p. 353).

Like the rest of their brethren, Transylvanian Hungarians had enjoyed political autonomy since the 1867 *Ausgleich*, though this hardly caused them to pursue an enlightened policy towards other minorities. As the dominant nation in the province until 1918, they should take some of the blame for the dismemberment of historical Hungary, for the policy of rapid and enforced Magyarization hardly encouraged the Romanian, Saxon and other minorities to rejoice at the prospect of a future led by Budapest. Yet, having once lost their majority status, there was, again, a not inconsiderable tradition of group, and even some limited individual, autonomy that Transylvania's Hungarians could call on in their attempt to resist encroachment in their earlier privileged status by 'Greater Romania's' rulers. The 1867 Austro-Hungarian 'compromise' facilitated the emergence of a native bourgeoisie which, unlike in the neighbouring United Romanian Principalities, could serve as a bridge between state and society. Furthermore, even before 1867 the ruling Hungarian elite had based its residual power on an authentic native institution, the county *megye* system, and a similar, if somewhat vaguer role, was played by the Diet, with the result that the local Hungarian gentry successfully resisted repeated attempts by the Habsburgs to take away its liberties. Consequently, litigiousness and legalism became a dominant feature of Hungarian political culture and tribunals, which were at least partially autonomous, contributed to the birth of individualistic, autonomous propensities (Schöpflin, 1983b). This was significantly different from the situation in the *Regat* (Moldavia and Wallachia), where politics and politicking, nepotism and clientelism, could do and undo virtually everything (see later). A further difference stemmed from attitudes related to religion, for, unlike Orthodoxy, neither Calvinism nor Roman Catholicism were readily subservient to the state and neither of the two religions could easily be turned into an instrument of the state (Schöpflin, 1983b).

Finally, there was a significant gap between Transylvania and the other provinces of 'Greater Romania', on one hand, and among nationalities living in Transylvania, on the other, in as much as modernization and urbanization had produced a different map in the population's social structure. The 1914 census in the *Regat* had returned figures showing a proportion of 14.9 per cent of the population resident in towns (Ministerul Industriei şi Comerţului, 1919, p. 15). Most of these, however, lived in settlements which cannot really be called 'urban', for their principal source of livelihood was agriculture. The proportion of urbanites in Transylvania in 1920 was not significantly different—some 14.0 per cent of the total population. Literacy, however, was far higher among Transylvanians than among the *regăţeni*. In 1910 the proportion of illiterates residing in the urban settlements of the *Regat* was 34.1 per cent, while in Transylvania it was only 21.5 per cent. Part of the explanation may lie in the national composition of Transylvanian city dwellers, for the Romanians, who were by and large less exposed to education, made up just over 25 per cent of town residents, while the Hungarians' proportion was 45.8 per cent, with 14.6 per cent added by the Germans and 14.4 per cent by other nationalities (a figure including Jews, among whom illiteracy was very rare in Transylvania). By 1930, the proportion of illiterates in *Regat* towns stood at one quarter of the population, whereas in Transylvanian towns it was only 13.1 per cent (Illyés, 1982, pp. 55-8). Industrial development in Transylvania at the time of unification was considerably more advanced (Roberts, 1969, pp. 67-8) and though the support of the RCP in the inter-war period in the province was mainly secured by postures displayed towards the 'national question', some of it may have reflected a higher degree of class consciousness (King, 1980, p. 33).

The Village and the Larger Village:
Peasants and Workers in Ceauşescu's Romania

As can be observed from Tables 3 and 4 (Chapter 5), the industrialization drive pursued by the Romanian regime generated extensive social change. Whereas in 1950 over 75 per cent of the population were employed in agriculture, in 1981 the proportion of the labour force in this sector had decreased to less than 30 per cent. In 1948 more than three-quarters of all Romanian citizens lived in rural settlements, whereas by 1981 their proportion of the population had dropped to less than half. This is still very high, even by East European standards (Johnson, 1981, p. 31), yet there is no doubt that Romanian society undergoes significant shifts in patterns of social mobility. Illiteracy has declined, having disappeared in all but the oldest age groups (Gilberg, 1975), compulsory education has been extended to ten years and the number of students at tertiary level rose from under 72,000 in the academic year 1960-1 to almost 191,000 in 1981-2 (Republica Socialistă România. Direcţia Centrală de Statistică, 1982, p. 291). These developments had a considerable impact on the structure of both town and village, but increased social mobility did not necessarily generate immediate shifts in mentality. Conformity, passivity and deference to authority, while contradicting some of the modernizing objectives pursued by the regime, are none the less functional in that they encompass a web of attitudinal variables congruent with party domination of society. The *mămăligă*, as Sampson colourfully put it in a paper delivered at a conference in Avignon in 1983, does not explode (Sampson, 1984).

But why? Persuaded that 'social passivity requires a more complex explanation' than what he calls 'the Balkan mentality theses', Sampson builds his explanation around the concept of 'muddling through'. However, on closer examination, this proves to be self-contradictory as an alternative explanatory tool, to contradict some of his own well-made observations and, what may be worse, to defy everyday reality—surely the worst possible combination for any social scientist, but particularly for an anthropologist. Indeed, his insistence on the second economy and its corrupting but 'functional' role, on patronage and 'connections' (the RCP is said to stand for *'pile, cunoştinţe şi relaţii'*), on dissimulation (*dedublare*), etc., are hardly more than *part and parcel* of the 'Balkan mentality thesis', described by Sampson himself as 'a mentality denoted by *passivity, skepticism of public organizations, stress on individual solutions and strong links to the family'* (Sampson, 1984; emphasis mine). His affirmation that although Romania faces a food shortage, everyone's refrigerator is stuffed because of 'getting by' (muddling through), on the other hand, raised more than one eyebrow among participants from Romania, when his paper was presented at Avignon.[8]

So why doesn't the *mămăligă* explode? To paraphrase Sampson, the question begs a complex answer. First, social mobility is not necessarily—at least not immediately—conducive to destabilization. On the contrary, as Bialer remarks, mobility from rural to urban occupations and from unskilled to skilled labour is one that requires the least investment from the state, yet for those involved it signifies a considerable improvement in living standards (Bialer, 1980, p. 156). The Romanian urban worker may live miserably in comparison with his Hungarian, not to mention West German, homologue, but unless he is a member of one of the national minorities, with family ties in Hungary or the FRG, his frame of reference is neither Budapest nor the Ruhrland, but his native village.[9] In the early 1980s over 60 per cent of the urban workforce was made up of individuals born and raised in the countryside (Cole, 1981, p. 75). This puts the country in a very different category from that of the industrially more developed East European states where, as Walter D. Connor demonstrates, the frame of reference of second- and third-generation workers is urban and proletarian, resulting in an ever-increasing tendency to urge the regime to liquidate the debts of the 'deferred costs of success' (Connor, 1977). By 1980-81 both workers and peasants spent a larger proportion of their budget on food than their counterparts anywhere in the CMEA countries (including Poland!), but whereas a villager had to allocate nearly 63 per cent of his income to feed his household, a worker's family spent 'only' 45.6-46.8 per cent of its earnings on food (Jackson, 1983, p. 53; Republica Socialistă România. Direcţia Centrală de Statistică, 1982, p. 51). Wage differentials between the agricultural and the non-agricultural sector, although showing an indication of diminishing, are still substantial. In 1965 the current income earned in peasant agriculture (co-operative and private) was only half of the current average income. Owing to incentives introduced in the 1970s, including the granting of minimum incomes (see Chapter 8), peasant family incomes rose to 60-65 per cent of incomes in current prices. In 1979 the average net income of the active co-operative peasant stood at 66 per cent of the average net industrial wage, and by 1982 the ratio had significantly improved to 73 per cent (Jackson, 1977, pp. 394-6, 1980, pp. 256-7, 1983, p. 62).

Whatever the significance of such an improvement, differences in remuneration remain sustantial and, what is more, due consideration should be given to the low status associated with agricultural work, to differences in social benefits such as pensions and child allowances, and to the considerably improved educational opportunities that families benefit from in urban areas. Each of these elements, while helping to encourage migration to towns, diminishes levels of expectancy. The net result is that Romania's largely first generational proletariat has a low level of class awareness. As Sampson himself pointed out in his associated paper (Nørgaard & Sampson, 1982), 'the objective possibility for the emerging of class consciousness and political action is strengthened at the point where social mobility *slows down*' (emphasis mine). Comparative data produced by the two researchers from Denmark, based on Connor and on Soviet sources, clearly indicate that Romanian workers registered the highest proportion of provenance from peasant fathers, and the lowest proportion of worker-father origins in Eastern Europe—with the possible exceptions of Albania and of Yugoslavia, for which no estimates were provided.[10]

In the light of these findings, a second hypothesis for the 'state of the *mămăligă*' should perhaps be advanced. Daniel N. Nelson's research on the 'workers' councils', based on Romanian surveys, indicates that workers' perception of their bodies of 'self-management' are generally negative, but, perhaps more significantly, their attitude towards the entire mechanism seems to be dominated by hostile passivity, strongly reminiscent of peasant attitudes to inimical environments (Nelson, 1981b, p. 460). Low levels of expectancy, a sense of 'conviction of impotence', and, in general, 'apoliticality' are not necessarily new orientations in Romanian society, and it is probably not coincidental that similar values and attitudes were discerned in Soviet populations (Connor, 1975), with whom the Romanians share both the inheritance of a 'peasant society' and a heavily political environment. Conformity and/or deference to authority are states of mind congruent with the mind of the (communist) state.

In this connection, data provided by Tables 3 and 4 make intriguing reading. In 1981, out of nearly 50 per cent of the countryside dwellers, only 29.3 per cent were employed in agriculture and forestry. This means that an important proportion of the Romanian workforce is made up of commuting workers, i.e. by people whose families live and work in villages, while they themselves commute to and fro on a daily basis. According to Nørgaard and Sampson (1982), commuting workers constitute nearly 30 per cent of Romania's urban workforce. In 1973, in Braşov county, one of Romania's most industrialized areas, some factories employed as many as half their workforce from among commuting villagers (Cole, 1976b, p. 245). Most of these commuters are poorly educated, unskilled labourers. Between 1961 and 1965 some 1.23 million people entered salaried and wage employment, most of them, presumably, in the non-agricultural sector. Close to 70 per cent of them had only elementary (4 years) education. Two-thirds of this newly recruited workforce came from rural areas (Ronnas, 1984, p. 148). What is more, official statistics may underestimate the proportion of peasants who reside in towns on a semi-temporary basis. Ronnas's doctoral thesis demonstrates that in 1977 there was a considerable discrepancy between officially published and non-official estimates of city populations (Ronnas, 1984, pp. 79-80). In the same year, local officialdom in Braşov estimated that, in addition to the twenty-five to fthousand 'temporary' residents of the town, some twenty to twenty-five thousand resided there illegally (Sampson, 1979).

The phenomenon is also known as the 'extended family household' and is apparently quite rational from an economic angle (Cole, 1976b, 1981)—or at least it was so until very recently. It involves a strategy of 'distributing members of the household so that it has income from wage labor, the co-operative farm and private agriculture'. In such families 'the husband is usually employed as worker, the wife remains at home to tend the animals, to garden, and perhaps to do some weaving, while the parents of wife and husband work for the co-operative farm. Alternatively, the wife may work on the co-operative farm, while the parents remain at home' (Cole, 1976a, p. 257). Membership of the collective is essential, for the use of private plots is conditioned by household (*not personal*) affiliation to the APC. Consequently, as Sampson incisively observed, the Romanian peasants 'do not work *for* the collective, but *on* the collective, for their household enterprise' (Sampson, 1983, p. 70; emphasis mine). According to Cole, the extended family strategy 'results in a higher standard of living than would be achieved by independent worker households, whether employed in industry or agriculture' (1981, p. 91).

The rationale of the strategy, this scholar reveals, does not simply rest in the improvement of the family's own lot, but also in the creation of an informal socio-economic network affecting even those families who took up permanent residence in towns, but who, none the less, preserved strong ties with their relatives in the countryside. 'Agricultural and craft goods produced in rural households are channelled to relatives who live in nearby towns, while consumer goods purchased with the higher salaries earned by urban workers are presented to rural relatives' (Cole, 1981, pp. 90-1). Daniel Chirot concludes, on the basis of several Romanian studies, that a 'semi-urban society, extending even into village areas', has thus been created, and that Romania has thereby succeeded in avoiding the worst problems of urbanization (Chirot, 1978, p. 477). Such a high proportion of commuting workers and of a proletariat whose life is divided between town and countryside, however, means that what Chirot calls a 'semi-urban' society in the village produces *a highly rural society in towns*. The 'frame of reference' of this group is to a very great extent the countryside, where Orthodox ritual remains very strong, and around which family reunions, feasts, and other events are celebrated (Cole, 1981, p. 91).

Building on Cole's, as well as on his own (Sampson, 1983) observations, Sampson writes that 'the most important difference in access to consumer goods is that Romanian workers have a closer connection to the countryside than the Poles. Using this connection, they can obtain necessary foodstuffs from family and friends in the villages' (Nørgaard & Sampson, 1982). The statement, however, reflects a state of affairs which has apparently diminished very much in proportion. Famished city dwellers may still be able to purchase illegally some foodstuffs in the village, but the late 1981 measures directed in part at commuting workers (see Chapter 8) undermined to a large extent the extended family's rationale . On one hand, draconian food rationalization on the basis of residence made the purchase of state-subsidized foodstuffs (such as bread or oil) by country residents a criminal offence (Colas, 1982, p. 35). On the other hand, the food and energy crises led to the revision of earlier regime policies of migration to urban centres on permanent or 'daytime residence' basis, as well as to the implicit revaluation of 'homogenization' between town and countryside through the semi-urbanization of the latter.

The 'systematization' of Romania, adopted as a comprehensive programme at the National Conference of the RCP in 1972 and passed as law in 1974 (Sampson, 1976, 1982; Ronnas, 1984, pp. 64-6), envisaged, among other things, depopulation of some less developed villages and increased housing and population densities in other rural settlements, destined eventually to become future centres of urbanization. In the early 1980s the costs of construction and heating of two-storey houses envisaged by the systematization and, above all, the necessity to cultivate large agricultural areas, led to the discontinuation of the programme in practice. The most serious problem which had to be faced as a consequence of previously encouraged policies in agriculture was that of low productivity due to deterioration in the quality of manpower. Permanent migration of youth, as well as the extended family rationale, resulted in the ageing and in the femininization of the agricultural labour force (Jackson, 1977, p. 933, 1981b, p. 254). By 1977 women made up 63 per cent of the agricultural workforce (compared with some 54 per cent in 1956 and 57.5 per cent in 1966) and the average age of men employed in this sector had risen to 43.2 years (38.2 per cent in 1956 and 40.5 per cent in 1966). Even these figures do not give the whole picture, for in the APCs, where incomes are considerably smaller than on the state farms, women made up 70 per cent of the workforce (Ronnas, 1984, pp. 58, 148).

A conference discussion published in the theoretical party monthly *Era socialistă* (No. 3, 5 February 1982) indicated that there were serious second thoughts in the RCP about the outcome of policies hitherto pursued. Most participants agreed that low incomes and low prestige had depleted much of the agricultural workforce, and that these developments, in their turn, had produced a 'negative selection of future agricultural workers', for only children who did not succeed in passing entrance examinations to other institutions would apply to study in agricultural schools. Moreover, only half of those who graduated from such schools went to work in villages after graduation, and less than 15 per cent of these would still be working in agricultural units two or three years later.

Measures taken by the party to remedy this situation in the early 1980s were typically mobilizational. They included a decision of the PEC requiring most of the students who graduated from the eighth grade in rural schools to attend high school (especially agricultural and vocational) in their own area (*Scînteia*, 1 June 1982), in an attempt to stop rural migration, as well as a decision forcing commuting administrative personnel employed in a supervisory capacity to move to the locality of their work (*Buletinul oficial*, 2 December 1981). The decree issued by the Council of State on 24 January 1982 stated that even the retired and the young would be obliged to help in agricultural work. In the course of the same month, and in August 1982, Ceauşescu stated categorically that in agricultural peak seasons, everyone in the village, including children from the age of ten, would be required to participate in the effort. Schools must close down, if need be, to allow the pupils to weed the fields 'as was customary to do it before [the advent of socialism!]' and, where 'there is a factory in the village, it should also close down for a few days, unless the fire must be kept going non-stop' (Ceauşescu, 1970-83, Vol. 23, pp. 239-40; *Scînteia*, 21 August 1982). Apart from the virtual enserfment of the peasantry, provided for in the Council of State's dispositions concerning the transfer of labour from unit to unit and from county to county (see Chapter 8), it was decided in early 1982 that at least 60-65 per cent of the total population connected with each APC should work in the co-operative (Jackson, 1983, p. 60). Once more, this destroyed the economic rationale of the extended family. Consequently, for first-generation urbanites bonds with the village lost much of the *economic* value attributed to them by Nørgaard and Sampson in their elucidation of the absence of restlessness among Romania's working class. What remains as valid as before, on the other hand, is the sociological explanation attributing this absence to the inherent weakness of autonomous propensities among Romania's urban and rural proletariat, and to low levels of expectancy.

The Intelligentsia: Dissimulation, Co-optation and Nationalism

A rural frame of reference can only partially account for the quiescence of Romanian society, for conformity is even more pronounced among the intelligentsia. This attitude towards power is to be accounted for by several, mutually reinforcing, explanations. As we turn to this category, it is essential to distinguish between the technical and the creative intelligentsia, for quiescence and acquiescence, though outwardly similar for both sub-categories, are probably differently induced. In so far as the former is concerned, social mobility might play a role similar, if not identical, to that which it fulfils in the case of peasants and workers, resulting in a similar, if not identical, relative low level of expectancy. By 1974, over 63 per cent of estimated non-manual workers in Romania were sons of workers and peasants (Connor, 1979, p. 128). It must be assumed that most of these were either 'functionaries' or belonged to the technical intelligentsia, whose mobility on the social ladder had been promoted by the industrialization process. This assumption is validated by official statistics on the number of university graduates by field of specialization. These indicate a clear trend of growth in the proportion of graduates in technical or related professions (see Table 17).

In the 'extensive' phase of development in which Romania still partly finds herself, divergences between the technical intelligentsia and the party are usually 'issue' rather than 'system' conflicts,[11] i.e. both are driven by the common ethos of producing more and better, with disagreements arising over *the means* most likely to facilitate these common aims. This does not imply, on the other hand, that conflicts between 'red' and 'expert' cannot become systemic, as the example of Czechoslovakia in the 1960s amply demonstrated. 'Narrow professionalism', as Chapter 6 indicates, is perceived by the Romanian leadership as a potentially threatening quality. However, it should be kept in mind that the technical intelligentsia in Romania faces a different set of problems to those faced by its Czech and Slovak counterparts in their attempt to bring about reforms suitable to 'intensive' development (Golan, 1971, pp. 50-8); it also faces a leadership which, for the time being, is not divided by serious intra-party factionalism. Moreover, it is probably to this category of intellectuals (though not solely to it) that Nørgaard and Sampson's

Table 17   University Graduates by Field of Specialization, 1960/1-1980/1*

	1960/1 %	1965/6 %	1970/1 %	1975/6 %	1980/1 %
Technical	39.9	35.6	36.1	47.7	58.5
Medicine-pharmacy	17.4	6.5	5.4	6.4	9.8
Economics	9.3	5.6	15.2	13.3	12.3
Jurisprudence	8.6	2.4	3.7	4.2	3.2
Biology, geology, geography	3.3	4.2	2.5	2.2	1.5
Chemistry	1.8	1.8	1.6	1.6	0.9
Mathematics-physics	3.2	3.4	3.1	5.5	3.6
Pedagogy	2.6	29.1	19.5	7.0	1.5
Humanities[†]	10.8	9.0	10.3	9.4	5.8
Arts	2.4	1.8	1.9	2.2	2.2

* Figures add up to less than 100 per cent because of calculation of first fraction only.
† Including philology, history and philosophy.
Source: Calculations from Republica Socialistă România. Direcţia Centrală de Statistică, 1982, pp. 293-4.

reference to the acceptance of industrialization as a party-directed, national, patriotic goal, is particularly applicable.

Conformism among the creative intelligentsia is altogether a different story. Although late nineteenth- and early twentieth-century 'traditionalist' currents advocated a return to village values as focuses of national identity, the Romanian creative intelligentsia at best adopted paternalistic attitudes towards the peasantry. Those who became its advocates did so less out of social identification than as part of the effort to mould the traits of 'national specificity'. The creative intelligentsia's conformist behaviour under the communist regime can consequently hardly be accounted for by rural frames of reference, even if the Romanian intellectuals of the inter-war period became to some extent subject to feedback from values they had been popularizing for several decades. Nor can intellectual conformism be attributed to an affinity with first-generation proletarian passivity. In listing their explanations for the absence of a mass protest movement, Nørgaard and Sampson (1982) quite accurately emphasize that in Romania, unlike Poland, there seems to be mutual suspicion (verging on hostility) between the intellectuals and the working class. Precisely because the creative intelligentsia perceives the social mobility of peasants and workers as being induced by the regime at its own expense, traditional cleavages have been widened instead of narrowed. Even those who climb the social ladder perceive the process in terms of *divorcing* themselves from their former social affiliation, rather than bridging the classes. They tend to look upon their less successful peers with scorn rather than compassion. I have often encountered complaints (including some uttered by intellectuals of rather recent vintage) concerning the (perceived) preferential salaries, housing or educational opportunities extended to 'the first generation in shoes'. Anti-intellectual postures adopted by the regime in matters such as freedom of expression and creativity, on the other hand, do not immediately alienate the working class, thus intensifying intellectual introversion. Consequently, a KOR-like strategy is very unlikely to emerge in the near future, Paul Goma's 1977 attempt (see later) notwithstanding.

Explanations for the creative intelligentsia's compliant attitude towards the RCP must therefore be sought elsewhere than in the deferred impact of a peasant society. Romanian emigré sources (Dumitriu, 1962, p. 75; Haupt, 1968, p. 684) suggest, as one possible explanation, the scarcity of communist intellectuals in pre-war Romania. Not without relevance, these sources point out that in Hungary, Poland and Czechoslovakia the leaders of intellectual dissent, known for their left-wing inclinations, could subsequently argue with the regime on Marxist lines. Indeed, in Chapter 6 it has been observed that a necessary, though not a sufficient, condition for inducing a process of political change in Eastern Europe is the presence of an intellectual 'revisionist' element, capable of formulating demands in an 'elite penetrative' jargon. The mass of Romania's creative intelligentsia, on the other hand, found itself in precisely the opposite position, for on the immediate instatement of the new regime, many philosophers, artists and writers could be (and were) blackmailed into collaboration by threats to 'reveal' their past.[12] Paradoxically, such figures were seen by the country's new rulers as more 'functional' to their purposes than the few intellectuals of left-wing inclinations, such as the poet Miron Radu Paraschivescu. Banished to oblivion by the RCP,[13] Paraschivescu, who had once left the party in protest against the Ribbentrop-Molotov pact, later took the role of father figure for a new generation of writers who, he hoped, would not give in to compromise. Most of his colleagues, on the other hand, were too stained by past nationalist and anti-communist positions to have any choice but compromise and collaboration, or to fade into oblivion and even face imprisonment.

An additional factor in the inducement of quiescence, valid throughout communist rule in Romania, is to be found in the long-entrenched Ottoman tradition of dissimulation and in the similarly imported, but deep-rooted, traditions of corruption, nepotism and bribery. A classic Romanian novel by Mateiu Caragiale (1885-1936), describing the atmosphere of such Turkish delights, bore the motto '*Que voulez-vous, nous sommes ici aux portes de l'Orient*' (Caragiale, 1970). The phrase had been coined by Raymond Poincaré, the future French president, who appeared as defence council in one of the more famous corruption trials in Bucharest. Before Romania decided to join the Triple Alliance in 1916, diplomats of the two opposing camps in Bucharest were competing to bribe newspapers for, as the Russian ambassador remarked in a dispatch to St. Petersburg, 'representatives of the local press are accustomed to receiving gratuities and . . . do not . . . work for nothing' (quoted in Conte, 1975,

Vol. 1, p. 131). By the early twentieth century Rădulescu-Motru remarked sarcastically:

Justice! Public institutions! . . . 'Do you have *somebody* at the Court of Justice?' 'Do you have *somebody* at the prefecture?' This eternal somebody! He does and undoes all and everything! This *somebody* may sanctify your scientist and even artist. He has his own newspaper, where his scribes might bark at you or glorify you. He has his own [literary] circle and his own Academy. This is how one becomes a scientist or an artist.

'The poet's odyssey', he added, 'will be a sad one', but not if he is ready to 'sing the politician's glory'. Although 'a beaten path', such willingness was sure remedy, leading straight to 'triumphal arches' (Rădulescu-Motru, 1904, pp. 137-8, 143. Emphasis in original).

It was a recipe that many established literary figures had little difficulty in following, once a new political elite came to power (Shafir, 1983b, pp. 401-2). The incentive to deference, dissimulation and conformity is not to be easily dismissed. Customarily employed 'positive sanctions' bestowed on the politically submissive in Eastern Europe were apparently more common in Romania than elsewhere. A group of Polish writers who visited Bucharest, Ghiţă Ionescu was told by a writer who defected in 1960, remarked to their Romanian hosts that while the Dej regime 'fed writers better, the communists in Poland allowed their writers to bark freely' (Ionescu, 1964, p. 180). In exchange for their silence, the Romanian writers were offered by the regime what Petru Dumitriu (1961, p. 786), a writer close to the highest party circles who defected to the West, called '*eine Art von komfortablem Kastratendasein*' (a sort of comfortable castrato's existence).

Under Ceauşescu, the regime pursues much the same policies. Writers suspected of having an independent mind were successfully tempted into silence or 'double talk' by being given positions of (more often than not) little political influence but substantial material affluence. Dumitru Radu Popescu, 'elected'[14] Chairman of the Writers' Union in 1981, for instance, was counted among the more courageous intellectuals, despite his membership of the Central Committee. Some of his plays were even temporarily banned after the 'mini-cultural revolution' of 1971. Since his election to the union's chairmanship he has joined the ranks of the submissive. Similarly, Marin Preda (1922-1980), author of several courageous novels,[15] became director of the 'cartea românească' publishing house, and soon after produced a novel remarkable for two reasons: it partially rehabilitated General Antonescu and his Bessarabian policies and it included a passage—totally unrelated to the plot itself—in which a young Communist brought to trial figures prominently. The only young militant prosecuted during the period covered by the novel had been—not unexpectedly—Ceauşescu himself.[16] Adrian Păunescu, to give just one more example, belongs to the new generation of writers who, in the mid-1960s, appeared to revolt against the constant compromises that had been imposed on the older generation, showing little patience or empathy for the circumstances of these compromises. The mentor of this generation was the perpetual heretic Paraschivescu, who in 1965, in a poem dedicated to his many young followers, urged them 'never betray yourselves'[17] (Paraschivescu, 1969, pp. 456-9). Păunescu was considered for a while the standard-bearer of this revolt. Eventually, however, he became the party leader's number one court troubadour and occasional personal companion. Among the pay-offs that accompanied this metamorphosis was the position of editor-in-chief of the Bucharest weekly *Flacăra*, to which he was appointed in 1973. Like most other members of his generation who pursued similar, if less successful, careers, he had quite forgotten Paraschivescu's testament. But he could march under 'triumphal arches', beating the sure path described by Rădulescu-Motru almost three-quarters of a century before.

Apart from the corrupting temptations of such incentives, traditional dissimulation probably contributes as heavily towards conformism. Tudor Arghezi's dictum 'What we smoke ain't what we talk' (quoted in Chapter 5) is said to have been uttered at a gathering of the Writers' Union, where the late Zaharia Stancu (1902-1974), a known political chameleon, was delivering a fiercely propagandist speech while chain-smoking Kent cigarettes. Nothing, a famous Romanian novelist confessed to this author, seemed more natural to him than to publish an article lavishly praising Ceauşescu's genius, in a tacit quid pro quo which substantially improved his chances of having a novel re-published ahead of schedule.

More than to any other factor, however, the quiescent attitude displayed by the Romanian creative intelligentsia is to be attributed to the nationalist line adopted by the party leadership in the early 1960s. Intellectuals were now allowed to give vent to hitherto suppressed nationalistic feelings, aimed at Romania's 'traditional enemies', the Soviet Union and Hungary, thereby channelling possible dissent and demands for reform from the domestic to the external sphere (see Chapter 5). Very few intellectuals resisted the temptation. Those who did were to become the outcasts of the regime, and, perhaps more crucial, of their own colleagues. In a book published in Paris, dissident writer Paul Goma had the following to say on the consequences of the Romanian independent foreign policy line on the intellectual community:

> I am no visionary but I see this . . . manifestation a bit in the following manner: take Peter or John, handcuff him, chain his feet as well, muzzle him, then pick up a club and tell him: 'Be independent, Peter, or ye'r dead. Be free, or I'll, I'll, . . . I don't know what I'll do if ye'r not' [Goma, 1973, p. 79].

A certain measure of limited liberalization, introduced at a time when the new Ceauşescu leadership was in need of support, began to show signs of vanishing as early as 1969 (Shafir, 1981a, pp. 357-419). Privately, these limitations were presented by the leadership as imposed by a desire to avoid the fate of Czechoslovakia. It was a cunning argument, since a considerable part of the creative intelligentsia rates national interest above any other, its self-perception remaining primarily that of 'defender of the nation'.

When the 'Eastern menace' does not appear to be imminent there is always the alternative of calling attention to the 'threat' from the West, i.e., the Transylvanian problem. Such regime-encouraged postures of 'defender of the nation' may trigger cognitive dissonance even among less conformist elements of the intelligentsia, thus serving to drive a wedge between ethnic Romanians and that permanent element of potential dissent which is the Hungarian intellectual community (see later). Romanian workers, Nørgaard and Sampson write (1982), are fragmented by nationality, and most ethnic Romanians would find it difficult to join any movement with anti-national overtones. The same applies to the intellectuals—but even more so. Conscious of this diversion, Ceauşescu's regime dos not discourage the publication of works with an obviously anti-Hungarian flavour. The opposite may be closer to the truth, particularly at times of internal stress.

An obvious case in point was offered by Ion Lăncrănjan, a writer belonging to the 'neo-traditionalist' school. His collection of essays *Cuvînt despre Transilvania* (*Discourse on Transylvania*) had fifty thousand copies printed, an unusually large circulation in view of official claims that Romania was facing a paper shortage. The book was full of invectives directed not only at what the author perceived as official Hungarian revisionist pronouncements on the injustice of the Trianon Treaty (among which he counted declarations by János Kádár),[18] but also at fellow writers of Hungarian origin, residents of Transylvania.

Moreover, with what must have struck a responsive chord even among Lăncrănjan's many personal adversaries, he did not forget to remind his readers that pro-Soviet postures had been pursued by the RCP at a time when ethnic Hungarians had figured prominently in the leadership, and even went as far as to claim that during the Stalinist purges Romanians had been subjected to harsher persecution than ethnic Hungarians, owing to the prominence of the latter in the security *apparatus*. In other words, in Stalinist Romania, the Hungarians had enjoyed preferential status (Lăncrănjan, 1982, pp. 174-5). To be sure, the book did little but repeat many of the arguments of official historiography, and, above all, the line on Romanian continuity in Transylvania.[19] However, it was the *tone* of the book that could not but draw attention, making it scandalously controversial—to be identified with or rejected. Among the many reviews published in the Romanian-language daily and literary press, not one was critical of Lăncrănjan.

The *Discourse*'s author can by no means be regarded as a dissident. His apparently courageous novels belong to a category of post-1965 literary products that should be qualified as 'police licensed', 'functional' criticism. The formula allows for the denunciation of mistakes made in the Dejist period, particularly in so far as emulation of the non-national, Soviet model is concerned, provided such literary effort reflects optimism in the party's ability to overcome the mistakes of the past. Lăncrănjan, however, has specialized in emphasizing the foreign origin of Romania's 'wrongdoers', whether Jews (Shafir, 1983a, pp. 230-2) or Hungarians. As I have demonstrated elsewhere (Shafir, 1983a, pp. 238-41), the 'neo-traditionalist' group, of which Lăncrănjan is a prominent member, enjoys the protection of the highest party levels. Its 'point of access to power' is as close to the apex of the pyramid as Mrs Ceauşescu and her ministerial son. Remarkably, a book written in 1983 by the President's brother, Ilie, entitled *Transylvania: Ancient Romanian Land*, employs language which is almost as offensive towards the Hungarian minority as Lăncrănjan's. In November 1983 excerpts from this book were published in the journal of the Young Communists' League, *Scînteia tineretului*, which is Nicu Ceauşescu's official mouthpiece. Whether officially inspired or not, the *Discourse* came at a most opportune moment, for once more, the regime could count on diverting attention from growing domestic discontent. Viewed from this angle, the protest published by intellectuals of Hungarian origin in the *samizdat* journal *Ellenpotok*, asking the Central Committee of the RCP to condemn Lăncrănjan's work (Reisch and Pataki, 1982), was, at best, naïve.

Most Romanian intellectuals would not risk the satisfaction of expressing their deep suspicion of Moscow and Budapest, under a leadership that does its utmost to exploit this safety-valve to its own ends. 'We have become so preoccupied with the danger of Soviet occupation', rebel writer Dumitru Ţepeneag declared at a meeting in 1968, 'that for all practical purposes, we have pre-occupied ourselves' (author's interview with Ţepeneag, Paris, 1973). In a similar manner, in his 1977 letter of support, addressed to the signatories of Charter '77, Goma wrote that the Romanians lived 'under Romanian occupation—ultimately more painful, more efficient than a foreign one' (*Dossier Paul Goma*, 1977, p. 88). It is doubtful whether the pain is widely shared. The Romanian creative intelligentsia may share with other East European intellectuals, such as the Poles, the sense of being a 'respository' of national values. Lacking, however, the Poles' traditional *szlachta* mentality, they are prone to acquiesce in the negation of an autonomy, which—throughout history—they had seldom enjoyed anyhow.

The Churches: Conformism as Credo and as Calvary

Relations between the state and the churches in communist Romania[20] do not easily lend themselves to analysis. They imply an intricate web, involving: systemic negation of autonomy in general, and of religious faith as a possible form of individual counter-identification in particular; the long-entrenched tradition of obedience to power, embodied by the institutionalized patronage of the dominant Church, which affects other denominations as well; and problems arising from the division of cults along national lines.

As early as August 1948 measures aimed at dismantling the foundations of church autonomy were enacted by the new regime. The Law of Cults subordinated the churches to a detailed control by the state. Among other things, it provided for complete state control of ecclesiastical administrative, financial and economic institutions, placing supervision of church affairs in the hands of the Mnistry of Religious Affairs, and restricting church activities to liturgical and pastoral concerns. This ministry was eventually abolished and replaced by a Department of Cults, which is subordinate to the Council of Ministers.

Already by 1948 the Law of Cults stipulated that all envisaged activities and functions of the churches had first to be endorsed by the Praesidium of the GNA. Legal recognition was extended to fourteen religious communities—as opposed to some sixty state-recognized cults under the previous regime. Yet even these were to regard recognition as contingent upon submission to the will of the state, for Article 13 of the law indicated that church activity could be revoked at any time 'in cases where this was justified'. The first Constitution of the Romanian People's Republic (April 1948) had virtually abolished confessional general schools, and the educational reform of 3 August 1948 (Deligiannis, 1971, pp. 85-9) abolished all private schools and religious teaching in the curriculum. Article 35 of the new educational law provided for the transfer of all ecclesiastical and private schools to the state system. Hand in hand with this measure, the property of the churches was expropriated without compensation.

While these measures affected all denominations, they were a particularly heavy blow to those cults identified with the national minorities. For centuries, self-management of community affairs has been founded on the ecclesiastical school system, particularly in so far as the German minority was concerned. Although the *Sächsische Nationuniversität* had already been abolished in 1937 (Illyés, 1982, p. 93), the self-supporting German confessional school system had survived intact. As for the Hungarian community, the role of its churches in the promotion and defence of autonomy became very important after Transylvania's unification with Romania in 1918.

The Romanian Orthodox Church is by far the major denomination in the country. There are no official statistics of church affiliation, but Western estimates ('Eastern Europe: Toward a "Religious Revival"?', 1984) indicate that roughly sixteen million people, or 70 per cent of the population, belong to it. Although the Orthodox Church took its toll when there was persecution of all creeds in the transformation period (Ionescu, 1964, p. 195), under Dej relations between the country's communist leadership and the Orthodox Church were somewhat ambivalent. On one hand, atheism was widely propagated, and church attendance discouraged. On the other hand, the regime made an obvious, if not overt, distinction between the Orthodox Church, which was viewed as loyal to the nation, and other sects, whose allegiance to the Romanian entity was, in its eyes, questionable. While the People's Republic Constitution of 1948 abolished the status of 'dominant' Church conferred on Orthodoxy by the 1923 Constitution, the Orthodox Church fared far better than did other denominations. This was due to a great extent to Patriarch Justinian Marina (1901-77), whose accession to office in 1948 is said to have been facilitated considerably by the fact that he had hidden Gheorghiu-Dej in his house during the period of illegality. Patriarch Justinian adopted a declared policy of 'double fidelity' (*Biserica Ortodoxă Română*, Nos 7-8, 1970, pp. 649-52), which was criticized by his opponents abroad, who accused him of being a 'red priest'. His supporters, on the other hand, claim that his leadership and the tactics of accommodation which he pursued, saved the Church from widespread persecution. On his death in 1977 he was succeeded by Patriarch Justin Moisescu, who is believed to be even closer to the RCP than his predecessor.

Under the new Patriarch ecclesiastical submission to state authority has reached new dimensions. 'Consistently passive in the face of the regime's attacks on the most basic religious values and religious rights', a survey on the churches in Eastern Europe published in 1984 by Radio Free Europe, indicates, 'the Orthodox hierarchy in Bucharest insists against all evidence that it functions under conditions of religious freedom' ('Eastern Europe: Toward a "Religious Revival"?', 1984). Although several historical places of worship, such as the Voroneţ Monastery, are known to be rapidly deteriorating, the Orthodox Church's officialdom does not break its silence. It is common knowledge in Romania that Voroneţ is a case of personal vendetta, conducted by Mrs Ceauşescu in retaliation for having been ignored by the nuns, who did not interrupt prayers upon her arrival for a visit to the convent. However, other monasteries and churches are also known to be in poor condition, and some historical religious sites in Bucharest and elsewhere have been demolished in recent years.

Even more incomprehensible is the Orthodox Church's repeated collaboration with the authorities in silencing those priests who spoke up against these, or similar, policies. A secret report on the consequences of such submission was smuggled to the West in 1979 (Stolojan, 1981, p. 16). The most notorious instance is that of Father Gheorghe Calciu Dumitreasa, whose sermons denouncing atheism (Calciu, 1979) were very popular with the younger generation, which triggered his expulsion from the theological seminary of Bucharest in 1978. The measures which the authorities took against him were simply endorsed by the patriarchy (Ligue pour la défense des Droits de l'Homme en Roumanie, 1981b), and his subsequent sentencing to ten years in prison is not known to have been protested either.[21]

The contrast with the Catholic Church in Poland could not be greater. Traditional submission, increased by the threat of sanctions, makes the dominant church in Romania a tool in the hands of the authorities, and by no stretch of the imagination can the Romanian Orthodox Church be envisaged as fulfilling a central role in the emergence of trends in societal autonomy.

Within the framework of the nationalist campaign, on the other hand, the Orthodox Church has been used by the authorities both as an instrument for recruiting popular support, and as one aimed at propagating a 'liberal' image in the West. In 1966 Ceauşescu visited the Putna Monastery, which was then celebrating 500 years in existence, and in 1967 the entire press carried detailed descriptions of similar festivities at the Curtea de Argeş Monastery. Representatives of the Orthodox (and of the Evangelical) Church participated in international ecumenical conferences in the 1960s and, in 1979, when Romania's MFN status appeared to be endangered by her internal policies, some high-ranking inter-denominational figures (including Chief Rabbi Moses Rosen) were hurriedly dispatched to the United States. In a similar manner, a Moslem delegation of ecclesiastics was sent to Iran in 1979, in an attempt to persuade Khomeini to allow petroleum deliveries under terms guaranteed by the Shah.

Collaboration between the regime and the Romanian Orthodox Church has extended over the issue of the Uniate Church as well. The Uniates (known also as

Greek Catholics or as members of the Catholic Church of the Byzantine Rite), broke away from the Orthodox Church by a union with Rome in the late seventeenth and early eighteenth century. In what was more a political than a religious act, the Uniates hoped to achieve for the Transylvanian Romanian community the status of a 'privileged' instead of merely 'tolerated' religion, and thereby bring about the abolition of serfdom for their brethren. They acknowledged Papal authority but were allowed to keep the Orthodox ritual, canon and calendar (Georgescu, 1984, pp. 53-4). The Uniates played a very prominent part in asserting their co-nationals' political rights in the province. In recognition of this historical role, the Constitution of 1923 specified that the Uniate Church, together with the Orthodox Church, constituted the 'national church'.

By 1948 this denomination counted some 1,700,000 members ('Eastern Europe: Towards a "Religious Revival"?', 1984). Subservient to Stalin's directives, the rulers of the People's Republic emulated the Soviet Ukrainian policies of persecution of the Uniates (Stolojan, 1981, p. 17), just as the leadership of the Communist Party of Czechoslovakia proceeded to do in Ruthenia (Ulč, 1974, pp. 13, 123-4). However, the ordeal of the Uniate Church cannot be attributed to immediacy alone. Friction between the two 'national churches' had been substantial in inter-war Romania (Durandin, 1983). Soon after the coup of August 1944 the Orthodox Metropolitan of Sibiu, Nicolae Bălan, wrote to his Leningrad homologue, Alexie, that the weakness of the Romanian nation was the outcome of the schism which had occurred in the Orthodox Church in the early eighteenth century (G. C., 1982). A tacit agreement with the authorities brought about the forced unification of the Romanian Uniate Church with the Orthodox Church in December 1948.

In what must have been an unusual appeal, coming as it did from an atheist government, the Council of Ministers in September 1948 called on adherents of the Uniate Church to convert to Orthodoxy. This was followed by massive arrests of Uniate clergy and the faithful. One thousand four hundred priests and some five thousand believers were sent to prison during the persecutions. Two hundred at least were simply assassinated while serving their term, and many others died of disease, hunger or exhaustion ('La question uniate . . .', 1983). With only one exception all the Uniate bishops died in prison. In preparation for the envisaged 'unification', the Law of Cults stipulated that in case of conversion of members of one faith to another, the property of the former was to be transferred to the latter in proportion to the number of converts, and that if 75 per cent of adherents were to switch their confessional allegiance, the entire wealth of the deserted denomination, including churches, was to pass into the hands of the newly embraced faith. The GNA Decree No. 358 of 1 December 1948 officially sanctioned the abolition of the Uniate Church.

The attitude of the regime under Ceauşescu *vis-à-vis* the Uniates shows no indication of changing. In one of the articles on Transylvania published by Ilie Ceauşescu in *Scînteia tineretului* (21 November 1983), there was praise for 'resistance to Roman Catholic pressure . . . to give up the traditional confession', homogeneity of faith being listed as one of the elements contributing to the unitary character of the Romanian inhabitants of the three historical provinces. Yet the Uniates continue a precarious existence as an 'underground Church'. Three bishops were secretly ordained by the Vatican and Iuliu Hossu, the only bishop who survived the imprisonment, was made a Cardinal *in pectore* by Pope Paul VI before his death in 1970 (R.Al. de F., 1981). In August 1977 a clandestine Committee for the Salvation of the Romanian Uniate Church addressed a letter to Ceauşescu, forwarding a copy to the Romanian representative on the UN Human Rights Commission (Moore, 1978a). The letter put the Romanian President in a somewhat embarrassing position, for it stressed the role played by the Latinist School in fostering Romanian national rights in Transylvania (see Chapter 1).

This role is highlighted in Ceauşescu's nationalistic speeches (Ceauşescu, 1968-9, Vol. 1, p. 601, 1970-83, Vol. 5, p. 109, Vol. 13, pp. 38-9), which fail, however, to mention that the leaders of the movement had been Uniate clergymen. The three bishops of the Church appealed to the Madrid follow-up meeting of the Conference on Security and Co-operation in Europe, reiterating the historical merits of Uniates and demanding the full restoration of their rights, in accordance with the provisions of the Constitution concerning freedom of worship (*Catacombes*, November-December 1980). In early 1982 Pope John Paul II publicly expressed concern over the fate of the Uniates, supporting their demands. The reaction of the Romanian Orthodox authorities was swift and unambiguous. Patriarch Justin and the Holy Synod dispatched an 'energetic reply', protesting such 'unfriendly and inconsiderate action', which was deemed to constitute 'interference in the internal affairs' of the Romanian Orthodox Church. Moreover, the Pope's public statement was said to reveal 'a hegemonical and imperialist complex' reflecting 'disregard of the history of our country's Church' (quoted in 'La question uniate . . .', 1983). Concomitantly, Patriarch Justin sent a telegram to Ceauşescu, expressing 'indignation at the attempt to reactivate the Uniate Church' and assuring the President of the 'profound respect, firm affection and total adhesion of the Romanian faithful in these troublesome hours provoked by neo-fascist circles' (*România liberă*, 14 January 1982; La question uniate . . .', 1983).

The Romanian Catholic Church[22] has some 1,200,000 followers, most of whom are either Hungarian or German Swabians. Ethnicity, together with suspicion towards 'the Pope's divisions', contributes to the mistrust manifested by the regime toward Roman Catholics, although in the late 1970s and early 1980s their situation has somewhat improved. Decree No. 358 of 1948 had abolished the Concordat and the Law of Cults forbade religious bodies and their representatives to have any connection with foreign religious communities, institutions or personalities, thus practically attempting to abolish Papal jurisdiction over Catholics in Romania. In the circumstances, the Roman Catholic authorities were unable to submit their statutes for approval, as required by law, and in retaliation the regime reduced the number of sees from five to two. By 1953, Vatican sources indicated that fifty-five priests, monks and nuns had been executed, two hundred and fifty had died or had been exiled, two hundred had been sentenced to forced labour and a similar number had been imprisoned. Among the latter were the two bishops of the surviving sees, Áron Márton and Anton Durcovici. Only Bishop Márton, a Hungarian, managed to come out alive, but he remained under house arrest until 1967. He died in 1980, being succeeded as bishop of Alba Iulia by his co-national, Mgr. Jakab Antal. The other Roman Catholic see, the archbishopric of Bucharest, was held by Mgr. Francisc Augustin, an ethnic German from Bukovina, whose appointment was never recognized by the Vatican, and who died in 1983. Like all other heads of religious denominations, Mgr. Augustin became a member of the National Council of the Front of Socialist Unity. Simulated change is a new station on the Romanian creeds' Via Dolorosa.

The bishoprics of Iaşi, Oradea-Satu Mare and Timişoara, however, were unilaterally abolished by the regime in 1949, being administered by Ordinaries since 1978 (Iaşi) and 1983 (Oradea-Satu Mare and Timişoara). The appointment of these Church officials signified an arrangement with the Vatican, with the Romanian state informally acquiescing to the Holy See nominations, in what appears to be a minor, but not insignificant, improvement in Bucharest's relations with Rome, which can be traced back to a visit paid by Ceauşescu to the Vatican in May 1973. Yet the situation of the Roman Catholic Church remains precarious, for its statutes are not legalized because of the provisions of the Law of Cults and other laws, which the Catholics cannot accept. As such, the Church is merely tolerated, existing in fact but not in law (Socor, 1983b). Celebration of the liturgy takes place under the supervision of the Department of Religious Affairs, and the appointment of bishops requires formal approval of the state. Priests, although appointed by the bishops, must also be approved by the Department of Religious Affairs.

Protestant denominations in Romania include the Reformed (Calvinist) Church, which is entirely Hungarian, with a membership of approximately 700,000 according to official figures, but 850,000 according to Western estimates; the Unitarians (Anti-Trinitarians), also a Hungarian church, for whom estimates vary between 50,000 and 75,000 (Institute of Political Sciences and of Studying the National Question, 1976, p. 23, and Illyés, 1982, pp. 231, 234, respectively); the Lutheran Church, the mass of whose followers are Transylvanian Saxons (no official figures for the number of faithful—though 166,000 according to Illyés, 1982, p. 232), but having a number of adherents among Hungarian nationals (30,000 in data provided by the Institute of Political Sciences, and 35,000 according to Illyés, 1982, p. 234); and several neo-Protestant cults, half of whose members are Hungarians, such as the Baptists (200,000), the Seventh-day Adventists (70,000), the Pentecostalists (75,000), and others (figures from Illyés, 1982, p. 234).

To the dismay of the regime, the neo-Protestant cults have been rapidly growing in numbers in recent years, with the Baptists showing particular success in proselytizing. An article published in the student weekly *Viaţa studenţească* in April 1982 indicated that the popularity of traditional religious denominations among young people was decreasing, and even established Protestant denominations were not doing too well; on the other hand, there was a significant increase in the number of recruits to legal neo-Protestant denominations, as well as to 'unauthorized religious groups' (quoted in Shafir, 1982). Such tendencies must worry the regime, for they indicate not only failure in atheist propaganda, but also an identification with those denominations not discredited by acquiescence—whether of recent or more traditional vintage. Most converts came from the Orthodox Church ('Eastern Europe: Towards a "Religious Revival"?', 1984), but some were Saxon Lutherans, most probably dissenting from their pastoral leadership's acceptance of limitations placed by the regime on the free practice of religion (Illyés, 1982, pp. 232-3).

A press campaign aimed at discrediting these cults was launched in the late 1970s and appears to be continuing (*Scînteia*, 25 April 1982, 23 May 1982 and 5 and 12 March 1983; *Scînteia tineretului*, 27 November 1982, 9 and 27 April 1983, 25 May 1983, 25 June 1983, 21 January 1984 and Bălaşa, 1984). Hand in hand with the propaganda machine, harsh measures were taken against members of the Baptist, Adventist and Pentecostalist denominations. Many were threatened with job dismissal, attempts were made to remove elected community leaders, heavy fines were imposed on congregations and the most outspoken activists were arrested and forced to emigrate ('Religion Under "Real Socialism"', 1979; Stolojan, 1981, p. 18; Ligue pour la défense des Droits de l'Homme en Roumanie, 1981a; 'Eastern Europe: Towards a "Religious Revival"?', 1984).

A strange incident involving a Romanian *émigré* who taught Transcendental Meditation under the auspices of the *securitate* at the Bucharest Education and Psychology Research Institute occurred in 1982. This former Romanian citizen was invited to teach in his country of origin and pursued his activities without problems for several years (*Le Matin*, 15 May 1982). In winter 1982, however, he was expelled, the institute was disbanded, and several prominent intellectuals and high party and state officials lost their jobs (*Le Monde*, 4 May 1982; *Le Matin*, 14 May 1982). Among these was Mrs Ceauşescu's protégé, Aneta Spornic, who was dismissed from the position of Minister of Education and Instruction. Eventually she made a comeback, in 1984, being appointed Chairwoman of the State Committee for Prices.

The Moslem community of Romania is made up of Turks and Tartars. Both groups are concentrated in the Dobruja region, and according to the 1977 census their combined number is some 41,000 (see Table 18, p. 166). As a religious community they are organized in a *muftilik*, headed by Mehmet Iacub. The Koranic seminary at Megedia was closed down by the authorities in 1967, and in 1977-8 the Islamic League complained of infringements of Moslem cultural and religious liberties (Berindei, 1980b, pp. 41-2).

Once one of the largest communities in Eastern Europe, the Jews of Romania are nowadays but a token presence. According to the 1977 census, their number was a mere 25,686 (see later), but the figure was probably slightly higher, since some respondents may have chosen to indicate Romanian nationality. In 1978 the Federation of Jewish Communities estimated a membership of some 40,000, organized in sixty-eight communities and twenty-one congregations. At present, Romania's Chief Rabbi puts the figure at 28,000 (private conversation, Tel Aviv, July 1984), of whom some two-thirds are over sixty years old (Fischer, 1983a,

p. 202). Most of those who survived the Holocaust emigrated to Israel, where there are now some 380,000 Jews of Romanian origin.

In Ceauşescu's Romania the Jews enjoy what is possibly the greatest measure of autonomy among all denominations. This is explained by several factors: first, their shrinking number, transforming the community into one of elderly introverts who pose no threat to the regime; second, the authorities' endeavour to project a positive image in the West, particularly in the USA; and, last, but not least, the personality of Chief Rabbi Moses Rosen.

Adopting a declared position of dual loyalties and serving as regime emissary in more than one 'delicate' mission abroad, Rabbi Rosen has been able to obtain concessions that are hard to imagine in places like the Soviet Union, Czechoslovakia or Poland. To be sure, there are some odd prices that must be paid. For example, the 1983-4 calendar published by the Federation lists such significant historical landmarks as Ceauşescu's birthday and the date of his election to the Presidency. On the other hand, the community is allowed to publish the four-language bi-monthly *Revista cultului mozaic* (where, typically, there are occasionally minor, but significant differences of nuance between articles published in Yiddish, Hebrew, or English and their somewhat diluted Romanian-language version), to run a chain of kosher restaurants and to extend other services to members of congregations.

The Jews of Romania were persecuted for their Zionist sympathies in the late 1940s and 1950s and emigration was stopped several times. The property of those who left the country illegally was confiscated in 1947 and in 1948, following Stalin's lead, the regime launched a public attack on Zionism. The first anti-Zionist trials began in 1949-50. Yet emigration continued until 1952, when Moscow directives, combined with the downfall of the Pauker faction and the first wave of anti-Jewish purges in the RCP, put an end to it for some six years. In 1958 Jews were once more allowed to emigrate, but soon after a further interruption occurred, with Romania's gates closing again until 1961. Ever since, and particularly after the establishment of diplomatic relations with Israel in 1967, the regime has adopted what is termed a 'humanitarian' approach to the problem of 'family reunion', although instances of difficulty occur regularly. With similar regularity, many such cases find their 'solution' on the eve of discussions in the US Congress concerning the yearly renewal of Romania's MFN status. To be sure, the authorities in Bucharest are 'helped' in adopting such 'humanitarian' postures by both the Jewish Agency and the World Jewish Congress, in what is universally acknowledged as an 'open secret'.

Yet neither such aid, certainly important at a time when Romania faces a shortage of hard currency, nor Rabbi Rosen's policies, can guarantee the safety of those Jews who do not (or cannot) leave the country. A Bucharest-enacted version of 'anti-semitism without Jews' is not entirely unfeasible, for the party-supported 'neo-traditionalist' group of Romanian intellectuals, led by writer Eugen Barbu, has attempted several times in the course of the last decade to revive anti-semitism (Shafir, 1983a). The latest (recalcitrant) 'hero' of such outbursts was the young poet Corneliu Vadim Tudor, who in 1983 even managed to include in one of his books a personal attack on Rosen, full of anti-semitic venom, alongside other poems of blatant anti-Jewish tenor (Tudor, 1983). The Chief Rabbi's demand that Tudor be put on trial fell on deaf ears, and the community was not allowed to publish in *Revista cultului mozaic* a resolution castigating the incident (Socor, 1984). The most autonomous of all religious denominations, as it turns out, is not *that* autonomous, the more so when its complaints are directed at the regime's most reliable supporters—the extreme nationalists. 'Dual loyalty', after all, may generate 'dual response'.

The National Minorities: 'Co-inhabiting' or 'Co-inhibited'?

There is hardly an issue more sensitive in Romanian politics than the problem of national minorities in general, and that of the Hungarian minority in particular. Divided as they might be over practically every other social and political aspect, supporters and opponents of the regime, including emigration, usually adopt identical positions whenever the issue of infringement of the rights of minorities is raised. Complaints of this nature are immediately equated with irredentist postures and with designs to dismember Transylvania from the body of the nation. At best, Romanian *émigré* circles would acknowledge that minorities are mistreated, but would attribute this to the plight of all Romanian citizens in the 'Multilaterally developed socialist society'. Such lack of empathy for the sensitivities of minorities, to be sure, is matched by over-sensitivity on the opposite side. Elemér Illyés's book on the national minorities in Romania (1982), for instance, employs terminology that often verges on the pathetic, while *Witness to Cultural Genocide*, a collection of documents published by the American Transylvanian Federation, might have been ill-served by its title. Only rarely (e.g. Berindei, 1980a, 1980b, respectively, Schöpflin, 1978) does one encounter a case where a 'former' Romanian or Hungarian strives to remain scientifically objective.

That national minorities share with the rest of the population the 'benefits' of simulated change is beyond argument. 'Participatory' structures aimed at diffusing grievances were set up in 1968, at a time when the leadership was troubled by the possibility that the Soviet Union might attempt to exploit dissatisfaction among the national minorities as a pretext for intervention in Romania. These structures were the Council of Workers of Hungarian, German or Serb nationality (subsequently, a similar council for the Ukrainian minorities was also established). These bodies perform their activities within the framework of the Front of Socialist Unity and Democracy, but, as with the Front itself, are nothing but pre-emptive structures, devoid of any power and influence. The councils operate under the daily supervision of the RCP's Central Committee Secretariat, and are financed from its budget (Fischer, 1977a, p. 509). The 'leading role of the party' is thereby structurally ensured, and no stretch of the imagination would define such allegedly 'representative' bodies as autonomous.

Károly Király, a former county party First Secretary, member of the CC and Vice-President of the Hungarian council, protested in 1977 and 1980, in letters addressed to prominent party officials, against the manipulation of the Council of Workers of Hungarian Nationality, pointing out that there was 'a great gap between theory and practice'. The councils, according to Király, do little else but hold occasional plenary sessions where nothing is said but praise for the regime's policies towards the national minorities. They have no headquarters, no office hours, discussions must be held in the Romanian language and are inhibited by awareness of the presence of rapporteurs, and their resolutions are mere formalities.[23]

The national minorities are subjected to the same blatant discrepancy between the *pays légal* and the *pays réel* that affects all other spheres of life in Romania. The Constitution makes generous provisions for minority facilities, as do a battery of other laws providing for minority rights (Schöpflin, 1978, p. 8). Article 22, for example, specifies that in counties populated by non-Romanian nationals, all bodies and institutions must use in speech and writing the language of the nationality concerned and should appoint officials from its ranks or from among citizens who know the way of life of the local population. On paper, these provisions are strictly respected, in so far as a façade representation of the minorities on bodies such as the GNA, CC or the local councils are concerned. Strictly proportional parliamentary representation is ensured by having Hungarian run against Hungarian or German against German in districts where multi-candidacy is allowed, and the proportion of the minorities on the CC reflects their proportion in the population, at least according to the official statistics (Fischer, 1979, p. 13, 1983a, p. 206). However, the minorities have no real influence on bodies where real policy-making is involved and even those who are supposed to represent them in other structures are hand picked by the party and mistrusted by their co-nationals. According to Király, in the mid-1970s there were no Hungarians on the party bureaux of such sizeable Magyar-populated counties as Maramureş, Arad or Timiş. The minority 'representatives', on the other hand, sometimes even refused to talk to their brethren in Hungarian, 'letting them know this way that perhaps someone prohibited them from using their mother tongue'. On the other hand, the same 'representatives' are viewed with suspicion by their Romanian comrades, who are sceptical as to their true loyalty.

Negation of the right of any genuine form of self-management, or autonomy, it can be argued, is not confined to particular attitudes *vis-à-vis* minorities. While valid, such an argument fails to take into consideration the sensitivity of national minorities everywhere when faced with policies perceived to endanger their separate identity. Trond Gilberg (1981a, pp. 199-200) quite rightly observes that the mobilization of the ethnic majority's intelligentsia to such campaigns as the 'scientific discovery' of the Geto-Dacian civilization, aimed at proving that the ancestors of the Romanian people inhabited Transylvania and Bessarabia long before Magyar or Slavic tribes arrived in those lands, is perceived by the minorities as an attempt to deny them historical rights of their own, and to lower them to the position of merely being tolerated. The Romanian regime, writes Mary Ellen Fischer, distinguishes individual equality and individual rights from group equality, and this distinction bears heavily on the issue of regime attitudes towards demands for autonomy generated from among the national minorities. Individual rights are threatened by definition, and for *all* Romanian citizens, by a party claiming the right to settle all social priorities. The threat, however, is perceived by the minorities as particularly severe, because in their eyes 'nationality rights are essentially collective rights, since the nationality is a form of communal existence' (Fischer, 1983a, pp. 192-3). An individual member of a minority group, Gilberg specifies, 'is concerned with possible individual discrimination against him, based on ethnicity', but to no lesser extent, 'if the cultural autonomy of the ethnic group to which he or she belongs is somewhat impaired . . . that individual considers such restrictions on *group autonomy* as a violation of his *individual* rights' (Gilberg, 1981a, pp. 195-6, emphasis in original). To restrict these rights, in the words of a Transylvanian Hungarian quoted by Fischer, is to deprive the nationalities of any rights.

It is precisely such collective rights, however, that the Romanian regime has strived to obliterate. For a number of years group and territorial autonomy were inseparable issues. In an attempt to find a solution for the large (at that time, over a million and a half) Hungarian minority in Transylvania, a Hungarian Autonomous Region was set up in 1952,[24] without, however, enjoying a status different to that of the country's other administrative provinces. The 1952 Constitution had provided for the establishment of a Council of State of the Autonomous Region, but the body was never set up. On the other hand, the existence of the region served as a pretext for not opening Hungarian cultural facilities in other parts of the country, although the territory included only slightly over a quarter of Hungarians living in Romania. Moreover, such partially representative collective institutions as the Hungarian People's Alliance were dissolved soon after, and many cultural facilities were withdrawn. The Autonomous Region thus had the dubious quality of satisfying no one, for what appeared to be the inadmissible existence of a 'state within a state' to the Romanian majority, was considered a Bucharest-managed ghetto by its Hungarian inhabitants.

Following some spill-over effects of the 1956 Hungarian events, the Romanians apparently convinced Moscow of the necessity to further curtail minority cultural rights. In 1959, at a meeting presided over by then CC Secretary Nicolae Ceauşescu, the Hungarian Bolyai University of Cluj was merged with the local Romanian university. The Rector of the Bolyai University, László Szabédi, subsequently committed suicide. In 1960 territorial re-organization was introduced, altering the population structure and weakening the region's Hungarian majority. The province was now re-named *Mureş* Autonomous Hungarian, thereby emphasizing its connection with the Romanian centre. The Constitution of 1965 defined Romania as a 'unitary' state, implicitly rejecting what Cesauşescu was to reject explicitly a year later: the Comintern designation of inter-war Romania as a multinational state (Ceauşescu, 1968-9, Vol. 1, pp. 360-1). The territorial reorganization of 1968, instituted as part of the RCP's endeavour to exchange derivative for

intra-systemic legitimacy, re-instituted the pre-communist territorial organization, clearing away (for whatever they were worth by now) the last vestiges of
Hungarian autonomy. The authorities had initially promised that the entire area
inhabited by the Szeklers would be united into a single *judeţ*. However, when the re-
organization was finally carried through, it turned out that the area was split into
three counties, of which one had a mixed Romanian-Hungarian population and
the remaining two were among Romania's economically weakest developed areas.

Individual rights of members of minorities, according to the Romanian view,
should be ensured through policies of equalization, as the result of industrial
modernization. According to the RCP Programme of 1974 (p. 150) 'In the phase of
edification of the multilaterally developed socialist society and the transition to
communism, hand in hand with the impetus development of production forces
over the entire territory of the country, the conditions for a full manifestation of all
citizens in social life, irrespective of nationality, for their active participation in the
leadership of society, will constantly improve'. In a speech delivered at a meeting of
the Hungarian and German nationalities' workers' councils in April 1974,
Ceauşescu stressed that in the Hungarian-inhabited counties which in 1968 were
counted among the country's least developed areas (Hargita and Covasna),
industrialization had proceeded at an intensive rate, bringing them to levels equal
to those of Romania's other regions (Ceauşescu, 1970-83, Vol. 10, p. 39). According
to Király who, as former party secretary of Covasna should be well informed, the
industrialization process which Ceauşescu mentioned may have equalized *regional*,
but not *national* differences. Regional development has been accompanied by
massive migration of workers, technicians and engineers of Romanian ethnic
origin into Hargita and Covasna, whereas ethnic Hungarians saw cities such as
Tîrgu Mureş, Cluj, Oradea or Arad virtually sealed off to them.

The evaluation of these policies is no easy matter. First, as Mary Ellen Fischer
indicates, available data can be used to support radically different conclusions. In
the absence of information concerning individual incomes by nationality, one
must resort to comparison of county statistics. However, such an approach immediately triggers a second problem, namely: is the comparison going to include the
more developed areas inhabited by the national minorities, or is it to be restricted to
the less developed counties? The conclusions may be widely different, since many
of Transylvania's most developed areas inhabited by national minorities could be
counted among the county's more developed regions. In its turn, this generates a
third, perhaps insurmountable difficulty, for evaluation of regime intentions *by the
national minorities themselves* is construed on previous patterns of political socialization and of historical experience. The party's policies of equal distribution of
production forces, according to Ceauşescu's speech of April 1974, 'are not suffi-
ciently understood' (Ceauşescu, 1970-83, Vol. 10, p. 39).

From available statistical data, analysed by Mary Ellen Fischer, it may be
concluded that the less developed areas of 'nationality counties' were not deprived
economically between 1965 and 1975. With the exception of Cluj, Bihor and Mureş
(all of which had started out well above average and could consequently be

expected to register lower growth rates), all other counties showed gross industrial production which was well above average, and most of them were above average in both investment and in per capita sales. From 1976 to 1979, on the other hand, *none* of the major Hungarian counties (Covasna, Hargita, Satu Mare, Sălaj, Cluj, Bihor and Mureş) registered above average growth. Moreover, out of the ten counties which were singled out for special efforts in economic and social development in the 1981-85 Five-Year Plan, only one (Mureş) has a substantial Hungarian population (Fischer, 1983a, pp. 208-11).

Sensitivities among national minorities, as indicated, can run particularly high and occasionally impair objectivity. Awareness of sensitivities should help those claiming to speak in the name of ethnic majorities to refrain from reinforcing traditional suspicions. It should—but it does not! A perfect case in point was provided by Ceauşescu in April 1974. After stating that members of national minorities are inclined, 'as a matter of course' to attribute instances of 'injustice' to ethnic distinctions, the Secretary General proceeded to reject complaints concerning the absence of educational facilities in minority languages, stressing that when Romanian specialists are sent to Arab countries, they are required to learn Arabic. In other words, while first displaying understanding (if not approval) of ethnic minority sensitivity, he ended by letting his audiences understand that they were merely *Gastarbeitern* in Romania (Ceauşescu, 1970-83, Vol. 10, pp. 42 and 46, respectively).

The incident was more than symptomatic, for minority dissatisfactions are strongly reinforced by policies consciously pursued by the regime. Despite provisions concerning educational facilities and the free use of national minority languages, assimilation is encouraged by several modalities: first, through migration of Romanian ethnics *into* Transylvania and dispersion of non-ethnics outside the region; second, through the (partially consequential) shrinkage in the number of schools and institutions providing teaching in minority languages; and, finally, through promotion of Romanian as the one language whose mastery is essential both for the country's economic progress and for the minorities' social mobility. The irony rests in the fact that precisely the same policies have been pursued by the Soviets in the Moldavia SSR, and precisely for the same purposes (Dima, 1982).

To be sure, these policies may stir controversy as to intent and outcome, and they were not without advocates among Western observers. Some of these have argued that, while it was true that economic change and population shifts had had a strong impact on areas inhabited by the national minorities, the percentage of economic elites among them had been higher than among Romanian ethnics, and consequently it was natural that Romania's social revolution had initially affected them more negatively. The intention, according to this argument, was not one of discrimination, but of equalization of conditions. Furthermore, regime-induced migration is said to reflect the same fundamental strategies, since the proportion of Romanian urbanites had been smaller than that of Hungarians, Germans or Jews. 'Given Romanian plans to expand industry and stimulate urban growth in all parts of the country, and that Hungarians make up less than 8 per cent of the population of Romania', it is claimed, 'it is inevitable that the proportions of Hungarians to Romanians in these cities will continue to shrink'. As for enforced or encouraged outward migration, individuals are said to be 'assigned' or to accept jobs away from their homes because that is where their skills are needed. The requirements of the economy, not ethnic affiliation or place of origin, have determined the distribution of labour. Admitting that there has been a reduction in the number of minority schools at primary and secondary level, the champions of Bucharest's national policies claim that the number of Romanian language schools has also been reduced and that 'in both cases, this has resulted from closing of tiny village schools in favour of larger, better equipped consolidated schools' (Romanian Research Group, 1979).

Minority sources from Transylvania have a different story to tell. According to Király, the practice of encouraging migration of Romanian ethnics into Transylvania was accompanied by the use of secret 'internal regulations' ordering plant directors to limit the number of personnel from among the national minorities (particularly technical and engineering). In parallel, two dispositions published in 1976, making it compulsory for graduates to take up jobs assigned by the state, directed towards combating 'parasitism', were also used for the purpose of depopulating Transylvania of national minority intelligentsia.

Another 'internal regulation' (Schöpflin, 1978, pp. 11–12) provided that university study groups in the languages of the minorities could be established if the students numbered a minimum of fifteen. However, care was usually taken to distribute students among groups in such a manner that their number would never be greater than fourteen. A similiar policy was followed with regard to primary and secondary level, where, since 1973, minimum numbers of twenty-five and thirty-six respectively, were required before permission could be given to open a class giving instruction in the language of a minority. On the other hand, the rule was not applied to pupils of Romanian ethnic origin, for the law stipulated that 'Romanian language sections and classes shall be organized regardless of the number of pupils'.

The educational law of 1973 was geared, among other things, to transforming the educational system by making it two-thirds technical and one-third humanities, in keeping with the policy of rapid industrialization. However, this has not been applied to Hungarian language instruction, where by 1974–5 only 1.4 per cent of technical schooling was in the native language. Similarly, technical textbooks were seldom translated into the languages of the minorities. As a consequence, and aware that their children's future might have to suffer in a country where social mobility is determined in great measure by the acquisition of technical education, parents of Hungarian or German children may have actually encouraged them to register in Romanian-language schools and institutes of higher learning. At the 1974 meeting with members of the nationalities' councils there were apparently some complaints about this state of affairs. Ceauşescu, however, rejected them energetically, claiming that it was not the language, but the *content* of teaching that mattered. Pursuing this subject, he added that no factory could work with translators and that, consequently, children of minority groups had to study Romanian as the only means of pursuing careers in all sectors of 'activity' (Ceauşescu, 1970-83, pp. 46-8). Consequently, it follows that, in the official Romanian view, equalization of conditions, or 'homogenization', is to lead, in the long run, to the solution of the problem of 'co-inhabitant nationalities' (as the minorities are officially termed), not only because of the disappearance of social contradictions, but also because of unavoidable cultural assimilation. Progress implicitly signifies 'Romanianization'.

There is some ambiguity in official documents and pronouncements concerning this matter. According to Schöpflin (1978, p. 8), no serious distinction is made in Romania between citizenship of the state (*Staatsangehörigkeit*) and membership of the Romanian nation (*Volkszugehörigkeit*). This is not accurate. In resolutions adopted at different party forums, in Ceauşescu's speeches, as well as in other publications (e.g. Florea, 1974; Institutul de ştiinţe politice şi de studiere a problemei naţionale, 1977; 'Contribuţia P.C.R. . . .', 1983), a distinction is made between *naţiune* (nation), which comprises all the inhabitants of the country regardless of ethnic affiliation, and *naţionalitate* (nationality), which designates ethnicity. The *naţiune*, stipulates that the party's Programme of 1974, will continue to exist in the period of socialist construction, as well as for some considerable time under communism, as indeed will the national state (*Programul*, 1975, p. 145; see also Ceauşescu's speech at the National Conference of the RCP, *Scînteia*, 17 December 1982). The nationalities, according to the 1974 Programme, will also 'preserve their entire importance in the period of forging the multi-laterally developed socialist society and the gradual transition to communism'. They 'will continue to exist for a prolonged [period of time], both in the period of socialist edification and in that of communist construction' (*Programul*, 1975, p. 148). However, addressing yet another meeting of the nationalities' Workers' Councils in December 1975, Ceauşescu appeared to have changed his mind about the matter, for he stated that 'socialism and communism cannot be forged according to nationality; there is no [such thing as] a Romanian socialism, a Hungarian one, another which is German, Bulgarian, French or I don't know what else' (Ceauşescu, 1970-83, Vol. 12, p. 235). This curious fit of inter-nationalism was not accompanied, it should be added, by a parallel *change d'avis* concerning *the nation*'s survival, which continues to serve the regime's nationalist campaigns.

Be that as it may, the Romanian authorities appear to make a special effort to help the national minorities 'homogenize' themselves into the body of the ethnic majority not only through the assimilationist policies reviewed above, but also by statistical manipulation. A glimpse at the returns of censuses conducted in 1956, 1966 and 1977 (see Table 18) demonstrates that the proportion of Romanian ethnics in the population is allegedly constantly rising, a performance that is unmatched by any of the national minorities except the gypsies. It is highly unlikely that the figures provided for the Hungarian minority are reliable. First, in 1977 the Romanian census separated for the first time the Szeklers from the body of their former ethnic identity, as indeed they did with the Saxons and the Swabians, and with the Lipovans, who were actually 'invited' to opt for ethnic categories never employed before. Very few respondents from either community, however, chose to do so. Second, were one to take the returns of the 1977 census at face value, one would be faced with an inexplicable phenomenon, in as much as natural increase among Romanian ethnics would outstrip that of the Hungarians in implausible proportions. As Table 16 demonstrates, only in the years 1967 and 1968, following Ceauşescu's measures to promote demographic growth, were natural increase figures for all populations of Romania (which, conceivably, reflected a particular growth among the ethnic majority) outstandingly high. Comparing these figures with data on natural increase in the heavily Hungarian-populated counties of Hargita, Covasna and Satu Mare, Mihnea Berindei (1980a, p. 38) discovered that only in 1967 and 1968 was the increase in these areas smaller than the county average, whereas between 1969 and 1978 the Hungarians there appeared to have a *higher fertility*. Finally, according to a Romanian propaganda brochure (Institute of Political Science and of Studying the National Question, 1976, p. 23), there were 1.48 million Hungarians attending the different minority churches. This would represent over 86 per cent of the combined number of Hungarians and Szeklers, which as Schöpflin (1978, p. 6) points out, is a highly unlikely proportion in a communist society.

If one adds to such 'hard data' the subjective factor, i.e. the natural suspicion of national minorities which is only enhanced by regime-inspired postures (e.g. the Lăncrănjan book or the 1980 celebrations of the 2,050th anniversary of Burebista's Dacian state), one cannot but conclude that the 'co-inhabitant' nationalities are not merely *co*-inhibited—they are inhibited without prefix. In other words, this is not simply a case of negation of individual autonomy and it is more than one of the system's negation of group autonomy. It verges on negation of a separate national identity.

Much of what has been said throughout this section of the Hungarian minority is also applicable to the Germans.[25] However, unlike the Hungarians, the Germans are not perceived as a threat to territorial or national integrity. Furthermore, their 'problem' appears to be gradually being solved by emigration, an option the Hungarians do not have, and probably do not want. Although they are the second largest national minority, their number has been shrinking since the end of the Second World War. About 100,000 of them left Romania with the German army, and, of the remaining, some 75,000 were deported to the Soviet Union from January 1945. Of these, 10,000 did not survive the labour camps. In 1948 and 1949 most deportees were allowed to return but about half of them went to Germany and to Austria. Some Swabians had to suffer deportation within Romania's borders, being forcefully removed to the Bărăgan plains between 1951 and 1956. During 1956, possibly in an attempt to drive a wedge between minorities at the time of the Hungarian uprising, German property confiscated after the war was returned or compensated for. In 1957, following an agreement signed between the government and the German Red Cross, emigration became

Table 18   Romania's Population by Nationality, 1956, 1966, 1977*

	1956	%†	1966	%†	1977	%†
Romanians	14,996,114	85.7	16,746,510	87.7	19,207,491	89.1
Hungarians	1,587,675	9.1	1,619,592	8.5	1,705,810	7.9
Szeklers	—	—	—	—	1,064	‡
Germans	384,708	2.2	382,595	2.0	348,444	1.6
Saxons	—	—	—	—	5,930	‡
Swabians	—	—	—	—	4,358	‡
Gypsies	104,216	0.6	64,197	0.3	229,986	1.0
Ukrainians	60,479	0.3	—	—	54,429	0.2
Ukrainians and Ruthenians	—	—	54,705	0.2	—	—
Ruthenians	—	—	—	—	988	‡
Serbs, Croats and Slovenes	46,517	0.3	44,236	0.2	—	—
Serbs	—	—	—	—	34,034	0.1
Croats	—	—	—	—	7,617	‡
Slovenes	—	—	—	—	707	‡
Russians	38,731	0.2	—	—	20,253	‡
Russians and Lipovans	—	—	39,483	0.1	—	—
Lipovans	—	—	—	—	11,494	‡
Jews	146,264	0.8	42,888	0.2	25,686	0.1
Turks	14,329	‡	18,040	‡	23,303	0.1
Tartars	20,469	0.1	22,151	0.1	23,107	0.1
Slovaks	23,331	0.1	22,221	0.1	22,037	0.1
Czechs	11,821	‡	9,978	‡	7,756	‡
Bulgarians	12,040	‡	11,193	‡	10,467	‡
Greeks	11,166	‡	9,088	‡	6,607	‡
Poles	7,627	‡	5,860	‡	4,756	‡
Armenians	6,441	‡	3,436	‡	2,436	‡
Macedo-romanians	—	—	—	—	1,179	‡
Aromanians	—	—	—	—	644	‡
Others and Undeclared	17,522	0.1	6,990	‡	4,203	‡
Total	17,489,450		19,103,163		21,559,416	

* As declared by respondènts.
† Calculation of first fraction only.
‡ Less than 0.1 per cent.
Source: *Recensămîntul*, 1959; *Recensămîntul*, 1968; *Scînteia*, 14 June 1977.

an option, but, as in the case of the Jews, one that would intermittently be closed. In 1967, when Romania became the first country in Eastern Europe to establish diplomatic relations with West Germany, not less than 60,000 German ethnics asked for permission to emigrate. This wave continued throughout the following years, the more so since, as West Germany became one of Bucharest's most important trading partners, it had the means to employ 'convincing' arguments when necessary. When the former Federal Chancellor Helmut Schmidt visited the Romanian capital in January 1978, Ceauşescu reportedly (dpa, 7 January 1978) pledged that 11,000 ethnic Germans would be granted permission to leave each year. By that time, the German proportion of the population had decreased from 2.2 per cent in 1956 to 1.6 per cent, and 80,000 already had their entry visas to West Germany (Berindei, 1980a, p. 39).

Despite these promises, in 1977 Ceauşescu launched a massive campaign against emigration, the main target of which were the Saxons and the Swabians. In a speech delivered at a joint meeting of the CC, the GNA and the Supreme Council of Economic and Social Development in March, the Secretary General declared that:

> ... we cannot but take notice disapprovingly of the fact that behind the so-called interest in humanitarian problems, in some countries there is ample activity to instigate Romanian citizens of different nationalities to leave their motherland and emigrate. It must be understood that the emigration problem does not even come close to being one of a humanitarian nature but constitutes an important political issue of each people, of relations between states. Consequently, we consider activities pursued abroad, aimed at instigating some Romanian citizens to emigrate, as an unfriendly attitude. The allurement of citizens of other nationalities to leave our country is ultimately directed at disorganizing certain sectors of our society's activity, at creating difficulties to the Romanian state. This is why our government firmly rejects such acts, considering them a serious intervention in Romania's internal affairs [Ceauşescu, 1970-83, Vol. 14, pp. 198-9].

The declaration obviously reflected awareness of the dangers posed to the economy by the massive emigration of a community which counted among its members a high proportion of skilled workers, technicians and engineers.

Driven by the same motives, in early November 1982 Romania announced an 'education tax', to be imposed on would-be emigrants, requiring the restitution of what was said to constitute the state's investment in the training and schooling of those about to leave. The sums involved were astronomical (up to $20,000 in some instances) and, what is more, they were to be paid in hard currency, despite the fact that no Romanian citizen is allowed to possess foreign money. Following heavy pressure exerted by West German, American and Israeli circles, which varied from threats to withdraw Bucharest's MFN status and apply the Jackson–Vanik Amendment to actions by German financial circles affecting Romanian efforts to re-schedule foreign debts, the tax was not applied—but it remains in force. Moreover, young men of German nationality who apply to emigrate are often drafted into 'disciplinary' military units, where some are known to have met their death by hard labour (Berindei, 1980b, p. 41). But then, according to Eduard Eisenburger, one of his co-national 'representatives' as Chairman of the Council of Working People of German Nationality, 'tendencies toward emigration' are only present among people whose 'patriotic and political consciousness is underdeveloped' (*Scînteia*, 31 March 1983). And the 'Multi-laterally *developed* socialist society' apparently can do without 'underdevelopment'.

Dissent

Romanian dissent, I was recently told by a Western specialist in East European affairs, lives in Paris and his name is Paul Goma. The affirmation may be a slight exaggeration, but it attests to the meagreness of the phenomenon.

Goma's name only became familiar to Western observers in 1977, but the saga of Romanian intellectual dissent actually starts with 'Paraschivescu's boys', or rather with those few young writers who remained loyal to their mentor's credo. Among these, a prominent part was played by the '*oneirists*' (a term deriving from the Greek *oneiros*, i.e. dream), a group formed in the early sixties around the young writers Dumitru Ţepeneag and Leonid Dimov. The *oneirists* were closely associated with Goma, though this association pertained more to the basic political implications of their writing than to aesthetic beliefs.

It is difficult (perhaps impossible) to provide a concise description of *oneirist* aesthetics. It was undoubtedly affiliated with, and had strong roots in, both Romanian and Western surrealism, and romanticism. The young Romanian *oneirists*, however, rejected what they regarded as surrealism's claims to authenticity and its pseudo-scientific, deterministic and Freudian character. Instead, they opted for the absolute autonomy of art, which, they held, may be achieved in a dream-like world, where distinctions between past, present and future (time) and between the 'here' and the 'there' (space), are completely dispensed with. At the same time, a distinction was drawn between the early 'romantic *oneirists*' and the new, 'structural *oneiricism*'. Unlike the former, the latter did not necessarily consider itself metaphysical, i.e. it was not concerned with 'truth beyond' but rather with 'form here'. While the romantics' aim in using the dream had been cognition, and art had been for them a corollary of truth, the structural *oneirists*' aim was articulation *qua* articulation and art had no other corollary but artistic expression (Ţepeneag, 1975a, 1975b; see also de Bosschere, 1969; Schlesak, 1972; Gabanyi, 1975, pp. 145-7; Shafir, 1981a, pp. 262-70 and *passim*).

Such absolutism of 'art for art's sake', with its clear anti-deterministic point of departure and with its rejection of any limits imposed on the freedom of expression, had obvious political implications, despite the fact that the *oneirists* were not initially necessarily politically motivated. Defending their autonomous postures against the (then incipient) coalition of nationalist and 'party-minded' writers who enjoyed the support of the regime, the *oneirists* were driven to a political response—and for some, such as Ţepeneag and the young writer Virgil Tănase, there would be no way back to 'pure literature'. The foes of *engagement* were paradoxically transformed into *engagés* by those promoting partisan art.

To his dismay, Ţepeneag found himself on political barricades, and in the early 1970s, while studying on a scholarship in Paris, he became the unofficial *porte parole* of the Romanian literary resistance. When the 'mini-cultural revolution' was launched in July 1971 he conducted open protest campaigns in the press and elsewhere. His attempts to return to Romania (it was against Paraschivean ethics to fight the regime from the relative security of the French capital) met with stubborn resistance, and only threats to provoke an international scandal eventually secured his return. Four years later, however, while again in Paris, he was stripped of his citizenship by presidential decree, in a series of new East European tactics for dealing with dissidence, later publicized by the Solzhenitsyn case.

The Romanian authorities falsely accused Ţepeneag of having asked for political asylum. His real 'crime', however, had been to launch a literary journal in France, aimed at bringing East European literature to the notice of Western intellectuals. Demanding to be told why Ţepeneag should be expelled from the Writers' Union, Geo Bogza, a courageous elderly writer, was given the terse reply: 'No need for explanations, *we* know why'. The only member of the Union who dared come out openly against these measures was Goma. He sent an open letter to the Union, in which, with a superb sense of irony, he demanded to 'enjoy the same rights' as Ţepeneag, since they had both committed the same 'crime' (*Dossier*, 1977, pp. 49–66).

Born in Bessarabia in 1935,[26] Goma spent his childhood in the Transylvanian town of Sibiu and in the Făgăraş district, where his parents were village teachers. At the age of sixteen he was briefly detained, being accused of intending to join the partisans. His second arrest in 1956 was a more serious affair; it came after he had dared to read aloud parts of a novel, the hero of which wished to organize a student movement similar to that in Hungary. Goma was sentenced to two years in prison, which were followed by five years of 'obligatory residence' in the Bărăgan region. It was only in 1962 that he regained his freedom. The writer made his official literary debut in 1966. A second book, *Ostinato*, offered for publication in 1967, described the reminiscences of a young Romanian intellectual, about to be freed from prison after having served a two-year term. This was not the first time that the delicate subject of injustice and humiliation had been tackled in the Ceauşescu years. Nevertheless, Goma's book was far more outspoken, not only in what the writer *dared* to put on paper, but more importantly, in what he *refused* to put. To put it in a nutshell, there was no trace of optimism about the future, and the 'crimes' were not attributed to 'deviation' by relatively unimportant officials. In the eyes of the censor, for instance, it was inadmissible that one of *Ostinato*'s characters should hold the rank of captain in the security forces. As Goma himself described the incident:

I was told: captain is not proper, make him an NCO . . . Officers cannot abuse [power]. If they did, the reader might be led into believing the institution itself was wrong . . . Also, you must carefully weight the end of the book . . . One must, at all costs, see the future shining brightly [*Dossier*, 1977, p. 44].

Unlike most of his colleagues, however, Goma was not prepared to compromise and accept the recipe of nationalist exaltation and 'optimist' criticism. After four years of 'negotiations' with the censors, *Ostinato* was published in West Germany and France in 1971.[27] Virgil Cândea, a Romanian historian and the President of the regime-sponsored 'Romania Association', explained in an interview on French television that the book had not really been banned by any official decision: the printers, allegedly, had refused to set up the type for such an obviously venomous script. In March 1970 Goma sent the publisher the manuscript of *The Door* (Goma, 1974). Alexandru Ivasiuc, a novelist who shared Goma's cell in prison (he later died in the earthquake of 1977), alerted the authorities that one of the novel's characters had been modelled on Mrs Ceauşescu. The calumny was sufficient to seal his fate and Goma's name became taboo.

In January 1977 Goma made public the contents of an open letter of solidarity, addressed to Pavel Kohout and other signatories of the Czechoslovak Charter '77. Posted to several Western diplomats in Bucharest, the letter was broadcast to Romania by Radio Free Europe in early February. At that time he also wrote a letter to Ceauşescu (significantly addressed to him at 'the Royal Palace'), explaining with sutble irony why the Romanian President should join him in support of the Chartists. The signatories of the Charter, he wrote, were no reactionaries but genuine socialists, whom Ceauşescu had supported back in 1968, when he had denounced the Soviet intervention in Czechoslovakia:

> I turn to you in despair. You are my last hope . . . Ever since Charter 77 was published . . . I can find no rest, and, I am sure of it, neither can you . . . I try to convince my acquaintances to join in the action of the Czechs and of the Slovaks, but I fail . . . Please believe me, my fellow-citizens' attitude has deeply grieved me: all our neighbours move . . . Only we, Romanians, keep silent . . . The Romanians fear the security forces . . . It consequently seems that only two persons in the country do not fear them: Your Excellency and myself . . . An entirely different situation would be brought about, should Your Excellency send a similar letter, a declaration of support to Charter '77. I am deeply convinced that millions of Romanians would follow you [*Dossier*, 1977, pp. 90-2].

More than any other dispatch, however, the authorities were enraged by an appeal Goma addressed to the Belgrade follow-up conference of the Helsinki agreements, in which he simply demanded the implementation of the Romanian Constitution's provisions concerning basic human rights (*Dossier*, 1977, pp. 93-5). By April the appeal had some 200 signatures. Many of them, however, joined because of repeated official refusals to allow them to emigrate, which partially explains why a substantial proportion of the signatories were ethnic Germans or Jews. Some were in fact subsequently granted exit visas, which soon led to a new idiom in Romania—the 'Goma passport'. Only two intellectuals dared attach their signatories to Goma's appeal. One of them, the literary critic Ion Negoiţescu, was forced to make public repentance (evoking national values) (*România literară*, 14

April 1977) and some six years later defected to the West. The other was the psychiatrist Ion Vianu, who in October 1976 had managed to publish in the Writers' Union's monthly *Viaţa românescă*, an article which pointed out the dangers of the misuse of psychiatry for political purposes. Like many other signatories, Vianu was badly harassed, though eventually granted a passport. By any standard, intellectual reponse to Goma's appeal was virtually insignificant.

If dissidence (or rather opposition) is to be viewed not merely in terms of the occasional publication of 'unorthodox' articles or books,[28] but as calling, at the end of the day, for *action*, with its attendant risks, then the Romanian intellectual community has very little to show for itself. During the years that have elapsed since the 'Goma affair', two writers (the former Stalinist Dan Deşliu and Dorin Tudoran) and a journalist (Victor Frunză, now in exile) are known to have resigned in protest from the RCP. In the academic world, a prominent young historian, Vlad Georgescu, dared to work on a manuscript denouncing, among other things, nationalist manipulations of history (Georgescu, 1981). For such audacity, he paid the familiar price: imprisonment, and (after Western intervention on his behalf), exile.

The same fate awaited Paul Goma. In a speech delivered in February 1977, the Secretary General castigated 'traitors of their country, slanderers who would not hesitate, from wherever they happened to be', to betray it 'like Judas, for a few more pieces of silver' (Ceauşescu, 1970-83, Vol. 14, pp. 46-7). Replying to the President, the writer sent him one more open letter. 'The *Traitors* and the *Enemies*', he wrote, 'are neither those who dare express their discontent, nor those who claim their elementary rights, nor those who—driven to desperation—chose the bitter road of exile. *The Traitors, Romania's Enemies* are policemen of all ranks, uniforms and functions, I mean the *Police System*' (*Dossier*, 1977, p. 97; emphasis in original). This was nothing but *lèse-majesté*. Having previously failed to intimidate him either by anonymous telephone calls from 'indignant patriots', or by being badly beaten by a former boxing champion, and having proved once more unsuccessful in trying to tempt him into compromise (Nicolae Breban, himself a 'part-time' dissident writer, acted as intermediary between Goma and the leadership), the regime arrested Goma on 1 April 1977 (Goma, 1977, p. 13-170). When I met him in Paris in the autumn, he still bore the marks of his detention.

Goma's liberation had been secured by Western intervention, but before he was allowed to leave he was warned that 'the revolution's arm' was long and unforgiving. Since the warning was ignored, and Goma (together with Virgil Tănase) persisted in criticizing the regime and Ceauşescu personally, the 'revolution's arm' attempted to reach him in 1982. The defection of an agent dispatched to kill him and Tănase foiled the plot (Goma, 1973; Tănase, 1983). Such 'multilateral' measures directed against vociferous critics are not to be wondered at. Yet in themselves, they do not explain the tranquillity of the *mămăligă*. Ominous as the activities of the Romanian *securitate* may be, its powers are not as tremendous as those intellectuals who explain their passivity in terms of their fear would make them out. 'A thousand, ten thousand times', Goma wrote in one of his books (1973, p. 80), 'I told myself and my fellow prisoners: blind submission does not ease the chains. They replied sagely: "Why stir them up?" "Let's not provoke them!" "If we leave them in peace, they will leave us in peace"'.

In conversations with Romanian intellectuals I was often impressed that these unfamiliar postures in particular create a sense of hostility towards the hard core of dissent. Goma, I was sometimes told, is but a quixotic figure who gets his kicks from 'provocation'. Intellectuals, it was granted, have a difficult time under Ceauşescu, but 'as always', it is still possible to 'live', provided one pays lip-service. In other encounters I could discern hostility *vis-à-vis* dissident refusal to join the nationalist chorus. And it is not irrelevant that, once Goma and Ţepeneag settled in the West, *émigré* circles whose connections with Romania's fascist past are well established, accused them of being agents for the *securitate*. Yet the same circles are known to cultivate a very close relationship with Bucharest nowadays, and some of their more prominent figures are even received in audience by Ceauşescu. 'Patriotism Dîmboviţa style' undoubtedly draws together strange bedfellows.

For the time being, intellectual dissent in Romania is probably best served by an epitaph. And one could hardly think of one more suitable than the words of Andrei Amalrik: 'no oppression can be effective without those who are prepared to submit to it' (Amalrik, 1970, p. 97).

According to Alexander Matejko, for the intelligentsia 'political freedom was and is a primary need, whereas for the blue-collar workers it is only a secondary need' (1974, p. 14). Obviously, this is not so in the Romanian case. Not only was the proportion of workers among the signatories of Goma's appeal by far more impressive than that of intellectuals, but working-class discontent was registered in more than one instance.

Already in September 1972 there were indications that not all was well and multilaterally developed in the mining area of the Jiul Valley. Unrest among miners is particularly ominous for the RCP, for the movement's extremely thin record of 'class struggle' includes only two major strikes in the whole inter-war period—one of them by miners in 1929. During a visit Ceauşescu paid to this region, the miners complained about high norms, low wages and lack of adequate machinery (Shafir, 1982). Five years later, the confrontation was violent (Amnesty International, 1980, pp. 5-6). In early August 1977, some 35,000 miners went on strike over a variety of grievances, foremost among which were a new pension law, poor housing and inadequate food. They demanded that the party leader come to talk to them personally, but when he finally arrived—on the third day of the strike—he was greeted with shouts of 'Down with proletarian bourgeoisie'. The chief organizers of the walk-out were two engineers, most probably 'first generation' non-manuals. They both died in 'accidents', which, according to Amnesty International, were never satisfactorily investigated. Some four thousand strikers were later dismissed, and many others were transferred to distant areas.

In October 1981 demonstrations broke out in several villages in the mining region of Motru, spreading later to the Jiul Valley. The headquarters of the party was occupied in Motru and the *securitate* had to be brought in to put down the demonstrations. Ceauşescu's personal appearance did little to calm the situation (Colas, 1982, p. 36). Miners went on strike again in the Maramureş area when they were handed their paycheques, following the introduction of the NEFM, in September 1983. The minister in charge of the industry, who came to talk to the strikers, promised certain changes in the system of remuneration . . . and left behind some 2,000 troops of the security forces. Strikes are also known to have broken out at the 'Steagul roşu' tractor plant in Braşov after the introduction of the NEFM (Berindei & Colas, 1984a, p. 39).

The harsh reaction of the regime to these, and similar incidents, stands witness to its attitude towards any centrifugal propensities in society. When a group of workers and 'white collars' announced the foundation of a Free Trade Union of Romanian Workers (SLOMR) in February 1979 (Amnesty International, 1980, pp. 6-7; Berindei, 1981, pp. 41-2), the leadership reacted with apparent panic, sentencing some to long terms of imprisonment, confining others to psychiatric institutions, and causing at least one of the founding members, Vasile Paraschiv, who had responded to the Goma appeal, to disappear for a long time. Three months later the movement had practically been crushed, and attempts to revive it since have never lasted more than a couple of days (Georgescu, 1984, p. 336).

A similar reaction had been experienced in May 1978 by a group of neo-Protestant believers who formed a movement in that month called the Romanian Christian Committee for the Defence of Freedom and Religious Conscience (ALRC) (Amnesty International, 1980, pp. 5-7; Stolojan, 1981). Among other demands, ALRC requested freedom of worship and an end to state interference in church affairs. The most important aspect of the organization's short history, however, may have been its collaboration with SLOMR and the adherence of several members of the Romanian Orthodox clergy, headed by Father Claciu. Most leading members of the ALRC were arrested or persuaded to emigrate—some of them by means of threats.

These accounts do not necessarily refute the previous analysis of autonomous and conformist propensities in Romanian society. The Orthodox Church is still by far the dominant religion for Romanian believers. While not unique, Father Claciu's defiance of political and patriarchal hierarchies remains a unique gesture. The miners' strikes are impressive, but they are so precisely because set against a background of long acquiescent conformity. Most other instances of working-class unrest, in as much as one can judge from foreign reports, are anomic, and there is little, if any, political sophistication in the demands made. The absence of any significant number of intellectuals in the Romanian dissident movement partially accounts for the unrefined character of the demands, with the notable exception of the SLOMR manifesto. From 'down with proletarian bourgeoisie' to the sophisticated Polish eighties there is yet a long road to tread. Its course may also necessitate building bridges between divided national sections, a task as difficult as any. Not only a difference in traditional patterns of protest activities is involved here (significantly, there is no *samizdat* in Romania except for the Hungarian-language *Ellenpotok*) but above all mutual distrust. It is significant that none of the Hungarian intellectuals who at one time or another raised their voices in protest at infringements of minority rights (such as Lajos Takács or András Süto)[29] denounced other forms of oppression, and, conversely, that none of *their* demands are known to have been supported by ethnic Romanians, with the possible exception of Goma.

True, the diffusion of political innovation *is* possible, and it is precisely such diffusion that the party leaders seem to fear. Demands included in the SLOMR manifesto indicate acute awareness of Solidarity's evolution, and an open letter by a group of Romanian women to Mrs Ceaușescu bluntly states that they 'have learnt something from the Polish people' (Berindei, 1981; 'Lettre ouverte . . .' 1981, p. 31). Yet demands for autonomy, while liable to imitation, can neither be copied nor imported. They must be rooted in local traditions and/or spring out of local situations. And while Romanian society might just be embarking on what Bauman defines as that process of 'historical learning' which leads to the liberation of 'civil society' (Bauman, 1981, pp. 49, 52), one would be well advised to remember that, by definition, historical processes are prolonged. And so are states of political stagnation.

Part V
Foreign Affairs

10   Simulated Permanence:
Romania in the Soviet Sphere

While simulated change constitutes the backbone of the internal policies pursued by the RCP, Romania's international politics are probably best defined antonymously. Constrained by the presence of the Eastern 'bear', the Romanian 'fox' has been forced to simulate a permanent presence in Moscow's organizational (Warsaw Treaty, CMEA) forest. Yet at the same time, Bucharest has been pursuing policies designed to weaken as much as possible its actual participation in the structural set-up of the Soviet sphere and, while keeping the façade of affiliation, to cultivate such ties as would render the permanency of allegiance to the system dominated by Moscow virtually minimal. Ronald H. Linden's fable metaphor (*Bears and Foxes*, 1979) provides a heuristic background against which the strategies of 'simulated permanency' pursued by the Romanian leadership since the early 1960s can be understood.

These strategies can also be seen, as Robert L. Farlow (1971, 1978) shows, as a case of 'partial alignment'. According to Farlow, partial alignment obtains when a state pursues a policy that stresses the primacy of national interests and goals, as these are defined by its own political elite, over any collective or general interests, as the latter are defined by other members of the alignment system of which that state is a component part. This results in antagonism, which is most prominent in the relations between the deviant state and the leading member of the system. The non-conforming state avoids overtly provoking the more powerful ally and consequently will not disengage formally from the system. For its part, the leading state is not willing to employ force, because in cost-benefit terms such measures might prove unproductive; yet, at the same time, the dominating element in the alliance is also unwilling to accept deviance. This situation results in a pattern of conflict and co-operation (Farlow, 1978, pp. 192-3).

For a policy of partial alignment to succeed, then, it is necessary for the less powerful state to avoid creating a situation where the superpower would be faced with no other alternative than that of terminating the partiality of the relationship. This is why permanency in the alliance must be emphasized by the less powerful state, even in pursuing policies that are conducive to weakening the bonds that tie it to the organization and to its leading member. The Romanians are known to be warm advocates of the dissolution of both the Warsaw Treaty Organization (WTO) and NATO. While advocacy of such measures is known to have served Moscow's propaganda purposes, the Romanians, as Alex Alexeiev remarks, 'have introduced an important nuance, by claiming that all military blocs (and not only NATO) are an obstacle to peace and co-operation among peoples' (1981, p. 11). Ever since the beginning of their 'deviance', the Romanian leaders have taken measures such as ending WTO manœuvres on Romanian soil and restricting Romanian participation in manœuvres elsewhere to symbolic dimensions;[1] advocating reorganizational measures aimed at ending the domination of the Pact's command structure by the Soviet military;[2] condemning WTO intervention in Czechoslovakia and adopting in its wake a new Defence Law and an 'all horizons' military defence doctrine of 'people's war' geared to resisting Soviet invasion;[3] refusing to raise defence expenditures against Soviet insistence, etc. However, it is not without relevance that Bucharest has always been careful to pay lip-service to its allegiance to the 'socialist camp'. For example, in May 1967, Ceauşescu stressed that 'like all other socialist countries', Romania wished to see both the WTO and NATO liquidated, hastening to add that 'whether the Warsaw Pact will exist or not, should imperialism unleash war, Romania, a socialist state, would fight alongside other socialist states'.

Moscow's sensitive ear probably perceived the declaration in precisely the terms intended, i.e. that Romania would not participate in an *offensive* WTO operation against the West, just as Bucharest's repeated (if veiled) insistence on the strictly *European* defensive character of the Warsaw Pact were not lost on the Kremlin at the time of the Ussuri River incidents in 1969 and on other occasions. Hand in hand with these declarations and (more importantly) their accompanying measures, Romania cultivated ties with China and Yugoslavia, became the first East European country to establish diplomatic relations with West Germany in 1967, refused to break diplomatic ties with Israel after the Six Day War, did not support the Soviet intervention in Afghanistan or the USSR-backed Vietnamese intervention in Kampuchea, and so on. Yet if and when a shift in any of these 'principled' stances is perceived to be necessary to avoid possible Soviet sanctions, the tone and nuance of the Romanian position undergoes significant change, as it will be observed below.

At first sight, the simulated change-simulated permanence antonym might appear to be contradicting any link between the internal and the external dimensions of policies. In reality, the opposite is the case. It is precisely owing to the RCP's attachment to the Leninist ethos of the party's leading role, reflected in its attitude towards society, that Moscow has grudgingly condoned 'Romanian deviance' in foreign affairs. In other words, the Romanian state (party) has been able to achieve a certain degree of autonomy in its international stance because no doubts arose in the Kremlin as to its capacity to pre-empt and to contain autonomy internally. Simulated permanence, in other words, is a corollary of *autonomous, but not of independent*, postures, for, as Aurel Braun emphasizes, in view of the fact that Romania continues willy-nilly to be a member of the Soviet sphere, and is compelled to stress occasionally the immutability of the affiliation, 'independence' is hardly a suitable description of Bucharest's situation in relation to Moscow (Braun, 1978, p. xi).

The basic aims of Romanian foreign policy were established in the famous 'Statement' of the RWP (*Scînteia*, 23 April 1964) and have hardly changed since:

Bearing in mind the diversity of the conditions of socialist construction, there are not, nor can there be, any unique patterns and recipes; no one can decide what is, and what is not correct for other countries and parties. It is up to every Marxist-Leninist party, it is a sovereign right of each socialist state, to elaborate, choose or change the forms and methods of socialist construction.

There does not and cannot exist a 'parent' party and a 'son' party, or 'superior' parties and 'subordinate' parties ... No party has, or can have, a privileged place, or can impose its line and opinions on other parties.

Whether at the United Nations or at international disarmanent talks, whether at world communist gatherings or in behind-the-scenes diplomatic contacts, the primary objective of this policy has been, and remains, the augmentation of Romanian autonomy, with the purpose of checking any possible Soviet design of forcing Bucharest 'back into the fold'.

The nature of Romania's manifold contacts or semi-alliances, established for this strategic purpose, differs in scope and intensity. It is, however, possible to classify them into a three-dimensional scheme: the international communist movement, the Third World, and the Western world.

The foremost partners in the first dimension have been China and Yugoslavia, and the most immediate opponents (though not necessarily for identical reasons) were Romania's 'traditional' enemies, the Soviet Union and Hungary.

The Sino-Soviet split, which first burst into the open at the Romanian party congress in 1960, was a *sine qua non* condition for the success of the Dejist challenge to Khrushchev (Fischer-Galati, 1966). The Romanian leader would hardly have dared oppose the Soviet premier had not Khrushchev's hands been tied at the time by internal party strife *and* by his endeavours to neutralize Mao. Bucharest adopted a position of strict neutrality in the conflict, the implications of which could be fully grasped only in juxtaposition with postures displayed by Moscow's other East European allies. By 1963 the Romanian ambassador had returned to Albania, whence Bucharest had withdrawn its diplomatic representative together with the Soviet Union in 1961, owing to Tirana's support of Chinese-backed 'anti-revisionism'. When Moscow and Beijing exchanged acrimonious letters in June 1963, *Scînteia* published both letters, thus hinting of a negation of the Soviet right to 'excommunicate' any communist party from the international movement. For their part, the Chinese, who earlier had had to cope with their own saga of Soviet economic pressure, proved sympathetic to the Romanian grievances. Significantly, one of the letters from the Chinese Communist Party (CCP) addressed to the CPSU and published by *Scînteia* expressed support for Bucharest's stand in the Comecon dispute with Moscow (King, 1972, p. 375).

In 1964 a Romanian delegation headed by Bodnăraş visited the Chinese capital, ostensibly in an effort to mediate between the two adversaries. One of the members of the Romanian team was the relatively inexperienced Politburo member Nicolae Ceauşescu. Despite endeavours to bring about a dialogue between Mao and Khrushchev, the Romanians began to realize that a policy of autonomy would be 'best served by continued Soviet-Chinese differences, but with both parties continuing to remain acknowledged members of the socialist camp' (King, 1972, p. 376). Consequently, from now on the RCP would oppose all Soviet attempts to convene an international conference of the communist parties with the purpose of ostracizing the CCP and other 'deviants'. The RCP did not send a delegation to the abortive conference of 1965 and in February 1968 its delegation walked out of the Budapest preparatory conference, criticizing statements made against the CCP. In his speech at the 1969 gathering of communist parties, Ceauşescu reiterated the Romanian position that no criticism of another party was admissible and that each party had the right and the obligation to pursue its own line. There was, according to the Romanian party leader 'no necessity for any kind of leading centre' in the movement, since no one could 'claim to be the holder of the magic key that answers all problems' (Ceauşescu, 1970-83, Vol. 4, pp. 78-83, 98). A similar line was adopted at the East Berlin conference of European parties in June 1976, when the Romanian Secretary General once more stressed that relations between parties must be based on 'complete equality, observance of each party's right to work out its [own] political line and its [own] revolutionary strategy', adding that it was 'definitely no longer either possible or necessary to have an international centre' (Ceauşescu, 1970-83, Vol. 13, pp. 212-13). When, in April 1980, the Polish and French parties sponsored another international conference of European parties in Paris, Bucharest turned down the invitation, suspecting Soviet attempts to rally the participants to support Moscow's invasion of Afghanistan, which contradicted the position of the Chinese, that of some West European parties, and indeed Romania's own party (Devlin, 1980; Radio Free Europe Research, Situation Report/5, Romania, 12 May 1980).

It is not irrelevant that Bucharest has on several occasions adopted the Chinese jargon when explaining its position concerning the necessity to promote relations based on respect for strict equality of rights among communist parties and states. On the day of CCP Secretary General Hu Yaoband's arrival in Bucharest on a 'friendly visit' in 1983, for example, *Scînteia* published an article written by Foreign Minister Ştefan Andrei, according to whom true 'international solidarity' was 'opposed to any subordination in relations among parties, to every *hegemonic* conception' (*Scînteia*, 5 May 1983; emphasis mine). Similarly, in an article published in the RCP's theoretical monthly in early 1984, PEC member Dumitru Popescu engaged in a veiled dispute with Soviet concepts of national sovereignty, qualifying Moscow's criticism of countries which 'adopt a firm position in defence of [their] national independence', as symptomatic of 'political *hegemonism*'. Popescu, furthermore, managed to link the Romanian and Chinese positions with those of Third World countries, which were said to struggle against 'imperialist domination, interference in internal affairs and consolidation of spheres of influence, and against the policy of *hegemonism*' (*Era socialistă*, No. 5, 10 March 1984; emphasis mine).

That Moscow viewed, and views, these developments with little patience is beyond doubt, the more so since Chinese support for the Romanian position was sometimes volunteered in formulas utterly unacceptable to the Soviets. Shortly before the Romanian resuscitation of the Bessarabian issue, for example, Mao spoke in one breath of Russian expansionism in the Far East and in Eastern Europe, linking Japanese claims to the Kurile Islands with his own grievances over Mongolia and other territories in Asia and with Romanian claims to Bessarabia (*Pravda*, 2 September 1964, reproduced in Doolin, 1965, pp. 42-4). More sensitive to the limitations of their autonomous postures, the Romanians made no mention of the Chairman's remarks in their media (Lendvai, 1969, p. 314). In a similar display of caution, Zhou Enlai's attack on 'modern revisionists' who were 'uniting with US imperialism', was edited out of the Romanian version of the speech he delivered during his 1966 visit to Bucharest, and the rally scheduled for the capital had to be delayed for two hours since Ceauşescu would not permit his guest to launch yet another critical assault on Moscow (King, 1972, pp. 379-80; Socianu, 1978, pp. 175-6). At times, however, the Romanians themselves have proved close to underestimating Soviet reaction. Ceauşescu's 1971 visit to Beijing, for instance, coming as it did in the wake of rumours concerning the active role played by the Romanians in the Sino-American *rapprochement*, triggered a strong reaction in the Kremlin, the more so since this display of autonomy had been preceded by refusal to allow the passage of Soviet troops through Romanian territory on their way to Bulgaria. In an obviously intimidating move, Warsaw Pact manoeuvres were conducted in the southern part of the Soviet Union while Ceauşescu visited China and North Korea. The implicit threat was clear enough to make the Romanian leader stop off in the Soviet capital on his return journey, in an obvious effort to soothe Brezhnev (Braun, 1978, pp. 133-4).

This incident was symptomatic of the nature of the Chinese-Romanian relationship. 'Distant waters', as Zhou Enlai put it in an interview with the Yugoslav publication *Vjesnik* in August that year (quoted in Braun, 1978, p. 119), 'cannot quench local fires'. The lesson was certainly not lost on the Romanians, who already in 1968 must have realized that Beijing could do little else for them but express verbal support. Yet the realization of the limitations of a semi-alliance does not necessarily lead to its being discontinued. Both partners may find that, while limited in nature, collaboration may still be mutually advantageous. Ceauşescu paid visits to China in May 1978 and in April 1982, and Prime Minister Dăscălescu visited Beijing in November 1983. For their part, the Chinese value their Romanian-Yugoslav 'Balkan connection', the more so since Beijing is unlikely to return to Tirana's good graces as long as Hoxha is still around. Chairman Hua Gofeng visited Bucharest and Belgrade in August 1978, and so did his nominal successor at the CCP's helm, Secretary General Hu Yaoband, who paid 'friendly political visits' to the two capitals in May 1983. Foreign Minister Wu Xuequian was also in Bucharest in March-April 1984.

Even if it is unlikely that Beijing still envisages the setting up of a communist

Balkan pro-Chinese military alliance, as Enver Hoxha claims they attempted to
do in 1968 (Zanga, 1978), there are enough mutual 'services' that the Chinese and
the Romanians can perform for each other. Bucharest, for example, is reported to
have extended its 'good services' in an attempt to mediate between China and
Vietnam (*Far Eastern Economic Review*, 17 March 1983) and Romania is China's
most important trading partner in CMEA (Ciorănescu, 1983a). For their part, the
Romanians are known to have purchased in China not only petroleum and other
raw materials, but also twenty-eight fast attack gunboats and twenty torpedo-
equipped hydrofoils (Linden, 1981, p. 252). The two sides have often exchanged
visits of military delegations, the value of which, though symbolic, rests in
emphasizing their determination to pursue their respective separate, though
occasionally intersecting, paths.

Similar considerations have determined the development of Yugoslav–
Romanian relations. Belgrade's long experience of successful confrontation with
Moscow, as well as Yugoslav prestige in the Third World, made Tito Romania's
natural ally once the rift with Moscow had reached the point of no return.
Following Ceauşescu's advent to power, the relationship intensified considerably.
In April 1966 Tito came to Romania in what subsequently proved to be the first in
a series of regular annual encounters designed to co-ordinate policies and to
develop economic and technical co-operation. After Tito's death these ties still
continued. Yugoslav party leader Dušan Dragosavać went to Romania in
February 1982 and his successor, Mitja Ribičić, visited Bucharest in April 1983.
For his part, Ceauşescu visited Yugoslavia in October 1982 and in April 1984.

The most impressive evidence of Romanian-Yugoslav economic co-operation
is given by two projects on the Danube designed to provide electricity and to
improve rail and water communications. More importantly perhaps, on the
military side, the Romanians have clearly modelled their doctrine of 'all people's
war' on the Yugoslav blueprint (Braun, 1977), which is not surprising, for
Yugoslavia is likely to be Romania's only partner in attempts to resist eventual
Soviet intervention. Moreover, the two countries have collaborated in the construction of a twin-jet fighter equipped with Rolls-Royce engines, the first non-
Soviet plane to be introduced in a Warsaw Pact country (Alexeiev, 1981, p. 10).
This does not signify, on the other hand, that Belgrade and Bucharest view every
issue from the same perspective. Not only have the two states had to 'agree to
disagree' on issues such as reaction to the Arab-Israeli war of 1967 (Belgrade
followed the Soviet example of breaking off diplomatic relations with Israel), but
the Yugoslavs are probably disturbed by Ceauşescu's only too obvious attempts to
step into Tito's shoes in the non-aligned movement, already hastily demonstrated
at the Yugoslav leader's funeral (Braun, 1982, p. 55).

From similar, if not identical, considerations, the RCP pursued, within the
international communist movement, a policy of close collaboration with the
Euro-communist parties. In a speech delivered in December 1977 Ceauşescu
stated that it was 'perfectly natural that the communist parties should define
autonomously, with no outside interference, their political line, including a

number of new concepts related to their revolutionary strategy and tactics' and, as a case in point, specifically mentioned 'the concept of Euro-communism' (Ceauşescu, 1970-83, Vol. 15, p. 328). Santiago Carillio and Enrico Berlinguer's speeches were the only addresses to the 1969 world gathering of communist parties that *Scînteia* published in full—except, of course, Ceauşescu's own speech and, as a measure of counterbalance, that delivered by Brezhnev (Mujal-León, 1978, p. 232). Both Euro-communist leaders visited Romania frequently and were always extended an enthusiastic welcome. These affectionate receptions stemmed from their acceptance in Bucharest as being yet another link in the chain of semi-alliances destined to *unchain* Romania from her ideological and other forms of subservience to Moscow. It was quite obvious why, for instance, at the time of Berlinguer's visit to Bucharest in January 1977, the official communiqué stressed complete agreement on foreign policy issues and specifically on the absolute right of each party to decide its own line (*Lumea*, 13 January 1977). When a split occurred in the Spanish Communist Party in early January 1984, Ceauşescu condemned the setting-up of the 'parallel' pro-Moscow faction (*Scînteia*, 27 January 1984), in strong contrast to the reaction the event produced in Moscow and elsewhere in Eastern Europe (Devlin, 1984).

On the other hand, just as Romania's support for the Czechoslovak reform in 1967-8 had not signified RCP willingness to emulate democratization in its own ranks, so the support expressed towards Euro-communism was carefully qualified to indicate that the ruling Romanian elite envisaged no adoption of Italian, French or Spanish stances *vis-à-vis* Romanian society (Tőkés, 1978, p. 489). On 5 July 1977 *Scînteia* made it clear that 'communists ... must refrain from comparing the experience of parties in socialist countries, which acted under different conditions, with the methods proposed for the building of the new system by communist parties in capitalist countries'. This may partly explain why, despite official support for Euro-communism, or rather *because* of it, the doctrine showed little indication of enjoying support among Romanian dissidents, in contrast to countries such as Czechoslovakia, Poland and East Germany (Wesson, 1982, p. 72).

The leitmotif of Romania's relations with the Soviet Union since 1968 has been Bucharest's explicit rejection of the 'Brezhnev Doctrine' and the implicit measures taken by the RCP to render credibility to its determination to resist Soviet intervention. These have been analysed in depth by Aurel Braun (1978) and need not occupy us in detail within the restricted context of the present scrutiny. What must be stressed, however, is that in the 1970s and 1980s Bucharest made no concession on this matter. On the contrary, it has striven to use every possible domestic and foreign channel of communication in order to convey to Moscow its unambiguously entrenched autonomous position. On the other hand, the need to assuage Soviet suspicions has occasionally prompted the Romanian leadership to make concessions on particular issues, the immediate importance of which was highly valued in Moscow, whereas the cost of deference was relatively low in Bucharest. Afghanistan (see later) is a typical example of this. Such tactics should be viewed primarily in terms of *reculer pour mieux sauter*, although they also provide evidence as to the limits of autonomy.

The new treaty of friendship and mutual aid signed by the Soviet Union and Romania in 1970 (*Scînteia*, 8 July 1970) is more than indicative of Bucharest's adamantine postures. Unlike the similar document signed by Moscow and Prague (Braun, 1978, p. 92), the treaty made no mention of the obligation of the socialist community to come to the rescue of socialist achievements. On foreign policy issues the two sides merely agreed to 'consult'. Such 'consultations' have only occasionally proved fruitful from Moscow's point of view. A visit paid by Foreign Minister Andrei Gromyko to Bucharest in January–February 1984, with the purpose of bringing the Romanians closer to bloc positions on a variety of issues, for example, ended in apparent failure. Soviet displeasure with their reluctant ally's simulated presence was symbolically expressed in 1970 by Brezhnev's absence from the singing ceremonies, with Ceauşescu seemingly untroubled by the cancellation of the visit (King, 1980, p. 144) and retaliating in kind by boycotting the festivity himself.

Even when Moscow appears to win some concessions, the Romanians unfailingly hurry to set the record straight by making it clear that their backward step was nothing but a tactical withdrawal in preparation for a two-step forward reaffirmation of familiar positions. Shortly after the release of a declaration of the Warsaw Pact Political Consultative Council, concerning, among other things, the 'new type of relations between socialist countries' in early 1983 (*Scînteia*, 7 January 1983), *România liberă* published an article which was extensively reviewed in the English summary of the official news agency, Agerpres. The author started by complaining that the right of nations to build socialism in the way they chose was paid only lip-service by some communist parties (as indeed the declaration released by the Prague WTO Political Consultative Council did), whereas in reality some (unspecified) countries assumed 'the right to claim that one's own socialism [is superior] to that built in other countries' (*România liberă*, 10 January 1983). The implication, it should be noted, came not long after the new Soviet party leader, Yuri Andropov, had stated that, while the best forms of socialist construction were those that corresponded to each country's own interests and traditions, the 'basic principles of the socialist system . . . its *class nature* and its essence, *are the same for all countries and for all peoples*' (*Pravda*, 23 April 1982; emphasis mine).

Ceauşescu and Andropov were not on very close terms, the more so since, whether with good reason or not, the Romanian leadership suspected Andropov of pro-Hungarian sympathies. Moreover, the Romanian Secretary General had apparently failed his 'Kremlinology' course, for he is reported to have told former US President Richard Nixon that Andropov's chances of inheriting Brezhnev's mantle were not very good, owing to his identification with the KGB (Nixon on ABC TV, 12 November 1982, as quoted in Ciorănescu, 1983b). Andropov's succession by Chernenko, however, is not likely to bring about a significant improvement in relations with the Soviet Union. Disregarding the temporal nature of the succession itself, the former First Secretary of the Moldavian SSR is unlikely to view with benevolent eyes the continued, if somewhat diluted,[4] Romanian hints at the historical injustice of the 'Bessarabian question'. Moreover, Chernenko's position on the issue of party equality is hardly different from that of his two predecessors. History, according to the present Secretary General of the CPSU, 'has demonstrated that there is not, nor can there be, any path of socialism in circumvention of the general laws discovered by Marxism-Leninism and *confirmed by the experience of the USSR and other countries of existing socialism*' (TASS, 4 January 1983; emphasis mine).

While, by promoting the 'class criterion' as the unique determinant of inter-party relations, the Soviets advance the view that 'real socialism' is essentially similar everywhere (or must become similar) and that, consequently, any conflicts among members of the socialist community are by definition 'non-antagonistic' (or should become non-antagonistic), the Romanians reject both the axiom and its implications. According to an article published in *Era socialistă* at the end of 1982:

> Marxist studies have employed for a long time a model of contradictions, and, in general, of political relations among states which presupposed their reduction to class antagonisms and to class relationships . . . Consequently, for a long time it was considered, for example, that elimination of class contradictions must bring along, by itself, the disappearance of antagonisms and contradictions between nations and states . . .
>
> However, particularly in the international arena, the national state is far from being merely 'another name' for 'class' . . . It expresses a distinct reality, entrenched not only in class criteria . . .
>
> Consequently, contradictions in the international life will develop . . . in connection with differences, opposition and even antagonisms specific to the problem of affirmation of values or of essential determinants of the nation and its state: the set-up, maintenance and consolidation of the national state; ensurance of a true and multilateral independence and sovereignty; materialisation of interests and of [the state's] own aims of economic and political development and manifestation of its capability to adopt a certain [line in] internal and external politics, to participate in international interactivities and to influence the environment in which it acts [Secăreş, 1982, pp. 23-4].

The 'class' criterion, in other words, cannot be evoked for interference in the internal affairs of a member of the 'socialist community', for its uniqueness in determining relations among the members of that community is by no means axiomatic. Socialist states are national not only in form, but also in content, and hence 'proletarian internationalism' reads in Bucharest as inter-*nationalism*. This may also be the reason why the terminology itself is never employed by the Romanians, who speak rather of 'international solidarity'—a term whose implications extend to the Third World and occasionally cut across East-West divisions. The author of the article in *Era socialistă*, for example, deplored the simplification of international conflicts to mere reflections of 'East-West' class confrontation, stating that this position infringed 'the freedom to choose one's own road of development, including one's own road to socialism' (Secăreş, 1982, p. 25). In a similar, if not identical, manner, an article in the Bucharest weekly *Contemporanul*, on 5 March 1982, insisted on the importance of the 'national-state' criterion, adding that in the contemporary world the main contradictions were not those dividing capitalist from socialist states, but rather those between 'rich and poor' countries. The latter contradictions, according to the author, Vasile Ioţa, did not stem 'from the difference in their social order but from the difference between the potential and the level of economic, technical and scientific development'. As such, similar contradictions could 'arise in relations between socialist states'.

These pronouncements undoubtedly aim at diminishing the effects of anticipated Soviet wrath by enlarging the circle of Romania's semi-allies—in this case by emphasizing the common bonds that allegedly link Bucharest with the nations of the Third World. For their part, the Soviets often chose to react to Romania's display of simulated permanence *by proxy*, and it is certainly no accident that the most vociferous critics of Bucharest's attitude to 'proletarian internationalism' have been the Hungarians. In the tacit terms that link Bucharest, Moscow and Budapest the implications of any explicit Hungarian criticism of Romania's nationalist postures are certainly not lost on either side of the triangle. Moreover, general Hungarian disapproval of Bucharest's infringements of 'internationalism' has been accompanied by the airing of specific criticism concerning the situation of the Magyar national minority in Romania, which, even if not always officially inspired, must have been at least condoned by both the Hungarian authorities and by Moscow.

Soon after Ceauşescu's famous speech of May 1966, in which he castigated Soviet policies in the Comintern and raised the Bessarabian question, Zoltán Komócsin, the chief ideologist of the Hungarian party and a member of the Politburo, published in *Problems of Peace and Socialism* a strongly-worded article in which the Romanian arguments in favour of party autonomy were rejected one by one (Komócsin, 1966). The incident was followed by a declaration by Kádár, in the course of an interview with a UPI correspondent,[5] in which he referred to the Trianon Peace Treaty as to a '*diktat*' that had 'dismembered the territory of Hungary', and by the Hungarian party leader's reference to Trianon in his address to the Ninth Congress of his party in November 1966 (see Chapter 9).

With Romania refusing to join in the chorus of WTO critics of the 'Prague Spring', and later criticizing the invasion of Czechoslovakia, a new crescendo was reached in Hungarian-Romanian polemics. Although Kádár could by no means be counted among the proponents of military intervention against Czechoslovakia, he openly criticized the Romanian position in a speech delivered before the National Assembly on 18 April (*Népszabadság*, 19 April 1968). In an article published in the Soviet *Pravda* two days later, Transylvanian-born István Szirmai, the head of the ideological section of the Hungarian CC, warned against the danger of neglect of internationalist duties caused by the pursuit of selfish national interests. Neither Kádár nor Szirmai made any mention of the Hungarian minority in Romania, but shortly afterwards, at a gathering of the Hungarian Writers' Union, a number of literary critics who took the floor mentioned the 'double responsibility' which Hungarian writers should hold *vis-à-vis* Magyar creations produced not only within Hungary's own borders, but also by Hungarian minorities living in neighbouring countries (*Elet és Irodalom*, 18 May, 15 June 1968). The initiative was by no means contradictory to the offical line, for on 19 October the party daily specified that 'No people would sever its ties with its torn-away parts, which speak the same language and have an identical history and culture . . . We have an inalienable duty to preserve and cultivate these relations' (*Népszabadság*, 10 October 1968).

The Romanians were obviously concerned that the grievances of the Hungarian national minorities could be used as a pretext for intervention. This was attested not only by Ceauşescu's visit, in the immediate wake of the invasion, to areas inhabited by Hungarians (Ceauşescu, 1968-9, Vol. 3, pp. 417, 425-54, 469-70, 502-35), but also by meetings with intellectuals of the national minorities (*Scînteia*, 28 June, 4 July 1968) and by the recruitment of such intellectuals in endeavours to reject the Budapest-supported 'double responsibility' thesis (Szász, 1968. Cf. also the declaration of the commission for national minorities' literature published in *Gazeta literară*, 29 August 1968).

According to an American visitor to Romania in the summer of 1968, one of the more persistent rumours following the invasion of Czechoslovakia was that Hungarian tanks had 'accidentally' strayed over the border and been welcomed with flowers by the Hungarian villagers on the Romanian side of the frontier. Another rumour held that Hungary's reluctance to participate in the invasion had been overcome only by a promise that the next stage of the operation would be Romania (Stuart, 1970, p. 115).

This was probably very little but hearsay and some of it might have been promoted by the Romanian leadership itself. Yet in March WTO manœuvres had been conducted in Hungary (Braun, 1978, p. 130) and the leadership of the RCP now undertook the first measures designed to cope with invasion by Romania's 'allies'. According to a law passed by the GNA shortly before the intervention in Czechoslovakia, the Romanian parliament is the only body entitled to authorize the entry of foreign troops into the country. With the adoption of the 'Bill on the Organization of the National Defence' in 1972 (Braun, 1978, p. 150 ff.), Romania's defensive strategies became very obviously geared *against* its partners in the WTO, and the USSR in particular (Volgyés, 1982, pp. 16-17).

As already indicated, manœuvres were held close to Romania's borders during Ceauşescu's visit to China in 1971, and, once more, it must have been with Moscow's knowledge and encouragement that Komócsin chose this time in particular to launch yet another attack on Romania's position *vis-à-vis* the bloc. Addressing parliament on 24 June, the Hungarian chief ideologist now spoke in one breath of differences of 'assessment of certain international problems' and of Hungarian interest in 'having the inhabitants of both our country and

Romania—*including those of Hungarian nationality living there*—come to understand that the fate and destiny of our peoples is inseparable from socialism'. The Hungarian party, he insisted, had a right to comment, on a Marxist basis, on the fate of Hungarians living in Transylvania (*Népszabadság*, 25 June 1971; emphasis mine). Komóscin's Romanian homologue, party ideologist Paul Niculescu-Mizil, angrily rejected these remarks, expressing surprise 'that *it is at this particular moment* that it has been deemed proper to pose . . . the question of the existence of differences in the Hungarian and Romanian strands on matters of principle and in their assessments of certain international issues'. To both accusations, the Romanian ideologist responded that 'We have never taken the liberty of teaching others, of interfering in the internal affairs of other fraternal countries and parties. At the same time, we cannot permit anyone, any outside forum, to pronounce sentence or to interfere in any way in the internal affairs of our party and state'. In Romania, he added, all problems, including the 'progress of co-inhabiting nationalities are decided on and solved by those living in this country, by our party and state leadership' (*Scînteia*, 9 July 1971; emphasis mine).

In June 1977 Ceauşescu and Kádár met on their common border. Apart from the more amusing sides of the encounter (Kádár is reported to have been amazed by the fact that the Romanian leader was accompanied by a food-taster, in the best tradition of the times of Dracula), the two leaders agreed to set up consulates in Cluj-Napoca and Debrecen, respectively. The Romanian side was obviously none too eager to implement these provisions, suspecting, as it did, attempts to establish links with the Hungarian minority in Romania. Consequently, Bucharest dragged its feet, and the two consulates were not inaugurated until August 1980 and December 1981, respectively.

Romanian reluctance to let Budapest open its consulate in the heavily Hungarian-populated city of Transylvania may have been increased by the publication of a two-part article written by the patriarch of Hungarian letters, the writer Gyula Illyés (*Magyar Nemzet*, 25 December 1977, 1 January 1978). Illyés called attention to the problem of Hungarian ethnics living abroad, and, in a rather veiled manner, accused Romania (the name of which, however, was not specifically mentioned) of pursuing discrimination against minorities. In a stiff reply, Mihnea Gheorghiu, President of the Romanian Academy of Social and Political Sciences, accused Illyés of 'anti-Romanian obsessions' and of having become a tool in the hands of 'the hateful nationalist agitation of the fascist circles of *émigré* Magyars' (*Luceafărul*, 6 May 1978).

During recent years, witness the Lăncrănjan book (see Chapter 9), mutual recrimination has become more and more personal. In two instances, in October 1982 and in March 1983, the Hungarian party daily published satires and a cartoon of Ceauşescu, ridiculing the personality cult and the Daco-Roman mania (*Népszabadság*, 3 October 1982, 13 March 1983). And when two high Hungarian cultural officials paid a visit to Bucharest in late 1982 *Scînteia*, which is usually very careful about retouching the photographs it prints, showed their faces in a grimace (1 December 1982). Whatever may float down the River Tisa, which flows from the Soviet Union to the Romanian frontier, to the Hungarian plain, it is certainly not 'brotherly socialist' love.

Negation of the right of one party or one state to interfere in the affairs of another, combined with endeavours to evince the common bonds uniting Romania with Third World countries, led Bucharest to adopt a different position from that of the Soviet bloc on Kampuchea and Afghanistan. Yet in both these instances, but particularly in the latter, the Romanians demonstrated that, if and when the need arises, they are perfectly capable of signalling to Moscow that they understand when concessions prompted by the Kremlin order of priorities have to be made.

Romania is the only country in the Soviet bloc that has a standing treaty with the Khmer Rouge (signed during Ceaușescu's visit to Phnom Penh in 1978) and has never accepted the legitimacy of the Heng Samrin regime. In 1979, following the Soviet-supported Vietnamese invasion of Cambodia, Romania became the first member of the WTO to cast an anti-Soviet vote in the UN General Assembly, where, alongside China, Yugoslavia and the countries of the Third World, it supported the Khmer Rouge representative as his country's legitimate delegate. The Vietnamese delegation at the Twelfth Congress of the RCP was conspicuously low key. In March 1980 Bucharest once more symbolically displayed its willingness to castigate Hanoi's occupation of Kampuchea, by publishing in *Scînteia* a message of congratulation addressed to Ceaușescu by Kieu Shamphan, on the occasion of his re-election to the presidency (Radu, 1981, pp. 244, 247). However, by early 1983, when Soviet pressure on Romania seemed to intensify, for a variety of reasons contingent on issues regarded in Bucharest as of more immediate concern, the Romanian attitude on the Kampuchean question appeared to be mellowing considerably. Ceaușescu's message to the New Delhi summit of non-aligned countries, for example, made no mention at all of the Vietnamese invasion (*Scînteia*, 8 March 1983), and the Romanian press avoided mentioning pronouncements by other participants on this issue.

Neither did the Romanian President's message make any mention of Afghanistan, thereby illustrating the gradual shift registered in Bucharest's attitude on an issue of primary importance to Moscow. According to Ronald H. Linden (1983, p. 51), Romania's approach to the Soviet intervention had been, from the start, significantly more 'restrained' than towards the invasion of Czechoslovakia. Considering the proximity of the danger in the latter case, this is hardly to be wondered at. By any reasonable standard, Bucharest's caution was nevertheless blatant in its defiance of Moscow's global interests. Although Romania did not vote for the non-aligned resolution demanding immediate withdrawal of foreign troops from Afghanistan in January 1980, neither did it join the rest of the camp in voting against it. In a declaration printed in all major newspapers, Teodor Marinescu, Romania's ambassador to the UN, declared that his country could not vote in favour of the majority proposal, because of the damage to *détente* the resolution generated, but neither could it condone interference in the internal affairs of a non-aligned state, since this constituted an infringement of international law and of Romania's often reiterated foreign policy principles (*Scînteia*, 15 January 1980). Consequently, the Romanian delegation 'voted with its feet', absenting itself from the ballot. Furthermore, together with North Korea, Bucharest refused to sign the February 1980 communiqué issued by the Sofia meeting of parliamentary delegations from twelve communist countries, which expressed support for Soviet intervention (Laux, 1981, p. 114).

Nevertheless, several months later, Soviet pressure must have determined Romania to reconsider the situation. On 27 April *Scînteia* published a message of congratulation addressed by Ceauşescu to Babrak Karmal on the occasion of the anniversary of the Afghan 'revolution', in which the Romanian leader expressed his conviction that relations between the two countries 'would develop further to the benefit of both peoples, of the policy of peace, *détente*, independence and progress'. In May Ceauşescu attached his signature to the declaration issued by the WTO summit which endorsed Moscow's position (*Scînteia*, 13 May 1980), and similar views were included in the joint statements issued after the Romanian leader's encounters with Bulgaria's Zhivkov and East Germany's Honecker in June (Radu, 1981, p. 247). Yet in December 1982, at the UN, Romania voted together with China for new investigations of charges that the USSR had waged chemical warfare in Laos, Cambodia and Afghanistan (Ciorănescu, 1983b).

As revealed in Chapter 8, the economic rationale of Romania's courtship of the Third World proved to have been quite mistaken. Instead of finding itself an exporter to the markets of 'the South', Bucharest ended by importing huge quantities of petroleum, most of which cannot be exchanged on barter terms, and the opportunities offered by recognition as a 'developing' country were largely missed by economic mismanagement. What Romania has been left with is diplomatic pomp and the questionably valuable diplomatic support of some Third World countries for its autonomous policies *vis-à-vis* the Soviets.

Romania was granted full membership status in the 'Group of 77' at the Manila meeting of February 1976 (*Scînteia*, 8 February 1976) and subsequently became a member of GATT, of UNCTAD, of the IMF and of the World Bank. In April 1975 former Foreign Minister George Macovescu requested Yugoslavia to support his country's application for observer status at the non-aligned summit conference, scheduled for Colombo in 1976 (*Tanjug*, 29 April 1975, as quoted in King, 1978, pp. 883-4). In an interview granted to *Le Monde* on 21 July 1975, the Romanian President explained that his country was 'objectively' both a member of the socialist camp and of the developing countries and it was in the latter capacity that it was requesting observer status in the non-aligned movement, since 'these states are, almost in their totality, developing countries as well'. In principle, however, Romania was also 'firmly in favour of abolishing military blocs', of 'concomitant liquidation of both the NATO bloc and the Warsaw Treaty' (Ceauşescu, 1970-83, Vol. 11, pp. 941-2). At the Lima conference of the non-aligned states, in August 1975, however, the participants decided to grant only guest-status to the Romanians, and neither efforts in Colombo nor in New Delhi in 1983 met with further success. Romania's permanent guest-status, despite its membership of the WTO, is balanced by the similar status extended to Portugal, a member of NATO.

In view of Bucharest's drive for further economic relations and its identi-fication with the developing countries, Robert R. King writes, 'establishing links with the non-aligned movement was merely the next logical step' (King, 1978, p. 882). However, the implications of such links are too important to be viewed as a mere extension of economic interests. In Bucharest's perception, semi-official membership of the non-aligned movement is designed to provide yet another example of the imposed nature of Romania's permanence in the Soviet sphere.

Although the Romanians are careful to emphasize that 'socialism and non-alignment have the same vision of the new principles that are to underline the future relations among all states of the world' (N. Mielcioiu, 'The Non-aligned Movement', as quoted in Radu, 1981, p. 242), from other pronouncements it can easily be inferred that not *all* socialist states are to be credited with such generous designs for the future world order. While 'contradictions' among socialist states, once viewed as 'non-antagonistic', are nowadays, according to the official Romanian line, of a possibly 'antagonistic nature', those occurring between the non-aligned countries remain 'non-antagonistic', for these states (including Romania) are united in the common struggle against the common foe—the more developed nations (of the West *and of the East*, as it has been observed) which attempt to impose their hegemony and domination.

Although Romania is known to have occasionally delivered arms to the more radical countries of the Third World, such as Mozambique (Kanet, 1983, p. 241), this should by no means be interpreted as if Bucharest's autonomous foreign policy were merely a smoke-screen for Soviet manipulation, as one observer is known to have suggested (Socor, 1976). The Romanians are also known to have cultivated good relations with states such as Gabon, Zaire, Costa Rica and, in the Arab world, Sadat's Egypt, Somalia and the Sudan—hardly regimes described by the Soviets as 'progressive' following the expulsion of their military and/or diplomatic staffs. Dumitru Popescu's statement, in the *Era socialistă* article of March 1984 is, from this point of view, more than significant. Romania, the PEC member wrote, 'does not consider itself obliged to identify automatically with a bloc policy of confrontation and tension', trying to promote in its stead a policy of peace and *détente.*

Détente is indeed perceived by Bucharest as potentially contributing to the entrenchment of its autonomous policies for, as Braun puts it, in so far as Romanian interests are concerned, a Soviet Union that does not feel strategically on the defence makes for a greater degree of security. When Moscow does not feel under pressure, the need to seek unquestioning obedience from its less important allies diminishes (Braun, 1978, pp. 115-16). For these reasons, the Romanians have been known to adopt positions which, more often than not, are aimed at bridging the gap between East and West and, above all, at pursuing their own long-term strategic political objectives. At times, these may clash with Soviet interests, but this is not necessarily always the case. For example, the resuscitation of Romania's proposals for demilitarization of the Balkans, which can be traced back to proposals first put forward by Bucharest on behalf of the WTO in 1957, would perfectly well suit Moscow's purposes, since the practical outcome of implementing these proposals, now demanding the denuclearization of the region (*Lumea*, Nos. 12-24, 17 March to 9 June 1983), would be neutralization and withdrawal of NATO and US forces. Consequently, the WTO supports the Romanian suggestions. This coincidence of interests, on the other hand, should not be read as subservience. The Romanians have attempted to play an active role in defusing *any* danger of an outbreak of hostilities, and even of growing tension between the superpowers, for no such scenario can be envisaged as serving Bucharest's attempts to resist Moscow's pressure for 'policy co-ordination'. And if the proposal for Balkan denuclearization coincides with Moscow's interests, in other instances Bucharest has taken initiatives that can hardly be seen as reflecting the position of its 'allies' in the WTO.

Romania's support for the Helsinki agreements, for example, can be attributed to no small extent to the provisions included in the second document of the first 'package', which deals with confidence-building measures. Having on several occasions experienced attempts by Moscow to intimidate them by military manœuvres close to their borders, the Romanians were enthusiastic supporters of the provision that required prior notification of any manœuvres involving over 25,000 troops and taking place within 250 km. of national frontiers. Further-more, as Braun indicates, the Romanian ambassador to the talks, Valentin Lipatti, insisted that confidence-building measures must include not only a prohibition on the use of force, but also on the *threat* of that use (Braun, 1978, p. 116). At the Stockholm Conference on Confidence and Security-Building Measures and Disarmament in Europe, in early 1984, Bucharest proposed—without Moscow's prior knowledge or approval—that the twenty-one days' advance notice of manœuvres agreed on at Helsinki be extended to thirty days, and that prior notification be required for manœuvres exceeding 18,000, as opposed to 25,000 troops (*Era socialistă*, 25 January 1984).

The most blatant discrepancy between Romanian and Soviet positions in so far as disarmament parleys are concerned occurred when the USSR decided to take counter-measures in response to the deployment of American Pershing missiles in Europe, at the end of 1983. Not only did Bucharest refrain from following the example of the other Soviet allies in blaming the situation on the US alone, but once the Soviets decided to retaliate in kind, the PEC, the Council of State and the government issued a declaration stating, '*All* these measures . . . push Europe and the whole world toward nuclear catastrophe' (*Scînteia*, 26 November 1983; emphasis mine). Several initiatives were taken by Bucharest in order to promote the resumption of the Geneva talks, and when the Soviet missiles were about to be installed in East Germany and Czechoslovakia, the GNA expressed deep concern over 'the installation of new medium-range missiles in certain Western *and* Eastern states of Europe' (*Scînteia*, 13 November 1983; emphasis mine). Furthermore, addressing the GNA session, Ceauşescu referred to the 'deployment of new medium-range US missiles in Europe *and the setting of new Soviet missiles in* retaliation', describing both as measures which 'ignored international public opinion' (*Scînteia*, 17 November 1983; emphasis mine). Finally, another appeal addressed by the GNA to the parliaments of Europe and Canada (i.e. including those of the GDR and Czechoslovakia), once the missiles had been deployed, urged a halt to installation, pending agreement between the superpowers (*Scînteia*, 25 March 1984).

Another Romanian proposal which reflects only an apparent identity of views with other members of the WTO concerns the freezing of military budgets. On 5 May 1984 the Romanian government submitted to the NATO countries a memorandum on behalf of its allies in the pact, proposing to hold preliminary consultations, attended by all members of the two alliances, with a view to starting talks on a mutual agreement not to increase military expenditures, as a first step towards reducing them. The Romanian proposals were based on the plan advanced by the WTO leaders at their meetings in Prague and Moscow, in January and June 1983. Since most military expenditure in the Soviet Union and its East European allies is hidden under other budget heads, the proposals were hardly likely to be accepted by NATO. But as far as the Romanians were concerned, this was 'sweet revenge', for in their attempt to forestall Soviet pressure for further integration of the pact, they had refused to increase military spending in 1978. In fact, Romania is the only Warsaw Pact state to have actually implemented the proposals—to Soviet dismay, it should be added. In December 1978 some five hundred million lei from the military budget were said to have been directed to the budget for children's allowances. In September 1980 military expenditure was again reduced by two thousand million lei, 1981 saw a further reduction in this budget, while in 1983 and 1984 military expenditure was kept at the level of the previous years (Cioránescu, 1984).

At times, Bucharest endeavours to defuse situations of potential friction likely to generate renewed Soviet pressure for integration and co-ordination, brought about Romanian attempts to play a mediating role in the international arena. It is relevant that none of these attempts met with Moscow's approval. Apart from the yet unconfirmed endeavour to serve as mediator between Vietnam and Kampuchea, the most famous instances of Romanian involvement in world affairs were the role played in the US-Chinese *rapprochement* and in the preliminary stages of the Israeli-Egyptian talks that led to the Camp David agreements.

In neither instance were economic interests absent, for both the United States and Israel had come to play significant, though proportionately different, roles in Romania's quest for hard currency.[6] In the former case, total trade between the two countries had jumped from some 70.6 million lei in 1965 to 6,222.5 million lei in 1980 and, although constantly deficient, the balance of trade between the two countries showed signs of closing the gap until 1979 (Republica Socialistă România. Direcţia Centrală de Statistică, 1979, p. 507; 1980, p. 262). In the latter case, the balance of trade has been constantly favourable to Bucharest since 1967—a price Israel certainly paid not unwillingly in exchange for the position adopted by the Romanian leadership since the eve of the outbreak of the 1967 Arab-Israeli hostilities.

Bucharest's economic interests notwithstanding, mercantilist considerations were certainly not the sole factor behind the Romanian stand. Obviously, recruiting support in the West was a high priority in the Romanian capital, one which, it should be added, had prompted Ceauşescu again to display his autonomous stand in 1967, causing friction with Moscow—the establishment of diplomatic relations with West Germany. A second consideration, certainly present in the case of American-Chinese feelers, clearly stemmed from the benefits Bucharest stood to derive from a prospective collaboration between the Soviet Union's most powerful adversaries. Yet these tactics could also prove counterproductive for, once again, an insecure Kremlin does not necessarily make for a secure Bucharest.

The Romanian dilemma of foreign policy initiatives consequently lies in having to decide whether to promote measures conducive to the weakening of (a) Soviet *motivation* to exercise pressure, such as *détente*; or (b) Soviet *capabilities* to acquire superiority over adversaries, the results of which would be nefarious in as much as autonomous Romanian stances are concerned. Like the American–Chinese *rapprochement*, the *pax Americana*, which the Camp David agreements initially seemed to lead to, belongs to the second category. Bucharest certainly had no reason to regret the expulsion of Soviet military advisors from Egypt or the subsequent break in diplomatic relations between Cairo and Moscow, and its role in bringing about the Egyptian-Israeli dialogue could not have been cheered in Moscow.

For precisely the same reason, seen from the other side of the superpowers' table, American-Romanian relations received a boost with Nixon's visit to Bucharest in 1969 (the first such trip by an American President to a Warsaw Pact country), shortly after Romania denounced the invasion of Czechoslovakia. In August 1975, after having granted MFN status to Romania (in March), President Ford visited Bucharest and in September 1983 Vice-President Bush visited the Romanian capital. Among the important American visits paid to Romania were those by Secretary of State Haig (following the declaration of martial law in Poland), in February 1982, and by Assistant Secretary of Defense Frank Carlucci, in October 1983, at a time of increased tension between East and West. For his part, Ceauşescu visited the United States in December 1970, in January 1973 and in April 1978.

During the first part of 1983, relations between the two states were overshadowed by the American decision to react to human rights infringements by the Romanian regime (the 'educational tax', see Chapter 9) by threatening to withdraw Romania's MFN status. However, the problem was settled on Bucharest's agreement not to enforce the legislation, and although regular inquiries in the US Congress concerning various forms of discrimination in Romania are likely to continue, no American administration is likely to pursue a course feared to lead to the enstrangement of the 'maverick'. Moreover, American public opinion is likely to be more impressed by such displays of autonomy as the decision to participate in the Los Angeles Olympic Games of 1984, alongside China and Yugoslavia, than by an item buried in the inside pages of the *New York Times* concerning the fate of would-be emigrants or the occasional Romanian dissident.

Western Europe has also fulfilled an important role in Romania's stratagems for autonomy entrenchment. The EEC in general (see Chapter 8), and West Germany and France in particular, are significant economic partners. By 1980 the Federal Republic was Romania's most important trade partner in the Western world and, what is at least as important, Romanian exports to this country exceeded imports in 1970-1, 1977 and in 1980-1. Trade with France, while deficient in every year except 1980, was second only to West Germany among Romania's EEC partners in 1981 (Republica Socialistă România. Direcţia Centrală de Statistică, 1975, p. 387; 1980, p. 502; 1982, pp. 256-7). In addition, both countries participate in several joint-production schemes, one of the most important of which involves the manufacture of French cars under licence. Great Britain, France and West Germany have all been involved in the Romanian effort to produce military equipment, which was triggered by Soviet reluctance to deliver modern armaments to an unreliable ally, as well as by Romania's attempt to give credibility to its determination to resist intervention (Braun, 1978, p. 170). In 1977 a joint equity venture was signed with the German-Dutch VFW Fokker company. It provided for the production of a hundred twin-engined transport aircraft over a period of ten years. Although the project was never implemented, it contributed to the development of expertise (Laux, 1981, p. 111). French helicopters of the Alouette III and Puma types have been built under licence since 1977 and 1978, respectively (*World Armament and Disarmament*, 1982, p. 245). Romania also assembles BAC-111 passenger and freight transport aeroplanes and it has produced some 360 Pilatus Britten-Norman BN-2 Islander aircraft, also under contract. The latter plane is known to have a multi-purpose military version—the Defender and the Maritime Defender (*Aviation Week and Space Technology*, 13 December 1982; *Jane's All the World Aircraft 1981-1982*, pp. 256-7).

No survey of Romanian foreign affairs can be concluded without reference to the personality factor. Like all other aspects of life in this Balkan state, foreign policy-making has been completely dominated by one man—Nicolae Ceauşescu. More than other aspects of life, however, the process came to reflect a gradual but constant replacement of rationality by empty grandiosity. For example, Romania's role in the Middle East settlement has served rational purposes, and even the most severe critics of the regime would credit Ceauşescu with a splendid performance. His subsequent insistence that his country (i.e. its President) be represented at a prospective international summit on the Middle East alongside the superpowers, on the other hand, serves no other purpose but that of satisfying the Romanian leader's thirst for personal glorification. Moreover, as Aurel Braun observes, some of Romania's challenges to the Soviet Union in recent years have been gratuitous, being probably generated by the 'imperial syndrome' to which Ceauşescu is succumbing (see Chapter 6). Likewise, his 'courting of various Third World leaders seemed almost farcical at times, and undertaken more for the gratification of his ego than for the sake of tangible benefits to Romania' (Braun, 1982, p. 55). In short, from a busy and appreciated politician, Ceauşescu turned into a somewhat comical political busybody.

It is true that prominence in international affairs may contribute to internal legitimization, the more so since Ceauşescu's exaggerated involvement in world affairs should be viewed as very much a part of what Linden terms '"the psychic payoffs" paid to the population in the currency of Romanian nationalism'. The deplorable state of the Romanian economy, on the other hand, is reported to generate some doubts as to the wisdom itself of the autonomous course. The Hungarians and the Bulgarians, it is nowadays occasionally remarked, may have no foreign policy of their own, but they have enough to eat. It therefore looks as if Linden's doubts as to the Romanian regime's continued ability to 'purchase legitimacy with a nationalized foreign policy' are beginning to materialize. Present signs, writes the American scholar, as if reporting from Ceauşescu's speeding train, 'point to a tunnel at the end of the light' (Linden, 1981, pp. 238-9). But who is to say that the tunnel itself is not haunted by the odd dialectical couple with which we started our journey into Romanian lands—the spectre of communism and the ghost of nationalism. Their ubiquity may be the only non-simulated presence around. As for the rest, *plus ça change, plus c'est simulé.*

Notes

Chapter 1

1. In this, as in other chapters, I am expanding on Shafir, 1981b, pp. 589-639.
2. Already by the sixteenth century the 'chroniclers' of the principalities were speaking of the Latin origins of all Romanians, but with no apparent political impact (Iorga, 1969, Vol. 1, pp. 139-40, 224-7; Giurescu, 1967, p. 109). The short-lived unification of the three provinces under Michael the Brave between 1599 and 1600 can hardly be said to have generated a 'national awareness', but it was to become part of the Romanian side of the Transylvanian 'myth'. According to President Ceauşescu, for instance, this union 'expressed the will of the Romanians to have their own unitary state, heralding the formation of the national unitary state later, in 1918'. The unification under Michael the Brave, he stated, should be emphasized, for it constitutes a 'reply' to those [Hungarian] 'historians who today attempt to propagate the theory of the alleged existence, in a certain period, of a void in the Carpathian-Danubian space' (Ceauşescu, 1982, p. 6).
3. Detailed accounts of the Sovietization of Romanian historiography are to be found in Ghermani, 1967a and Georgescu, 1981. Cf. also Rura, 1961. An incisive and concise presentation is that of Schöpflin, 1974.
4. The letters 'â' and 'î' are pronounced similarly in the Romanian language, but while the former may be traced back to Latin origins, the latter evolved from the Cyrillic character. A government decree issued in September 1953 and enforced in April 1954 obliterated the letter 'â' from the alphabet. This 'ortographic reform' was partially altered in 1965 when the regime's neo-nationalist line 'reformed the reform'. Compare Academia Republicii Populare Romîne. Institutul de Linguistică, 1960, pp. 3-4 and Academia Republicii Socialiste România. Institutul de Linguistică din Bucureşti, 1965, p. 3.
5. 'Group autonomy'—often called 'personal autonomy'—indicates (to employ Karl Renner's terminology) the 'state-exempted societal spheres', while 'individual autonomy' refers to intra-group attitudes and is defined in sociological terms as the 'ability of an individual to select personal values and to withstand social pressure for conformity', thereby being capable of acting 'independently of norms of an immediate group situation in favour of his own personal norms, or convictions' (K. Renner, *Das Selbststimmungsrecht der Nation in Besonderer Anwendung auf Österreich*, as quoted in Boehm, 1930, p. 335; G. A. Theodorson & A. G. Theodorson, 1969, p. 24). For a discussion of autonomy versus conformity in Romania cf. Shafir, 1982, on which the following presentation is partially based.

Chapter 2

1. The following is based on Shafir, 1984b. Cf. also Roberts, 1969, pp. 243-4, 276-81 and *passim*; Haupt, 1967; Kitch, 1977; Jowitt, 1978b; Voicu, 1970; Hurezeanu, 1970 and 1975; Ornea, 1982.
2. Expelled from Romania in 1881, Russel (Sudzilovski) settled down in Sofia, as a general practitioner. Later, however, he emigrated to France, from whence he left for the USA. By 1891, under the name of Kauka Luchini, he was in Hawaii, where he became President of the Senate after an armed rebel insurrection. Following defeat, Sudzilovski-Russel-Luchini

was once more on the run, and after a short spell, during which he became the owner of a large sugar plantation in a Pacific island, this unrepentant dissident arrived in Japan, where he engaged in revolutionary propaganda among Russian prisoners of war. He met his death in China in 1930, aged eighty-three (not before he had married a Japanese noblewoman (Ornea, 1982, pp. 208-9n)).

3. Similar criticism, however, was expressed as late as 1961. Cf. Gheorghiu-Dej, 1961, pp. 426-7.

4. Unless otherwise indicated, the following is based on Rakovsky's autobiography, in *Deyateli SSSR i Oktyabr' skoi Revoliutsii: Entsiklopeditcheski slovar' russkogo bibliografitcheskogo Instituta 'Grant'*, Vol.2, Moscow 1927, column 170 ff., translated in G. Haupt & J. J. Marie, 1974, pp. 385-98. Apart from sources quoted below, on C. Rakovsky see also Rothchild, 1955; Ionescu, 1964, pp. 2-7, 9-10, 22-3 and *passim*; Deutscher, 1970a, pp. 207-8 and *passim*, Deutscher 1970b, pp. 66-7, 78-81 and *passim*, Deutscher, 1970c, pp. 202-3, 385-6, 434-40 and *passim*; Oren, 1971, pp. 38-9, 89 and *passim*.

5. Because of his purge in the Soviet Union, Rakovsky was ignored by post-war Romanian party historiography, while his pro-Russian position in the inter-war period was an impediment to full rehabilitation under Ceaușescu. Partial rehabilitation, however, occurred in 1968, with the publication of a collection of documents dealing with socialist activities between 1907 and 1916 (Institutul de studii istorice, 1968). Cristescu's article should be considered a further step in this direction.

6. In 1920, however, he opposed action against Romania on grounds very similar to those which had determined Lenin to veto his plans a year earlier, namely that the action would unite the major powers against the Soviet state. Lenin had opposed Rakovsky's plan in 1919 because he feared it would weaken his troops' capacity to wipe out Denikin's forces. Compare King, 1980, p. 28 and Conte, 1975, Vol. 1, pp. 240-6, respectively.

Chapter 3

1. For a discussion of RCP attitudes to the 'agrarian question' in the inter-war period cf. Roberts, 1969, pp. 250, 287-8; Jackson, 1966, pp. 252-4; King, 1980, pp. 23-5.

2. This is yet another 'revision' of post-war historiography. In the early sixties anti-Comintern activities by Romanian socialists were still branded 'social-democrat intrigues' and 'reactionary plots' (Ghermani, 1977, p. 13).

3. These are included in *Istoria Partidului Communist Român: Sinteză* (Bucharest: Institutul de studii istorice și social-politice de pe lîngă CC al PCR), n.d., pp. 28-9, a document for strictly internal circulation, as was revealed to me by a high-ranking Romanian party historian in 1983. These figures, however, are also included in Graham, 1982, pp. 30-1. The Romanian historian was obviously surprised and annoyed that the American author had managed to gain access to the book, and in my presence made a note of the fact, the purpose of which was, naturally, not revealed to this author.

4. See the illuminating article by Vago, 1972. It is interesting to remark that the RCP did not hesitate to attempt to exploit anti-semitism in its favour. The Third Congress, for instance, called for struggle against 'Jewish capital' (Vago, 1974, p. 47).

5. For a list of leaders liquidated in the USSR, and rehabilitated in April 1968, cf. *Plenara*, April 1968, p. 75).

6. Statistics for the 1919, 1920 and 1922 elections are often confusing and contradictory. Absolute figures on a national basis are misleading, because different voting systems were used in the different provinces of the newly established Greater Romania. Parties did not run candidates in all provinces, and there is some disagreement concerning the provinces in

which the RCP participated in elections. According to Ziemer (1969, p. 1061), the communists ran candidates in the Old Kingdom only, whereas according to Shapiro (1981, pp. 41-5), the 0.8 per cent includes Bessarabia too. The latter source, however, has the 0.8 per cent under the 'Socialist Party' category, and has no entry whatever for the communists. The figures cited for other provinces by Shapiro do not correspond to Ziemer's figures on the separate socialist list. The RCP received 63,131 votes in 1922, but this is less impressive than it might look at first sight for, according to the 1918 electoral law for the Old Kingdom, Dobrudja and Bessarabia, the electorate could vote for more than one candidate. Consequently, a voter could give all his votes to the same list, up to the number of deputies elected by his district (Shapiro, 1981, p. 44).

7. For a short spell of a few months, the Popovici group had acted independently as the Socialist Party of Romania (Scurtu, 1982, p. 139).

8. Following King Carol II's coup of February 1938, the party-system was abolished in March. In December the King instituted a single-party system, with himself at the head of the Front of National Rebirth (Nedelcu, 1973, pp. 265-92; Roberts, 1969, pp. 206-8).

Chapter 4

1. Of these, Nano and Cretzianu are valuable primary sources, for both were actively engaged in the negotiations. Simion is the first comprehensive regime-approved version of the events.

2. This had included, in addition to the RCP, the Ploughmen's Front, the Union of Patriotic Defence, the Socialist-Peasant Party and the MADOSZ (Magyar Dolgozók Országos Szovetsége), a left-wing Hungarian organization under Communist tutelage. Initially, the SDP had also agreed to join, but shortly afterwards it withdrew, making membership conditional on the participation of the two other 'historical' democratic parties, the NPP and the NLP (Jurca, 1978, p. 162; Scurtu, 1980, pp. 259-6).

3. The latter accounts are particularly evident in Lee, 1955 and in Franck, 1977, both of whom rely heavily on the reminiscences of the King and the Court.

4. The new anthem is described as the 'symbol of the indestructible cord between the achievements of the socialist years, the present internal and external policies of the country, the future perspectives on the path of multilateral progress and the Romanian people's long past of struggle for liberty and social justice' (Surpat *et al.*, 1980, p. 272).

5. This argument was first presented by Axenciuc, 1965.

6. The NDF was set up in October 1944, thereby splitting the NDB. It included the RCP, the SDP, the Ploughmen's Front, the Union of Patriots, and the United Trade Unions. Later, it was joined by MADOSZ (Ionescu, 1964, p. 99; Vago, 1977, p. 128).

Chapter 5

1. This may or may not indicate that Niculescu-Mizil was opposing Ceauşescu's bid for absolute power in 1969. The former chief ideologist's constant shift from one position to another in the hierarchy (though by no means confined to him alone), as well as the fact that he was forced to drop the 'Mizil' from his name, lest he sound more 'noble' than Ceauşescu, would appear to substantiate such 'Kremlinological' speculation.

2. For a Romanian version of these events see Fătu, 1972. For a Western account of the Maniu-Brătianu resistance activities in the period 1944-7 consult Quinlan, 1977.

3. This is attested by a letter published in *Glasul Patriei* (a publication destined for use as propaganda among *émigrés* in the West) on 20 December 1955, in which he claimed to have erred when entering into an alliance with the NPP in the late forties.

4. The most detailed studies of the industrialization drive are Montias, 1967 and Jackson, 1977.

5. For an incisive discussion of 'truth blending' in Romanian statistical records, and a comparison with Western evaluations of the country's economic growth see Jackson 1981b.

6. For a subsequent revision of the author's arguments in this article see Huntington, 1971.

7. The following is based on Shafir, 1982.

8. The 'deviation' apparently did generate some friction with the Soviets and other 'loyal' parties. According to Ceauşescu, 'some comrades abroad, and even some in [our] country, ask: why does our party's Programme formulate the thesis of moulding a multilaterally developed socialist society, whereas other socialist countries formulated that of a developed socialist society? Formulation of a new strategic objective undoubtedly constitutes the [separate] task of each party. Each [party] establishes it, taking into consideration both the general laws [of socialist construction] and [its own] concrete realities . . . We are similarly asked: why don't we use the thesis of real socialism? Our vantage point, once more, is that it is the right of each party to characterize, in one form or another, the socialism it is building. Were we to use the term "real socialism" for our country, some comrades could possibly infer that we make an absolutization of our form of socialist construction, that we consider it the only valid form, and that, in one way or another, we deny the reality of other ways and forms of socialist construction' (Ceauşescu, 1982, p. 26).

9. To promote productivity, the depositor would earn 6 per cent per year if the enterprise fulfilled its planned profits, 8 per cent if these profits were exceeded, but only 5 per cent if plan implementation were deficient.

10. See Conquest, 1966, pp. 35-7. Conquest, however, does not provide a definition of the term. One would be tempted to employ Jerry Hough's concept of 'petrification', were it not for the author's own disavowal of such interpretation of Soviet-type systems, and for the fact that 'petrification' tends to be (wrongly) associated with 'eternity'. See the discussion in Hough, 1977, pp. 19-47.

Chapter 6

1. This section is based on Shafir, 1985.

2. Such references, to be sure, are also to be found in Dej's pronouncements, dealing with the struggle against his rivals; but these are instances of personal, rather than generational, orientation.

3. For example, the decision of Ochab to step down in Gomulka's favour in Poland in 1956, could partially be attributed to determination to end factional strife and allow the rallying of the Polish United Workers' Party around a leadership which promised to be both 'national' and 'socialist' oriented at the same time.

4. For a critical review of Bunce's thesis cf. Brown, 1982, pp. 227-31; Breslauer, 1982, p. 287n.

5. Unlike the other members of the Dejist team, Ceauşescu had not formally been a member of the 1954 inner core of national leadership. He became a full member of the Politburo shortly after Pătrăşcanu's liquidation. Consequently, unlike the other lieutenants of Gheorghiu-Dej, he could decline responsibility for Pătrăşcanu's execution. But the formal side of the affair is not likely to reveal the true picture. After all, Drăghici was not a member of the Politburo at that time either, and the consecutive promotion of both future power contenders to the leading party organ in 1955 indicates that Dej was trusting both to implement his line in the two most strategic pillars of the structure of power: the party and the security apparatus. It should also be pointed out that Foriş, who was also rehabilitated in April 1968, was castigated by Ceauşescu at the November-December 1961 CC plenum as an 'agent' of Antonescu's secret police (*Scînteia*, 13 December 1961). This hardly substantiates Ceauşescu's attempt to portray

Drăghici as the one and only member of the former leadership who 'was persuaded he could do anything because of his connections with Gheorghiu-Dej' (Ceauşescu, 1968-9, Vol. 3, p. 195). One should grant that Ceauşescu was less involved than Drăghici (who had been Minister of the Interior since 1952) in the decision to liquidate Pătrăşcanu. Nevertheless, his promotion to candidate membership of the Politburo in April 1954, following Pătrăşcanu's execution, indicates he had certainly not opposed the move, despite subsequent attempts at presenting a different image of those events. I am alluding here to the play *The Power and the Truth* published in 1973, which had originally served as a script for a film (Popovici, 1973; Shafir, 1983b, pp. 413-14). It is possible, however, that Ceauşescu was accurate when he revealed in 1968 that Dej had opposed an attempt by the remainder of the Politburo members to remove Drăghici in 1956, while he had personally supported the attempt (Ceauşescu, 1968-9, Vol. 3, pp. 194-5). This incident could be described as an earlier version of the 'struggle against power', as well as one of personal rivalry for the mantle of the heir presumptive. Whatever the angle of perspective, it had nothing in common with opposition to Dej's former purges.

6. The title of Secretary General was restored in the Soviet Union in 1966 and in Czechoslovakia in 1971 (Rush, 1974, p. 289).
7. The other four were Drăghici, Moghioroş, Mihai Dalea and Leonte Răutu.
8. '*Dej-rein*' (German) means 'clean of Dej', in fact 'clean of Dej supporters'. It is derived from '*Juden-rein*' (clean of Jews), which the Nazis used in reference to the desirability of getting rid of semites (editor's note).
9. 'Camarilla' is mainly associated in Romania with King Carol II's corrupt entourage.
10. For a detailed analysis of her career and the animosities associated with it, see Fischer 1983b in Wolchik & Meyer, forthcoming. My good friend Mary Ellen Fischer was kind enough to let me benefit from this manuscript before publication.
11. According to a Romanian historian who happens to hold Central Committee membership, one of the mysteries of the present century—likely to remain one of history's great puzzles—is 'who were Mrs Ceauşescu's colleagues at University?' Private conversation. This has not stopped respectable Western seats of learning from bestowing honorary degrees and titles upon the Romanian 'First Comrade'.
12. The differences between the Hohenzollerns and the Ceauşescus, according to a joke current in Bucharest, rests in the fact that the former ruled the country one *after* the other.
13. The absence of Poland, a most obvious 'candidate' for the pattern described in this paragraph, is however, striking. While patronage and political clientelism is widespread in communist Poland (Tarkowski, 1983), there were no instances of 'familialism' at the top of the hierarchy. This is probably explained in part by the high rate of marriages with Jews among party leaders who held prominent positions until 1970. To have advanced one's kin to high posts would have increased animosity, as well as played into the hands of political adversaries of M. Moczar's type. In Hungary the absence of 'familialism' in the post-1956 leadership is probably best explained by the 'personality factor' (see the discussion below).
14. This argument is further developed in Jowitt, 1983.
15. See also Fischer, 1981, pp. 133-4.
16. See the stimulating analysis of the reaction of Husák and Kádár to similar circumstances in Gitelman, 1981.
17. According to the decision of a CC plenum of June 1965.
18. According to the RCP statutes, members can join at 18, but for those under 26 years this is conditioned by prior membership of the Union of Communist Youth, the age limit for membership of the latter organization being 30.

19. On 31 December 1980 the age breakdown of party members was as follows: 23.60 per cent under 30; 52.49 per cent 31-50; 16.36 per cent 51-60; and 7.55 per cent over 60 years of age (*Scînteia*, 28 March 1981). No figures concerning the age composition of the RCP were published after this date.

Chapter 7

1. This figure was calculated from data included in the Central Intelligence Agency, 1982, pp. 25-32, 46-52.
2. Apart from the Ceauşescu pair and Ilie Verdeţ, whose positions figure in Table 11, other members of the family who hold multiple positions in party and state are Nicu Ceauşescu, Manea Mănescu and Gheorge Petrescu (see Chapter 6).
3. 'Workers' self-management' and enterprise 'self-administration' were launched by Ceauşescu in July 1977. See Ceauşescu, 1970-83, Vol. 14, pp. 543-609.
4. This situation of 'responsibility without control' (Nelson, 1980, pp. 47-8) is clearly reflected in Ceauşescu's speech of 7 September 1979, in which the party leader put before the Central Committee the main points of the envisaged extension of 'self-management' to the peoples' councils. See Ceauşescu, 1970-83, Vol. 18, pp. 657-8.

Chapter 8

1. Among East European countries, Romania's debt service ratio was second only to Czechoslovakia in 1980. Even in 1981 debts per capita were a third less than in Hungary, the GDR or Yugoslavia. See Jackson, 1983, p. 9.
2. According to *Scînteia* of 6 February 1982, Romanian industry uses 20-25 per cent more electricity to produce identical products. Earlier, in a speech delivered at the Second Congress of the Working People's Council in 1981 (*Scînteia*, 25 June 1981), Ceauşescu stated that the annual per capita consumption of primary energy will represent 5,000kgs. of conventional fuel by 1985, and that per capital consumption of electric power will surpass 3,500 kWh, which gives Romania equal or even higher consumption rates than those registered for the industrial developed countries, the national income of which is 2 to 3 times higher than that of the SSR.
3. Although the Soviet Union also raised prices for raw materials, trade with 'acceptable' CMEA partners between 1976 and 1984 was based on long-term agreements which reflected a five-year moving average of preceding years' market prices, calculated annually. Even these were generally used only as the starting point for an intricate bargaining process, and the USSR's other partners benefited from long-term loans (Kanet, 1981, p. 304; Lawson, 1982-3, p. 34). The CMEA summit of June 1984 decided to bring Soviet oil prices nearer to average world market prices.
4. The largest such enterprises are in the Middle East, the Banyas oil refinery in Syria being the biggest of all.
5. For details concerning previous feelers in this direction, the earliest of which dates from April 1972, see King, 1978b, p. 880.
6. It should be mentioned, however, that in 1981 prices for deliveries of products to the state were increased twofold, and a further increase was decreed in 1983 (*Scînteia*, 24 January 1982, 29 March 1983; Jackson, 1983, pp. 57-8). The effect of the incentive, none the less, remains controversial. An American economist was told by his Bucharest acquaintances that peasants were no longer interested in coming to town to sell products, because they were paid higher prices for deliveries to the state (Jackson, 1983, p. 57). On the other hand,

in an interview with *Scînteia* on 2 April 1983, a Romanian agricultural official admitted that some peasants had not delivered 'even an egg' to the state.

7. This can be deduced from the speech of Finance Minister P. Gigea in the GNA, explaining why defence spending in 1982 and 1983 differed by 8.8 per cent, despite Ceauşescu's declaration that military expenditure had been kept at the same level (*Scînteia*, 10 December 1982).

8. While in 1979 the decisions had applied equally to industry and consumers, this time electricity consumption in the industrial sector was reduced by only 10 to 15 per cent (*Scînteia*, 9 December 1982). For details of the damages incurred by industry during the power cuts see *România liberă* 17 and 19 December 1981 and 19, 20, 28, and 29 January 1982, as well as *Scînteia tineretului*, 29 January 1981.

9. According to Al. Andriţoiu, a Romanian poet, Ceauşescu symbolizes 'the lightspot of continuity' in the history of the country. Another poet, Ion Văduva-Poenaru, described the RCP as the 'party of light', while for his colleague Ion Potopin, Romania itself was the 'fatherland of light'. See 'Pecetele de lumină ale continuităţii', *Scînteia*, 21 October 1973; 'Unirea Românilor', *Luceafărul*, 24 September 1983 and 'În patria luminii', *Luceafărul*, 4 February 1984, respectively. For a description of on-the-spot checks on the use of forbidden electrical appliances see *România liberă*, 30 January 1984.

10. For details concerning Romania's handling of its foreign debt, see Jackson, 1983.

11. In 1977 the number of industrial centrals was increased to 112 (Smith, 1981, p. 70).

12. The following is based mainly on Smith, 1981, which is the best treatment of the NEFM.

13. This disposition was officially encoded on 1 January 1981. According to the new law on foreign trade, 'Planned imports will be permitted only proportionally, as planned export returns and payments are achieved, or if export contracts ensure the necessary currency resources. In cases where such resources are not ensured, the ministries and other central local bodies, centrals and enterprises, are obliged to re-establish the volume of imports according to the framework of planned currency balances' (*Buletinul oficial*, 24 December 1980).

14. The previous system guaranteed an income of 1,500 lei, provided the farmer had worked the number of days stipulated by law (*Buletinul oficial*, 31 December 1976).

15. In his speech at the National Party Conference in July 1972, the Secretary General called for the gradual introduction of a 40-44-hour week by 1980. The 1975 Programme of the RCP mentioned a target of 44 hours, to be achieved in 1976-80, and of 40-42 hours, by 1990 (*Programul*, 1975, p. 92). These directives were changed at the National Conference of the RCP in 1977 (*Scînteia*, 12 December), where it was decided to introduce a 46-hour week during 1978-80, and a 44-hour week in 1981-3. At a meeting with geologists and other specialists in the mining industry in 1983, however, Ceauşescu mentioned the introduction of the 44-hour week as a target for the end of 1985 (*Scînteia*, 30 January 1983).

Chapter 9

1. I am indebted to my friend Steven Sampson for letting me benefit from the insights of this study.

2. The last argument is strikingly familiar to the notion of 'limited good', discussed in Chapter 6.

3. In this presentation I expand on Shafir, 1982.

4. See the distinction made in Note 5, Chapter 1.

5. The Romanian principalities were not united at this point in history.
6. For details on Blaga's theory of the 'mioritic space' (derived from the title of a folk-ballad, 'Miorița)', see Shafir, 1983b, pp. 405-6.
7. The following is based on descriptions provided by the American anthropologist Marlyn McArthur (1976), but the conclusions are entirely my own.
8. Sampson opts for the 'muddling through' concept since he is persuaded that Romania is neither a society 'in crisis' nor one facing political stagnation. But when attempting to refute my argument in favour of the latter approach, he defines stagnation in terms totally different from those I used at the Avignon conference and in this book. See Sampson, 1984, forthcoming, in *International Journal of Romanian Studies*. Whatever the merits of his alternative definition of stagnation, elucidation of the argument becomes impossible where there is no agreement on terms. I am, once more, grateful to Sampson for having sent me a draft of his paper.
9. Apart from Connor, this is clearly reflected in the writings of both Bialer and Nørgaard & Sampson: 'An extremely important dimension in evaluating one's standard of living', Bialer writes (1980, p. 162) 'concerns the reference point used as base'. According to Nørgaard & Sampson (1982), the 'political question of living standards in Eastern Europe is not a matter of "absolutes" but of "relatives": it is a question of how people themselves experience development. The working classes of Eastern Europe have tended to judge these shortages by comparing them with their own historical experience (the depression or wartime years as peasants or unemployed workers) or *with the relatively less well-off peasants of today'* (emphasis mine).
10. In 1970 65.4 per cent of blue-collar workers in Romania came from families in which the father was a peasant, and only 30.5 per cent were sons and daughters of workers. This compares with 32 per cent versus 50 per cent in the Soviet Union (1967, reference to an investigation conducted by O. Skaraton in Kazan), 37.5 versus 53.6 per cent in Czechoslovakia (1967), 43.6 versus 50.4 per cent in Poland (1972), 54.0 versus 42.8 per cent in Hungary (1973) and 61.5 versus 33.3 per cent in Bulgaria (1967).
11. For a discussion of the difference between 'issue' and 'system' conflicts see LaPalombara, 1974, pp. 315-16. This is what Huntington has in mind when he writes:

'The managers' demands are usually concrete and limited; those of intellectuals more diffuse and general. To grant the demands of the intellectuals would be to jeopardize the authority of the entire system. To grant the demands of the managerial elites for functional autonomy is to improve the efficiency and performance of the system without posing any real threat to the position of the political leadership' [Huntington, 1970, p. 37].

N. S. Khrushchev seems to have made a similar distinction in his memoirs:

'The technological intelligentsia—that is, the sector whose intellectual energy is realized in the creation of equipment and other practical objects—is an area where we haven't had too many problems. By the very nature of its activity, the technological intelligentsia does not interfere in the more complicated spheres of social life, namely in ideology' [Khrushchev, 1974, p. 72].

12. See the 'reminiscences' of a former Romanian censor on his successful attempt to convince the poet and playwright Victor Eftimiu to collaborate with the regime, 'Victor Eftimiu . . .', 1968.
13. Paraschivescu's gradual disillusionment with communism as implemented in Romania

was already obvious at a very early stage of the transformation period. See his diary, part of which was published posthumously in France. Paraschivescu, 1976, pp. 165 ff.

14. His 'election' was actually imposed by the regime (author's conversation with writers who participated at the session).

15. See Shafir, 1981a, *passim.*

16. See Preda, 1975. I cannot share the enthusiasm that greeted Preda's last novel in Romania (as well as in the West), although the tragic circumstances of his premature death partly explain such a response (see Preda, 1980). As with many other Romanian writers, Preda avoided extending his critical review of Romanian society beyond the Dej period, and the few glimpses of that period which *were* provided (the Stalin-Dej encounter, the life of the 'New Class') hardly justify the effort of going over 1,200 pages of what remains a poorly written piece of romantic fiction. As a political document, the novel is disappointing. As a spiritual testament, it only proves that compromise cannot be easily discounted.

17. For a translation see Shafir, 1983b, p. 415.

18. Although at the Helsinki Conference of European Peace and Security Kádár did mention that 'the territory of defeated Hungary was reduced to a third of what it used to be', as Lăncrănjan quotes him saying (without, however, mentioning his name), he did *not* state at the Ninth conference of the Hungarian Party (1966) that the 'Trianon Treaty was an imperialist *diktat* which divided up Hungary and gave Transylvania to Romania' (the Lăncrănjan version, attributed to the 'speaker from Helsinki'), but that the 'imperialist *diktat* of Trianon ... served as a pretext for the ruling classes to take nationalist and chauvinist passions and hatred directed against neighbouring peoples to extremes'. The difference is important, for Kádár's statement blamed, by implication, the ruling classes in both Hungary *and* Romania for incitement to chauvinism. Lăncrănjan, on the other hand would have the Hungarian party leader take up a less Marxist, more straightfowardly nationalist Romanian-like position. The discrepancy between the actual and the attributed version was revealed by the Hungarian writer György Száraz in an interview with Radio Budapest on 25 October 1982. See BBC Summary of World Broadcasts, East Europe/7168, 28 October 1982. For the Romanian writer's version of these pronouncements see Lăncrănjan, 1982, p. 132.

19. On this issue, Romanian pronouncements in 1982-3 have been very frequent and often polemical. Cf. Muşat & Tănăsescu, 1982; Preda, 1983a, 1983b, Daicoviciu, 1983a, 1983b, 1983c; Olteanu, 1983; Socaciu, 1983; Muşat, 1983a, 1983b; Muşat & Ardeleanu, 1983; Mitrofan, 1983; Netea, 1983; Ardeleanu, 1983; Pascu, 1983a, 1983b, 1983c; Giuglea, 1983; Gheorghiu, 1983b, Ştefănescu, 1983.

20. Unless otherwise indicated, this discussion is based on information from Suttner, 1977 and Illyés, 1982, pp. 213-37.

21. According to as yet unconfirmed reports, Father Calciu was freed in September 1984.

22. See ibid, and Socor, 1983b.

23. The text of his letters may be found in the pamphlet distributed by the Committee for Human Rights in Romania on 30 January 1978, *New York Times*, 1 February 1978 and *Esprit*, March 1978. Cf. also Schöpflin, 1978. The text of the 1980 letter addressed to Prime Minister Verdeţ appears in *Congressional Record*, 5 June 1980, and is quoted in Radio Free Europe-Radio Liberty, Situation Report (Romania), No. 10, 22 July 1980.

24. On the history of the Autonomous Region and on the situation of the Hungarian minority cf. also King, 1973, pp. 25-44; Gilberg, 1976; Berindei, 1980a, 1980b; Illyés, 1982, pp. 114-17 and *passim.*

25. The discussion of this aspect is based on McArthur, 1976; Berindei, 1980a, 1980b; Fischer, 1983a.

26. The following is a résumé of Shafir, 1978.
27. See Goma, 1971 for the French version.
28. To be sure, intellectual opposition begins with such defiant gestures. Among the more prominent Romanian writers who would belong to this category are Marin Sorescu, Augustin Buzura and Ana Blandiana. For a discussion of their work, as well as of other instances of intellectual resistance to regime pressure, see Shafir, 1981a.
29. Cf. Schöpflin, 1978; Illyés, 1982, p. 148.

Chapter 10

1. The last WTO exercises with troop participation on Romanian soil were held in October 1962, with Soviet, Bulgarian and Romanian units (Braun, 1978, p. 129). Romanian troops have not participated in manœuvres abroad since 1967 (Jones, 1981, pp. 117-18). General staff exercises (i.e. not involving troops) were occasionally held on Romanian soil, but these were merely symbolic. For example, in March 1984 an exercise was held in Romania, but only Romanian officers participated in the operation.
2. For details cf. Braun, 1978, pp. 110-11; Jones, 1981, pp. 133-4; Alexeiev, 1981, p. 13.
3. Cf. Braun, 1978, pp. 120-2, 150-5, 173-8; Jones, 1981, pp. 82-92, 156-8; Volgyés, 1982, pp. 41-59.
4. In 1976, in an attempt to appease the Soviets, Ceauşescu paid an official visit to Soviet Moldavia. However, Romanian publications are full of veiled allusions to their brethren beyond the Prut River, and to their contribution to national culture and state-building. Cf., for recent examples, *Flacăra*, 18 March 1983, 24 May 1984, *Contemporanul*, 1 April 1983, *Luceafărul*, 2 April 1983, *Scînteia tineretului*, 2 April 1983. Ceauşescu himself hinted at mistreatment of Romanians in the Moldavian SSR in his speech delivered at the National Party Conference of December 1982 (*Scînteia*, 17 December 1983). For other post-1976 developments cf. Moore, 1978b, 'Bessarabia Again on the Tapis', 1978; Cioranescu, 1979; Maier, 1984.
5. Quoted by György Száraz in his interview on Radio Budapest, 25 October 1982, BBC Summary of World Broadcasts, Eastern Europe/7168, 28 October 1982.
6. On American-Romanian economic relations cf. Burgess, 1977; Forrest, 1982. On the economic background to Romania's policies in the Middle East see Shafir, 1974.

References

A. G., 1982. 'New draft bill on the duties of the people's councils', Radio Free Europe Research, Situation Report. Romania/14, 9 September.

Academia Republicii Populare Romîne, 1960-64. *Istoria Romîniei*. Bucharest, Editura Academiei Republicii Populare Romîne, 4 vols.

Academia Republicii Populare Romîne. Institutul de linguistică din Bucureşti, 1960. *Îndreptar ortografic şi de punctuaţie*. Bucharest, Editura Academiei Republicii Populare Romîne.

Academia Republicii Socialiste România. Institutul de linguistică din Bucureşti, 1965. *Îndreptar ortografic, ortoepic şi de punctuaţie*. Bucharest, Editura Academiei Republicii Socialiste România.

Academia Ştefan Gheorghiu, 1975. *Dicţionar politic*. Bucharest, Editura politică.

Alberti, A. (ed.), 1979. *The Socialist Republic of Romania*. Milan and Bucharest, Edizioni del Calendario and Institutul de studii istorice şi social-politice de pe lîngă CC al PCR.

Alexeiev, A., 1981. 'Romania and the Warsaw Pact: the defense policy of a reluctant ally'. *Strategic Studies*, No. 1.

Alton, T. P. *et al.*, 1983. *Research Project on National Income in East Central Europe*. Occasional Papers Nos. 75-79, New York, L.W. International Financial Research Inc.

Amalrik, A., 1970. 'Open letter to Kuznetzov'. *Survey*, No. 74-75.

Amnesty International Briefing, 1980. *Romania*. Nottingham, Amnesty International.

Anderson, E. E., 1983. 'Central planning and production instabilities in Eastern Europe'. *Slavic Review*, No. 2.

Andriţoiu, A., 1983. 'Pecetele de lumină ale continuităţii'. *Scînteia*, 21 October.

Anescu, V., Bantea, E. & Cupşa, I., 1966. *Participation of the Romanian Army in the Anti-Hitlerite War*. Bucharest, The Military Publishing House.

Ardeleanu, I., 1983. 'Însemnătatea istorică a făuririi statului naţional român'. *Era socialistă*, No. 15.

Avineri, S., 1969. 'Introduction' in S. Avineri (ed.), *Karl Marx on Colonialism and Modernization*. Garden City, N.Y., Anchor Books, Doubleday.

Axenciuc, V., 1965. 'Cu privire la unele trăsături economico-sociale ale României în primele două decenii ale secolului al XX-lea'. *Analele institutului de studii istorice şi social-politice de pe lîngă CC al PCR*, No. 6.

Bacon, W. M., 1978. 'The Military and the Party in Romania' in D. R. Herspring & I. Volgyés (eds), *Civil-Military Relations in Communist Systems*. Boulder, Co., Westview Press.

—— 1983. 'Romania' in R. Wesson (ed.), *Yearbook on International Communist Affairs*. Stanford, Ca., Hoover Institution Press.

Badrus, G., 1983. 'Viabilitatea deplină a principiilor fundamentale ale colaborării şi cooperării in cadrul C.A.E.R.'. *Era Socialistă*, No. 4.

Baker, R. H., 1982. 'Clientelism in the post-revolutionary state: the Soviet Union' in C. Clapham (ed.), *Private Patronage and Public Power: Political Clientelism in the Modern State*. New York, St. Martin's Press.

Bălaşa, A., 1984. 'Specificul ideologiei religioase promovate de cultele şi sectele neoprotestante'. *Revista de filozofie*, No. 1.

Bauman, Z., 1979. 'Comment on Eastern Europe'. *Studies in Comparative Communism*, No. 2-3.

—— 1981. 'On the maturation of socialism'. *Telos*, No. 47.

Bell, J. D., 1982. 'Bulgaria: the silent partner' in M. M. Drachkovich (ed.), *East Central Europe: Yesterday—Today—Tomorrow*. Stanford, Ca., Hoover Institution Press.

Berindei, M., 1980a. 'Les minorités nationales en Roumanie'. *L'Alternative*, No. 3.

—— 1980b. 'Les minorités nationales en Roumanie (suite et fin)'. *L'Alternative*, No. 4-5.

—— 1981. 'La Roumanie à l'heure polonaise'. *L'Alternative*, No. 8.

Berindei, M. & Colas, A., 1984a. 'De l'obscurité à l'obscurantisme'. *L'Alterantive*, No. 26.

—— —— 1984b. 'L'abolition du salariat'. *L'Alternative*, No. 25.

Berza, M., 1966. 'Putna'. *Contemporanul*, 8 July.

'Bessarabia Again on the Tapis', 1978. Radio Free Europe Research, RAD Background Report/224 (Romania), 11 October.

Bialer, S., 1980. *Stalin's Successors: Leadership Stability and Change in the Soviet Union*. Cambridge, Cambridge University Press.

—— 1983, 'The political system' in R. F. Byrnes (ed)., *After Brezhnev: Sources of Soviet Conduct in the 1980s*. Bloomington, Indiana University Press.

Bielasiak, J., 1981. 'Workers and mass participation in "Socialist Democracy"' in J. F. Triska & Ch. Gati (eds) *Blue Collar Workers in Eastern Europe*. London, George Allen & Unwin.

—— 1982. 'Party leadership and mass participation in developed socialism' in J. Seroka & M. D. Simon (eds), *Developed Socialism in the Soviet Bloc: Political Theory and Political Reality*. Boulder, Co., Westview Press.

Blaga, L., 1969. *Trilogia culturii: Orizont și stil. Spațiul mioritic. Geneza metamorfozei și sensul culturii*. Bucharest, Editura pentru literatură universală.

Boboș, I. & Deleanu, I., 1979. 'Mass and public organizations in the socio-political evolution of the country' in I. Ceterchi, O. Trăsnea and C. Vlad (eds), *The Political System of the Socialist Republic of Romania*. Bucharest, Editura științifică și enciclopedică.

Bochiș, I., Dumitrescu, S. & Oprea, A., 1965. 'Manualul de istorie al doctrinelor economice'. *Lupta de clasă*, No. 4.

Boehm, M. H., 1930. 'Autonomy' in E. R. A. Seligman (ed)., *Encyclopaedia of the Social Sciences*. New York, vol. 2.

Bogdan, C., 1983. 'Noul echilibru mondial și interesele păcii și independenței poparelor'. *Era socialistă*, No. 7.

Bornstein, M., 1977. 'Economic reform in Eastern Europe' in *East European Economies Post-Helsinki: A Compendium of Papers Submitted to the Joint Economic Committee, Congress of the United States*. Washington, D.C., US Government Printing Office.

Braham, R. L., 1964. 'Rumania: onto the separate path'. *Problems of Communism*, No. 3.

Braun, A., 1977. 'The Yugoslav-Romanian concept of People's War', *Canadian Defense Quarterly*, No. 7.

—— 1978. *Romanian Foreign Policy Since 1965: The Political and Military Limits of Autonomy*. New York, Praeger.

—— 1982. 'Romania's travails'. *Problems of Communism*, No. 3.

Breslauer, G. W., 1982. *Khrushchev and Brezhnev as Leaders: Building Authority in Soviet Politics*. London, George Allen & Unwin.

Brown, A., 1980. 'The power of the General Secretary of the CPSU' in T. H. Rigby, A. Brown & P. Reddaway (eds), *Authority, Power and Policy in the USSR*. New York, St. Martin's Press.

—— 1982. 'Leadership succession and policy innovation' in A. Brown & M. Kaser (eds), *Soviet Policy for the 1980s*. Bloomington, Indiana University Press.

Brown, J. F., 1963. 'Rumania steps out of line'. *Survey*, No. 49.

—— 1965. 'Eastern Europe'. *Survey*, No. 64.

— 1966. *The New Eastern Europe*. New York, Praeger.

Bruchis, M., 1982. *One Step Back, Two Steps Forward: On the Language Policy of the Communist Party of the Soviet Union in the National Republics (Moldavian: A Look Back, A Survey and Perspectives 1924-1980)*. New York, Columbia University Press.

Bulborea, I., 1969. 'Idei economice şi sociale în publicistica eminesciană'. *Anale de istorie*, No. 2.

Bunce, V., 1981. *Do New Leaders Make a Difference?: Executive Succession and Public Policy Under Capitalism and Socialism*. Princeton, N.J., Princeton University Press.

Burda, Şt., 1983. 'Mărturii ale culturii şi civilizaţiei româneşti'. *Magazin istoric*, No. 5.

Burgess, J. A., 1977. 'An analysis of the United States-Romanian long-term agreement on economic, industrial and technical co-operation' in *East European Economies Post-Helsinki: A Compendium of Papers Submitted to the Joint Economic Committee, Congress of the United States*. Washington, D.C., US Government Printing Office.

Burks, R. V., 1966. 'The Rumanian national deviation: an accounting' in K. London (ed.), *Eastern Europe in Transition*. Baltimore, Md., Johns Hopkins Press.

Calafeteanu, I., 1977. 'Eforturile diplomaţiei româneşti în vederea realizării unităţii de acţiune a statelor din sud-estul Europei în faţa expansiunii fasciste (martie 1938-iulie 1939)' in Institutul de studii istorice şi social-politice de pe lîngă CC al PCR, *Probleme de politică externă a României 1918-1940: Culegere de studii*, Vol. II. Bucharest, Editura militară.

Calciu, G., 1979. *Sapte cuvinte către tineri*. Munich, Jon Dumitru Verlag.

Campus, E., 1966. 'Nicolae Titulescu şi politica pentru apărarea integrităţii teritoriale a României'. *Studii*, No. 2.

— 1968a. *Mica înţelegere*. Bucharest, Editura ştiinţifică.

— 1968b. *The Little Entente and the Balkan Alliance*. Bucharest, Editura Academiei Republicii Socialiste România.

Caragiale, M., 1970. *Craii de curte veche*. Bucharest, Editura Eminescu.

Ceauşescu, I., 1983. *Transylvania: An Ancient Romanian Land*. Bucharest, The Military Publishing House.

Ceauşescu, N., 1968-69. *România pe drumul desăvîrşirii construcţiei socialiste*. Bucharest, Editura politică, 3 vols.

— 1970-83. *România pe drumul construirii societăţii socialiste multilateral dezvoltate*. Bucharest, Editura politică, 20 vols.

— 1982. 'Expunere cu privire la stadiul actual al edificării socialismului în ţara noastră, la problemele teoretice, ideologice şi activitatea politică, educativă a partidului prezentată la plenara largită a Comitetului Central al Partidului Comunist Român'. *Anale de istorie*, No. 4.

Central Intelligence Agency. Directorate of Intelligence, 1982. *Directory of Officials of the Socialist Republic of Romania: A Reference Aid*. CR 82-13770, Washington, D.C.

Ceterchi, I., 1979. 'The exercise of self-management in the political system of socialist Romania' in I. Ceterchi, O. Trăsnea and C. Vlad (eds), *The Political System of the Socialist Republic of Romania*. Bucharest, Editura ştiinţifică şi enciclopedică.

— 1981. 'Concepţia Partidului Comunist Român cu privire la rolul statului socialist în înfăptuirea societăţii socialiste multilateral dezvoltate şi înaintării ţării spre comunism'. *Anale de istorie*, No. 4.

Cherestesiu, V. & Copoiu, N., 1967. 'Participarea oamenilor muncii din România la apărarea şi sprijinirea Marii Revoluţii Socialiste din Octombrie' in *Marea Revoluţie Socialistă din Octombrie şi România: Culegere de studii*. Bucharest, Editura politică.

Chiper, I., 1969. 'Istoriografia străină despre insurecţia armată din august 1944 din România'. *Studii*, No. 4.

Chirot, D., 1976. *Social Change in a Peripheral Society: The Creation of a Balkan Colony.* New York, Academic Press.

—— 1978. 'Social change in communist Romania'. *Social Forces*, No. 2.

—— 1980. 'The corporatist model and socialism: notes on Romanian development'. *Theory and Society*, No. 2.

Churchill, W. S., 1962. *The Second World War: The Hinge of Fate*, vol. IV. New York, Bantham Books.

—— 1962. *The Second World War: Triumph and Tragedy*, vol. VI. New York, Bantham Books.

Ciorănescu, G., 1979. 'Moldavian and Western interpretations of modern Romanian history'. Radio Free Europe Research, RAD Background Report/198 (Romania), 19 September.

—— 1983a. 'Hu visits Ceauşescu'. Radio Free Europe Research, RAD Background Report/143 (Eastern Europe), 23 June.

—— 1983b. 'Romanian-Soviet relations at the start of the new year'. Radio Free Europe Research, RAD Background Report/13 (Romania), 19 January.

—— 1984. 'Romania and military spending proposals'. Radio Free Europe Research, Situation Report, Romania/6, 4 April.

Cismărescu, M., 1976. 'An original experiment in Romania: the party and state bodies'. *Review of Socialist Law*, No. 2.

Cîncea, P., 1974. *Viaţa politică din România în primul deceniu al independenţei de stat.* Bucharest, Editura ştiinţifică.

Clark, C. V., 1927. *Bessarabia: Russia and Roumania on the Black Sea.* New York, Dodd, Mead and Co.

Colas, A., 1982. 'Une situation explosive'. *L'Alternative*, No. 14.

Cole, J., 1976a. 'Familial dynamics in a Romanian workers' village'. *Dialectical Anthropology*, No. 3.

—— 1976b. 'Field work in Romania: introduction'. *Dialectical Anthropology*, No. 3.

—— 1981. 'Family, farm and factory: rural workers in contemporary Romania' in D. N. Nelson (ed.), *Romania in the 1980s.* Boulder, Co., Westview Press.

Congresul al IX-lea al Partidului Comunist Român, 1966. Bucharest, Editura politică.

Congresul al X-lea al Partidului Comunist Român, 1969. Bucharest, Editura politică.

Congresul al XII-lea al Partidului Comunist Român, 1981. Bucharest, Editura politică.

Congresul Partidului Muncitoresc Român 21-23 februarie 1948, 1948. Bucharest, Editura Partidului Muncitoresc Român.

Connor, W. D., 1975. 'Generation and politics in the USSR', *Problems of Communism*, No. 5.

—— 1977. 'Social change and stability in Eastern Europe'. *Problems of Communism*, No. 6.

—— 1979. *Socialism, Politics and Equality: Hierarchy and Change in Eastern Europe and the USSR.* New York, Columbia University Press.

Conquest, R., 1966. 'Immobilism and decay'. *Problems of Communism*, No. 5.

Constituţia Republicii Socialiste România, 1969. Bucharest, Editura politică.

Conte, F., 1975. *Christian Rakovski (1873-1941): Essai de biographie politique.* Lille, Université de Lille III, 2 vols.

'Contribuţia PCR, a secretarului său General, tovarăşul Nicolae Ceauşescu, la îmbogăţirea teoriei despre naţiune şi relăţiile naţionale în lumea contemporană' 1983. *Era socialistă*, No. 2.

Copoiu, N., 1963. 'Unele probleme ale istoriei Romîniei în lucrările lui Karl Marx'. *Analele institutului de istorie a partidului de pe lîngă CC al PMR*, No. 2.

Cretzianu, A. (ed.), 1956. *Captive Rumania.* London, Atlantic Press.

—— 1957. *Lost Opportunity.* London, Jonathan Cape.

Cristescu, G., 1972. 'Amintiri despre Cristian Racovski'. *Anale de istorie*, No. 1.

Cruceanu, M., 1967. 'Elek Köblös (1887-1937)'. *Analele institutului de studii istorice şi social-politice de pe lîngă CC al PCR*, No. 4.

Cruceanu, M. & Ciobanu, E., 1970. 'Mişcarea muncitorească din România în cele două decenii premergătoare creării partidului comunist'. *Anale de istorie*, No. 5.

Cruceanu, M. & Tănăsescu, F., 1971. *Al. Dobrogeanu-Gherea*. Bucharest, Editura politică.

Cultura socialistă în România, 1974. Bucharest, Editura politică.

Daicoviciu, C., 1954. 'Pozitia anti-ştiinţifică a istoriografiei burgheze romîne cu privire la Dacia'. *Studii*, No. 1.

Daicoviciu, H., 1983a. 'Din nou despre romanizare'. *Steaua*, No. 2.

—— 1983b. 'Forţa adevărului istoric'. *Era socialistă*, No. 8.

—— 1983c. 'O judecată sănătoasă'. *Steaua*, No. 10.

Daniels, R. V., 1971. 'Soviet politics since Khrushchev' in J. W. Strong (ed.), *The Soviet Union Under Brezhnev and Kosygin*. New York, Van Nostrand.

de Bosschere, G., 1969. 'Le groupe de six a Bucarest'. *Preuves*, No. 217.

Degras, J. (ed.), 1953. *Soviet Documents on Foreign Policy*. London, Oxford University Press.

Deligiannis, E. A. D., 1971. 'Education in the Socialist Republic of Romania', unpublished doctoral dissertation, University of Southern California, Faculty of the Graduate School.

Deutsch, K. W., 1961. 'Social mobilization and political development'. *American Political Science Review*, No. 3.

—— 1966. 'Nation building and national development: some issues for political research', 'Introduction' in K. W. Deutsch & W. J. Foltz (eds), *Nation Building*. New York, Atherton Press.

Deutscher, I., 1970a. *The Prophet Armed. Trotsky: 1879-1921*. London, Oxford University Press.

—— 1970b. *The Prophet Unarmed. Trotsky: 1921-1929*. London, Oxford University Press.

—— 1970c. *The Prophet Outcast. Trotsky: 1929-1940*. London, Oxford University Press.

Devlin, K., 1980. 'European Communism's Conference of Disunity'. Radio Free Europe Research, RAD Background Report/99 (World Communist Movement), 2 May.

—— 1984. 'Spain's other Communist Party'. Radio Free Europe Research, RAD Background Report/8 (World Communist Movement), 27 January.

'Dezbaterile privind macheta volumului al VI-lea din tratatul "Istoria României"', 1969. *Studii*, No. 3.

Dima, N., 1982. *Bessarabia and Bukovina: The Soviet-Romanian Territorial Dispute*. New York, Columbia University Press.

Directivele Comitetului Central al Partidului Comunist Român cu privire la perfecţionarea conducerii şi planificării economiei naţionale corespunzător condiţiilor noii etape de dezvolatre socialistă a României, 1967. Bucharest, Editura politică.

Dobrogeanu-Gherea, C., 1956. *Studii Critice*. Bucharest, Editura de stat pentru literatură şi artă, 2 vols.

—— 1972. *Corespondenţa*. Bucharest, Editura Minerva.

—— 1976-8. *Opre comlete*. Bucharest, Editura politică, 8 vols.

Documente din istoria Partidului Communist din România, 1953. Editura pentru literatură politică.

Doolin, D. J., 1965. *Territorial Claims in the Sino-Soviet Conflict*. Stanford, Calif, Hoover Institution Press.

Dossier Paul Goma: L'écrivain face au socialisme du silence, présenté par V. Tănase, 1977. Paris, Albatros.

Dumitriu, P., 1961. 'Gescheirte Koexistenz: Skizze einer Literaturgeschichte Rumäniens im letzten Jahrzehnt'. *Osteuropa*, Nos. 11-12.

—— 1962. 'Social structure and tensions in Rumania'. *The Review* (Brussels), No. 4.

Durandin, C., 1983. 'Roumanité et orthodoxie: Un débat de l'entre deux guerres'. Paper presented at the Second International Congress of Romanian Studies, Avignon, France.

'Eastern Europe: toward a "religious revival"?', 1984. Radio Free Europe Research, RAD Background Report/88 (Eastern Europe), 23 May.

Farlow, R. H., 1971. 'Romanian foreign policy: a case of partial alignment'. *Problems of Communism*, No. 6.

—— 1978. 'Romania and the policy of partial alignment' in J. A. Kuhlman (ed.), *The Foreign Policies of Eastern Europe: Domestic and International Determinants*. Leyden, A. W. Sijthoff.

Fătu, M., 1972. *Sfîrşit fără glorie: Partidul Naţional Tărănesc (Maniu) şi Partidul Naţional Liberal (Brătianu) în anii 1944-47*. Bucharest, Editura ştiinţifică.

—— 1979. *Alianţele politice ale Partidului Comunist Român 1944-1947*. Cluj-Napoca, Editura Dacia.

—— 1983. 'Semnificaţia istorică a unităţii politice şi organizatorice a mişcării muncitoreşti din România: 35 de ani de la făurirea partidului unic'. *Era socialistă*, No. 3.

Federation of Jewish Communities of the Socialist Republic of Romania, 1978. *Jewish Life in Romania in 1978*. Bucharest, Federation of Jewish Communities of the Socialist Republic of Romania.

Feifer, G., 1975. 'The case of the passive minority' in R. L. Tőkés (ed.), *Dissent in the USSR: Politics, Ideology and People*. Baltimore, Johns Hopkins University Press.

Felea, I. & Tănăsescu, F., 1980. 'O viaţă dăruită idealului socialist' in L. Ghelerter, *Scrieri social-politice*. Bucharest, Editura politică.

Fischer, M. E., 1977a. 'Nation and nationality in Romania' in G. D. Simmonds (ed.), *The USSR and Eastern Europe in the Era of Brezhnev and Kosygin*. Detroit, University of Detroit Press.

—— 1977b. 'Participatory reforms and political development in Romania' in J. F. Triska & P. M. Cocks (eds), *Political Development in Eastern Europe*. New York, Praeger.

—— 1979. 'The Romanian Communist Party and its Central Committee: patterns of growth and change'. *Southeastern Europe*, **6**, pt. 1.

—— 1980. 'Political leadership and personnel policy in Romania: continuity and change 1965-1976' in S. Rosefielde (ed.), *World Communism at the Crossroads*. Boston, M. Nijhoff.

—— 1981. 'Idol or leader? The origins and future of the Ceauşescu cult' in D. N. Nelson (ed.), *Romania in the 1980s*. Boulder, Co., Westview Press.

—— 1982. 'Nicolae Ceauşescu and the Romanian political leadership: nationalism and personalization of power'. Skidmore, Skidmore College, Edwin M. Mosley Faculty Research Lecture.

—— 1983a. 'The politics of national inequality in Romania' in D. N. Nelson (ed.), *Communism and the Politics of Inequality*. Lexington, Mass., Lexington Books.

—— 1983b. 'Women in Romanian politics: Elena Ceauşescu, pronatalism and the promotion of women' in S. Wolchick and A. G. Mayer (eds), *The Changing Status of Women in Eastern Europe*. Forthcoming.

Fischer-Galati, S. (ed.), 1957. *Romania*. New York, Praeger.

—— 1966. 'Rumania and the Sino-Soviet Conflict' in K. London (ed.), *Eastern Europe in Transition*. Baltimore, Johns Hopkins University Press.

—— 1967. *The New Rumania: From People's Democracy to Socialist Republic*. Cambridge, Mass., MIT Press.

—— 1970. *Twentieth Century Rumania*. New York, Columbia University Press.

—— 1971. 'The origins of Romanian nationalism' in P. F. Sugar and I. J. Lederer (eds), *Nationalism in Eastern Europe*. Seattle, Washington University Press.

— 1975. 'The communist takeover of Rumania: a function of Soviet power' in Th. T. Hammond (ed.), *The Anatomy of Communist Takeovers.* New Haven, Yale University Press.

Florea, E., 1974. *Naţiunea românã şi socialismul.* Bucharest, Editura Academiei Republicii Socialiste România.

Forrest, R., 1982. 'Romanian-American relations, 1947-1975' in S. Fischer-Galati, R. R. Florescu & G. R. Ursul (eds), *Romania Between East and West: Historical Essays in Memory of Constantin C. Giurescu.* New York, Columbia University Press.

Foster, G. M., 1967. 'Peasant society and the image of Limited Good' in J. M. Potter, M. N. Diaz & G. M. Foster (eds), *Peasant Society: A Reader.* Boston, Little, Brown.

Franck, N., 1977. *La Roumanie dans l'engrenage: Comment le Royaume est devenu République Populaire (1944-1947).* Paris, Elsevier Sequoia.

Friedgut, T., 1974. 'The Democratic movement: dimensions and perspectives' in R. L. Tőkés (ed.), *Dissent in the USSR: Politics, Ideology and People.* Baltimore, Johns Hopkins University Press.

G. C., 1982. 'John Paul II on the Romanian Uniates', Radio Free Europe Research, Situation Report, Romania/2, 26 January.

Gabanyi, A. U., 1975. *Partei und Literatur in Rumänien seit 1945.* Munich, R. Oldenbourg Verlag.

Gafton, P., 1982. 'Selling the Workers Their Own Property'. Radio Free Europe Research, Situation Report, Romania/19, 12 November.

— 1983. 'The 1983 State Budget'. Radio Free Europe Research, Situation Report, Romania/1, 13 January.

— 1984. 'Romania's Eastern Trade Trends', Radio Free Europe Research, Situation Report, Romania/5, 14 March.

Gafton, P. & Moore, P., 1984. 'Milking Private Agriculture'. Radio Free Europe Research, Situation Report, Romania/2, 30 January.

Georgescu, T., 1970a. 'De la revoluţionarii democraţi la întiiul partid politic al clasei muncitoare P.S.D.M.R.'. *Anale de istorie*, No. 5.

— 1970b. 'Liga muncii' in I. Popescu-Puţuri *et al., Organizaţii de masă legale şi ilegale create, conduse sau influenţate de PCR: 1921-1944.* Bucharest, Editura politică.

Georgescu, V., 1971. *Political Ideas and the Enlightenment in the Romanian Principalities (1750-1831).* New York, Columbia University Press.

— 1981. *Politică şi istorie: Cazul comuniştilor români 1944-1977.* Munich, Jon Dumitru Verlag.

— 1984. *Istoria românilor de la origini pîna în zilele noastre.* Los Angeles, American Romanian Academy of Arts and Sciences.

Ghelerter, L., 1980. *Scrieri social-politice.* Bucharest, Editura politică.

Gheorghiu, M., 1983a. 'O strategie umanistă a dezvoltării: Poziţia României cu privire la noua ordine economică şi politică internaţională'. *Era socialistă*, No. 7.

— 1983b. 'Peste hotare, un larg răsunet'. *Luceafărul*, 3 December.

Gheorghiu-Dej, G., 1952. *Articole şi cuvântări.* Bucharest, Editura pentru literatură politică.

— 1961. *Articole şi cuvîntări 1959-1961.* Bucharest, Editura politică.

— 1962. *Articole şi cuvîntări 1961-1962.* Bucharest, Editura politică.

Ghermani, D., 1967a. *Die kommunistische Umdeutung der rumänischen Geschichte unter besonderer Berücksichtigung des Mittelalters.* Munich, R. Oldenbourg Verlag.

— 1967b. 'Wandlungen der rumänischen Historiographie im Spiegel der ersten vier Bände der "Istoria Romîniei"?. *Südost-Forschungen*, **26**.

— 1977. 'Die Rumänische Kommunistische Partei', in K. D. Grothusen (ed.), *Rumänien.* Göttingen, Vandenhoeck & Ruprecht.

212   *References*

Ghermani, D., 1981. *Die nationale Souveränitätspolitik der SR Rumänien.* Munich, R. Oldenbourg Verlag.
Gilberg, T., 1974a. 'Ceauşescu's Romania'. *Problems of Communism,* No. 4.
—— 1974b. 'Romania: Problems of the multilaterally developed society' in Ch. Gati (ed.), *The Politics of Modernization: Testing the Soviet Model.* Washington D.C., Praeger.
—— 1975. *Modernization in Romania Since World War II.* New York, Praeger.
—— 1976. 'Ethnic minorities in Romania under socialism' in B. L. Faber (ed.), *The Social Structure of Eastern Europe.* New York, Praeger.
—— 1979. 'The Communist Party of Romania' in S. Fischer-Galati (ed.), *The Communist Parties of Eastern Europe.* New York, Columbia University Press.
—— 1981a. 'Modernization, human rights and nationalism: the case of Romania' in G. Klein & M. J. Reban (eds.), *The Politics of Ethnicity in Eastern Europe.* New York, Columbia University Press.
—— 1981b. 'Political socialization in Romania: prospects and performance' in D. N. Nelson (ed.), *Romania in the 1980s.* Boulder, Co., Westview Press.
Gitelman, Z., 1972. 'Beyond Leninism: political development in Eastern Europe'. *Newsletter on Comparative Studies of Communism,* No. 3.
—— 1981. 'The world economy and elite political strategies in Czechoslovakia, Hungary and Poland', in M. Bornstein, Z. Gitelman & W. Zimmerman (eds), *East-West Relations and the Future of Eastern Europe: Politics and Economics.* London, George Allen & Unwin.
Giugela, G., 1983. *Cuvinte româneşti şi romanice.* Bucharest, Editura ştiinţifică şi enciclopedică.
Giurescu, C. C., 1966. 'Ştefan cel Mare sau epoca de glorie a Moldovei'. *Ramuri,* No. 3.
—— 1967. *Transilvania în istoria poporului român.* Bucharest, Editura ştiinţifică.
Gogoneaţă, N. & Ornea, Z., 1965. *A. D. Xenopol: Concepţia socială şi filozofică.* Bucharest, Editura ştiinţifică.
Golan, G., 1971. *The Czechoslovak Reform Movement: Communism in Crisis, 1962-1968.* Cambridge, Cambridge University Press.
—— 1975. 'Elements of Russian tradition in Soviet Socialism' in S. N. Eisenstadt & Y. Azmon (eds), *Socialism and Tradition.* Atlantic Highlands, Humanities Press.
Goma, P., 1971. *La cellule des libérables.* Paris, Gallimard.
—— 1973. *Gherla.* Paris, Gallimard.
—— 1974. *Elles étaient quatre.* Paris, Gallimard.
—— 1977. *Le tremblement des hommes.* Paris, Seuil.
—— 1983. *Chassé croisé: Recit.* Paris, Hachette.
Graham, L., 1982. *Romania: A Developing Socialist State.* Boulder, Co., Westview Press.
Granick, D., 1975. *Enterprise Guidance in Eastern Europe.* Princeton, N.J., Princeton University Press.
Grigorian, V., 1950. 'Strategiia i taktika leninizma boevoe oruzhie bratskih kompartii'. *Bolshevik,* No. 7.
Gruber, H., 1974. *Soviet Russia Masters the Comintern: International Communism in the Era of Stalin's Ascendancy.* Garden City, N.Y., Anchor Books.
Gumpel, W., 1977. 'Die Wirtschaftsystem' in K. D. Grothusen (ed.), *Rumänien.* Göttingen, Vandenhoeck & Ruprecht.
Hammer, D. P., 1971. 'The dilemma of party growth'. *Problems of Communism,* No. 4.
Hammond, Th. T., 1975. 'The history of communist takeovers' in Th. T. Hammond (ed.), *The Anatomy of Communist Takeovers.* New Haven, Conn., Yale University Press.
Harasymiw, B., 1971. 'Application of the concept of pluralism to the Soviet political system'. *Newsletter on Comparative Studies of Communism,* No. 1.

Haupt, G., 1967. 'Naissance du socialisme par la critique: La Roumanie'. *Le Mouvement social*, No. 59.

— 1968. 'La genèse du conflict sovieto-roumain'. *Revue française de science politique*, No. 4.

Haupt, G. & Marie, J. J. (eds), 1974. *Makers of the Russian Revolution: Biographies of Bolshevik Leaders*. Ithaca, N.Y., Cornell University Press.

Heer, N. W., 1971. *Politics and History in the Soviet Union*. Cambridge, Mass., MIT Press.

Hejzlar, Ž., 1982. 'Poland: a failed attempt at emancipation'. *Social Affairs*, No. 5.

Hitchins, K., 1968. 'The Russian Revolution and the Romanian Socialist Movement 1917-1918'. *Slavic Review*, No. 2.

— 1971. 'The Rumanian Socialists and the Hungarian Soviet Republic' in A. C. Janos & W. B. Slottman (eds), *Revolution in Perspective: Essays on the Hungarian Soviet Republic*. Berkeley and Los Angeles, University of California Press.

— 1976. 'Rumanian Socialists and the nationality problem in Hungary 1903-1918'. *Slavic Review*, No. 1.

Hodnett, G., 1975. 'Succession contingencies in the Soviet Union'. *Problems of Communism*, No. .

— 1981. 'The pattern of leadership politics' in S. Bialer (ed.), *The Domestic Context of Soviet Foreign Policy*. Boulder, Co., Westview Press.

Hough, J., 1977. *The Soviet Union and Social Science*. Cambridge, Mass., Harvard University Press.

Hough, J. & Fainsod, M., 1980. *How the Soviet Union is Governed*. Cambridge, Mass., Harvard University Press.

Huntington, S. P., 1965. 'Political Development and Political Decay'. *World Politics*, No. 3.

— 1970. 'Social and institutional dynamics in one-party systems' in S. P. Huntington & C. H. Moore (eds), *Authoritarian Politics in Modern Society*. New York, Basic Books.

— 1971. 'The change to change: modernization, development and politics'. *Comparative Politics*, No. 3.

Hurezeanu, D., 1970. 'Gîndirea lui Dobrogeanu-Gherea în "Neoiobăgia"'. *Anale de istorie*, No. 2.

— 1975. 'Constantin Dobrogeanu-Gherea: Un eminent teoretician al socialismului în România', *Era socialistă*, No. 10.

Ierunca, V., 1973. 'La phénomène concentrationnaire en Roumanie' in P. Goma, *Gherla*. Paris, Gallimard.

— 1976. 'Zece ani dela moartea lui G. Călinescu'. *Limite* (Paris), No. 21.

Illyés, E., 1982. *National Minorities in Romania: Change in Transylvania*. New York, Columbia University Press.

Institute of Political Sciences and of Studying the National Question, 1976. *The Hungarian Nationality in Romania*. Bucharest, Meridiane.

Institutul central de statistică, 1938. *Recensământul general al populaţiei României din 29 decemvrie 1930*, **2**. Bucharest, Institutul central de statistică.

Institutul de studii istorice a partidului de pe lîngă CC al PMR, 1964. *Presa muncitorească şi socialistă din România*, vol. 1 (1865-1900), pt. 1 (1865-1889). Bucharest, Editura politică.

Institutul de studii istorice şi social-politice de pe lîngă CC al PCR, 1968. *Presa muncitorească şi socialistă din România*, vol. 2. (1900-1921). Bucharest, Editura politică.

Institutul de studii istorice şi social-politice de pe lîngă CC al PMR, 1969. *Documente din istoria mişcării munciotoreşti din România 1893-1900*. Bucharest, Editura politică.

Institutul de ştiinţe politice şi de studiere a problemei naţionale, 1977. *Naţiune, suveranitate, independenţă*. Bucharest, Editura politică.

Ionescu, E., 1965. 'Momente din timpul doborîrii dictaturii militare fasciste'. *Analele Institutului de istorie a partidului de pe lîngă CC al PCR*, No. 1.

Ionescu, G., 1964. *Communism in Rumania 1944-1962*. London, Oxford University Press.

—— 1970. 'Romania' in G. Ionescu and E. Gellner (eds), *Populism: Its Meanings and National Characteristics.* London, Weidenfeld and Nicolson.

Ioniţă, G. I., 1969. 'Cercetarea istoriei contemporane a României în ultimul sfert de veac'. *Anale de istorie,* No. 6.

—— 1971. 'Locul şi rolul Partidului Comunist în opoziţia politică din România anilor 1934-februarie 1938: Linia politică-tactică. *Studii,* No. 3.

—— 1983. 'Caracterul unitar al istoriei în viziunea Secretarului General al Partidului Comunist Român. *Revista de istorie,* No. 1.

Iorga, N., 1915. *Istoria românilor din Ardeal şi Ungaria (Dela mişcarea lui Horea până astăzi).* Bucharest, Editura Casei şcoalelor.

—— 1969. *Istoria literaturii române în secolul al XVIII-lea (1688-1821).* Bucharest, Editura didactică şi pedagogică, 1962, 2 vols.

Ivaşcu, G., 1964. 'Patriotismul lui Eminescu'. *Contemporanul,* 12 June.

Jackson, G. D., 1966. *Comintern and Peasant in Eastern Europe 1919-1930.* New York, Columbia University Press.

Jackson, M. R., 1977. 'Industrialization, trade and mobilization in Romania's drive for economic independence' in *East European Economies Post-Helsinki: A Compendium of Papers Submitted to the Joint Economic Committee, Congress of the United States.* Washington, D.C., US Government Printing Office.

—— 1981a. 'Perspectives on Romania's economic development in the 1980s' in D. N. Nelson (ed.), *Romania in the 1980s.* Boulder, Co., Westview Press.

—— 1981b. 'Romania's economy at the end of the 1970s: turning the corner on intensive development' in *East European Economic Assessment. Part 1: Country Studies 1980. A Compendium of Papers Submitted to the Joint Economic Committee, Congress of the United States.* Washington, D.C., US Government Printing Office.

—— 1983. 'Romania's debt crisis: its causes and consequences', Arizona, Arizona State University, Faculty Working Papers, forthcoming in *East European Economies in the 1980s. Part 1: Country Studies 1983. A Compendium of Papers Submitted to the Joint Economic Committee, Congress of the United States.* Washington, D.C., US Government Printing Office.

Jane's All the World Aircraft 1981-1982, 1982. London, Jane's Publishing Company.

Janos, A. C., 1978. 'Modernization and decay in historical perspective: the case of Romania' in K. Jowitt (ed.), *Social Change in Romania 1860-1940: A Debate on Development in a European Nation.* Berkeley, Institute of International Studies, University of California.

Johnson, Ch., 1970. 'Comparing communist nations' in Ch. Johnson (ed.), *Change in Communist Systems.* Stanford, Calif., Stanford University Press.

Johnson, P. M., 1981. 'Changing social structure and the political role of manual workers' in J. F. Triska & Ch. Gati (eds), *Blue Collar Workers in Eastern Europe.* London, George Allen & Unwin.

Jones, C. D., 1981. *Soviet Influence in Eastern Europe: Political Autonomy and the Warsaw Pact.* New York, Praeger.

Jowitt, K., 1971. *Revolutionary Breakthroughs and National Development: The Case of Romania, 1944-1965.* Berkeley and Los Angeles, University of California Press.

—— 1974a. 'An organizational approach to the study of political culture in Marxist-Leninist systems'. *American Political Science Review,* No. 3.

—— 1974b. 'Political innovation in Rumania'. *Survey,* No. 4.

—— 1975. 'Inclusion and mobilization in European Leninist Regimes'. *World Politics,* No. 1.

—— 1978a. *The Leninist Response to National Dependency.* Berkeley, Institute of International Studies, University of California.

—— 1978b. 'The sociocultural basis of national dependency in peasant countries' in K. Jowitt (ed.), *Social Change in Romania 1860-1940: A Debate on Development in a European Nation.* Berkeley, Institute of International Studies, University of California.

—— 1983. 'Soviet neotraditionalism: the political corruption of a Leninist regime'. *Soviet Studies,* No. 3.

Jurca, N., 1978. *Mişcarea socialistă şi social-democratică din România.* Bucharest, Editura Litera.

Kanet, R., 1981. 'Patterns of East European economic involvement in the Third World' in M. Radu (ed.), *Eastern Europe and the Third World.* New York, Praeger.

—— 1983. 'Eastern Europe and the Third World: the expanding relationship' in S. L. Wolchik & M. J. Sodaro (eds), *Foreign and Domestic Policy in Eastern Europe in the 1980s.* London, Macmillan.

Karatnycky, A., Motyl, A. J., & Sturmthal, A., 1980. *Workers' Rights East and West: A Comparative Study of Trade Union and Workers' Rights in Western Democracies and Eastern Europe.* New Brunswick, League for Industrial Democracy, Transaction Books.

Kaser, M. C., 1967. *Comecon.* London, Oxford University Press.

Kelley, D. R., 1982. 'Developed socialism: a political formula for the Brezhnev era' in J. Seroka & M. D. Simon (eds), *Developed Socialism in the Soviet Bloc.* Boulder, Co., Westview Press.

Kesselman, M., 1973. 'Order or movement?: the literature of political development as ideology'. *World Politics,* No. 1.

Khrushchev, N. S., 1974. *Khrushchev Remembers: The Last Testament.* London, Andre Deutsch.

King, R. R., 1972. 'Rumania and the Sino-Soviet conflict'. *Studies in Comparative Communism,* No. 4.

—— 1973. *Minorities Under Communism.* Cambridge, Mass., Harvard University Press.

—— 1976. 'The escalation of Rumanian-Soviet historical polemics over Bessarabia'. Radio Free Europe Research, RAD Background Report/38 (Rumania), 12 February.

—— 1978a. 'The blending of party and state in Rumania'. *East European Quarterly,* No. 4.

—— 1978b. 'Romania and the Third World'. *Orbis,* No. 4.

—— 1980. *History of the Romanian Communist Party.* Stanford, Calif., Hoover Institution Press.

Kitch, M., 1975. 'Constantin Stere and Rumanian Populism'. *Slavonic and East European Review,* No. 131.

—— 1977. 'Constantin Dobrogeanu-Gherea and Rumanian Marxism'. *Slavonic and East European Review,* No. 1.

Komócsin, Z., 1966. 'Patriotism, national interest, internationalism'. *Problems of Peace and Socialism, World Marxist Review,* No. 6.

Korbonski, A., 1976. 'Leadership succession and political change in Eastern Europe'. *Studies in Comparative Communism,* Nos 1-2.

—— 1977. 'The "Change to Change" in Eastern Europe' in J. F. Triska & P. M. Cocks (eds), *Political Development in Eastern Europe.* New York, Praeger.

Kőrősi-Krizsán, S., 1966. 'Rumania and the Comintern'. *East Europe,* No. 12.

Kővary, A., 1979. 'The Rumanian national mystery: myth-makers under the microscope'. *Crossroads,* No. 3.

'La question uniate et Jean Paul II', 1983' in *Roumanie: Crise et répresion. L'Alternative,* numéro spécial supplément au No. 20, janvier.

Lache, St., & Ţuţui, G., 1978. *România, şi conferinţa de pace 1946.* Cluj-Napoca, Editura Dacia.

Lahav, Y., 1977. 'Soviet Policy and the Transylvanian Question (1940-1946)'. Research Paper 27, Jerusalem, The Soviet and East European Research Centre, The Hebrew University of Jerusalem, mimeo.

Lăncrănjan, I., 1982. *Cuvînt despre Transilvania.* Bucharest, Editura Sport-Turism.

LaPalombara, J., 1974. *Politics Within Nations.* Englewood Cliffs, N.J., Prentice-Hall.

Laux, J. K., 1981. 'The limits of autonomy: Romania in the 1980s' in *East European Economic Assessment. Part 2: Regional Assessment. A Compendium of Papers Submitted to the Joint Economic Committee, Congress of the United States.* Washington D.C., US Government Printing Office.

Lawson, C. W., 1982-3. 'The Soviet Union and Eastern Europe in Southern Africa: is there a conflict of interests?' *International Affairs*, No. 1.

—— 1983. 'National independence and reciprocal advantages: the political economy of Romanian-South relations'. *Soviet Studies*, No. 3.

Lee, A. G., 1955. *Crown Against Sickle: The Story of King Michael of Rumania.* London, Hutchinson.

Lendvai, P., 1969. *Eagles in Cobwebs: Nationalism and Communism in the Balkans.* London, Mac-Donald.

'Lettre ouverte à Madame Ceauşescu', 1981. *L'Alternative*, No. 13.

Lewtzkyj, B. & Stonynowski, J., 1978. *Who is Who in the Socialist Countries.* New York, K. G. Saur Publications.

Ligue pour la défense des Droits de l'homme en Roumanie, 1981a. 'Des cas de persécution religieuse'. *L'Alternative*, No. 9.

—— 1981b. 'Le prêtre Gheorghe Calciu Dumitreasa'. *L'Alternative*, No. 8.

Linden, R. H., 1979. *Bears and Foxes: The International Relations of the East European States.* New York, Columbia University Press.

—— 1981, 'Romania's foreign policy in the 1980s' in D. N. Nelson (ed.), *Romania in the 1980s.* Boulder, Co., Westview Press.

—— 1983. 'Romanian foreign policy in the 1980s: domestic-foreign policy linkages' in S. L. Wolchik and M. S. Sodaro (eds), *Foreign and Domestic Policy in Eastern Europe.* London, Macmillan.

'L'itinéraire d'un syndicaliste', 1981. *L'Alternative*, Nos. 16-17.

Liveanu, V., 1962. 'Date privind pregătirea şi desfăşurarea Congresului I al Partidului Comunist din Romînia'. *Studii şi materiale de istorie contemporană*, No. 2.

Lowenthal, R., 1970. 'Development vs. Utopia in Communist policy' in Ch. Johnson (ed.), *Change in Communist Systems.* Stanford, Calif., Stanford University Press.

—— 1982. 'The post-revolutionary phase in China and Russia'. *Studies in Comparative Communism*, No. 3.

Luftman, E., 1982. 'Can the World Bank salvage the Romanian oil industry?' Radio Free Europe Research, RAD Background Report/132 (Romania), 14 June.

McArthur, M., 1976. 'The Saxon Germans: political fate of an ethnic identity'. *Dialectical Anthropology*, No. 4.

McCauley, M., 1983. 'Leadership and the succession struggle' in M. McCauley (ed.), *The Soviet Union After Brezhnev.* London, Heinemann Education.

Maciu, V. *et al.*, 1964. *Outline of Rumanian Historiography Until the Beginnings of the 20th Century.* Bucharest, Publishing House of the Academy of the Rumanian People's Republic.

Maier, A., 1980. 'Ceauşescu Deified on his 62nd Birthday'. Radio Free Europe Research, RAD Background Report, Romania/34, 11 February.

—— 1983a. 'Ceauşescu's Birthday Extravaganza'. Radio Free Europe Research, Situation Report, Romania/3, 19 February.

—— 1983b. 'Ceauşescu's Personality Cult Abroad'. Radio Free Europe Research, Situation Report, Romania/2, 29 January.

—— 1983c. 'Romania's Western Trade: Problems and Prospects'. Radio Free Europe Research, Situation Report, Romania/20, 31 December.

— 1984. 'Romania Commemorates Foundation in 1918'. Radio Free Europe Research, RAD Background Report, Romania/30, 1 March.

Markham, R. H., 1949. *Le Roumanie sous le joug soviétique*. Paris, Calman-Levy.

Marx, K., 1964. *Însemnări despre români (Manuscrise inedite)*, A. Oţetea & S. Schwann (eds.). Bucharest, Editura Academiei Republicii Populare Romîne.

Matejko, A., 1974. *Social Change and Stratification in Eastern Europe*. New York, Praeger.

Măgereanu, F., 1984. 'URSS—principalul partener comercial al României'. *Revista economică*, No. 6.

Meyer, A. G., 1970. 'Historical development of the communist theory of leadership' in R. Barry Farrel (ed.), *Political Leadership in Eastern Europe*. London, Butterworth.

— 1972. 'Legitimacy and power in East Central Europe' in S. Sinanian, P. C. Ludz & I. Deak (eds), *Eastern Europe in the 1970s*. New York, Praeger.

— 1983. 'Communism and leadership'. *Studies in Comparative Communism*, No. 3.

Micu, D., 1975. *Gîndirea şi 'gîndirismul'*. Bucharest, Editura Minerva.

Miller, J. H., 1982. 'The Communist Party: trends and problems' in A. Brown & M. Kaser (eds), *Soviet Policy for the 1980s*. Bloomington, Indiana University Press.

Ministerul Industriei şi Comerţului. Direcţiunea Generală a Statisticii, 1919. *Anuarul statistic al României 1915-16*. Bucharest, Tipografia Curţii regale F. Göbl & Fii.

Mitrofan, I., 1983. 'Înfloritoarea aşezare romană de la Micăsasa'. *Scînteia*, 10 July.

Moisiuc, V., 1969. 'Cu privire la originile şi caracterul celui de-al doilea război mondial'. *Anale de istorie*, No. 6.

— 1971. *Diplomaţia României şi problema apărării suveranităţii şi independenţei naţionale în perioada martie 1938-mai 1940*. Bucharest, Editura Academiei RSR.

Moisiuc, V. et al., 1977. *Probleme de politică externă a României 1918-1940*. Bucharest, Editura militară.

Montias, M., 1964. 'Background and origins of the Rumanian dispute with Comecon'. *Soviet Studies*, October.

— 1967. *Economic Development in Communist Rumania*. Cambridge, Mass., MIT Press.

— 1970. 'Types of communist economic systems' in Ch. Johnson (ed.), *Change in Communist Systems*. Stanford, Ca., Stanford University Press.

Moore, P., 1978a. 'Dissent in Romania: An Overreview'. Radio Free Europe Research, RAD Background Report, Romania/112, 5 June.

— 1978b. 'The Return of the Bessarabian Polemic: The Soviet Contribution'. Radio Free Europe Research, RAD Background Report, Romania/160, 13 July.

— 1979, 'The Romanian Communist Party's 12th Congress: A Preliminary Review'. Radio Free Europe Research, RAD Background Report, Romania/263, 28 November.

— 1983. 'Romania in 1983'. Radio Free Europe Research, RAD Background Report, Romania/294, 30 December.

Mujal-León, E. M., 1978. 'The domestic and international evolution of the Spanish Communist Party' in R. L. Tőkés (ed.), *Eurocommunism and Détente*. New York, New York University Press.

Muşat, M., 1983a. 'Lupta românilor din Transilvania pentru libertate şi unitate naţională'. *Era socialistă*, No. 21.

— 1983b. 'Originea daco-romană şi continuitatea în spaţiul carpato-danubio-pontic—caracteristici fundamentale ale poporului român'. *Era socialistă*, No. 9.

Muşat, M. & Ardeleanu, I., 1971. *Viaţa politică în România, 1918-1921*. Bucharest, Editura politică.

— 1981. *Unitate, continuitate şi ascensiune în mişcarea muncitorească din România 1821-1948*. Bucharest, Editura Academiei Republicii Socialiste România.

— 1982. *Political Life in Romania 1918-1921*. Bucharest, Editura Academiei Republicii Socialiste România.

Muşat, M., & Ardeleanu, I., 1983. *De la statul geto-dacic la statul român unitar.* Bucharest, Editura ştiinţifică şi enciclopedică.

Muşat, M., & Tănăsescu, T., 1982. 'Stravechea Dacie—pamînt românesc generos'. *Anale de istorie,* No. 4.

Nano, F. C., 1952. 'The First Soviet double-cross'. *Journal of Central European Affairs,* No. 3.

National Conference of the Romanian Communist Party July 19-21 1972: Documents. N.p., Romanian News Agency Agerpres.

Nedelcu, F., 1983. *Viaţa politică din România în preajma instaurării dictaturii regale.* Cluj, Editura Dacia.

Nelson, D. N., 1980. *Democratic Centralism in Romania: A Study of Local Communist Politics.* New York, Columbia University Press.

—— 1981a. 'Development and participation in communist systems' in D. E. Schulz & J. S. Adams (eds), *Political Participation in Communist Systems.* New York, Pergamon.

—— 1981b. 'Romania' in W. E. Welsh (ed.), *Survey Research and Public Attitudes in Eastern Europe and the Soviet Union.* New York, Pergamon.

—— 1981c. 'Vertical integration and political control in Eastern Europe: the Polish and Romanian cases'. *Slavic Review,* No. 2.

—— 1981d. 'Workers in a workers' state' in D. N. Nelson (ed.), *Romania in the 1980s.* Boulder, Co., Westview Press.

—— 1982a. 'Developing socialism and worker-party conflict' in J. Seroka & M. D. Simon (eds), *Developed Socialism in the Soviet Bloc.* Boulder, Co., Westview.

—— 1982b. 'People's councils deputies in Romania' in D. N. Nelson & S. White (eds), *Communist Legislatures in Comparative Perspective.* Albany, State University of New York Press.

Netea, I., 1983. 'Şi azi ca ieri luptători pentru adevăr, pentru dreptate'. *Flacăra,* 15 June.

Niculescu-Mizil, P., 1969. 'Preocupări actuale ale partidului nostru în domeniul activităţii ideologice'. *Lupta de clasă,* No. 11.

Niri, A., 1962. 'V. B. Uşacov—"Politica externă a Germaniei Hitleriste"'. *Analele institutului de istorie a partidului de pe lînga CC al PMR,* No. 5.

Nørgaard, O. & Sampson, S., 1982. 'Poland's crisis and East European socialism: structural, specific and conjuctural implications'. Paper prepared for *Kapitalistate,* International Conference on the State, Cosenza, Italy.

Oldson, W. O., 1973. *The Historical and Nationalistic Thought of Nicolae Iorga.* New York, Columbia University Press.

Olteanu, S., 1983. 'Comunităţi rurale neîntrerupte între secolele III-XI'. *Contemporanul,* 13 May.

Omagiu tovarăşului Ceauşescu, 1973. Bucharest, Editura politică.

Oprescu, P., 1983. 'Permanenţe ale istoriei poporului român'. *Era socialistă,* No. 20.

Oren, N., 1971. *Bulgarian Communism: The Road to Power.* New York, Columbia University Press.

Ornea, Z., 1972. *Poporanismul: Momente şi sinteze.* Bucharest, Editura Minerva.

—— 1975. 'Falansterul de la Scăieni şi tradiţiile mişcării socialiste româneşti'. *Era socialistă,* No. 3.

—— 1980. *Traditionalism şi modernitate în deceniul al treilea.* Bucharest, Editura Eminescu.

—— 1982. *Viaţa lui C. Dobrogeanu-Gherea.* Bucharest, Editura Cartea românească.

Oţetea, A., 1969. 'Dezvoltarea ştiintei istorice romîneşti după 23 august 1944'. *Studii,* No. 4.

P. G., 1982. 'Food Prices Go Up'. Radio Free Europe Research, Situation Report, Romania/4, 13 February.

—— 1983. 'Resumption of Food Rationing'. Radio Free Europe Research, Situation Report, Romania/23, 11 November.

Pano, N. C., 1982. 'Albania: the last bastion of Stalinism' in M. M. Drachkovitch (ed.), *East*

Central Europe: Yesterday-Today-Tomorrow. Stanford, Calif., Stanford University, Hoover Institution Press.

Paraschivescu, M. R., 1969. *Scrieri*, vol. 1. Bucharest, Editura pentru literatură.

— 1976. *Journal d'un héretique*. Paris, Olivier Orban.

Park, K., 1982. 'North Korea under Kim Chong-il'. *Journal of Northeast Asian Studies*, No. 2.

Pascu, Şt., 1983a. *Ce este Transilvania*. Cluj-Napoca, Editura Dacia.

Pascu, Şt., 1983b. 'Independenţa şi unitatea-temelie peste veacuri'. *Contemporanul*, 16 September.

— 1983c. 'Transilvania străvechi pamînt românesc'. *Era socialistă*, No. 22.

Pânzaru, P., 1968. 'Democraţie şi umanism'. *Contemporanul*, 5 July.

'Pentru dezvoltarea spiritului militant al ştiinţei istorice', 1977. *Studii*, No. 6.

Perlmutter, A. & LeoGrande, W., 1982. 'The Party in uniform: toward a theory of civil-military relations in communist political systems'. *American Political Science Review*, No. 4.

Petrescu, Titel C., 1944. *Socialismul în România*. Bucharest, Biblioteca socialistă.

Petric, A. & Tutui, G., 1967. *L'unification du mouvement ouvrier de Roumania*. Bucharest, Éditions de l'Académie de la République Socialiste de Roumanie.

Plenara Comitetului Central al Partidului Comunist Român din 22-25 aprilie 1968, 1968. Bucharest, Editura politică.

Popescu-Puţuri, I., 1966. 'România în timpul celui de-al doilea război mondial'. *Analele institutului de studii istorice şi social-politice de pe lîngă CC al PCR*, No. 6.

— 1981. 'Îndemn la creaţie' (I). *Anale de istorie*, No. 5.

Popescu-Puţuri, I. & Zaharia, G. *et al.*, 1965. *La contribution de la Romanie à la victoire sur le fascisme*. Bucharest, Éditions de l'Académie de la République Socialiste de Roumanie.

Popişteanu, C. & Pânzaru, P., 1974. *Romanian Historical Itinerary: 1944-1974*. Bucharest, Editura Enciclopedică română.

Popovici, T., 1973. 'Puterea şi adevărul'. *Teatru*, No. 1.

Potopin, I., 1984. 'În patria luminii'. *Luceăfarul*, 4 February.

Pravda, A., 1983. 'Trade unionism in East European communist systems: toward corporatism?'. *International Political Science Review*, No. 2.

Preda, C., 1983a. 'A XVI-a sesiune naţională de arheologie'. *Revista de istorie*, No. 1.

— 1983b. 'Marile dovezi ale continuităţii'. *Contemporanul*, 13 May.

Preda, M., 1975. *Delirul*. Bucharest, Editura Cartea românească.

— 1980. *Cel mai iubit dintre pămînteni*. Bucharest, Editura Cartea românească, 3 vols.

Prifiti, P. R., 1978. *Socialist Albania Since 1944: Domestic and Foreign Development*. Cambridge, Mass., MIT Press.

Programul Partidului Comunist Român de făurire a societăţii multilateral dezvoltate şi înaintare a României spre comunism, 1975. Bucharest, Editura politică.

Prost, H., 1954. *Destin de la Roumanie*. Paris, Berger Levrault.

Quinlan, P. D., 1977. *Clash Over Romania: British and American Policies Towards Romania 1938-1947*. Los Angeles, American Romanian Academy of Arts and Sciences.

R. Al. de F., 1981. 'The Uniate Church Appeals to the Madrid Conference'. Radio Free Europe Research, Situation Report, Romania/19, 23 September.

Radu, M., 1981. 'Romania and the Third World: the dilemmas of a "free rider"' in M. Radu (ed.), *Eastern Europe and the Third World: East vs. South*. New York, Praeger.

Rakovski, K. G., 1925. *Roumanie et Bessarabie*. Paris, Librairie du Travail.

— 1974. 'Autobiography' in G. Haupt and J. J. Marie (eds), *Makers of the Russian Revolution: Biographies of Bolshevik Leaders*. Ithaca, N.Y., Cornell University Press.

Raţiu, I., 1975. *Contemporary Romania: Her Place in World Affairs*. Richmond, Surrey, Foreign Affairs Publishing Company.

Rădulescu-Motru, C., 1904. *Cultura română și politicianismul.* Bucharest, Libraria Soccecu, & Co., 2nd edn.

—— 1936. *Românismul: Catehismul unei noi spiritualiți.* Bucharest, Fundația pentru literatură și artă 'Regele Carol II'.

—— 1937. 'Psychology of the Romanian people'. *Revista de filozofie,* **2,** reprinted in *Romanian Sources,* **2,** pt. I, 1976.

Recensămîntul populației din 21 februarie 1956, 1959. Bucharest, Direcția centrală de statistică.

Recensămîntul populației și locuințelor din 15 martie 1966, 1968. Bucharest, Direcția centrală de statistică.

Reisch, A. & Pataki, J., 1982. 'Hungarian-Romanian Polemics over Transylvania Continue'. Radio Free Europe Research, RAD Background Report, Hungary/238, 15 November.

'Religion Under "Real Socialism"'. Radio Free Europe Research, RAD Background Report, Eastern Europe/123, 31 May.

Republica Socialistă România. Direcția Centrală de Statistică, 1965-82. *Anuarul Statistic al Republicii Socialiste România.* Bucharest, Direcția centrală de statistică.

Rigby, T. H., 1972. 'The Soviet Politbureau: a comparative profile 1951-1971'. *Soviet Studies,* No. 1.

—— 1977. 'Stalinism and the mono-organizational society' in R. C. Tucker (ed.), *Stalinism: Essays in Historical Interpretation.* New York, W. W. Norton.

—— 1980. 'A conceptual approach to authority, power and policy in the Soviet Union' in T. H. Rigby, A. Brown & P. Reddaway (eds), *Authority, Power and Policy in the Soviet Union.* New York, St. Martin's Press.

Roberts, H. L., 1969. *Rumania: Political Problems of an Agrarian State.* N.p., Archon Books.

Rogers, E. M., 1969. *Modernization Among Peasants: The Impact of Communication.* New York, Holt, Rinehart and Winston.

Roller, M., 1951. *Probleme de istorie: Contribuții la lupta pentru o istorie științifică a R.P.R..* n.p., Editura Partidului Muncitoresc Român, 3rd printing.

—— (ed.), 1956. *Istoria R.P.R..* Bucharest, Editura de stat didactică și pedagogică.

Romanian Research Group, 1979. 'Transylvanian ethnicity'. *Current Anthropology,* No. 1.

Ronnas, P., 1984. *Urbanization in Romania: A Geography of Socialist Economic Change.* Stockholm, Economic Research Institute.

Rothchild, J. A., 1955. *Rakovsky.* Oxford, St. Antony's College.

—— 1979. *East Central Europe Between the Two World Wars.* Seattle, University of Washington Press, 3rd printing.

Rura, M., 1961. *Reinterpretation of History as a Method for Furthering Communism in Rumania: A Study in Comparative Historiography.* Washington, D.C., Georgetown University Press.

Rusenescu, M., 1969. 'Istoriografia românească privind insurecția antifascistă din august 1944 și urmările sale'. *Studii,* No. 4.

Rush, M., 1974. *How Communist States Change Their Rulers.* Ithaca, N.Y., Cornell University Press.

Sampson, S., 1976. 'Feldioara: The city comes to the peasant'. *Dialectical Anthropology,* No. 4.

—— 1979. 'Urbanization—planned and unplanned: a case study of Brașov, Romania' in T. French (ed.), *The Socialist City.* London, John Wiley

—— 1982. *The Planners and the Peasants: An Anthropological Study of Urban Development in Romania.* University Centre of South Jutland: Institute of East-West Studies, Monographs in East-West Studies, No. 4.

—— 1983. 'Rich families and poor collectives: an anthropological approach to Romania's "Second economy"'. *Bidrag Till Östsatsforskningen,* No. 1.

— 1984. 'Muddling through in Romania (or why the mămăligă doesn't explode)'. Paper presented at the Second International Congress of Romanian Studies, Avignon, France, forthcoming, *International Journal of Romanian Studies*.

Schlesak, D., 1972. 'Politische Schule der Träume'. *Merkur*, No. 9.

Schmitter, Ph.C., 1978. 'Reflections on Mihail Manoilescu and the political consequences of delayed–dependent development on the periphery of Western Europe' in K. Jowitt (ed.), *Social Change in Romania 1860-1940: A Debate on Development in a European Nation*. Berkeley, Institute of International Studies, University of California.

Schönfield, R., 1977. 'Industrie und gewerbliche Wirtschaft' in K. D. Grothusen (ed.), *Rumänien*. Göttingen, Vandenhoeck & Ruprecht.

Schöpflin, G., 1974. 'Rumanian nationalism'. *Survey* Nos. 2-3.

— 1978. 'The Hungarians of Rumania'. Minority Rights Group Report No. 37, London, Minority Rights Group.

— 1982a. 'Hungary between prosperity and crisis'. *Conflict Studies*, No. 136.

— 1982b. 'Normalisation in Eastern Europe: the reimposition of the Soviet system'. *Millenium*, No. 2.

— 1983a. 'Poland and Eastern Europe' in A. Brumberg (ed.), *Poland: Genesis of a Revolution*. New York, Vintage Books.

— 1983b. 'Rumänien, Ungarn und Siebenbürgen'. *Europäische Rundschau*, No. 1.

Schulz, D. E., 1981. 'On the nature and function of participation in communist systems: a developmental analysis' in D. E. Schultz & J. A. Adams (eds), *Political Participation in Communist Systems*, New York, Pergamon.

Scurtu, I., 1982. *Viaţa politică din România 1918-1944*. Bucharest, Editura Albatros.

Secăreş, V., 1982. 'Contradicţiile vieţii internaţionale în etapa actuală'. *Era socialistă*, No. 24.

Seton-Watson, H., 1956. *The East European Revolution*. New York, Praeger, 3rd edn.

Shafir, M., 1974. 'Rumanian policy in the Middle East 1967-1972'. Research Paper No. 7, The Soviet and East European Research Centre, The Hebrew University of Jerusalem, mimeo.

— 1978. 'Who is Paul Goma?'. *Index on Censorship*, No. 1.

— 1980. 'Campus Eliza: The Little Entente and the Balkan Alliance'. *Südost-Forschungen*, **39**.

— 1981a. 'The Intellectual and the Party: the Rumanian Communist Party and the creative intelligentsia in the Ceauşescu period,,1965-1971', unpublished doctoral dissertation, Jerusalem, The Hebrew University of Jerusalem.

— 1981b. 'The Socialist Republic of Romania' in B. Szajkowski (ed.), *Marxist Governments: A World Survey*, vol. 3. London, Macmillan.

— 1982. 'Autonomy and conformity in Romania'. Paper presented at the 1982 Convention of the American Society for the Advancement of Slavic Studies, Washington, D.C.

— 1983a. 'The men of the Archangel revisited: Anti-semitic formations among communist Romania's intellectuals', *Studies in Comparative Communism*, No. 2-3.

— 1983b. 'Political culture, intellectual dissent and intellectual consent: the case of Romania'. *Orbis*, No. 2.

— 1984a. 'Political stagnation and Marxist critique: 1968 and beyond in comparative East European perspective'. *British Journal of Political Science*, No. 4.

— 1984b. 'Romania's Marx and the National Question: Constantin Dobrogeanu-Gherea'. *History of Political Thought*, forthcoming.

— 1985. 'Leadership and succession in communist Romania' in M. McCauley & S. Carter, *Leadership and Succession in the USSR, Eastern Europe and China*. London, Macmillan, forthcoming.

222   *References*

Shapiro, P., 1981. 'Romania's past as challenge for the future: a developmental approach to inter-war politics' in D. N. Nelson (ed.), *Romania in the 1980s*. Boulder, Co., Westview Press.

Sharlet, R. S., 1969. 'Systematic political science and communist systems' in F. J. Fleron, Jr. (ed.), *Communist Studies and the Social Sciences: Essays on Methodology and Empirical Theory*. Chicago, Rand MacNally.

Shoup, P., 1981. *The East European and Soviet Data Handbook*. New York, Columbia University Press.

Simion, A., 1979. *Preliminarii politico-diplomatice ale insurecţiei române din august 1944*. Cluj-Napoca, Editura Dacia.

Smith, A., 1980. 'Romanian economic reforms' in Economics Directorate, NATO, *Economic Reforms in Eastern Europe and Prospects for the 1980s*. Oxford, Pergamon Press.

— 1981. 'The Romanian industrial enterprise' in I. Jeffries (ed.), *The Industrial Enterprise in Eastern Europe*. Eastbourne, Praeger.

Socaciu, E., 1983. 'O relevatoare cronică a Transilvaniei'. *Contemporanul*, 13 May.

Socianu, H., 1978. 'The foreign policies of Romania in the sixties' in J. A. Kuhlman (ed.), *The Foreign Policies of Eastern Europe: Domestic and International Determinants*. Leyden, A. W. Sijthoff.

Socor, V., 1976. 'The limits of national independence in the Soviet bloc: Rumania's foreign policy reconsidered'. *Orbis*, No. 2.

— 1983a. 'Ceauşescu Bestows More Honors on Members of His Family'. Radio Free Europe Research, Situation Report, Romania/10, 7 June.

— 1983b. 'Changes in the Situation of the Romanian Catholic Church?' Radio Free Europe Research, RAD Background Report Romania 277, 27 December.

— 1984. 'Anti-Semitism in Official Publications Re-occurs'. Radio Free Europe Research, Situation Report, Romania/9, 14 June.

Sozan, M., 1979. 'Reply'. *Current Anthropology*, No. 1.

Spechler, M. C., 1983. 'The bankrupt success of Eastern Europe and the failure of growth policy'. *Slavic and Soviet Series*, No. 1-2.

Spigler, I., 1973. *Economic Reform in Rumanian Industry*. London, Oxford University Press.

Staar, R., 1981. 'Checklist of communist parties and fronts 1980'. *Problems of Communism*, No. 2.

Stahl, H. H., 1969. *Les anciennes communautés villageoises roumaines*. Bucharest and Paris, Academie roumaine and C.N.R.S.

Stănică, G., 1984. '"Breed, comrade women, it's your duty"'. *The Guardian*, 3 April.

Stolojan, S., 1981. 'Persecution et résistance religieuse en Roumanie'. *L'Alternative*, No. 9.

Streinu, V., 1966. 'Clopotele mînăstirii Putna'. *Luceafărul*, 9 July.

Stroe, C., 1983. 'Contradicţii sociale şi procesul făuririi societăţii socialiste'. *Era socialistă*, No. 4.

Stuart, A., 1970. 'Ceauşescu's Land'. *Survey*, No. 76.

Surpat, G., 1980. *Naţionalizarea şi semnificaţia sa istorică pentru dezvoltarea României pe calea socialismului*. Bucharest, Editura politică.

— 1981. 'Întărirea continuă a unităţii moral-politice şi coeziunii întregului popor în procesul edificării societăţii socialiste multilateral dezvoltate'. *Anale de istorie*, No. 5.

Surpat, G., *et al.*, 1980. *România în anii socialismului 1948-1978*. Bucharest, Editura politică, Institutul de studii istorice şi social-politice de pe lîngă CC al PCR.

Suttner, E. C., 1977. 'Kirchen und Staat' in K. D. Grothusen (ed.), *Rumänien*. Göttingen, Vandenhoeck & Ruprecht.

Szajkowski, B., 1982. *The Establishment of Marxist Regimes*. London, Butterworth.

— 1983. *Next to God . . . Poland*. London, Frances Pinter.

Szász, J., 1968. 'O răspundere inalienabiliă'. *Gazeta literară*, 25 July.

Ştefănescu, Şt., 1983. 'Process cu profunde determinări istorice'. *Era socialistă*, No. 20.

Tănase, V., 1983. *C'est mon affaire.* Paris, Flamarion.

Tarkowski, J., 1983. 'Patronage in a centralized socialist system: the case of Poland'. *International Political Science Review*, No. 4.

Theodorson, G. A. & Theodorson, A. G., 1969. *A Modern Dictionary of Sociology*. New York, N.Y. Crowell.

Thompson, J. B., 1964. 'Rumania's struggle with Comecon'. *East Europe.* No. 6.

Tismăneanu, V., 1983. 'Critical Marxism and Eastern Europe'. *Praxis International*, No. 3.

Tőkés, R. L., 1978. 'Eastern Europe in the 1970s: détente, dissent and Eurocommunism' in R. L. Tőkés (ed.), *Eurocommunism and Détente.* New York, New York University Press.

Totu, I. V., 1984. 'Dezvoltarea şi perfecţionarea colaborării dintre ţările socialiste membre ale C.A.E.R.'. *Revista economică*, No. 4.

Triska, J. F. (ed.), 1968. *Constitutions of the Communist Party States*, Stanford, Ca., Hoover Institution Press.

Tudor, C. V., 1983. *Saturnalii.* Bucharest, Albatros.

Turczynski, E., 1971. 'The background of Romanian fascism' in P. F. Lederer (ed.), *Native Fascism in the Successor States 1918-1945.* Santa Barbara, Calif., ABC-Clio.

Turnock, D., 1974. *An Economic Geography of Romania.* London, G. Bell.

Ţepeneag, D., 1975a. 'Quelques idées fixes et autant de variables'. *Cahiers de l'Est*, No. 4.

—— 1975b. 'Şotron'. *Ethos* (Paris), 2.

Ţuţu, G., 1983. 'Contribuţia economică a României la victoria în războiul antifascist'. *Revista economică*, No. 18.

Ulč, O., 1974. *Politics in Czechoslovakia.* San Francisco, W. H. Freeman.

United Nations, 1983. *Economic Survey of Eastern Europe in 1982.* New York, United Nations.

Ursul, G. R., 1982. 'From political freedom to religious independence: the Romanian Orthodox Church, 1877-1925' in S. Fischer-Galati, R. R. Florescu & G. R. Ursul (eds), *Romania Between East and West: Historical Essays in Memory of Constantin C. Giurescu.* New York, Columbia University Press.

Vago, B., 1972. 'The Jewish vote in Romania between the two World Wars'. *Jewish Journal of Sociology*, No. 2.

—— 1974. 'The attitude towards Jews as a criterion of the "left-right" concept' in B. Vago & G. Mosse (eds), *Jews and Non-Jews in Eastern Europe.* New York, John Wiley and Sons.

—— 1977. 'Romania' in M. McCauley (ed.), *Communist Power in Europe, 1944-1949.* London, Macmillan.

Văduva-Poenaru, I., 1983. 'Unirea românilor'. *Luceafărul*, 24 September.

Verba, S., 1965. 'Conclusion' in L. Pye & S. Verba (eds), *Political Culture and Political Development.* Princeton, N.J., Princeton University Press.

'Victor Eftimiu meets the censor', 1968. *East Europe*, No. 5.

Voicu, Şt., 1966. 'Pagini din lupta partidului Comunist Român împotriva fascismului, pentru independenţă şi suvcranitate naţională'. *Lupta de clasă*, No. 6.

—— 1970. 'Constantin Dobrogeanu-Gherea'. *Anale de istorice*, No. 3.

Volgyés, I., 1982. *The Political Reliability of the Warsaw Pact Armies: The Southern Trier.* Durham, N.C., Duke University Policy Studies.

Voturin, D., Petrov, P. & Slepenchuk, F., 1965. 'Pod krasnym znamenem revoliutsii'. *Kommunist Moldavii*, No. 4.

Weber, E., 1964. *Varieties of Fascism.* Princeton, N.J., Van Nostrand.

Weber, E., 1966. 'Romania' in H. Rogger & E. Weber (eds), *The European Right*. Berkeley and Los Angeles, University of California Press.

Wesson, R., 1982. 'Eurocommunism and Eastern Europe' in M. M. Drachkovitch (ed.), *East Central Europe: Yesterday-Today-Tomorrow*. Stanford, Calif., Hoover Institution.

—— 1983. 'Checklist of communist parties, 1982'. *Problems of Communism*, No. 2.

Wharton Econometric Forecasting Associates, 1983. 'Soviet foreign trade performance in 1982' in *Centrally Planned Economies: Current Analysis* (April).

Willerton, J. P., Jr., 1979. 'Clientelism in the Soviet Union: an initial examination'. *Studies in Comparative Communism*, Nos. 2-3.

Witness to Cultural Genocide, 1979. New York, America Transylvanian Féderation Inc., and Committee for Human Rights in Rumania.

World Armament and Disarmament: SIPRI Yearbook 1982, 1982. London, Taylor and Francis, Ltd.

Zach, K., 1979. 'Rumäniens Bodenreformen des 20 Jahrhunderts in der politischen Diskution: Vorgeschichte, Hintergründe, Ausblick. Ein historisch-deskriptive Unretsuchung'. *Münchener Zeitschrift für Balkankunde*, 2. Band.

Zagoria, L., 1982. 'Number Three Man in the Albanian Leadership on the Way Out'. Radio Free Europe Research, RAD Background Report/241 (Albania), 16 November.

Zaharia, G., 1966. 'Cu privire la politica externă a României în prima etapă a celui de-al doilea război mondial'. *Analele institutului de studii istorice și social-politice de pe lîngă CC al PCR*, No. 5.

—— 1969. 'Partidul Comunist Român-forța conducătoare a insurecției din anul 1944'. *Anale de istorie*, No. 4.

Zaharia, G. & Botoran, C., 1981. *Politica externă de apărare națională a României în contextul europeean interbelic 1919-1939*. Bucharest, Editura militară.

Zaharia, G. & Petri, A., 1966. 'Partidul Comunist Român în fruntea luptei poporului pentru apărarea independenței naționale a țării, împotriva fascismului'. *Analele institutului de studii istorice și social-politice de pe lîngă CC al PCR*, No. 2-3.

Zanga, L., 1978. 'The Albanian Letter—A Retaliatory Document'. Radio Free Europe Research, RAD Background Report, Albania/178, 11 August.

Ziemer, K., 1969. 'Rumänien' in D. Sternberger & B. Vogel (eds), *Die Wahl der Parlamente und anderer Staatsorgane: Ein handbuch*. Berlin, Walter de Gruyter et Cie.

Index